The American Establishment

THE
AMERICAN
ESTABLISHMENT

LEONARD SILK

&

MARK SILK

Basic Books, Inc., Publishers

NEW YORK

Grateful acknowledgement is made to the following for permission to reprint excerpts from:

"Those were the Days," words and music by Gene Raskin; TRO- © Copyright 1962 and 1968, Essex Music, Inc., New York, New York. Used by permission.

R.N.: The Memoirs of Richard Nixon, Copyright © 1978 by Richard Nixon. All rights reserved. Reprinted by permission of Grosset and Dunlap, Inc.

Library of Congress Cataloging in Publication Data

Silk, Leonard Solomon, 1918–
 The American establishment.

 Includes bibliographical references and index.
 1. Elite (Social sciences)—United States.
2. Social institutions—United States. 3. Power
(Social sciences) 4. Influence (Psychology)
I. Silk, Mark, joint author. II. Title.
HN90.E4S54   973.92   80–50533
ISBN: 0–465–00134–3

TO BERNICE AND TEMA

Good Friends

"What redeems it is the idea only. An idea at the back of it; not a sentimental pretence but an idea; and an unselfish belief in the idea—something you can set up, and bow down before, and offer a sacrifice to . . ."

—JOSEPH CONRAD,
Heart of Darkness

CONTENTS

Preface   *ix*

Chapter 1
The American Establishment: The Third Force   *3*
What Is the Establishment? / Key Attributes / Origins: The
Church of Massachusetts / From Eliot to Lippmann /
The Third Force

Chapter 2
Elitism for All: Harvard   *21*
Liberalism Pays/TheAnti-CrimsonTide/TheOpenDoor/
The Limits of Tolerance / The Battle of Memorial Church /
"Be Serviceable" / The Playing Fields of Cambridge

Chapter 3
Church, State, and Counting House:
The New York Times   *66*
A Family Business / Addressing Vietnam / Nixon and Other
Enemies / Crisis over the Pentagon Papers / Sulzberger vs.
Oakes / Member of the Club / The Business of the Press

Chapter 4
Investing in Virtue: The Ford Foundation   *104*
The Gospel of Carnegie / Rockefeller's Baptism /
The Ludlow Trauma / The Philanthropoid's Creed / The
Coming of Ford / Go-Go Years / Hard Times / Thomas of
Bed-Sty / Results, Results

Chapter 5
The Dismal Science of Reform: Brookings   *153*
The Policy Network / Horatio Alger Goes to Washington /
Big Wind from Chicago / Making Peace with the New Deal /
The Plan to Bomb Brookings / Conservative Competition: The
American Enterprise Institute / The Professors and Politics

CONTENTS

Chapter 6

Mission on Sixty-Eighth Street:
The Council on Foreign Relations   *183*

Home from Versailles / Men of All Faiths / Bucking
Isolationism / Waging the Cold War / The Era of Bad
Feeling / In Search of a New Consensus / Bundy vs.
Kissinger / Going Public

Chapter 7

Big Business and the Establishment   *226*

Creed of Big Business / Croly Rescues Hamilton / The
Progressive Tycoon / Birth of the CED / The Mission
Abroad / Business Bootlegs Keynes / Inflation and Reaction:
The Business Roundtable / Byrom's Synthesis / The Struggle
Within

Chapter 8

The Establishment in the Political Ring   *268*

A Puritan in Politics / Modern Republicanism / The Best of
Enemies / The New Majority / Trilateralism: Rise and Fall /
Inside Looking Out: Carter / Free at Last

Chapter 9

The Prospects of the Establishment   *311*

The Anti-Establishment Habit / The Populist Attack / The
"Free-Enterprise" Challenge / Liberty, Now and Then

Notes   *329*

Index   *337*

PREFACE

THE LATE Richard Rovere, in his essay, "Notes on the Establishment in America," published in 1961, explained the nature and operations of an institution whose very existence was unknown to (or at least denied by) the great majority of its own members. Yet Rovere persevered, confidently believing in the existence of the American Establishment. We are grateful to him for his pioneering work.

Since Rovere wrote, the term *Establishment* has been on everyone's lips. By working stiffs and business executives, radicals and reactionaries, wardheelers and Presidents, the term is used pejoratively. For instance, on July 6, 1979, President Jimmy Carter, when asked by one of the authors of this book how he would characterize the Establishment, replied: "Well, this will be derisory—snobbish, arrogant, distrustful, especially of people like us." Mr. Carter was by no means the only recent President to disclose a strong animus against the Establishment. President Richard Nixon's prejudice against it and fear of it were so deep and obsessive that in the end they consumed his administration.

The absence of a clear concept of the Establishment has fed prejudices against it. The loose use of the term to denote virtually any form of institutional authority has permitted the real Establishment to be missed among a welter of literary, educational, cultural, civic, business, sports, and other "establishments." In becoming a cliché, the Establishment has lost its original metaphorical significance. For the term derives from the concept of an Established Church, specifically the established Church of England, a religious body that enjoys the exclusive recognition and material support of the State—a type of relationship which in this country the Constitution sought to prevent.

In our efforts to trace the American Establishment we have received invaluable help from many people at the institutions we have covered in this book. We wish especially to thank Joseph Pechman and Roland Hoover of the Brookings Institution, James Keogh of the Business Roundtable, Richard Magat and Sandra Markham of the Ford Foundation, Sol Hurwitz of the Committee for Economic Development, Porter McKeever and Peter Johnson of the office of the late John D. Rockefeller 3d, Patsy Gesell of the Council on Foreign Relations, and Paul Greenfeder and Gray Peart of *The New York Times*.

We also wish to thank all those we interviewed, many of whom are cited by name in the following pages. It was kind and generous of them to give us so much of their time and thought.

We have discussed parts of this book with a number of friends, and particularly thank, for valuable suggestions, criticism, and encouragement, Jacob Cohen, Meryl Cohen, Fred Hechinger, Walter Jackson, David Kaiser, Roslyn Kaiser, William Lanouette, Kim McQuaid, Marshall Robinson, Adam Silk, Andrew Silk, Guy Stroumsa, and Helena Wall.

Our editor, Martin Kessler, has been a constant source of stimulus and wise counsel. Harold Proshansky, president of the Graduate Center of the City University of New York, aided us by making office space and research facilities available. We are

Preface

most indebted to Amelia North and Susan Tobin for careful and imaginative research assistance.

Finally, the authors wish to thank each other, warmly. *Finis coronat laborem.*

L.S.
M.S.

June, 1980
Hulls Cove, Maine

The American Establishment

Chapter I

The American Establishment:

The Third Force

ONE DAY in the late spring of 1962, John D. Rockefeller 3d received a cable at his New York office in Rockefeller Center from Frederick E. Nolting, Jr., the American ambassador to South Vietnam. The cable caused Rockefeller to telephone John B. Oakes, the editor of the editorial page of *The New York Times.* Rockefeller told Oakes he would like to have lunch with him to discuss something "very serious." Oakes, who was well acquainted with Rockefeller and admired him, readily agreed.

They met for lunch on May 25 at the Century Club at 7 West Forty-third Street, two blocks down from the *Times.* Both Rockefeller and Oakes were "Centurions," the title members of the club bestow upon themselves. It is considered bad form at the Century for members to get out papers while they are lunching, but Rockefeller produced Nolting's cable and handed it to Oakes. The cable said that the *Times,* by repeatedly criticizing Ngo Dinh Diem and the Nhu family for their corruption and authoritarian rule, was undermining the Diem government and jeopardizing the American position in Vietnam. The *Times* was thus damaging efforts to stop the advance of communism in South East Asia. Was there anything Rockefeller could do, asked Nolting, to persuade the *Times* to stop attacking the Diem regime?

Rockefeller told Oakes he was sympathetic to Nolting's position. He had met Nolting in Saigon a few weeks earlier when he was taking a swing through Burma, Laos, Cambodia, and South Vietnam in connection with his interests—and those of the Rockefeller Foundation—in land reform and population control. The *Times* was a strong supporter of such Rockefeller missions; Arthur Hays Sulzberger, who had just retired as publisher of the *Times*, had served on the board of the Rockefeller Foundation from 1948 until 1962.

On his foreign tours for the Foundation, Rockefeller did not ordinarily call on American ambassadors, but he had gone to the embassy in Saigon to meet Nolting because Rockefeller's son Jay, a student at Harvard and later the Governor of West Virginia, was dating Ambassador Nolting's daughter, a student at Radcliffe.

Rockefeller's manner was diffident as he tried to persuade Oakes to be less critical of Diem. He suggested that the *Times* might be hurting the American position and helping the Communists inadvertently. To Oakes, Rockefeller seemed almost apologetic for intervening on the issue. Oakes thanked Rockefeller for his interest and concern, but said the *Times* looked at the problem differently; he and his associates thought South Vietnam could be saved from communism only if it had a government that could win the trust and support of its own people.

After the Oakes-Rockefeller luncheon at the Century Club, the *Times'* editorial policy on the Diem regime did not change. If anything, it became more critical. A year later, on June 13, 1963, an editorial declared:

> It is time Mr. Diem realized that he cannot discriminate against a majority of the people of South Vietnam and win his war against the Communists. If he cannot genuinely represent a majority then he is not the man to be President. He seems to feel that since he is

supported by large-scale American aid he does not have to be supported by the Vietnamese people. No more dangerous error could be made.

Diem continued to reject such criticism. In his view, all underdeveloped countries were, by virtue of a "historical and general phenomenon," ruled by dictators and autocrats, whose existence "corresponded to a historical need for centralization of power." Dismissing press criticism, Diem declared that it could not possibly be constructive but was designed only "to give me a complex of guilt, which I can never have."[1]

Rockefeller did not, after the May 25 luncheon, again attempt to persuade Oakes to stop the *Times'* criticism of Diem. Instead, United States policy changed. The Kennedy administration, in the face of spreading insurgency against the Diem regime, gradually withdrew its support of Diem. In August, 1963, Henry Cabot Lodge was sent to replace Nolting. On November 1, 1963, Diem and his younger brother Ngo Dinh Nhu were murdered by South Vietnamese officers inside an American-built M-113 armored personnel carrier on the streets of Saigon.

Had the American Establishment, of which Rockefeller and Nolting were the very embodiment, failed? Or had the American Establishment, embodied in *The New York Times* and the foreign policy chiefs of the Kennedy administration, prevailed?

What Is the Establishment?

Many Americans feel suspicious and antagonistic toward that thing called the Establishment, a vague body that they believe plays a powerful role in the American society. They accuse it of wrongs ranging from foreign adventuring and the looting of the world's wealth to the suppression of the democratic freedoms of its own people. Others see it as nothing more than a bunch of influential people, living in the Northeast corner of the country and gradually losing their influence as the nation's wealth and power shift to the South and the West. But some Americans see in the Establishment an enduring force that has long held, and continues to hold, a vast and discordant society together, balancing and mediating between the even more powerful forces of popular democracy and corporate capitalism.

Our way of trying to resolve these contending views has been to take a close look at some of the institutions and people grouped around the concept of an Establishment, an institution which, maddeningly, seems both to exist and not exist. This existential ambiguity may be inherent in all institutions—bodies that from one perspective look like corporeal blocs of people, buildings, files, contracts, and from another like ideas that blow away when their time is past.

Yet nations are made of institutions, and the characteristic danger of great nations, as Walter Bagehot observed, is that "They may at last fail from not comprehending the great institutions which they have created." That is a danger now facing the United States, which has been undergoing a loss of confidence in its own great institutions.

The Establishment existed long before it acquired its present name, which it did only about the middle of the twentieth century. But long before it had a name, here or anywhere else, it was recognized as a thing. In fact, "The THING" is precisely what William Cobbett, the early nineteenth-century English pamphleteer, called it in his country.

To Cobbett, the Thing was that network of individuals and institutions that coined the money, invented and preached the morals, created and ran the best schools, passed out the honors, and upheld the System. It included the aristocracy and the gentry, the gentlemen's clubs and the gentlemen's universities, the high churchmen, and the top editors of what Cobbett called "The bloody old *Times.*" And as the Thing upheld the State, the State upheld the Thing.

Credit for the first use of the term the *Establishment* as a label for the Thing belongs to the British historian, A. J. P. Taylor. Taylor used it in an article about Cobbett in *The New Statesman and Nation* of April 19, 1953, in which he wrote: "Trotzky tells how, when he first visited England, Lenin took him round London and, pointing out the sights, exclaimed: 'That's *their* Westminster Abbey! That's *their* Houses of Parliament!' Lenin was making a class, not a national, emphasis. By *them* he meant not the English, but the governing classes, the Establishment."[2] This Establishment, said Taylor, "talks with its own branded accent, eats different meals at different times from the rest of the populace, has its privileged system of education, its own religion, its powerful offices both visible and invisible." (The *Oxford English Dictionary* mistakenly attributes the first usage of the Establishment to the journalist Henry Fairlie for his article in *The Spectator* of September 10, 1955.)

The word caught on in England in the 1950s. The British Establishment had emerged from the war with much of its old vigor—too much, some thought. It was accused by its critics, especially on the left, of using pseudo-ecclesiastical powers to thwart progress. The very term *Establishment* symbolized, as Hugh Thomas put it, "the assumption of the attributes of the state church by certain powerful institutions and people."[3] The charge was that this phoney church was helping to perpetuate aristocratic and imperial habits of thought and policy left over from the nineteenth century, when England was supreme among nations. The road to a healthier and more democratic society was being blocked by its efforts to revive a collapsed past.

The term *Establishment* quickly crossed the Atlantic—not just because there is a rapid two-way traffic in coinages and fads between Britain and the United States but because the Establishment was reviving on the American side as well. There was, however, an important political difference. Where the British Establishment was under attack from the left as an antidemocratic force, the American Establishment had just survived the assault from the right of Senator Joseph McCarthy of Wisconsin and his followers, who accused it of sympathy with communism, or outright treason. With the downfall of McCarthy and McCarthyism, the American Establishment was about to emerge as pioneer of the liberal New Frontier of John F.

Kennedy. This is why the concept publicized by Richard Rovere's 1961 article and his 1962 volume[4] caught on so fast.

But in crossing from Britain to America, the concept of the Establishment seemed to have lost something; it was a metaphor without a clear referent. The British Establishment was understood as the broader, secular analogue to the established Church of England. Where, in the United States, was the established Church?

Yet, in our view, the metaphor remains valid on the American side for two reasons: its essential attributes and its actual link to a religious Establishment.

Key Attributes

The classic discussion of the attributes of a religious Establishment is that of William Paley, an eighteenth-century English theologian and Anglican priest. In his *Principles of Moral and Political Philosophy* (1785), Paley says established churches have a number of requisites, including a professional clergy, guaranteed financial support, and exclusivity—"confining the provision of maintenance of the clergy to the teachers of one particular sect." A secular Establishment has like attributes:

A Professional Clergy. The purpose of a religious establishment is to serve as a scheme for preserving and communicating religious knowledge. Such a scheme requires a class of professionals with expertise, such as linguistic training, knowledge of ancient texts, skills in theological reasoning and discourse.

A secular establishment has similar need of professionals: political scientists, economists, lawyers, mathematicians, administrators, possessors of skills in political-theological reasoning and discourse. Such professionals inhabit a select group of universities, research institutes, policy centers, foundations, and even a few business organizations, news media, and government agencies, such as the State Department or the Central Intelligence Agency. But their principal seminaries are in the private sector.

Guaranteed Support. Paley stressed that the professional clergy should be securely endowed because if it had to depend on voluntary contributions, the populace would have a financial incentive to avoid or reduce religion, or twist it to suit their own purposes. Preaching would become a sort of begging; the preacher would be tempted to adapt his doctrine and style to the desires of the capricious mob. Truth and conscience would be compromised.

Similarly, a secular Establishment is wary of being bought by any interest, financial or political. It shares Paley's fear that making its professionals and institutions too dependent on any corporation or on the State will introduce "numerous corruptions and abuses." Thus recent pleas of some conservative businessmen and their intellectual allies to capitalist donors to restrict their giving to universities and research institutions that support "capitalism" (as defined by the donors and their advisers) have raised Establishment hackles. True establishmentarians urge that money be given "without strings," so that disinterested professionals can pursue the truth, wherever it leads.

With inflation eating into old endowments, the Establishment has grown anxious about the financial health of some of its favored institutions. Before his death in an automobile crash in 1977, John D. Rockefeller 3d was devoting himself mainly to the mounting of a public crusade to rescue what he called *the Third Sector*—not business or government but those nonprofit institutions, such as colleges, universities and research centers, museums and orchestras, churches and social welfare agencies which he held to be crucial to the nation's cultural and moral life. Rich men alone, he said, could no longer carry the Third Sector; broad public support was needed: "This widespread participation is a key element in American pluralism. Ours is a pluralistic society precisely because we have the three broad and vigorous sectors, not just two as in most European countries. ... Opportunities and channels abound within which individual citizens can take initiative. Therein lies the diversity and much of the energy and creativity for which our society has always been noted."

Exclusivity. Financial support of a religious Establishment by the State, said Paley, should be confined to a single sect to minimize social conflict over clerical appointments and to avoid doctrinal warfare. He was not unsympathetic to the idea of having the State support all sects, but thought such a scheme would prove unworkable. Denominational churches would proliferate and would wind up scattered and poor. There would again be the danger of doctrinal competition for material reward.

The American Establishment *is* exclusive, not as a result of State decree or financial support, but of its peculiar history and selection process. Unlike the established church of the Paleyan model, however, it minimizes and sometimes even denies its exclusivity. It knows that in a liberal society the best means to exclusivity is maximum-possible inclusivity. If other sects and sectarian tendencies can be co-opted, then you become the only game in town.

Thus, in matters of public policy, the Establishment forswears definitions of orthodoxy. Its research studies commonly wind up with "options." It dislikes political polemics. It has no clearly enunciated ideology. It invites adherents of different values and creeds to debate, provided that the debate be civil and relatively low-keyed. It solicits the views of outsiders who will play and speak by the rules—respectable labor leaders, people with strong regional accents and styles, minority spokesmen, even the occasional radical.

Tolerance. This hospitality toward dissenting views does not contradict the Paleyan prescription; on the contrary, it conforms to it. Tests of faith, said Paley, should be kept to a minimum in an established church, for, while insuring some measure of order, they check inquiry, violate liberty, and "ensnare the consciences of the clergy, by holding out temptations to prevarication."

Lying was the cardinal sin. Dissidents should enjoy complete toleration, principally because their presence would serve the cause of truth (which would emerge from controversy) but also because the dissidents might be converted and co-opted.

Flexibility.   But the Establishment should not assume that it was everlastingly right in what it had believed. It needed to be flexible to survive. *"If,"* said Paley, *"the dissenters from the establishment become a majority of the people, the establishment itself ought to be altered or qualified."**

The American Establishment fully satisfies this Paleyan principle; it has moved left, right, and center with national ideological currents, and has swung from the East towards the West and the South, with the political winds. The reaching out of the so-called Eastern Establishment for the Southern Baptist Jimmy Carter was no contradiction but a validation of its essential Paleyan character.

Origins: The Church of Massachusetts

Though it has become an overwhelmingly secular institution, the American Establishment can trace its roots to a real religious establishment—the Unitarian church in Massachusetts.

It is often forgotten that, although the First Amendment to the United States Constitution banned the institution of an established church, this proscription did not originally apply to the several states. Not until 1940 did the Supreme Court ban established churches within individual states, and then by interpreting the due process clause of the Fourteenth Amendment (ratified in 1868) as embodying the First Amendment injunctions against interfering with freedom of religion.

In the early years of the Republic, many states did interfere in matters of faith by requiring test oaths for public office, enacting laws against non-Protestants, and the like. Such dis-

*Italics ours.

crimination lasted longer than actual religious establishments. The Anglican establishments of New York and the Southern states were gone by 1800, victims of Jeffersonian doctrine, sectarian pressures, and anti-British feeling. The Congregationalist establishments of New England, untarnished by a British connection, lasted into the nineteenth century. But after 1820 only the Massachusetts establishment remained.

Soon after the American Revolution, a split developed within the Congregationalist pastorate of Massachusetts. On one side was the party of orthodox Calvinism, whose strength lay in the farming population of the western part of the Commonwealth; on the other was the party of Unitarianism (or, as its devotees preferred to say, Liberal Christianity), which was confined to Eastern Massachusetts, where it was dominant among the commercial elite of Boston and other seaport towns.

The first major confrontation between the two factions occurred from 1804 to 1806 when, amid much bitter wrangling, the presidency and senior professorship of Harvard College were awarded to Unitarians. Harvard had been slipping away from orthodoxy for many years but this proved the final straw for good Trinitarians. They sent their sons off to sound places like Yale and Williams, and at Andover founded a seminary from which to obtain proper Calvinist ministers. The schism became irrevocable after 1815, when, thanks to rulings by a Unitarian judiciary, the orthodox abandoned scores of parish churches and built their own houses of worship rather than submit to the appointment of liberal ministers. The establishment was thus divided into Brahmin and undercaste segments; it is the former that concerns us here.

Harvard was the command center of the Unitarian wing of the church and part of the official apparatus of the Commonwealth of Massachusetts. Public officials sat on its Board of Overseers; it depended heavily on tax revenues allocated to it by the Massachusetts legislature.

The characteristic doctrines of Liberal Christianity were worked out at Harvard and communicated to generations of future ministers by such professors of moral philosophy and divinity as Francis Bowen, E. T. Channing, Levi Hedge, Andrews Norton, James Walker, and the Henry Wares, senior and junior. Liberal Christianity was a sanguine and rationalistic sort of religion which substituted a concern with morals for the traditional Puritan preoccupation with doctrine. The existence of moral values, not the arbitrary power of God, was the ultimate truth about the universe. The church's role was to promote moral and spiritual uplift, not to conserve dogma. Upholding the dignity of man, Liberal Christianity sought to school men's moral faculties; the good man was harmoniously balanced, ruled by conscience and prudence, motivated by disinterested affection.

The Harvard Unitarians, looking to occupy a middle ground between Calvinist orthodoxy and Enlightenment Deism, maintained customary Christian religious practices while demurring at the Godhead of Jesus and the depravity of man. Above all, they prided themselves on their commitment to toleration. They refused to articulate a specific creed and took pains to insure that the Harvard faculty be open to members of all Christian denominations. Indeed, in 1831 only six of the fourteen faculty members were Unitarians; the others included three Roman Catholics and a Quaker.

Unitarianism's most important bequest to Harvard was the atmosphere of tolerance which resulted from its principled denial of sectarianism; Harvard's President Kirkland (1810 to 1828) referred to his coreligionists as "the unsectarian sect." In the nineteenth century, this atmosphere set Harvard apart from all other American institutions of higher learning. There was a price paid for its virtues, however, as indicated by the subject set for Divinity students to address in 1826: "On ye connexion between enlightened views of Christianity, and lukewarmness in its cause."*

*Orthodox trinitarians had a point when they claimed that Liberal Christianity was merely a half-way house to atheism. New England Transcendentalism, which it spawned, was initially regarded at Harvard as (since Deism) "the latest form of infi-

If the Unitarian moralists rejected the theological authoritarianism of their forefathers, they nonetheless sought to maintain the traditional prestige of the pulpit in the community. This meant currying the favor of the merchants and businessmen of Boston. There was always a tension between the desire to prick the conscience of the rich and the need to engage in conservative apologetics for the rights of private property.

Beyond this, the Unitarian clergy realized that moral leadership could not be theirs alone; enlightenment required diffusion among the population at large. Harvard suited this purpose admirably. Henry Ware, Jr., told the graduating seniors of 1837 that they should act "like so much leaven, to affect the whole community, pervade it with higher tastes, and give it a better tone."[5] Educated gentlemen would help constitute a refined elite of clerics and laymen who could, in Ware's words, "see to it that the love of gold, the passion for display, the thirst for power, the appetite for pleasure, do not get the ascendency in the community."[6] Groups of literati did meet, and created such durable cultural institutions as the Boston Athenaeum and the *North American Review.*

"The men we particularly need," said Andrews Norton, "are those who may guide and form public opinion and sentiment in matters of taste, in morals, in politics, and in religion."[7]

Nevertheless, for their pains, Harvard's missionaries were attacked as hypocritical snobs who hid their ambitions for power behind a facade of social uplift. What most infuriated their opponents were their professions of openness and ecumenical principles while they doggedly held on to the privileges of establishment.

The end of the official Massachusetts establishment came in 1833. The trinitarian Congregationalists, fed up, joined forces with the nonestablished churches to push through a constitutional amendment of disestablishment. Thereafter the Unitarian clergy became increasingly apolitical.

---

delity." By the end of the century, though, Divinity School theologians had largely come under the sway of this idealist philosophy of romantic individualism.

From Eliot to Lippmann

The Unitarian establishment was formally laid to rest but the ethos it had cultivated survived, and passed from New England into the Establishment of today. Necessarily, this ethos underwent an evolution; it was further secularized, with leadership ultimately conceived as belonging to a class of professionals— lawyers, academics, businessmen—rather than to clerics and refined gentlemen. But the original ecclesiastical character did not disappear. Indeed, it was recognized and avowed by two of the Establishment's founding fathers (sons of Harvard both): Charles W. Eliot and Walter Lippmann.

Eliot, Harvard's president from 1869 to 1909 and the person most responsible for turning it into a great university, was a strong-willed Yankee of purest Brahmin stock. The spirit of Liberal Christianity was in his genes. "I did not *find* in the Unitarian faith inspiration and strength," he remarked late in life. "I was born into it, and brought up in it. . . . I am emphatically a birthright Unitarian."[8] At the time that a full-blown academic culture was materializing in this country, he fashioned the faith of his fathers into a noble and optimistic philosophy of education. The Unitarian devotion to toleration translated into a pioneering commitment to academic freedom. Unsectarianism meant encouraging diversity and even idiosyncrasy within fields, nowhere more evident than in the philosophy department of William James, Josiah Royce, and George Santayana. Faith in man's essential goodness bore fruit in Eliot's system of free electives for undergraduates. As one malicious faculty wit put it:

> Election,
> He held, almost with Calvin, was the one
> Way to salvation, and he dared expect
> Boys to be God-like, and like him to elect.[9]

Freedom was the key. Believing that "the essence of freedom is in equality of opportunities," Eliot fought to change admissions standards in order to make a Harvard education available to a wider range of students.

In "The Religion of the Future," an address delivered in 1909 to a summer session of the Harvard Divinity School, Eliot said society was progressing toward a "simple and rational faith" free from "metaphysical complexities or magical rites." He reinterpreted the "veritas" on Harvard's shield, which originally signified Christian truth, to mean the search for scientific truth, which would "progressively set men free."[10]

Knowledge and humanitarian service, said Eliot, would replace promises of future blessedness and superstitious rites in affording solace to human woe. Thus the "ministers" of the "new religion" would be doctors, scientists, teachers, urban planners, philanthropists—in sum, all those whose job it was to ameliorate this-worldly sources of "physical and moral evil." Apparently, the Harvard of the Future would still be in the business of producing an educated clergy, but not, it seemed, at the Divinity School.

In the same year that Eliot gave this speech, Walter Lippmann graduated from Harvard. Lippmann was neither a Brahmin nor a New Englander, but a New Yorker of German-Jewish family. While at Harvard he was an active socialist, but those days were long gone when, in 1929, he turned his attention to questions of faith and morals. In *A Preface to Morals* his voice is that of neither a Jew nor a radical, but of a Liberal Christian divine who had finally decided to jettison the last remnants of theistic doctrine.

Lippmann's theme was the crisis of the present age. The "acids of modernity" had eaten away at the religious base of society. In the past, moral principles had force because they were believed to have been instituted by God. Moral leaders had authority because God was thought to stand behind them. But now, with certitude in such matters lost, the world was in disorder. American society was in particularly bad straits because its acquaintance with traditional authority was so slight. "The American social system is migratory, revolutionary, and protestant. It provides no recognized leaders and no clear standards of conduct. No one is recognized as the interpreter of morals and the arbiter of taste. There is no social hierarchy, there is no acknowledged ruling class, no well-known system of rights and duties, no code of manners."[11] Something had to be found to replace the useful social fictions religion had once provided. Since no new revelation could be expected, the only answer lay in some sort of humanistic creed. Lippmann's proposal for a creed boiled down to one word: *disinterestedness.* This was the message of the great teachers of wisdom and, in an age which had lost its faith, it was the only way out. Here was a "religion of the spirit" that would untangle moral confusion.

Having found his creed, Lippmann turned to the real world to see if he could locate signs of creeping disinterestedness. He was fairly optimistic about business. To the extent that it was scientific it was on the right track. "It is no exaggeration to say that pure science is high religion incarnate."[12] Thus, the captains of industry were becoming regenerate through having to rely increasingly on research and development, scientific management, and other forms of technocratic expertise. About government Lippmann was less sanguine. True, hope could be found in the existence of a disinterested judiciary and civil service, likewise in "the use in all political debates of the evidence of technicians, experts, and neutral investigators."[13] But by and large the people were not likely to give up their special desires for the sake of a disinterested world-view. The need, then, was for disinterested political leaders—statesmen, not politicians— who would educate the people to desire only what it was possible for them to have. The people must be given "what they will learn to want."[14] Disinterestedness had to be imposed from above. For this a new class of moralists was necessary, its function not to preach or exhort, but to investigate reality, to seek insight, and to elucidate the good. The American Establishment had found its apologia.

The Third Force

In this book we have pursued the Establishment through some of the most important institutions it inhabits: Harvard, *The New York Times,* the Ford Foundation, the Brookings Institution, the Council on Foreign Relations, and the Committee for Economic Development. Not every person who is associated with those bodies is a member of the Establishment; some, indeed, are among its foes. And the institutions we have chosen to describe in the pages that follow are far from being the only ones which, on balance, can be said to belong to the Establishment. Among a long list of others worth considering (not all of them in the East) are Yale, Princeton, Columbia, the University of Chicago, Stanford, the Carnegie Endowment for International Peace, the RAND Corporation, the Twentieth Century Fund, the Russell Sage Foundation, the Century Association, even the boards of the Metropolitan Museum of Art, the Museum of Modern Art, and the Metropolitan Opera. We chose the institutions we did because we are focusing on the Establishment's role in American political affairs and public policy rather than in cultural or aesthetic matters. We regard these institutions as extremely important in their own right and broadly representative of others.

We see the Establishment as a collective entity, as a "third force" in the American polity, the other two being Business and Government. The Establishment is not a force wholly independent of these other two. On the contrary, it has links to both of them, and a certain amount of moving about occurs among their leading members, who sometimes are found attached to one sector and then to another, or even to two or all three of them simultaneously. Thus our two next-to-last chapters examine the relationships between the Establishment and Business, and the Establishment and Government.

Despite the commerce, or intercourse, among these three forces, we hold them to be independent of each other, quite different in their ethos, motivations, structures, goals. We shall not try to characterize these differences here; that is the job of the chapters that follow. But we might say, very briefly, that where the aim of business is profit, and where the aim of politics is power, the aim of the Establishment is disinterest and public morality—which is why, in our conception, it so resembles a state church. The individual institutions of the Establishment commonly have other and more specific functions: to further education, promote research, discuss foreign policy, give the news, etc. But we have concluded that the whole of the Establishment is greater than the sum of its parts; it is that Whole which is the *Third Force*—in effect, the core of John D. Rockefeller 3d's voluntary Third Sector.

The important element of voluntarism is what makes ours a distinctively *American* Establishment. As Tocqueville perceptively observed nearly a century and a half ago, Americans have a passion for joining together in voluntary associations for achieving public purposes. That passion has by no means disappeared, although there are reasons to fear that it may be eroding or may no longer be adequate to the jobs it once felt competent to discharge.* In our final chapter, we shall weigh those pressures and consider the future of the Establishment.

Our Establishment is distinctively American in still another sense. It is a *democratic* establishment, rather than an aristocratic or authoritarian one, and has been from the beginning. Its roots are in a liberal, democratic church; tolerance and openness were and remain its dominant principles. Proud of its traditions, proud of its role and status, seeking excellence, the American Establishment yet reaches out to the people.

This clearly involves some inner strain and contradiction—contradiction that outsiders note and often criticize. As we shall see, President Nixon accused the Establishment of liking humanity in the mass but not as individuals (as he asserted he did). The Establishment is hit from both sides—by the populists as elitist, and by the conservatives as liberal. It cannot escape this contradiction.

*This is the theme of Waldemar Nielsen's recent book, *The Endangered Sector* (New York, 1979).

No human institution, secular or religious, fully lives up to its own ideals, and certainly, as we hope the succeeding chapters make plain, the institutions of the Establishment do not. The people of these institutions have all the fallibility, and some of the venality, of people everywhere. The Establishment's links to business and government—that is, to people with quite specific vested economic and political interests—inevitably make for complexity, and something less than purity. The Establishment is often vulnerable to the extremely serious charge of pursuing the private interests of its members behind a mask of disinterest. Those who pretend to high standards of disinterest and morality had better live up to them or be despised as hypocrites.

But, in our view, America needs institutions and individuals willing to brave that accusation. The American Establishment represents the effort of many people to create a national force, outside government, dedicated to truth, liberty, and, however defined, the broad public interest.

The Establishment Thinks Big. It worries not only about the whole nation but about all humanity. It searches after the vast abstractions. It pursues the best, and it sometimes produces the worst.

Chapter 2

Elitism for All: Harvard

THERE ARE several great American universities, and some nearly equal to Harvard in Establishment character. But Harvard is the sun, and its light is diffused throughout the system.

Not only is Harvard the principal source of the Establishment's ethos; it is its foremost exemplar. The earliest American college, it was the first institution to try to provide the North American wilderness with an educated elite. In American higher education it never relinquished its position of preeminence. Although not the first to undertake graduate instruction in a serious way, it got in quickly with the most—resources, programs, students. Above all, it was the first American university to cherish *national* ambitions, seeking students from all parts of the country and, even more importantly, developing superior and *large* professional schools to train the nation's leaders. And it achieved the prestige it was after, gaining intellectual leadership and moral influence, attracting talent and wealth, and earning the envy and resentment of others.

Liberalism Pays

Never in Harvard's three and a half centuries was its dominance on the American intellectual scene so clear as during the period after World War II. With its celebrated Redbook on general education, Harvard led the way in curriculum reform. With its public resistance to the anti-Red witch hunt of Senator Joe McCarthy of Wisconsin, Harvard (fairly or exaggeratedly) was seen as the emblem of academic freedom. The best students sought to flock to Harvard. The best professors wanted to be there. Its graduate students and castoff faculty spread its influence everywhere. Its journals and institutes and prizes proliferated. Its endowment was the greatest. And its pride mounted.

The golden dream of Harvard's pride was the Kennedy presidency: his assassination shattered that dream. Although some of Kennedy's Harvard people stayed on under Lyndon Johnson, the magic was gone.

In the face of the Vietnam war, urban violence, the unsuccess of the Great Society, and the bitter student protests within the gates of the liberal university, the sense of righteous purpose dissolved. The cool, professional competence of the university was exposed as blockheaded; instrumentalism was shot to death in Southeast Asia. At home the new social order was a flop; the American war on poverty was routed by inflation.

A sense of moral failure was all-embracing. The Establishment had failed and therefore Harvard, at its heart, had failed. Suicidal impulses abounded. Watergate helped to dissipate them, but moral convalescence has been slow, as close observation of the Cambridge scene reveals.

October 20, 1978. Alumni in their station wagons are foregathering at Soldiers Field for the Dartmouth game. On the Charles, between the stadium and the bright foliage along Memorial Drive, oarspeople are plying their shells. And beyond the trees, on freshly sodded acreage of the former Massachusetts Bay Transportation Authority rail yard, a ceremony is getting under way. Harvard is dedicating the new home of the John Fitzgerald Kennedy School of Government, its belated tribute to a fallen son.

Aging pioneers of the New Frontier assemble: McGeorge Bundy, John Kenneth Galbraith, Richard Goodwin, Richard Neustadt, Edward Kennedy, Jacqueline Kennedy Onassis. But as the friends of the Kennedy School make their way to the folding chairs, with the Harvard Band playing college tunes under the baton of Arthur Fiedler, the nostalgia is rudely disturbed by sounds from Harvard's more recent, less pleasant past: the unmistakable rhythmic chanting of student demonstrators. They are arrayed at the back of the John F. Kennedy Memorial Park, behind a cordon of rope and policeman's blue, waving placards and handing out leaflets, and shouting:

> Hey, hey, Derek Bok,
> Throw away your racist stock.

The students are protesting Harvard's refusal to divest itself of its stockholdings in companies that maintain operations in the Republic of South Africa. President Bok had enunciated the policy the previous spring in response to student demonstrations against apartheid. The protesters have a specific reason for attending the dedication of the Kennedy School. They have discovered that the School has named its library for Charles Engelhard, a recently deceased American businessman (and a financial backer of JFK), in acknowledgement of a $1 million gift from the Engelhard Foundation.* Engelhard built a vast fortune by investing in numerous South African industrial enterprises, most notably in the Transvaal gold mines. More than that, he was an unabashed apologist for the apartheid regime.

The protesters want the name of the Engelhard Library changed. They keep up a steady chant. The Sheriff of Middlesex County calls the meeting to order. Now the plump young dean of the Kennedy School, Graham Allison, is at the rostrum. He

---

*This was not the only instance of the Kennedy School's tribute to a commercial benefactor. The main meeting place of the school is called the ARCO Forum of Public Affairs.

acknowledges the presence of the protesters, expresses sympathetic understanding of their distress, and offers a deal. If they promise not to disrupt the ceremony with chanting, one of them will be permitted to state their case at the end of the affair. Allison's offer is greeted with a mixture of catcalls and applause.

The Dean turns to an extended discussion of what he calls Parkinson's Second Law: that perfection of planning, design, and construction is a sure sign of institutional decay. The audience begins to fidget; the protesters lapse into sullen silence. The National Anthem. Invocation by a representative of the Boston Archdiocese. More speeches, from the Governor and the Metropolitan District Commissioner.

And now it is Bok's turn to speak. Suddenly the protesters come to life. They regard Bok as the villain of the piece, and they mean to keep up a steady volley of noise throughout his address. "Let us speak now, let us speak now." They do not relish the prospect of a mass walkout if and when their spokesman is given his chance. Within the ranks there is some desire to break through the barricade and march to the speaker's platform, but the leaders do not want this, and the presence of the policemen provides additional dissuasion. The demonstration remains exclusively verbal.

Bok, slim and still boyish despite graying hair, sets his jaw and plunges in. His theme is "excellence in government." Throughout the world there is general dissatisfaction with the quality of life. Is this the fault of an absence of leadership? No, the trouble is more deeply rooted. Problems have grown too large; there are no simple solutions. No single institution can remedy the situation, but each must look within itself. In that spirit, we at Harvard have decided to do what we can to improve the quality of government.

"Let us speak now, let us speak now!" Amid the cacophony, the people under the pavilion are growing restive. Muttered unpleasantries against the protesters.

Bok grimly carries on. The Kennedy administration had scores of experts, but they lacked serious, systematic preparation for government service. In the past decade, however, new methods of public administration have evolved; the requisite body of knowledge now exists. Government has assumed a role in solving all the problems we face today, but there is no tradition of preparation for public leadership. That is the principal missing link in higher education today. What we are doing here is building bridges between the world of public affairs and the academy.

Bok sits down. Senator Kennedy rises to nervous applause. Welcoming the protesters, he recalls how his brother Bob went to Cape Town and spoke out against apartheid there. He tells them that he and his family will stay to hear their speaker, and hopes everyone else will, too. A solid stroke. There will be no chanting while he is at the rostrum.

The Senator recalls how Jack, when competing intramurally for Winthrop House against other Houses with Yankee names like Lowell, Eliot, and Kirkland, never dreamed that there would one day be a building named Kennedy. He denounces Proposition 13 and those who are using Jack's name to justify their dubious tax proposals. The Kennedy School, he asserts, has set its face against those developments. Jack understood the power of ordinary citizens. Though attracted to journalism, he went into public affairs. "He loved the *Crimson,* but his mother was the mayor's daughter."

The younger brother declares his support for deregulation of industry and makes a pitch for his health insurance plan. The mullahs of the Kennedy School are more sympathetic to the former than the latter, but it is a rare opportunity to indulge in the unabashed liberalism of an earlier day. Towards the end, the Senator's voice breaks. "Now, at last, Jack has come back to Harvard." All join in singing "The Battle Hymn of the Republic."

Reverend Peter Gomes, the portly minister of Harvard's Memorial Church, offers the benediction. Gomes is a curious amalgam. He is black—his mother from a middle-class family resident in Boston since before the Civil War, his father a Portuguese-speaking immigrant from the Cape Verdean island of Brava. But Peter Gomes' voice is pure Boston Brahmin. He is a Baptist, conservative and evangelical in his theology; also a confirmed anglophile, with a love for all aspects of high church ceremonial. A young man, he is a great favorite of Harvard's Yankee old guard, who consider him a kindred spirit. He is on good terms with Harvard's black community as well, having paid his dues by spending two years as dean of freshmen and history instructor at the Tuskeegee Institute. Gomes has in the past lent his support to the anti-South Africa crusade, but his remarks do not refer to it. He contents himself with a generalized clerical caution. "The God to whom we pray . . . is not unacquainted with the vanity of human accomplishment and the foolishness of that power in which we delight."

Now it is the protesters' turn. As Mark Smith, a black student, ascends the speaker's platform, only a handful of disgruntled souls depart the scene. Everyone else follows the Kennedy example. Some, recalling SDS orators of the Vietnam years, brace for a graceless harangue. Smith states the circumstances of the protest briefly. Setting aside the complicated issue of investment policy, he focusses attention squarely on the symbolism of the library. "Naming a library after Charles Engelhard is a travesty and a damn shame."

His auditors, on this day, are well attuned to the significance of symbols; after all, if the Kennedy School is a living memorial to JFK, who can deny that the library is a living memorial to Engelhard?

"Talk at Harvard is cheap. But when money is mentioned, there is a wringing of hands and talk of tough decisions." The audience relaxes. Smith's argument is cogent, his rhetoric entertaining, and, whether he knows it or not, he can draw upon a certain reservoir of annoyance within the Harvard community at the administration's boundless enthusiasm for the Kennedy School. By the time he concludes with Frederick Douglass's "Power concedes nothing without a struggle," the crowd is on his side.

Enthusiastic applause. Senator Kennedy leaps up to shake Smith's hand. The assemblage disperses in great good humor. The administration has listened; the protesters have had their case presented according to the best traditions of reasoned debate. Harvard is still Harvard. Liberalism pays. The naming of the library was a mistake; perhaps the name will be changed. (It will.)

Have the protesters been co-opted? By nightfall some of them, placards and leaflets deposited in their rooms, will be assisting in tuxedos at Kennedy School cocktail parties. In the post-post-Vietnam era, push can come to clink. But the protest over investments will continue too.

The Anti-Crimson Tide

In the beginning, Harvard's liberalism was religious. The elders of Massachusetts Bay set up Harvard College in 1636 as an accessory to their Puritan religious establishment. It would provide the young colony with the means of educating its own clergy. Not coincidentally, the college was founded at a time when the establishment was under attack; Anne Hutchinson and her followers were disputing the authority of the official ministry to dictate on religious matters to the rest of the community. Harvard was intended to buttress that clerical authority.

Anne Hutchinson failed, and was exiled in disgrace. Henceforth the colony's "errand into the wilderness" would be shepherded by erudite pastors of the established faith, the divine science of John Calvin.

But book learning can undermine as well as prop up a given orthodoxy, and it soon became apparent to the more conservative Puritan clergy that Harvard was not living up to their expectations. Indeed, under the nose of Increase Mather, the college's rigid but often absent president, a dangerous religious liberalism had crept in. The belated but strenuous efforts of Increase, his son Cotton, and their allies to root out liberalism at Harvard failed.

The well-to-do merchants of Boston were themselves increasingly liberal. Free trade bred free thought; Adam Smith was not wrong about that. The proper Bostonians had no desire to see their college returned to the narrow Calvinism of the past. The election of the liberal John Leverett as president in 1707 set Harvard firmly on the path which led, a century later, to Unitarianism, and which earned it both the lasting distrust of orthodox and evangelical Protestants and a general reputation for freethinking.

But at the same time that Harvard was slipping the reins of Puritan orthodoxy, it was also gaining notoriety as a nursery of snobbism and upper-class pretention. In 1722, the pages of the *New England Courant* were enlivened by the attacks of young Benjamin Franklin on this polishing school for the dull offspring of Boston's emergent commercial aristocracy: a temple of learning "where, for want of a suitable Genius, they learn little more than how to carry themselves handsomely, and enter a Room genteely (which might as well be acquired at a Dancing-School)...." And yet, such popinjays aspired to social leadership.

> Long have the weaker Sons of Harvard strove
> To move our Rev'rence and command our Love,
> By Means, how sordid, 'tis not hard to say,
> When all their Merit lies in M. and A.
> The Knowing Sons of Harvard we revere,
> And in their just Defense will still appear;
> But every idle Fop who there commences,
> Shall never claim Dominion o'er our Senses,
> We judge not of their Knowledge by their Air,
> Nor think the wisest Heads have curled Hair.[1]

Liberalism and social elitism: long before the American Revolution, Harvard had become suspect on just those grounds that it is today. The two charges were connected. In the early eighteenth century, Harvard's liberalism consisted in its openness to the teachings of certain Anglican divines. This was a consequence of the increasingly close and admiring contact of Boston merchants with their affluent British counterparts. It was an English style that the undergraduate rakes were affecting.

Elitism for All: Harvard

Yet, despite latent or overt anglophilia, Harvard was proudly American; its students and alumni for the most part acquitted themselves bravely and patriotically in the Revolution. Nevertheless, after the Revolution the double grievance persisted. Harvard was the emblem of Massachusetts' eastern Federalist upper class, which was politically conservative, aristocratic of temper, and Unitarian (or, to some critics, godless) in religion. In the small towns and farming communities to the south and west, dominated by the forces of trinitarian Congregationalism and Jeffersonian democracy, Harvard symbolized a certain rottenness at the top, a lack of commitment on the part of society's leaders to the basic faiths responsible for that society's strength and very existence: the Christian faith of their fathers and the new democratic faith.

It was hard to move the reverence and command the love of the opposition. Harvard was avowedly in the business of schooling an elite; and, to a vigorously egalitarian populace, this could only be resented. Harvard's Unitarianism, though theoretically separable from the issue of elitism, was in fact bound up with it. The Unitarian moralists imagined that theirs was the religion of the future, and they presented it as a lesson to the rest of society, the example that others were to imitate. Wasn't this simply the spiritual component of the Boston patriciate's general pretension to leadership? That, more than the Unitarian heresy per se, was what stuck in the craw of the "less advanced" classes.

After the Civil War, Harvard began to lose its Unitarian cast, thanks particularly to the inroads of Episcopalianism on Boston's upper crust. Meanwhile, with the Irish immigration, Rome replaced Geneva as the symbol of "backwardness" in religion. To the Irish working class, even more than to their Calvinist predecessors, Harvard stood for aristocracy and irreligion.

The "Godless Harvard" of the nineteenth century was gradually replaced, in the twentieth, by what the old *Boston Post* used to call "the Kremlin on the Charles"; the issue was now godless communism. According to the new charge, Harvard, ancient betrayer of Calvinism, was now betraying that religious creed's secular ghost: the ethos of capitalism.

In the 1930s, Harvard harbored radicals, sent eager New Dealers down to Washington, and served as a command post for the infiltration of Keynesian economics into national economic policy making. After World War II, it was accused of shielding Reds while fighting the patriotic Senator McCarthy. It was deeply implicated in the welfare-statism (underminer of free enterprise) of John F. Kennedy's New Frontier and Lyndon B. Johnson's Great Society.

But once again the animus against Harvard seemed to have more to do with elitism than with ideological heresy. Harvard's new professionals were more heterogeneous and more democratically based than their Brahmin ancestors, yet they had assumed a like social role, combining refinement in taste, aloofness from ordinary folk, and a conviction that moral and intellectual superiority entitled them to the privileges of leadership.

If Joe McCarthy had been interested solely in ferreting out Communists, he would have found happier hunting grounds at other places than Harvard, which possessed virtually none. But the Senator's goal was to make the social elite of Cambridge sweat, to wage populist war against the patricians. Harvard returned the compliment; such aid and comfort as it afforded its leftists and dissidents signalled its contempt for vulgar populism, which the Senator from Wisconsin embodied.

To this day the charge of un-Americanism dogs Harvard. Indeed, it has never been stated more baldly than in the title of John LeBoutellier's autobiographical tract, *Harvard Hates America: The Odyssey of a Born-Again American.* [2] The author, a graduate of both Harvard College and the Harvard Business School, hurls brickbats at a variety of targets. From his undergraduate days he retails horror stories of student radicalism and dissipation, and of liberal bias or worse in the classroom. He paints an unpleasant picture of social snobbery among members of the Porcellian, Harvard's most exclusive "final club." For him, both leftists and "clubbies" provide evidence of "the inbred Harvard sense of superiority."[3] Later, after this Candide of the Right has left Cambridge to wander through the swamplands of Republican fundraising, he returns to the banks of the Charles only to find, to his dismay, that once again Harvard is inflicting a disservice upon the nation, now by using its Business School to create a smug breed of technically accomplished but utterly immoral capitalists, interested in nothing but money, power, and self-aggrandizement.

Harvard Hates America is a later but weaker version of the young William F. Buckley, Jr.'s *God and Man at Yale*. Buckley, writing in 1951, argued that Yale was giving short shrift in its undergraduate offerings to Christianity and laissez-faire economics. Yale's elitism did not bother him. The problem was rather that Yale seemed to be betraying its own upper-class role by yielding to the forces of secularism and socialism. The book is therefore couched as a call to Yale alumni, by and large members of the *haute bourgeoisie*, to bring pressure on their alma mater to redress the balance.

Yet LeBoutellier, from across the field in Cambridge, sees the crimson in triumph flashing. In his peroration, the voice of authentic Harvard pride emerges:

> In every field, whether it be business, law, medicine, or anything else, Harvard University should be leading the way, recognizing changing public attitudes and needs. Harvard should recognize its special role in America—that of being charged with the responsibility for educating leaders capable of solving problems, leaders dedicated to improving the welfare of the entire country, not followers devoted simply to "making money."[4]

If America hates Harvard, it is, LeBoutellier notwithstanding, precisely for arrogating to itself this "special role."

Harvard does not hate America; its Archibald MacLeishes and Samuel Eliot Morisons and Archibald Coxes want nothing more than to be of service to the nation. Yet Harvard's love for America is unrequited. Downstairs does not love upstairs.

The Open Door

The American Establishment has been shifting from a white Anglo-Saxon aristocracy towards a more ethnically diverse and ecumenical meritocracy. This has been a long and slow process, by no means simple to bring about. But it has been absolutely essential. To maintain its existence and increase its strength, the Establishment has had to reconcile opposing pulls: on the one side, it had to preserve exclusivity, its claim to social and moral as well as intellectual superiority; on the other side, it had to recruit the best talent available or see its pretensions undermined, widen its political base in the new and rising popular forces beyond its own gates, and, in the American democracy, practice or at least simulate a sincere belief in equality.

Ironically, the need for exclusivity seemed crucial to enhancing the Establishment's moral strength. The last decades of the nineteenth century saw the beginnings of what Christopher Lasch has called "the moral and intellectual rehabilitation of the ruling class." The old commercial elites of the Eastern seaboard, pressed politically by immigrant hordes and economically by an uncouth new industrial plutocracy, chose to fight rather than subside gently into provincial oblivion. Their fight was surprisingly successful, and resulted in the emergence of a new national bourgeoisie.[5]

The old Eastern elites succeeded by building on their social and cultural preeminence. Through such institutions as boarding schools, exclusive resorts, country clubs, city athletic and social clubs, and civic associations and charities, they established common identity, and civilized and assimilated the *nouveaux riches* while simultaneously holding the hyphenated Americans at bay.

In public affairs, an elevated moral tone was struck, and some political muscle developed, through municipal and civil-service reform movements. The evils of unguided democracy and unfettered capitalism were attacked with a new ideology of social orderliness which urged the interest of all citizens in economy and efficiency in government and state supervision of economic life.

In all this, the leading colleges and universities played a central role, affording not only another arena for upper-class socializing but also essential intellectual leverage. With the appealing hope of remedying social ills through the discovery and dissemination of knowledge, the colleges would supply experts and professionals to devise, rationalize, and carry out desired public remedies.

Higher education was becoming an increasingly accessible and promising mode of social advancement for Americans; the best institutions seemed to offer poor but deserving youth the opportunity to pass through ivy-covered classrooms and libraries into a Jeffersonian aristocracy of merit. But the new leaders, as they emerged, would be expected to share the norms of class and culture belonging to the older gentries. The conflict between elitism and the democratic dogma was deep, and nowhere more so than at Harvard.

Charles W. Eliot was Harvard's great progressive. Under his leadership, from 1869 to 1909, a proud but drowsy New England college flanked with small, apprenticing professional schools evolved into a university worthy of the name. Eliot's was the heroic age of American higher education. Not only at Harvard but in other parts of the country great feats of institution building were being performed by such exceptional academic leaders as James McCosh of Princeton, Andrew D. White of Cornell, Daniel C. Gilman of Johns Hopkins, James B. Angell of Michigan, William R. Harper of Chicago, and David S. Jordan of Stanford. Johns Hopkins, established in 1876, was the first of the true American universities, drawing its inspiration from the great German research faculties. Eliot had a hand in shaping the Hopkins' approach, the success of which he was able to use as a lever for getting Harvard quickly on the bandwagon of graduate education. The renovations of Harvard's law and medical schools were among his earliest and greatest accomplishments.

As a fervent believer in education's power to ameliorate social ills, Eliot had no peer, and he became a visible symbol of the academy's growing involvement in public affairs. He made pronouncements on any and all questions of faith, morals, and government policy. He stood for incorporating the ideals of public service of his Brahmin forebears into the country's new culture of professionalism; after retirement, he sat on the boards of the Rockefeller Foundation, the Institute for Government Research, and the Council on Foreign Relations. He was the nation's professor, known to Americans as the designer of the famous "five-foot shelf" of Harvard Classics, which included his guide to their contents and a fifteen-minute per day regimen for self-education.

Eliot was a democrat* who waged battles to make a Harvard education available to students who did not have all the benefits of first rate, "classical," secondary schooling. An aloof and somewhat humorless man himself, he had little use for conventional college spirit and was unconcerned with shaping collegiate life. His object was to offer a rich and open intellectual environment and to let undergraduates make their own way, as free as possible from outside interference. Outside of freshman English, students were permitted to select whichever courses they wished. The undergraduate community suffered some fragmentation. Wealthy students began to live on the fashionable "Gold Coast" along Mt. Auburn Steet and dined at their clubs, while the poor lived in rooming houses and ate at the Memorial Hall commons.

William James, the university's leading philosopher, gave Eliot's Harvard its most stirring testimonial in a 1903 commencement talk entitled "The True Harvard." Was there anything, James asked, that made Harvard specially worthy of devotion? Not the quality of its education. James chided Eliot for naiveté in imagining that "if the schools would only do their duty better, social vice might cease." For every vice, some Harvard advocate could be found. To be a Harvard man would guarantee no

*Also a Democrat. He bolted from the Republicans in the mugwump revolt of 1884, supporting Grover Cleveland rather than the Plumed Knight, James G. Blaine. Unlike most of his fellow mugwumps, Eliot changed parties for good.

more than educated cleverness "in the service of popular idols and vulgar ends." Moreover, James said, any college could foster mere "club loyalty."

There was, however, something special: an inner, spiritual Harvard, for which outsiders came "from the remotest outskirts of our country, without introductions, without school affiliations; special students, scientific students, graduate students, poor students of the College, who make their living as they go." Such students came to Harvard because they had heard of her "persistently atomistic constitution, of her tolerance of exceptionality and eccentricity, of her devotion to the principles of individual vocation and choice." They acquired a deeper and subtler loyalty to Harvard, the Harvard which was able to nurture "independent and lonely thinkers."[6]

The Limits of Tolerance

But there were those who felt that Harvard was too lonely and atomistic. Foremost among them was Eliot's successor, Abbott Lawrence Lowell, who assumed the reins of the university in 1909. Lowell, who stemmed from the most distinguished of the Brahmin dynasties, was a man of nothing if not strong convictions. After an undistinguished law career in Boston, he returned to his alma mater as a lecturer on government, becoming a full professor in 1900. From that post he engaged in a sniping campaign against the Eliot regime.

Lowell was, like Eliot, a good Unitarian, but he did not share Eliot's faith in mankind's natural goodness. When Harvard's new philosophy building, Emerson Hall, was erected, the assumption was that it would be inscribed with the appropriately Emersonian "Man is the measure of all things." Instead, Lowell supplied the more ambiguous "What is man that thou art mindful of him?" Twentieth-century angst had arrived.

Of the Harvard man at least, Lowell was always intensely mindful. He was convinced that undergraduates needed guidance in their studies; Eliot's system of free electives was scrapped in favor of "concentrations" (departmental majors), distribution requirements, and Oxbridge-style tutorials. Socially, Lowell believed that Harvard was a nice place if you came from the right secondary school, but lonely and alienating if you did not; he made it his business to house the undergraduates properly. He first built freshman dormitories and then, with a generous bequest from Yale alumnus Edward Stephen Harkness in 1928, created a system of residential Houses for the three upper classes. Lowell's purpose, according to his biographer, was "the encouragement of a democratic social life among the students."[7]

Social democracy meant, in effect, clubs for everybody. The Houses had their own libraries, common rooms, dining halls, and, in some cases, squash courts. All undergraduates not living at home were required to live on campus, and Lowell shrewdly insisted that everyone pay board. Eating together, he felt, was the surest way of breaking down social barriers; the prep school cliques would fall apart and the clubmen would be weaned away, at least partially, from their exclusive sanctuaries. Meanwhile, the outsiders would acquire style and polish.

Total democratization was not envisaged, simply the preservation of the college's traditional character. Elliott Perkins (class of 1923) recently recalled a conversation from his pre-House undergraduate days with his father, Thomas Nelson Perkins, then a fellow of the university's ruling body, the Harvard Corporation. "Dad said, 'Harvard will always appeal to the greasy grind; we've got the library, etc. And we'll keep our people for a while, because of club associations. But we're going to lose our backbone, the good middle-class American boy without much Harvard background. They won't think Harvard College is any fun. Then people like us, who like to think of ourselves as an aristocracy, will have no one to feel aristocratic about. We'll drop away, and nothing will remain of Harvard College.' And that," said Elliott Perkins, for many years the master of Lowell House, "is why the Houses are so important."

If the clubmen posed one kind of threat to a "democratized" Harvard, Jews, in Lowell's eyes, posed another. Since the 1880s, Jews had been coming to Harvard in growing numbers, drawn by the school's reputation for both academic excellence and religious tolerance. Between 1908 and 1920, their proportion of the undergraduate student body increased from 6 to 20 percent, and this was interpreted by some to mean that Harvard had a "Jewish problem."

Actually, the problem had as much to do with the altered character of the Jewish population as it did with numbers. Consider two representative Jewish students, the first a classmate of Nelson Perkins (class of 1891), the second a classmate of his son Elliott (class of 1923).

Victor Sydney Rothschild was born in New York City in 1870, attended public schools there as well as the Royal Gymnasium in Frankfurt, Germany, and was prepared for college at Dr. Julius Sachs' school in New York. At Harvard he pursued an interest in French literature, played principal viola in the college orchestra, and was a star member of the track team, setting a record in the 880-yard run which held up for many years. He was known for his sense of humor, and was often called upon to serve as toastmaster at class dinners; many of his witticisms were published in the Harvard *Lampoon.* In later life, he was a member of the New York Stock Exchange and a trustee of the United Hebrew Charities. He wrote monographs on Michel Montaigne, the French essayist and skeptical philosopher of Jewish descent, and spent his last years composing Montaigne's "autobiography" in sixteenth-century French.

Frank Shapiro, on the other hand, was born in Novgorod, Russia, in 1902. He attended the Boston Latin School. He also had a good sense of humor, but his Harvard experience was a far cry from Rothschild's.

Happy the man without traditions! Shortly after my mother and I left the grilled enclosure of Ellis Island and had settled in the

comforts of a palatial West End (of Boston) suite of three roomettes
—one sans window—my mother took me by tender hand and said:
"My son goes to Harvard!" We later moved to "The Hill" (Phillips
Street near West Cedar Street) rubbing shoulders with—but somehow never crossing border of—Louisburg Square, where "Harvard" was even more in the air. Thus, happily I was unfettered with
traditions of Yale or Princeton as was Ed Weeks of Chestnut Street
nearby.

But why was I scheduled for Harvard? Again my mother speaking: "Is it not so near, Froikeh—you could take your lunch with"
(as indeed I did and ate it daily in one of the empty salons of
Emerson) "and you could come home every night and do your
home-lessons and with your giving Hebrew lessons, we will manage
to get your tuition." Thus was Harvard fitted into the framework.
Thus, also, there wasn't much "college life."[8]

Harvard had no trouble accepting its V. S. Rothschilds, middle and upper class German Jews from New York and Cincinnati who came to Cambridge as fully acculturated (and often
highly cultured) Americans. The Frank Shapiros, however,
were another matter, and in 1920 they constituted the bulk of
Harvard's Jewish 20 percent. These Eastern European immigrants, commuting daily to Harvard Yard from their working-
class homes in and around Boston, seemed like creatures from
another planet. They talked, dressed, and carried themselves
differently. "In college," recalls Elliott Perkins, "I could tell a
Jew walking towards me a block away." College life was an
unaffordable luxury; they were there to study, and study they
did, wreaking havoc on Harvard's gentlemanly grading curves.
There was fear that their numbers would continue to increase,
if not to the more than 80 percent at New York's City College,
then perhaps to Columbia's 40 percent.

Lowell was not about to let it happen. In 1922, the university
announced that, as part of a general review of the issue of limiting enrollment*, it intended to address the subject of the proportion of Jews at the college. The announcement raised a storm of

*Until then, admission was based purely on written examination. Reassessment of
this policy was precipitated by a substantial expansion of enrollment following World
War I.

protest. The Boston City Council condemned the Harvard administration and, at the behest of the State legislature, a committee of investigation was appointed by the governor. *The New York Times* gave the story prominent play. Nelson Perkins told his son, "I wish the old man wouldn't shoot his mouth off when he doesn't know what he's talking about. There is no Jewish problem, just the latest unassimilated immigrant problem."

Lowell, though, was inclined to think of Jews as unassimilable, at least to the extent that they continued to observe the practices of their religion; moreover, the likelihood of assimilation was inversely proportional to the number of Jewish students. He proposed a Jewish quota of 15 or 16 percent, but this was rejected by the faculty committee he appointed to study the admissions question. (Of the thirteen men on the committee, three were themselves Jewish.) Instead, the committee recommended measures to gain a more geographically diverse student body and to permit administrative discretion in admissions as a means of limiting overall enrollment.

The measures more than accomplished Lowell's goal. Although there are no exact figures, it appears that by the time the House system got under way in 1930, the percentage of Jews in the college was down to about 10 percent. As instruments of Lowellian democracy, the Houses in the thirties admitted freshman applicants according to a system of distributive quotas: (1) Groton, St. Paul's, and St. Mark's; (2) Andover and Exeter; (3) Other private schools; (4) Public high schools; and (5) Category "X." Category "X" meant Jews. Prep school cliques and Semites were thus dispersed into a series of English-style melting pots.

In Lowell's eyes, Harvard was responsible for embodying the values of America's dominant culture. The Houses were to stand for the best traditions of Anglo-American democracy. Protestant civilization was symbolized by the imposing new Memorial Church, built by Lowell, over the objections of some, as Harvard's tribute to those of its sons who fell in the Great War.

Outsiders were welcomed, but within limits and not on their own terms. Harvard had long prided itself on its hospitality to black students, but Lowell did not want them living among whites. Eventually he was persuaded to allow those blacks who requested it to live on campus. Since precious few of them ever enrolled, the issue was largely symbolic. The Boston Irish might have threatened Harvard's traditional character; however, they, in obedience to the wishes of the country's Catholic authorities, for the most part confined their pursuit of higher learning to Church-sponsored colleges and universities. Such Catholics as made their way to Harvard seemed by their very presence to want to assimilate into the Protestant mainstream and that, to Lowell, was a fine thing. He was happy to arrange for his Irish Catholic friend and classmate, James Byrne, to become a member of the Harvard Corporation.

Thus it was the Jews, with their numbers and "foreign" manner, who constituted the menace. Anti-Semitism came to Harvard: Jews were money-grubbing and aggressive, aloof from others, wanting in social graces, incapable of refinement, unconscious of civic responsibility. Of course, there were exceptions. As Lowell was fond of saying, "Meet a scrupulous Jew and you meet the best of men and citizens. He is certain to be an idealist."[9] But then there were all those unscrupulous ones.

Genteel anti-Semitism, ensconced in corporate boardrooms, country clubs, and literary salons since the end of the nineteenth century, was not fully felt in higher education until after World War I, when flocks of applicants enabled formerly student-hungry colleges and universities to become selective. Exclusionary policies were most perceptible at those institutions which, by reason of geography or liberal reputation, had proved most attractive to Jewish students. Harvard, thanks to Lowell's characteristic forthrightness and unshakeable sense of his own rectitude, was unique in pursuing restriction openly. Other universities, notably Columbia, proceeded with greater discretion and dissimulation. But throughout the world of elite private education, the attempt to create a national leadership class meant stemming the Jewish tide. Only after World War II, when Hitler had given anti-Semitism a bad name, did the barriers start to come down.

Elitism for All: Harvard

As it happened, Harvard began to move into the "postwar" world a decade before it arrived—when James Bryant Conant was appointed in 1933 to succeed Lowell as president. Conant was a Yankee but not a Brahmin and had no great love for the Boston patriciate. He was, like Eliot, a chemist, and like him also, a "university" rather than a "college" man, concerned more with research and scholarship than with undergraduate life. Committed to academic excellence, he instituted a program of national scholarships to attract brilliant students and a system of ad hoc committees through which outsiders would evaluate all of Harvard's tenure appointments. Under Conant's leadership, the university began to stress intellectual merit over gentlemanship. Genteel anti-Semitism slowly faded until, like the Cheshire cat, there was nothing but its smile—and the memory of its claws.

The Battle of Memorial Church

Conant left Harvard in 1953 to become U.S. High Commissioner to Germany. The Harvard Corporation's search for a successor to Conant in the first months of 1953 coincided with the height of the McCarthyite attacks on Harvard as a breeding ground of Eastern elitism and a haven for godless communism. It was certainly politic, then, that the man chosen should turn out to be a pious midwesterner, Nathan Marsh Pusey.

Pusey had, to be sure, received both his A.B. and Ph.D. (in the Classics) at Harvard. He came, however, from Council Bluffs, Iowa, and had spent the previous nine years as president of Lawrence College in Appleton, Wisconsin. Appleton happened to be the home town of Joe McCarthy; by publicly opposing the Senator's reelection in 1952, Pusey had gained something of a reputation as a bearder of lions. He would lend midwestern respectability to Harvard's anti-McCarthyite posture. It helped that Pusey was a practicing Episcopalian—and this accorded with Harvard's needs in another way. The university had made a major commitment to revive its almost moribund divinity school, and a president who cared about religion could be of great assistance. Finally, Pusey was a humanist whose career had been spent at four-year colleges; he thus stood in useful contrast to his predecessor, a Lowell to Conant's Eliot.

But Pusey had his own crosses to bear. Not a distinguished scholar or a proper Bostonian, he had no natural constituency among the faculty or the Brahmin old guard. He struck many as bland, humorless, and remote. This impression of austerity was conveyed in a widely-circulated story which Samuel Eliot Morison put into an article on the Harvard presidency for *The New England Quarterly.*

It is said that the Corporation, after voting for Pusey, had qualms about his social habits, having heard that Lawrence was a teetotal institution. A Harvard graduate living at Appleton was asked to entertain him, and report. Shortly after, the Corporation received a telegram from this gentleman, which read: "Relax! Pusey Just Finished Third Old-Fashioned."[10]

If his teetotalism was mythical, Pusey's religious piety was not. Any doubts on this score were quickly erased by the first Harvard president in a hundred and fifty years to be an orthodox trinitarian Protestant.

A week after assuming office, Pusey addressed the opening convocation of the Harvard Divinity School with a speech entitled "A Faith for These Times." His purpose was to assert the importance of both theological studies and traditional Christian faith in the life of the university. He did this by criticizing the last address delivered by a Harvard president at the Divinity School: Eliot's "The Religion of the Future." In his 1909 speech, Eliot had brought Harvard's tradition of liberal Christianity to its logical culmination; the religion of the future was a creed of social meliorism divested of theological substance. It amounted to the liberal ideology of the modern secular university, and of the modern Establishment as well, promising mankind happiness through increased scientific knowledge, professionalism, and disinterested good works. This was the faith that Nathan Pusey attacked. Eliot's religion of the future, he claimed, "will not do for us"; events of the twentieth century "have made its easy optimism unpalatable." Creeds were not to be dispensed with, but to be inquired into and made adequate for our time, lest "truth . . . be lost in a formless and uninformed faith." Society's great need was for "leadership in religious knowledge, and even more, in religious experience—not increased industrial might, not more research facilities, certainly not these things by themselves."[11]

Pusey's speech provoked consternation within Harvard and, widely reported and reprinted, it reverberated through the ranks of the alumni. No one expected such sentiments from a Harvard president. In Italy, the aged connoisseur and art critic Bernard Berenson greeted a young Harvard professor whom he had never met before with the words, "Sit down and tell me what's going on. I'm furious about what he said, undoing what Eliot set out to do." Pusey had touched a deep institutional nerve. By attacking Eliot, he seemed to be calling Harvard's cherished liberalism into question. Even the more conventionally religious Lowell had been uninterested in theology and "religious experience," and had never addressed himself publicly to issues of faith.

In the opening years of his administration, Pusey did much to further the cause of religion at Harvard. As expected, he played an important role in the revival of the Divinity School, which had, through persistent neglect, become an embarrassment to the university. By the late forties, its faculty had shrunk to an aged few; its students were by and large meatballs. The rumor was that Conant, whose interest in religion was minimal, wanted to close down the school of religion and ship its magnificent library off to Oberlin. Against this prospect prominent alumni rebelled, so the only solution was to make the place respectable again. In 1951, Conant arranged for John Lord O'-Brian, distinguished Washington lawyer, Chairman of Harvard's Board of Overseers, and committed Episcopal layman, to set up and head a fundraising committee. Ultimately, with Pusey leading the way, $6 million was collected (increasing the school's endowment by 600 percent) and a first-class faculty set in place. The greatest catch was the world-renowned theologian Paul Tillich, who became a University Professor.

Pusey also persuaded one of America's leading preachers, George Buttrick, to leave New York's Madison Avenue Presbyterian Church for the post of Preacher to the University. Buttrick, an imperious ex-Briton with no previous Harvard ties, regarded it as his mission to turn Memorial Church into a going concern. What had been a poorly attended preaching station became a full-scale church, complete with sacraments, study groups, and Sunday school. On Sunday mornings, Buttrick's powerful sermons packed them in. It soon became apparent that, under Pusey, the religious revival of the Eisenhower years had reached even unto godless Harvard. This fact was deemed worthy of a cover story by both *Time* and *Newsweek*. For the secularists, however, there came a day of reckoning.

On March 28, 1958, the Harvard *Crimson* ran a long critique of Harvard's new religiosity. The author, William W. Bartley 3d (class of 1956), was a second-year graduate student in the Philosophy Department and a candidate for the Episcopal ministry to boot.* Bartley was certainly not opposed to religion, but he believed that Pusey, Buttrick, Tillich, and company had brought to Harvard a noxious and alien religious ideology that offered spiritual placebos in place of hard thought and exclusivist faith in place of ecumenical vision. Thus had "the hair shirt . . . become button-down." Although the case was overstated, Bartley's research was extensive, his prose pungent, and his polemical instinct acute. He pointed out, for instance, that the words of Eliot which Pusey had attacked in 1953 had, only two

---

*Bartley eventually became a professor of philosophy in California and, in 1979, published a sympathetic account of the life and purposes of Werner Erhardt, the founder of the psychological self-improvement regime EST.

years before, been praised by Conant as being "as relevant today as when they were uttered nearly 50 years ago."

This kind of troublemaking would have been to little effect, however, had Bartley not stumbled upon an issue capable of stirring discontent into action. To exemplify sectarian tendency, he asserted that, in a departure from traditional university policy, Buttrick was refusing to permit Jewish marriages in Memorial Church. The preacher was quoted as stating that "it would be intellectually dishonest for Christian and Jewish marriages to be carried on beneath the same roof." Bartley noted that the National Council of Churches did not regard Unitarians as Christians; yet surely these heirs of Harvard's dominant religious tradition would not be barred from Memorial Church. "The objection, apparently, is not to non-Christians, but to Jews."

Spring break delayed by a week the public airing of reactions to Bartley's article. On April 8, the *Crimson* ran an editorial condemning what it saw as "a fundamental—and disturbing— change of official policy." It also printed a letter from Robert S. Morison (class of 1930), head of medical and biological research for the Rockefeller Foundation and a former *Crimson* president. Morison wrote that the article had "made clear to many of us just why we have felt a growing uneasiness at the trend of Cambridge thinking on problems of faith and morals." He further emphasized, as had the editorial, that Memorial Church had been built with funds contributed by Harvard men of all faiths as a tribute to those who had died in World War I. The decision to restrict access now was "simple dishonesty." Lowell's chicken had come home to roost. The following day, Pusey responded. There had, he said, been no change in policy. Harvard's tradition was a Christian one; Memorial Church was a Christian church, albeit nondenominational. Because it was a place of Christian worship, the Corporation's policy had always been to deny its use for private, non-Christian ceremonies such as marriages or funerals. Those few that had taken place had been unauthorized.

News that the ruling was long-standing did nothing to quiet the troubled waters; at issue now was the policy itself and Pusey's clear approval of it. The entire campus, from Faculty Club to freshman dorm, resounded with heated debate about the place of religion at Harvard and the nature of a church. Notices were affixed to the doors of Memorial Church, reading "Do we or do we not believe in the equality of faiths and the brotherhood of man?" A Unitarian professor, known to be seriously ill, wrote in to ask whether, on the occasion of his death, an inquest would be held by the Preacher to the University "on the orthodoxy of my 'Christian' views." Another professorial missive addressed the following question to Pusey: "You have done, sir what you came to Harvard to do. Your end now is clearly accomplished. Nothing more in this direction seems possible or desirable. What, then, remains for you to do?" President Eliot's old private secretary and protege, Jerome Greene, sent word that Pusey's position had come as a "painful shock." Forums to discuss the subject were planned by the Harvard Liberal Union and the Congregational Presbyterian Student Fellowship. There was some defense of Pusey, but not much. Buttrick, by steadfastly maintaining a stony silence, did not help matters. Denunciations issued from Unitarian pulpits. The national press got hold of the story. An edited-down version of Bartley's article appeared in the *New Republic*.

On April 18, a large delegation of faculty members—including such big guns as Mark DeWolfe Howe, John Finley, Samuel Beer, J. K. Galbraith, and Arthur Schlesinger, Jr.—trooped over to Massachusetts Hall to present Pusey with a petition of protest. Invoking the spirit of William James's "True Harvard" ("a Harvard which should be as free and tolerant in religious matters as it is in all others which affect the lives of civilized men"), the petition asked that Memorial Church be opened to non-Christian nuptial and funeral rites. Among those who crowded into the president's office were some of Pusey's former teachers, including Perry Miller, the preeminent historian of New England puritanism, who happened to be a confirmed atheist. Miller demanded to know whether he would be permitted a funeral in Memorial Church. Visibly pale but strong in defense, Pusey replied, "You will, Perry, you will; if you can find a minister who'll do it." Finley made an elegant speech about the meaning of Harvard. "It's all right, John," said Pusey, "as long as you don't confuse Harvard with God." As Beer remarked years later, "That's exactly what we were doing. If there was ever a case of Harvard worship, that was it."

Pusey, however, had his own Harvard card to play. As Krister Stendahl, later Dean of the Divinity School, recalled: "Pusey said that we had to honor the Harvard tradition. I took the line that no, you cannot do this. What holds this community together is pluralism. We have a choice. We can think of Memorial Church as a Protestant Christian church, as an homage to our past; or that it should slowly transform itself into a place which can be used for cult by all. The anti-religious or agnostic ones there were intrigued with Pusey's position. Also, they detected in me a desire to strengthen religious faith."

The question posed by Stendahl—whether or not there should be an established Protestant church at Harvard—was the real issue for Pusey. He therefore regarded himself as vindicated when, a week later, the Corporation reaffirmed the Christian character of Memorial Church while opening it up to "private" non-Christian ceremonies. The ruling was satisfactory to most of his opponents as well, since they were more concerned about the principle of social exclusion than the underlying religious status quo. Significantly, the Jewish community at Harvard had been divided on the controversy. Self-described "secular Jews" like Morton White, Jerome Bruner, I B. Cohen, and Henry Aiken were leaders of the protest. Observant Jews, who had no interest in making ceremonial use of Memorial Church anyway, for the most part remained indifferent, and in some cases supported Pusey as a defender of religious values in general. Although Harvard was by now one-fourth Jewish, no one took the opportunity to urge the university to provide financial support for Jewish religious activity.

Most of Pusey's critics were not worried about the university's sponsorship of Christian cult, but about its willingness to restrict the use of its facilities. Memorial Church did not stand for Christianity, but for Harvard and its fallen sons. If Harvard was Christian in tradition, so be it, but all must be allowed their own access to the institutional shrine. The religion of Harvard was Harvard. Moreover, the university's image was at stake. As the faculty petition emphasized, restrictive legislation had to be rescinded "so that there can be no doubt as to where Harvard stands today and where it will stand in the future on the question of religious freedom and equality."

The world was watching. Postwar Harvard had dedicated itself to freedom and equality generally, and to an educational mission of national, even international, scope. But Pusey, in his handling of the Memorial Church episode, seemed to have cast his lot with the forces of darkness, a symbol of provincialism, narrowness of mind, and self-righteous religiosity.

Although the public controversy soon blew over, many faculty members never forgave Pusey. The extent of their alienation only became evident a decade later, when the takeover of University Hall by SDS members and their subsequent ejection by police plunged Harvard into weeks of chaos. Then Pusey needed all the faculty support he could get, but, as one professor recalled, "the conservative people whom he should have been able to depend upon just weren't there."

The religion of Harvard—and of the Establishment—had become decisively pluralistic and ecumenical. Anti-Semitism, anti-Catholicism, and virtually all the other antis, even anti-atheism, were in very bad taste. Anticommunism, however, remained an important article of faith.

Elitism for All: Harvard

"Be Serviceable"

When James Bryant Conant left Harvard's presidency to become High Commissioner to Germany in 1953, the figure who best personified the spirit of postwar Harvard was McGeorge Bundy, Dean of the Faculty of Arts and Sciences. David Halberstam's portrait of Bundy at Harvard in *The Best and the Brightest* is vivid: the brilliant and well-connected Brahmin from Groton and Yale coming to Cambridge before World War II as one of the elite Junior Fellows; his return to Harvard after distinguished wartime service (including helping to plan D-Day), time spent working on the Marshall Plan, doing political analysis for the Council on Foreign Relations, writing speeches for John Foster Dulles; his quick rise to tenure and then to the Deanship of the Faculty at the age of thirty-four.

Within Arts and Sciences, it was not from Pusey that all blessings were seen to flow.

> Mr. Bundy was a very remarkable Dean . . . remarkable in his hospitality to new ideas, in his recruitment of new talent, and in his devotion to academic freedom. Under his leadership Harvard completed an irreversible change, begun under James Conant, from an institution designed to serve the north-eastern upper class into a national university drawing on young men and women of all classes, colors and creeds.[12]

This testimonial (from fifteen faculty members, including J. K. Galbraith, Stanley Hoffmann, Carl Kaysen, and Arthur Schlesinger, Jr.) came in a 1977 letter to The *New York Review* defending Bundy against charges that he had pushed nontenured teachers, former members of the Communist party, out of the university during the McCarthy period. And indeed, Bundy disapproved of the so-called "Fifth Amendment Communists"—those who refused to name names before Congressional committees—and thought they did not belong at Harvard.

A love of freedom meant a willingness to fight the enemies of freedom, whether of the right or the left. Harvard's liberal faculty members saw no conflict between liberalism, anti-McCarthyism, and anticommunism. For them, the fifties were exciting times. They thought of themselves as the best; for more than a decade, ad hoc committees had filled their ranks by asking, "Is this the best person in the world for the job?" Their students were the best, too.

Yet, looking back on his years at Harvard from his post-Vietnam aerie as president of the Ford Foundation in New York, Bundy decided that the university had been smug and insufficiently self-critical. "We were proud of Harvard; were we perhaps too proud?" he asked.

In 1961, the question would not have occurred, for when Bundy, Galbraith, Kaysen, Schlesinger and the rest moved down to Washington to join the Kennedy administration, it seemed like the culmination of a destined mission. The best university in creation, having made itself a truly national institution, would now undertake the nation's business in earnest. As Bundy recalled, "Especially at Harvard there was a tendency to suppose that because a Harvard man was President, and a lot of professors were down there with him, somehow the university was running the country."[13]

In that Camelotian dawn, Harvard was well positioned on all fronts. Its economists, the leading apostles of American Keynesianism, would lead the new administration beside the still waters of smooth and steady growth; Paul Samuelson, a Harvard Ph.D. who had been sent down the river to MIT in the days of genteel anti-Semitism at Harvard,[14] began the instruction of John F. Kennedy in the principles of counter-cyclical fiscal policy during the 1960 electoral campaign. And Samuelson himself became the Elector of President Kennedy's Council of Economic Advisers—Chairman Walter W. Heller of Minnesota, James Tobin of Yale, and Kermit Gordon of Williams and the Ford Foundation.

In the realm of foreign affairs, Harvard had its area studies outfits: the Russian Research Center and the East Asia Study Center. For the total picture, there was Henry Kissinger's Center for International Affairs. The double-domes of Harvard roamed the world; Pakistan put its economy under the guidance of a team of Cambridge economists, and proud India accepted the tutelage of Ambassador John Kenneth Galbraith.

All in all, Charles Eliot would have been happy. The Religion of the Future had arrived. That inclusive creed, standing for broad consensus on basic values, substituted professional problem-solving for eschatalogical promises, and preached the triumph of reason and scientific knowledge over physical and spiritual ills. Its explicit motto was, "Be Serviceable."

Eliot's vision had been redeemed at Harvard; better yet, it was abroad in the land. Social scientists, wishfully, had begun to speak of America as a *post-industrial* society. This did not mean that industry was fading away but rather that industrial capitalism had gone as far as it could under old-fashioned business entrepreneurship. Further development depended on the ministrations of scientists, mathematicians, economists, planners—technocrats and intellectuals of all sorts. According to Daniel Bell, one of the leading theorists of post-industrialism, such experts held the key to the future.

> To say that the major institutions of the new society will be predominantly intellectual is to say, primarily, that the basic *innovative* features of the society will derive not from business as we know it today, principally the "product corporation," but from the research corporations, the industrial laboratories, the experimental stations, and the universities.[15]

JFK was the perfect emblem. Though an Irish Catholic outsider, he seemed patrician in style and culture; his Harvard education had served him well. He spoke the Establishment's gospel of service ("Ask not what your country can do for you . . . "). He was the right sort of liberal, humane but tough —extending his hand to a jailed Martin Luther King, empathizing with West Berliners, outstaring Khrushchev over Cuban missiles. He was something of an intellectual; he read books and wrote them, and he listened to professors. He was the ideal president for the age of the university. Indeed, with its supereducated advisors and crisis managers, his administration seemed to signal that the new national order had commenced. J. K. Galbraith emerged as the truest believer. In *The New Industrial State*, he postulated an efficient "technostructure" superseding the predatory drives of traditional capitalism. And he called for a new intellectual class to impose its own superior values and goals on business and government.

How quickly the bloom faded. By the time *The New Industrial State* appeared, in 1967, the liberal consensus was in disarray. The Vietnam war was turning into the nation's nightmare; Lyndon Johnson's Great Society, having promised more than it could deliver, was foundering and losing popular support. Responsibility lay with the brave new frontiersmen in Washington. Having pledged technical and managerial competence in the pursuit of noble goals, it had produced disaster abroad and bungling at home. The campuses exploded in student protest against the war and the schools' alleged complicity in it. In 1969, radical students at Harvard published a pamphlet entitled "How Harvard Rules," which detailed the university's connections with the federal government; they wanted no part of the mobilized university. A communitarian counterculture challenged the technological and meritocratic values of *the system*. *Liberal* became a dirty word. How had things gone so awry? Some, like Bundy, were willing to admit to the sin of pride. They had been too self-confident, had dared too greatly, had promised too much. But what was to be done now?

The 1969 student uprising at Harvard precipitated Pusey's early retirement. As his successor, the Corporation chose Derek Curtis Bok, scion of the wealthy Philadelphia publishing family and dean of the Harvard Law School. Youthful and dynamic, he looked to be a more flexible handler of undergraduate disturbances than the stiff-necked Pusey. Indeed, when his office was occupied by black students in the spring of 1972, Bok kept his cool.

But student activism, on the decline, was only one of the problems confronting Bok on taking office in 1971. Others included a two and a half million dollar budget deficit, a seriously depressed market for Harvard Ph.D.'s, and an administration in

Washington unsympathetic to higher education generally, and to Harvard in particular. The times seemed to call for reflection and consolidation, not bold new initiatives.

But Bok had no intention of pulling in the university's horns and moving it away from public affairs. On the contrary, his view was that far from being overly mobilized, Harvard had not been serviceable enough. It had become, he felt, too much of an ivory tower, too distant from the real world. In the early days of his administration, he advocated exposing undergraduates to nonacademic "role models." In his first annual report, he stressed the importance of the university's involvement with the community and with all levels of government; he also recommended that the university's professional schools adopt a "common basic curriculum in policy analysis and administration." This last recommendation hinted at what was to be the single most significant piece of institution building undertaken at Harvard during the seventies: the creation of the Kennedy School of Government as a freestanding professional school. Before becoming president, Bok had been involved in laying its groundwork. The issue of providing education for public service concerned him deeply, and he used his 1973 to 1974 report to issue a brief in its behalf.

The federal government, he wrote, suffered from having too many specialists who lacked general skills in administration and policy analysis. Lawyers were especially deficient. Businessmen had the skills, but were inexperienced in the political process and in dealing with intangibles. What was needed was "nothing less than a new profession." It would include elected and appointed officials, career civil servants—people working in all branches of government and in large nonprofit institutions as well. All shared "the common experience of holding important positions of responsibility involving planning, policy making and administration." The importance of training such a profession could, he said, scarcely be overemphasized, since we seemed to be entering an era of scarcity and restraint "in which the deficiencies of government cannot be papered over by constantly rising levels of prosperity." Nor, nowadays, was it possible for any important group to pursue its private interests free from government policy. Like it or not, public officials had to establish "the framework that determines the ability of each segment of society to determine its goals."

If Bok's statement was gauged to current realities, it was also a response to the lessons of the past. Inadequate training, it implied, had been at least partly responsible for the policy failures of the sixties, in which Harvard professors and alumni had played so prominent a role. Through no fault of their own, they had been amateurs in the business of running the country, and the country had suffered for it. Their deficiencies Harvard would now seek to remedy.

The dream of a profession of public service has of course been around for a long time; however, in the country's long romance with professionalism in general, it always presented the trickiest challenge. Since the mid-nineteenth century, professional status has held a particular appeal for Americans, offering niches of prestige and authority in a society subject to egalitarian anomie and committed by principle to classlessness. Social historians have noted the widespread use of the term "professor" to describe all kinds of teachers and charletans: professors of piano and violin, professors purveying snake oil and hawking sideshows. Today, beauticians are cosmetologists and garbage men are sanitary engineers.

At more exalted levels, higher education has played a crucial authenticating role. In the late nineteenth century ancient professions like law and medicine were brought firmly within the academic orbit, and since then the same has been done for hitherto inchoate occupations like schoolteaching and social work. Thanks to the trailblazing success of the Harvard Business School, even businessmen have come to see themselves as members of a profession dependent, to some extent at least, on academic certification. Nowadays all fields, even to a degree the news media, possess elites trained in the professional schools of universities.

As a defense against the manifest charm of professionalism,

Elitism for All: Harvard

Americans have maintained a healthy distrust of experts and professors, people who claim to know better. Who elected them? Because professional authority rubs against the democratic grain, the largest absentee in the ranks of the American professions has been public administration. Some responsibility for this belongs to the country's system of government; federalism and the separation of powers discouraged the development of a prestigious and professionally unified bureaucratic elite at the national level. Such structural disparateness, combined with popular fears and traditional love of political patronage, hampered even modest civil service reform. In the 1880s, the federal bureaucracy was depoliticized to some degree; the Pendleton Act of 1883 established a bipartisan Civil Service Commission, inaugurating a system of competitive examinations and offering a measure of job security to federal employees. Because of general hostility to having the government run by "a college-trained aristocracy," the first examinations were designed for those with an ordinary public school education. Not until 1920 was the actual principle of job tenure for government officials established, and the upper reaches of the bureaucracy have never been insulated from partisan politics.

Thus, decentralized power, job insecurity, and an underlying ideological hostility to government by unelected service elites militated against the growth of public administration as an independent profession in the United States. This contrasted dramatically with the situation in Europe, where governments deliberately encouraged the formation of elite cadres of bureaucrats. On the Continent, states provided their own specialist training, either on the job or in schools like the French Ecole Nationale d'Administration. In England, recruitment was accomplished through a single open competitive examination, designed to create an administrative class of generalists composed of the cream of Oxford and Cambridge graduates; for them government service was to be a lifelong career. Ambitious Americans were better advised to hedge against the insecurities of high-level government employment by choosing professions which could be pursued in the private as well as the public sector.

Despite the obstacles, efforts were made by good Progressives to devise a professional education for bureaucrats. To allay suspicions of antidemocracy, they adopted the convenient if fundamentally wrongheaded theory of public administration first advanced by Woodrow Wilson in the *Political Science Quarterly* in 1887: that policy and administration were separable. Administrators were simply managers, technicians who saw to it that policy was efficiently carried out. They constituted no threat to democratic government, since policy making itself was (properly) in the hands of elected officials. Shaping education in public administration in the early part of this century, this theory focused academic attention not on substantive issues but on the nuts and bolts of running agencies: handling personnel, budgeting, and the like. While such a course of study was useful, it was hardly designed to attract the best minds of a generation. Neither did it generate much in the way of academic prestige. Even those universities which, in the teens and twenties, set up programs or schools of public administration tended to give them short shrift. These early efforts have been judged "fragmentary, haphazard, and meager."[16]

Harvard first contemplated setting up a graduate school for civil servants and diplomats during the administration of Theodore Roosevelt, the first alumnus of the college to become President of the United States since John Quincy Adams. Career opportunities in the civil and diplomatic services seemed limited, however, and the decision was made to establish a school of business administration instead. The Business School was given a mandate to train government officials as well as businessmen, but it never undertook to do so. As a result, a program in public administration had to wait for the administration of another Harvard alumnus, Franklin Delano Roosevelt.

The gray eminence who presided over the birth of Harvard's School of Public Administration was Felix Frankfurter; funding came from the industrialist Lucius Littauer. Politically, the two were far apart. Frankfurter was a liberal Democrat and staunch Roosevelt supporter, about to leave his Law School professorship to join the Supreme Court. Littauer, a conservative Republican, had served as a congressman from upstate New York. Both, however, were devoted sons of Harvard, and German Jews with a common interest in supporting Judaic studies at their alma mater. Frankfurter convinced Littauer that, like it or not, the New Deal was here to stay, that the best way to minimize the evils of a large federal bureaucracy was to make sure that the bureaucrats were as competent and well informed as possible, and that the best way to achieve that end was to found a school of public administration at Harvard. In November 1935, Littauer offered the university $2 million for the venture; Conant accepted immediately.

The New Deal fostered the growth of university programs in public administration across the country, but it also tended to undermine the traditional Wilsonian dichotomy. The New Dealers were obviously planners and policy makers as well as administrators. Thanks to Frankfurter, the Harvard school took a different philosophical tack. A great anglophile, he regarded the British civil service as the proper model. "British experience," he wrote to Conant, "establishes that the civil service fares best with men of a high standard of general education who receive their specialized instruction in a probationary year in the departments."[17] The university should provide course work in substantive policy problems, not training in the techniques of administration.

Frankfurter's notion accorded well with prevailing economic constraints and intellectual prejudices. Littauer's bequest, part of which went to the construction of a new building, was insufficient to establish a full-fledged professional school; faculty members in Arts and Sciences were inclined to regard schools of "management"—whether for business or government—as intellectually second-rate.

The result was that the school became a jointly-held appendage of the economics and government departments, both of which were housed in its building, the Littauer Center. The student body consisted largely of mid-career government officials, who came for a year of academic recreation and a master's degree in public administration. No specific course of study was designed for them; they were free to shop around the university for what they wanted. Whatever special identity the school had consisted in a series of purportedly interdisciplinary seminars in such subjects as land use planning, fiscal policy, and water resources management. Actually, these were usually taught by a single faculty member and were unidisciplinary. On his retirement as president in 1953, Conant called the school a "complete failure" as an "experiment in interfaculty cooperation."

In 1956, Paul Herzog, the school's associate dean, received a grant from the Carnegie Corporation to write a report on the status of the school. Herzog saw that the school needed a more distinct identity and a coherent educational program of its own. He recommended the creation of a nucleus of faculty members whose primary commitment would be to the school; he also suggested the establishment of a core curriculum required of all students. He was less than enthusiastic about the principle of ignoring instruction in administration. "Whether or not 'public administration' is or can be a separate profession in the United States, it is clear that the Harvard School has never purported to train public administrators as such." That, Herzog claimed, had to be its goal. The Herzog Report was the school's first step towards the institutional grandeur of the Bok regime.

The Playing Fields of Cambridge

The shepherd for most of the way was Don K. Price, a shrewd and laconic Kentuckian, who became dean in 1958. Price, who looks more like an Appalachian mountain man than an Ivy League professor, did not come to Harvard via a traditional academic route. After graduating from Vanderbilt in 1931, he aimed to become a newspaperman and did, in fact, spend a couple of years working for *The Nashville Tennessean.* He won a Rhodes scholarship, however, and at Oxford was inspired with the ideal of improving American public administration by none other than Felix Frankfurter, who was a visiting professor there from 1934 to 1935.

On his return to the United States, Price forswore journalism and turned to public service and what might be called public service kibbitzing. He worked for the Central Housing Council and the Social Science Research Council, and did a short stint on the staff of the Bureau of the Budget. Between 1939 and 1953, he spent eleven years at the Public Administration Clearing House, then moved over to the Ford Foundation, first as associate director and finally as a vice-president. By the time he came to Harvard, Price was convinced that what the government needed was more sophisticated generalists in the upper ranks of the bureaucracy; too often administration devolved upon specialists who had no idea of how to run an agency. Here, he felt, was the proper mission for schools of public administration; at Harvard he could lead the way. "I did a lot of traveling for the Ford Foundation, and I was struck by Harvard's influence, even in other countries. To some extent I thought this unfortunate; I hated the snobbery. But when I decided to leave Ford, I realized that Harvard was the only school which could influence public administration in the whole country."

It took longer than Price expected, both to get Harvard's school off and running and to influence the rest of the country. The Kennedy administration helped, though more by its demise than anything else. Initially, it just drained away faculty members: Carl Kaysen to Bundy's National Security Council staff; David Bell to the Budget Bureau; Stanley Surrey to Treasury; Archibald Cox to the Solicitor General's office; Lincoln Gordon to Brazil; Galbraith to India. As Price wrote in his annual report, "Within the Faculty of Public Administration, the Dean is tempted to take a position somewhat like that of the general who complained that the war was ruining the Regular Army."

The "regular army" profited from the war's tragic end; after

JFK's assassination, the Kennedy family raised $10 million to set up an Institute of Politics as a permanent part of the School of Public Administration. The Kennedy Library was expected to be located at Harvard, and the idea was to make it more than just a tourist attraction and scholarly archive; the Institute, with its visiting politicians, student seminars, and faculty study groups, would make the place a "living" memorial to the dead president. Harvard, in return, decided to make the entire school a living memorial, renaming it "The John Fitzgerald Kennedy School of Government." Richard E. Neustadt, advisor of presidents and longtime Democratic sage, was prevailed upon to exchange his Columbia professorship for a Harvard one and become the Institute's first director. Neustadt eagerly involved himself and the Institute in Price's efforts to build up the school as a whole.

Price, Neustadt, and a small nucleus of committed faculty recognized that if they were to have a true professional school, they would need to do more than provide vacationing public officials with a year's worth of continuing education. A comprehensive course of study had to be devised for the training of future administrators.

But what should professional education for public service be? To answer that question, Price put together a committee of interested professors from throughout the university. What emerged was a way of transcending the old policy-administration dichotomy which, though widely acknowledged as false, remained an intellectual stumbling block for schools of public administration. An educational program would be aimed at the intersection of policy and administration, that is, on the planning, execution, and judging of public policy.

Sophisticated analytic techniques were first employed within the federal government during the sixties, most notably at the Pentagon under Robert S. McNamara, a product of the Harvard Business School and former president of the Ford Motor Company. Price's committee concluded that future administrators would have to be familiar with such arcana as operations research, decision theory, and microeconomics. Here was a task worthy of the Kennedy School. Derek Bok, then dean of the

Law School, urged his fellow committee members to push ahead quickly. Law students contemplating government service should, he felt, be able to get training in social science. (He himself had seen fit to acquire an M.A. in economics.) "If you guys won't do it for us," he told the Kennedy School people, "we'll have to do it ourselves."

The committee devised a two-year master's program in public policy. An intensive lobbying campaign was necessary to persuade both the economics and government departments and the Faculty of Arts and Sciences as a whole to go along. Thanks in large part to the efforts of the canny and battle-tested John Dunlop, economics professor and labor mediator, the program was finally voted through. The turning point in the faculty debate was a speech made by Howard Raiffa, a much respected professor of managerial economics at the Business School. "The trouble," he said, "is that you people in Arts and Sciences aren't interested in *teaching*. That's what we do at the Business School. You're only interested in graduate seminars." Underlying that trouble was the prevailing trend in economics, and to a lesser extent in political science, towards making the social sciences more mathematical and theoretical. Close involvement with issues of policy had increasingly given way to a concern with the invention of logical "models" of social, economic, and political behavior. This made the graduate seminar an inappropriate place—at once too sophisticated and too remote—for aspiring administrators. What the Kennedy School proposed was to apply social science to real problems in a way that potential administrators could grasp and use.

The public policy program, which began in 1969 with twenty-one students, turned out, for Price, "a good deal more technocratic in flavor than I personally would have gone in for." The first year "core" curriculum, required of all students, included full-year courses in analytic methods, microeconomics, statistics, a workshop in solving policy problems, and something called "political and bureaucratic analysis." This last subject, which provided some leaven to the hard-core analytics, owed its existence to Richard Neustadt. A worrier by nature, Neustadt had, since his days in the Truman White House, enjoyed pondering the mistakes and fiascos of U.S. policy: in the Korean War, the Suez crisis, the United States' decision to abandon Britain's Skybolt missile, and the Alliance for Progress.

In 1967, animated by a desire to discover why the results of Vietnam and the Great Society had been so out of line with intentions, Neustadt set up a faculty research seminar at the institute to study the relations of government bureaucracy, politics, and policy. Known as the "May Group" (after its first chairman, history professor Ernest R. May), the seminar sought ways of incorporating the less tangible aspects of government behavior, including historical experience, personal values, bureaucratic rivalry, and the organization of agencies, into the analysis of public policy. The Kennedy School's course in political and bureaucratic analysis came directly out of work done by the May Group. Its best known product was a study of the Cuban missile crisis written by the seminar's first rapporteur, Graham T. Allison. Allison urged the inadequacy of viewing the crisis as a kind of chess game played by two "rational actors." With its theoretical disquisitions, three "models" of explanation, and technocratic verbiage, Allison's *Essence of Decision* sought to incorporate a historian's detailed understanding of events into "scientific" strategy analysis. The book gained Allison a professorship at the Kennedy School, and helped make him Dean, succeeding Price, in 1977.

The public policy program was the foundation of the Kennedy School's growth during the first decade of the Bok administration. A $21 million fund-raising campaign was successfully waged; $12 million went into the construction of the new building on the banks of the Charles, able to house a core faculty of 50 and 600 or so full-time graduate students— including a couple of hundred mid-careerists from government.

New research centers were ticketed for the premises. The first of these, the Center for Science and International Affairs, got off to a quick start with a $4 million grant from the Ford

Foundation to study international security and arms control. Others dealing with regulatory issues, health policy, and energy have been launched, and more will come.

A school for executives, modeled on the Business School's advanced management program, is also under way; short courses of from three to thirteen weeks are given to senior government officials. The Kennedy School has the space to run nine programs of this sort, and aims at a yearly "student body" of about 700. Both Bok and John Dunlop believe the school's greatest impact will be in the area of executive training. (In election years, the Institute of Politics runs its own courses; newly elected mayors and congressmen regularly troop to Cambridge to be lectured at by Harvard and other Boston-area professors.)

Bok's overall goal has been to make the school the hub of public policy study for the entire university, a mustering ground for expertise. Relations with all the other professional schools, even Divinity, have been cultivated. Any issue of public concern, from waste treatment to professional ethics, is considered fair game for seminars, study groups, conferences, and colloquia.

A considerable degree of institutional imperialism is at work here. A number of the university's other schools—the Graduate School of Design, the School of Public Health, even the august Business School—have been forced, sometimes kicking and screaming, to embrace the new orthodoxies of public policy study. In 1979, it was announced that the Design School's Department of City and Regional Planning would be transferred to the Kennedy School. In Harvard's $250 million fund-raising campaign for the 1980s, the only substantive area earmarked for support is public policy education. Be serviceable—or else.

The Kennedy School has had an impact not only within Harvard but also, as Price originally hoped, in the outside world. Its educational emphasis on the development of analytic skills seemed "right" to many in the field. With financial support from the Ford and Sloan Foundations, similar programs sprang up at

Duke, Berkeley, Michigan, Yale, the RAND Corporation, the Hubert Humphrey School in Minnesota, and even the Lyndon Baines Johnson School in Texas. Kennedyites and Johnsonites could lie down, like lions and lambs, in the green pastures of academia.

But, after the overreaching pride and fall of the intellectuals in government during the 1960s and 1970s, humility is the order of the day in schools for public servants. "There is a great consciousness here," says Dean Allison of the Kennedy School, "of the 'best and brightest' syndrome, of the dangers in training Whiz Kids, new style technocrats." The school tries to combat too technocratic an approach through instruction in "bureaucratic and political analysis." Students ponder the morality of government decision making in ethics courses, a particular passion of Bok's. Conflicts of values, says Allison, lie at the heart of most policy debates. "The role for the best and the brightest is not to decide the hard value trade-offs but to clarify the problems so that choices can be made." Humility reshuffles the clichés.

And humility seems to lead to conservatism. The Kennedy School, for all its New Frontier roots, is close to the conservative mood of the country at large. "There is a general skepticism about the role of government," says Allison. "For the first time since the New Deal, questions about the proper role of government have been reopened."

Don Price, still a fatherly presence at the Kennedy School, sees the very enterprise of educating generalist administrators as "a mark of conservatism." Specialists, he suggests, lack a broad enough perspective to keep from becoming advocates of the agencies and interests they represent; greater government commitments will continue to be demanded unless there is "countervailing pressure from generalists." Students at the Kennedy School are being taught, says Price, "to analyze secondary effects—they're all economizers."

The effort at Harvard to professionalize public administration has thus embodied an important philosophical break with the optimistic view of government action which prevailed among liberals between the New Deal and the Great Society. It signals a return to the more cautious, probusiness liberalism of the Progressive era, stressing economy and efficiency. The effort likewise recalls the Progressive anxiety to create institutions which might provide the nation with more cohesive leadership. The worry, then as now, was that the country was beginning to fray apart.

Chapter 3

Church, State, and

Counting House:

The New York Times

I N THEIR STATEMENTS at college commencements and other high occasions, publishers regularly laud freedom of the press and their own concern for the public weal, but rarely mention another cardinal concern of theirs: making money. Arthur Ochs Sulzberger, publisher of *The New York Times,* suffers from no such pecuniary prudery. Asked to define the mission of his newspaper, he responds: "First of all, to be profitable. Isn't that a terrible way to put it? But if we're not profitable, we can't have any other mission."

The other mission, he says, is "to cover the news—to call the shots as we see them."

Does he think that it is also the *Times*'s mission to provide leadership? "No, not particularly," he replies. "But by doing our job, we do seem to provide leadership. It's a result of all we do. Leadership will follow if we do our job and call the shots as we see them. As a result you have an audience. Nobody calls down and says to a reporter or columnist, 'Write it this way.'

You call it the way you see it. That's what provides the leadership."

But what about the paper's editorial page? Sulzberger says he considers the editorial page as essentially his own voice. "The power to control editorial policy goes with ownership," he says. "Editorial writers have to be comfortable with the editorial policy of the publisher. If they don't like it, they should take some other job."

A Family Business

It was Adolph S. Ochs, grandfather of the present publisher, who acquired *The New York Times* in 1896 and built it into the premier newspaper of the American Establishment. From the beginning his aim was to publish a newspaper that would always be disinterested and *pure* (that was the meaning of the *Times* motto emblazoned on page one, "All the News That's Fit to Print"). Ochs used to describe the *Times* as a public trust, and himself as only a temporary trustee. He poured the bulk of its growing revenues back into the paper to improve and widen its coverage of foreign and domestic affairs, and to expand the boundaries of newspapering into new areas—science, literature, and the arts.

But he never neglected the business side of the paper. His strategy was to make it a paper that businessmen would respect and support. Ochs knew the newspaper business from the ground up; he had started learning it as a fourteen-year-old printer's devil on *The Knoxville* (Tennessee) *Chronicle* in 1872.

He was the oldest child of Jewish immigrants. His father had served with distinction as a captain in the United States Army in the Mexican and Civil Wars. While still in the army, he had begun investing in a textile business, made a small fortune immediately after the Civil War, but lost it all in 1867, a year of financial panic in the South. He had to sell the family estate "Ochsenburg,"—located in the country outside Knoxville—and move the family into an unpainted shack on Water Street in town.

His son Adolph left school to help support the family. He was a hard worker, and stubborn; his nickname as a boy was "Mooley," a farmer's term for a hornless ox. At the age of twenty, Ochs bought his first newspaper, *The Chattanooga Times.* At thirty-eight, he felt ready to move into New York. He first tried to buy a paper called *The New York Mercury.* But when he heard that the *Times* was dying, he went to the rescue like a melodrama hero untying a maiden from the railroad tracks. The *Times,* a pure and highminded newspaper even before he took it over, was his dream come true.

Ochs impressed the financiers Charles R. Flint, General Sam Thomas, J. P. Morgan, and August Belmont, who controlled the paper, as a smart newspaperman who might save their investment. They offered Ochs $50,000 a year (an enormous sum in those days) to run the paper, but he said he would not take the job, even for $150,000, unless he were given the opportunity to acquire majority control of the *Times* if he made good and restored it to profitability. The financiers agreed; at that point it was Ochs or certain bankruptcy.

In 1896, shortly after taking over management, he wrote out his aims for the paper. His wife Effie, summering in Atlantic City with their baby Iphigene, helped him polish the draft. The key paragraph said:

> It will be my earnest aim that The New-York Times* give the news, all the news, in concise and attractive form, in language that is parliamentary in good society, and give it as early, if not earlier, than it can be learned through any other reliable medium; to give the news impartially, without fear or favor, regardless of any party, sect or interest involved; to make the columns of The New-York Times a forum for the consideration of all questions of public importance, and to that end to invite intelligent discussion from all shades of opinion.

*The hyphen was dropped in December, 1896.

Church, State, and Counting House

This declaration was published as a "Business Announcement" on the editorial page on August 19, 1896. Ochs also stated in his announcement that there would be "no radical changes in the present efficient staff," and that Charles R. Miller, "who has so ably for many years presided over the editorial page," would continue as editor.

Nor, said Ochs, would there be any departure from the general tone and character of editorial policies on public questions which had distinguished the *Times* as a nonpartisan newspaper:

> "unless it be, if possible, to intensify its devotion to the cause of sound money and tariff reform, opposition to wastefulness and peculation in administering the public affairs and in its advocacy of the lowest tax consistent with good government, and no more government than is absolutely necessary to protect society, maintain individual vested rights and assure the free exercise of a sound conscience."

A more concise statement of the business ideology of his day can scarcely be imagined. Ochs did not, however, want his editorial page to sound dogmatic. He knew himself as strong-willed, but regarded assertiveness as offensive to others, and unpersuasive as well. He once told his daughter Iphigene, who had graduated from Barnard College and was working at the Henry Street Settlement, "Iphigene, I do not deny your right to speak what is on your mind on this or any other subject. I do quarrel with the arbitrary stand you take, and with the vehemence with which you present your views."[1] He made her memorize page 99 of Benjamin Franklin's *Autobiography*, which began, "I made it a rule to forbear all direct contradiction to the sentiments of others and all positive assertion of my own." When she forgot he would caution her, "Page 99, Iphigene."

Charles Miller, Ochs's chief editor, also preferred moderation on the editorial page. Near the end of World War I, however, Miller wrote one passionate editorial that plunged Ochs into a deep melancholia that lasted for years, and almost caused him to retire from the newspaper's management.

The *Times* had been fervent in support of the war. Indeed, even before America was in the war, it had urged strong American support to Britain and France and had been investigated for it by the Senate.*

But in the fall of 1918, with the Germans in full retreat on the Western front, Austria put out a peace bid, and Charles Miller, without consulting Ochs, dictated an editorial to the paper over the telephone from his home in Great Neck, Long Island; it was Sunday, September 15, and Mr. Miller was writing on deadline. His editorial stated that the Austrian bid for a "non-binding" discussion should be accepted—for reasons of humanity. "When we consider the deluge of blood that has been poured out in this war, the incalculable waste of treasure, the ruin it has wrought, the grief that wrings millions of hearts because of it, we must conclude that only the madness or the soulless depravity of some one of the belligerent powers could obstruct or defeat the purpose of the conference," Miller wrote.

Angry letters and telegrams poured in to the *Times*. Many of its readers demanded unconditional surrender of the Germans. The editorial's implications of "madness" or "depravity" outraged those who thought that their motives were as good as the *Times'*. Some prominent businessmen were in a fury. The Union League Club, then the bastion of the New York financial elite, scheduled a meeting for September 26, 1918, to consider public denunciation of the *Times* for the Austrian editorial. However, some members of the club, including Chauncey M. Depew, the leading orator of his day and the president of the New York Central Railroad, the jurist Elihu Root, and Frank W. Woolworth, of the 5-and-10-cent store chain, talked them out of it. Woolworth cabled that nothing should be done "to impair

*The *Times* was cleared of charges that it was secretly controlled by *The Times* of London and by British money. The chief interrogator, Senator Thomas R. Walsh, also suggested that *The New York Times* was backing the British cause because of its own interests in increasing advertising revenues; Senator Walsh noted that ship advertising was bringing the *Times* about $50,000 a year. Carr Van Anda, managing editor of the paper, replied: "I have not the slightest hesitation in saying that the payment of that or any other sum of money by shipping interests, or any other interests, would have not one iota's influence upon the conduct of The Times." Van Anda stonily stated that any such insinuation "could be attributed only to malice or credulity." Senator Walsh backed off and said his committee had no intention of interfering with freedom of the press.

the influence of *The New York Times*, which is foremost in its devotion to the welfare of the United States."

Charles Miller, distraught, turned to President Charles Eliot of Harvard for an independent opinion. President Eliot told Miller that he agreed with his reasoning but thought some of the phrasing indiscreet.

Ochs was urged by friends to separate himself from Miller's editorial by making it publicly known that he had not seen it before publication. But he refused. "I could not do such a thing," he said. "I have always accepted public praise and public approval of the many great editorials Mr. Miller has written for the *Times*. When there is blame instead of praise I must share that, too."

Addressing Vietnam

Wars and other national crises create special agonies for an Establishment newspaper like the *Times*. Principles of integrity, responsibility, and moderation clash when the nation is divided —and especially when the government is seen as untrustworthy.

The *Times* did not start out as an opponent of the Vietnam War. On the contrary, its thinking, like that of the American Establishment generally, was dominated by the so-called "containment doctrine," first spelled out by George Kennan, in a celebrated article in *Foreign Affairs*, signed X, in July, 1947. Kennan had urged that the Western response to Soviet "pressure" should be "firm and vigilant containment," and this doctrine had been generalized into a grand and monolithic design for the American response to communism anywhere in the world.

Accordingly, during the 1950s and well into the 1960s, the *Times* treated the defense of Vietnam against communism as vital to the "free world" and virtually the whole of humanity.

At the time of the French defeat at Dienbienphu in 1954, an editorial* declared that Dienbienphu was

> ... not even a decisive battle in the war for Indo-China. French officials and American officials with them have blown it up into a symbol out of all proportion to its importance as a position in the fluctuating war. Yet in another sense it is decisive. . . . It is a last stand in the most heroic French tradition, a display of sheer gallantry in a life-and-death situation that revives our faith not in France alone . . . but in the dauntless spirit of man. In that sense, too, the fortress in the jungle cannot be blown too big as a symbol. It has held long enough to renew the free world's faith in the victory of the cause for which it stands.

And the editorial concluded by hailing "the triumphant story of the defiant few who are fighting for us all."

However, in 1961, John B. Oakes, Princetonian, former Rhodes scholar, OSS officer, nephew of Adolph S. Ochs, and son of his brother George Washington (who changed his part of the family's name from Ochs to Oakes during World War I, in the mood of patriotic fervor) became editor of the editorial page. And as early as 1962, as Americans took over the former French role in South Vietnam, the *Times* began to warn that a major war was brewing and called for greater candor from the United States Government.

The paper was torn by its desire to contain communism and uphold democracy and by its unwillingness to see the conflict in Vietnam widen and build into a massive war on the mainland. On May 21, 1964 a *Times* editorial warned the American government that it "would be a mistake to enlarge the war further without establishing a reasonable, limited objective for its settlement."

Three weeks later, on June 12, 1964, the paper began to harden its stand against efforts to win a military solution in Vietnam:

> There is no ideal solution: but it has seemed to this newspaper that the most practicable one is, in the broadest possible terms, a

---

*Though *Times* editorials are published anonymously, this editorial of May 6, 1954 was written by Anne O'Hare McCormick, the paper's foreign-affairs columnist and the first woman member of the editorial board.

guaranteed neutralization of all states that formerly made up Indochina. . . . The entire problem deserves exploration in another conference of the fourteen nations, Communist China included, that have been concerned with Southeast Asia since the Geneva Conference of 1962. The decisive confrontation of the United States and Red China should be over a negotiating table, not with arms. In the long run, this will only be possible when Communist China is a member of the United Nations and when Washington can speak to Peking in the normal course of diplomatic exchanges between two nations that recognize each other.

Yet the paper's vision was clouded, and it remained torn between its desire for a negotiated settlement and its determination to use force if necessary to convince North Vietnam that it could not prevail. The *Times* supported President Johnson on the Gulf of Tonkin resolution, declaring on August 5, 1964:

> United States determination to assure the independence of South Vietnam, if ever doubted before, can not be doubted now by the Communists to the north of their allies. It is a grave moment, calling for open-eyed, cool-headed appraising of all the alarming possibilities—by North Vietnam as well as others.

But this did not mean that, in supporting President Johnson on the Tonkin Gulf resolution, the *Times* now favored escalation of the war; it interpreted the President's move as reminding Hanoi again that, "despite new provocation, the United States still seeks no wider war."

Indeed the paper's choice of Johnson over Barry Goldwater for the presidency in 1964 was based on the belief that Johnson would make a calmer and more restrained leader. The editors convinced themselves that Johnson's "firmness" would lead to a negotiated peace. Just before the election, an editorial stated:

> The nation's united confidence in its Chief Executive is vital. No one else can play the hand. That confidence will be best maintained by a continued adherence to the principles the President himself has enunciated of firmness, but a firmness that will always be measured —a firmness whose mission is peace.

But, as soon as he had won the election, Johnson escalated his attacks on North Vietnam and the Vietcong. The *Times* was chagrined. It seemed that the President was going for a military solution after all. A November 25, 1964 editorial declared that, with the election over, the "hawks were emerging from the dovecotes of the Johnson administration," and a reassessment of war plans was under way. All five members of the Joint Chiefs of Staff were pressing for a broadening of the war. If there was to be a new policy, said the *Times,* if an Asian war was to be converted into an "American war," the country had "a right to insist that it be told what has changed so profoundly in the past two months to justify it."

By February 14, 1965, the paper was warning that "history, good intentions and a concatenation of events have led the United States into a morass where we sink deeper each day."

On May 28, 1965, it said Johnson was taking the country into a huge land war in Asia "almost surreptitiously." He was escalating not only the fighting itself but the rhetoric, the principles, the allegedly high American purpose for waging the war. "Our national honor is at stake," President Johnson had declared. The *Times* retorted:

> A statement like the one Mr. Johnson made arouses uneasiness because of its categorical nature. The stakes in the Vietnamese conflict are being raised steadily. The Vietnamese conflict—and no one needs to tell this to Washington—holds within it the possibility of a war with Communist China and a world war.
>
> It is neither cynicism nor appeasement to point out that the word "honor" is not a scientific but an emotionally charged term of very high voltage. If President Johnson means that Americans would not accept a defeat so humiliating that it represents a loss of national honor, he is right. The risk comes in determining when, if or how honor would be lost. There are even such things as honorable defeats and dishonorable victories. And in between are all kinds of compromises that are neither one thing nor another—but sensible and realistic.[2]

The *Times* never relented thereafter in its opposition to Johnson's escalation of the war. The President was furious with the *Times.* He told friends and associates it was verging on treason.

The *Times* had become the first and foremost critic of the Vietnam War from within the Establishment. And for being "prematurely" against the war, it suffered the outrage of most of the Establishment, many of whose leaders accused it of having lost its sanity or patriotism (shades of World War I!) John Oakes even came to regard himself and the editorial page as "anti-Establishment." Though most of the Establishment eventually came around to the *Times'* position, it would be years before the paper would lose its reputation of having gone pink, if not red.

Nixon and Other Enemies

When Richard Nixon became president in 1969, he saw the political necessity of ending the draft and gradually pulling American troops out of Vietnam. But he was determined not to "bug out," not to "cut and run." Hence, while seeking to "Vietnamize" the war, Nixon went all out against those Americans who were demanding an early end to the fighting and bombing. With a flagrant disregard of the law and the Constitution that ultimately destroyed his presidency, Nixon attacked opponents of the war as his enemies. He was prepared to use the FBI, the CIA, the Internal Revenue Service, White House "plumbers"—whomever and whatever he needed—to harass and defeat those who opposed him on Vietnam.

The New York Times stood in the forefront of that opposition. Nixon himself had helped to deepen the paper's antipathy to the war, not only on the part of the paper's reporters and editors but also its publisher; there had long been dislike and distrust of Nixon on the fourteenth floor of the *Times,* where the publisher and his top executives sit.

To answer the question of why the *Times'* publisher was so opposed to Nixon, Punch Sulzberger says: "I think I have to look back—I think Dad* and some of the others who were

*Arthur Hays Sulzberger, publisher of the *Times* from 1935 to 1961.

around in more responsible positions than I was back during the time of the Helen Gahagan Douglas business had acquired a tremendous dislike of Nixon. I was away in colleges and overseas for the paper at that time. I just developed and inherited a distaste for that man, not helped by some of his subsequent actions.

"Dad, who was very close to Eisenhower, never liked Nixon at all, and I guess I must have absorbed some of that, because I never trusted the man one iota, and I didn't like him. I always thought he was a dishonest kind of person, and I found that feeling was shared by so many of my colleagues. We never really had a debate about Mr. Nixon. But I never presumed for a moment that he was so dishonest in the terms that finally came out."

Sulzberger says it was not Nixon's policies so much as his *character* that won the enmity of the *Times*. His father's views weigh heavily on him as he ponders the problem: "Dad was always *impressed* by Nixon. I never, to the best of my recollection, ever met him when he was Vice-President. Dad always used to come back and say that he was impressed by how much the man *knew*, but that he continued to dislike him."

Nixon cordially reciprocated this dislike. When the *Times* endorsed George McGovern for president in 1972, Nixon wrote in his diary:

> I said that I learned the news with relief because I didn't want anybody on the staff to urge me to meet with their editorial board and thank God we had not done so. Nobody had the temerity to suggest that I do so. And as I pointed out to Haldeman there should be a letter to the *Times* or a statement that the *Times* basically *should* endorse McGovern because he stood for everything they stood for —permissiveness, a bug-out from Vietnam, new isolationism, etcetera.[3]

When engulfed in Watergate, Nixon declared that "the Establishment" was dying, but that, before it did, it was determined to "get" him. What did he mean by that? The publisher of the *Times* thinks he was "painting with a fairly broad brush, but clearly he swept into it *The Washington Post* and *The New York Times*. I think he probably meant the universities too, the Harvards, Yales, Columbias, who were all pretty violently against him. I think they suspected he was a man of little morality." (Asked the same question, the banker David Rockefeller responded: "This is why I have grave questions as to the serious meaning of the Establishment, because I can't imagine what body of people who could be described as the Establishment would be out to 'get' Nixon in that sense, and I really have no idea what he meant. A lot of people didn't like Nixon, but it was hardly confined to what could be described as the Establishment. In fact, I would have thought there were more outside than in.")

It was Vice-President Spiro Agnew, Sulzberger recalls, who first spearheaded Nixon's attack on the press, and the *Times* in particular. "We were certainly one of his prime, his very prime targets," says Sulzberger. "We had supported Agnew for Governor of Maryland—that's often forgotten." But by the time Nixon chose Agnew for his ticket in 1968, the *Times* had uncovered evidence of Agnew's involvement in corruption with building contractors in Maryland. "Everybody knew that we thought Nixon was a terrible disaster, and we thought Agnew didn't add a goddam thing to the ticket, and we said so," says the publisher.

Was anti-Semitism involved in Agnew's assault on the press? "I'd like to think there really wasn't any," says Sulzberger, "but I think that's too simplistic. There must have been, whether it was aimed at us or the *Post*—you know Kay Graham is Jewish. There must have been some measure of it." In any case, he adds, "Agnew was a singularly unattractive crook, it turned out. He's going back to Maryland to pay up his taxes, so they don't put him in jail. He got out by the skin of his teeth."

Sulzberger doesn't think Nixon is anti-Semitic, but rather distinguishes between what he regards as "good Jews" and "bad Jews," or those who support him and those who don't. "I don't think Bill Safire would have operated with him if he truly thought he was anti-Semitic. He wasn't against all Jews by any means, far from it."

Sulzberger says he doesn't see anti-Semitism as being as much of a problem "out there" (in America) as "in here" (at *The New York Times*). "I don't want us to be known as a Jewish newspaper," he says. "We are not a Jewish newspaper. It just so happens that a lot of talented Jews go into journalism—leaving aside the ABC's, CBS's, NBC's, which are really entertainment centers more than news, regardless of what they say."

Before Punch Sulzberger became publisher of the *Times,* the paper had deliberately sought to downplay the Jewish background of some of its leading editors and writers. A. M. Rosenthal and A. H. Raskin, for instance, used initials rather than their first names, both of which are Abraham. (Both became widely known, however, as "Abe.") "Well, I'm more public," says Sulzberger. "I put their names on the masthead, and everybody can see it. When Dad was publisher, there were three names on the masthead—his own, Julie Adler, and Godfrey Nelson, secretary-treasurer, and nobody else. In the early days there weren't even bylines, so nobody knew who anybody was. That's changed a great deal, and I think changed for the good. I think that people are entitled to know who the managing editor is, and those kinds of things. It's all more obvious. But when you look at it, you say, 'Holy Golly,' you know."

Sulzberger believes that there should be a better balance between Jews and gentiles in the next generation of editors of the *Times*—as there was in earlier generations, under Charles Miller, Rollo Ogden, John Finley, Charles Merz, Carr Van Anda, "Jimmy" James, Turner Catledge, Clifton Daniel, and James Reston. "You look at your next generation," says Sulzberger, "and some are and some aren't, and that is exactly the hell the way it ought to be. That's very important, I think, for us. But I don't get a sense of our being perceived Jewishly. We get some reaction when we take stands on Jewish issues. People don't understand why we are not more supportive of Israel in some way, shape, and form. How can you be a Jew and not be 100 percent behind Israel, because there are plenty of others behind the Arabs? But other than that, we just don't catch it from anybody."

Sulzberger does not sense antipathy from that part of the upper crust of the New York business community that is not Jewish. "They're so mixed up," he says. "Many of the investment bankers are Jewish, the commercial bankers are not. I don't sense it, but it may be said behind my back."

Is there a regional antipathy from which the *Times* suffers as a New York newspaper? "I think one would be hard pressed to define it," says Sulzberger, "but I would have to say that undoubtedly it must be true. We are in New York and suffer along with the fate of our city, and are held up as being profligate— we're too easy on welfare, and indeed our editorial policy is a liberal one on welfare in many respects, but it's less liberal now than it was.

"And we were perceived as the give-away boys in our own industry. We were perceived as the give-away boys in terms of industrial relations for years and years and years. Much abuse was heaped on us because New York City led the way in industrial relations, and the *Times* led New York City. I am reminded on occasion that my father was supposed to have said, and probably did say, that never would *The New York Times* take a strike over an economic issue. It was an announced policy to the unions. So you can imagine the effect when we said to our labor relations people, in that context, 'go and negotiate.' *The Daily News* always felt that we collapsed on everything, and we probably did."

Though the *Times* had sought to remain independent in politics, its stands on social issues increasingly put it in the Democratic camp. But the *Times*, with its liberal traditions, had also been betrayed by history—not just by the election of Nixon but by the rightward movement of the Republican party. This made it more difficult for the *Times* to play its preferred role as a bipartisan, unifying force. The liberal principles it stood for had almost ceased to be Republican party principles. "The divided Republican party," says Sulzberger, "practically killed us."

Crisis over the Pentagon Papers

In the crisis over the *Times'* role as the newspaper of the Establishment, the showdown came with its decision, in the summer of 1971, to publish the Pentagon Papers, documents drawn from a massive history of the United States' involvement in the Vietnam War, written within the Department of Defense. Xerox copies of the papers had been given to *Times* reporter Neil Sheehan by a former Defense Department aide and RAND analyst, Daniel Ellsberg, who had become a bitter opponent of the Vietnam War.

The Pentagon Papers were classified "top secret," and the publisher, top executives, editors, and lawyers of the *Times* went through three months of intense argument over whether and how to publish them.

The newspaper's law firm, Lord, Day, and Lord, one of whose senior partners was Herbert Brownell, attorney general in the Eisenhower administration, strongly advised against publication, warning that it would bring vigorous and probably successful action against the paper by the government.[4]

Sulzberger was well aware that he was putting the newspaper's reputation, perhaps its very existence, on the line. The number two executive at the *Times,* Harding Bancroft, a former Naval officer and State Department official, was against any publication of the Pentagon Papers; he thought they might reveal codes or embarrassing diplomatic secrets. The editorial page editor, John Oakes, recommended paraphrasing the documents or quoting only brief excerpts from them rather than running the actual texts. The late Lester Markel, who had built the Sunday *Times* into a national institution in its own right, held that publication of the actual documents would be "irresponsible." To traditionalists like Markel, irresponsibility meant any action taken by the paper which would hurt the foreign policy or diplomatic position of the United States.

Those who favored publication of the Pentagon Papers felt,

however, that true responsibility meant one thing: telling the whole truth so that citizens could make up their own minds about the war. This was the powerfully held view of such key editors as James Reston, A. M. Rosenthal, Max Frankel, and James Greenfield, and of the reporters directly involved. As Neil Sheehan put it, the *Times'* job "was to report as accurately as possible" on the history of the war, as revealed by the Pentagon's own documents, and to enable "the average citizen and the professional historian" to judge the papers' own merits.[5]

Sulzberger's decision to publish much of the text of the Pentagon Papers, despite their top secret classification, was strengthened especially by the arguments of James C. Goodale, a young lawyer who headed the *Times'* legal department. Goodale's philosophy, the philosophy of a "newspaperman's lawyer," was: "There is always a way to get a story into print." Goodale prepared a long memorandum which concluded that, if the Pentagon Papers stories were done carefully, higher courts would never sustain an injunction or criminal conviction against the *Times.*

In retrospect, the publisher still thinks the *Times* was right to handle the Pentagon Papers as it did. Sulzberger says: "I think, looking back, we probably did it about as correctly as we could have. The big debate was whether we should do it all at once, get it all out, and be done with it, and then sort of thumb your nose at the government and say, 'Well, what can you do about it?' "

"I never even told my directors," he says. "We afterward sent them an explanation of what we had done. As they were directors of the company, were they entitled to know what we were doing before the fact and the dimensions of it? Good question. I never have resolved in my mind what the obligations are. It's a legitimate question; the board of directors doesn't discuss editorial matters, but this went beyond editorial judgments." Yet his instinctive decision was not to submit this decision to a board whose role was limited to business matters—even if the existence of the paper were at stake.

For Nixon, no clear necessity existed to try to stop publication of the Pentagon Papers. As Nixon later wrote, "We had only two choices: we could do nothing, or we could move for an injunction that would prevent *The New York Times* from continuing publication. Policy argued for moving against the *Times;* politics argued against it." (After all, it was primarily, he said, "a critique of the way Kennedy and Johnson had led the nation into war in Vietnam.") "Nevertheless," Nixon decided, "publication of the Pentagon Papers was certain to hurt the whole Vietnam effort. Critics of the war would use them to attack my goals and my policies."[6]

After the first installment of the Pentagon Papers was published on Sunday, June 13, 1971, Nixon and his advisers went into a series of meetings on how to stop further publication by the *Times.* On Monday afternoon, Attorney General John Mitchell and Robert Mardian, head of the internal security division at the Justice Department, met at Mitchell's apartment in the Watergate and drafted a telegram asking the *Times* to cease publication and threatening legal action if it did not. The telegram stated that the material was classified top secret and that disclosure was directly prohibited by the Espionage Law. "Further publication of information of this character," the telegram said, "will cause irreparable injury to the defense interests of the United States." Mardian sought to telephone the text directly to Sulzberger at the *Times* in New York, but was told that the publisher was in London.

In New York, there was a furious argument over whether to submit to the government's request. A. M. Rosenthal was absolutely against yielding and insisted that the publisher be called to make the decision. When Sulzberger was awakened that night at the Savoy Hotel in London, James Goodale took the phone and said, "We cannot afford for the future of this paper to stop publication now."* Sulzberger agreed, and the *Times* went ahead with its third installment.

The editors in New York drafted a reply to Mitchell, declin-

*Goodale, after being named Vice-Chairman of the New York Times Co. in 1979, resigned in January, 1980. Walter Mattson, who had risen through the ranks from his start as a printer, became president of the company.

ing his request and stating that the issue was for the courts to decide; the *Times* would oppose any request by the government for an injunction "for the same reason that led us to publish the articles in the first place."

The Nixon administration's effort to silence the *Times* was what really made the Pentagon Paper story—just as the attempted Watergate cover-up later made the Watergate story.

So the big excitement in the Tuesday, June 15 edition of the *Times* was not the third installment of the Pentagon Papers but the story slugged, "Mitchell Seeks to Halt Series on Vietnam but Times Refuses." Later Rosenthal said: "Think what it would have meant in our history and the history of the newspaper business if the headline had been 'Justice Department Asks End to Vietnam Series and Times Concedes.' I think it would have changed the history of the newspaper business."

The government succeeded in getting an injunction against the *Times* to stop publication of the Pentagon Papers—the first time in the nation's history that a newspaper had been subject to prior restraint. The case moved swiftly to the Supreme Court where the *Times,* which had been joined by *The Washington Post* in its appeal after the *Post* had similarly been silenced by an injunction, won a split verdict, six to three.

The decision was hailed as a highwater mark for freedom of the press, but if it had come a little later it might have gone the other way. For it was the last decision of what Sanford Ungar has called "the post-Warren Court."[7] Not long afterward, the liberal justices Hugo Black and William O. Douglas, both of whom took absolute First Amendment positions in defense of the newspapers, were gone, and it became a "Burger Court," or, as some preferred to say, "a Nixon Court."

Chief Justice Burger was clearly furious with the *Times.* He found it "hardly believable" that "a newspaper long regarded as a great institution in American life would fail to perform one of the basic and simple duties of every citizen with respect to the discovery or possession of stolen property or secret government documents. That duty, I had thought—perhaps naively—was to report, forthwith, to responsible public officers. This duty rests

on taxi drivers, justices, and *The New York Times.*" But the paper
had concluded that its overriding duty was to pursue and publish the truth, and to let the people decide what they wanted to
do about it.

Sulzberger vs. Oakes

Although the Pentagon Papers case may have been a triumph
for press freedom and for the democratic process under law, it
confirmed for many people—and not just Nixon sympathizers
but the more conservative members of the Establishment—that
the *Times's* editorial policy had gone "left."

This was a charge which, ironically enough, had been shared
by the publisher and his top news executive, A. M. Rosenthal.
In Chris Argyris's tape recordings,[8] done as management consultant for *The New York Times* during 1972 and 1973, Abe Rosenthal (designated as "R") is quoted as telling the publisher and a
group of *Times* editors that he had become "terribly concerned
that the paper, in the last few years, had gone toward the left
politically."[9]

"This," he said, "has bothered me more than anything else in
my professional life. And I would feel equally strong if it went
to the right. The editorial page has gone toward the left, the
columnists are liberal to liberal left, and many of the bright
reporters have come out of an atmosphere of advocacy. All of us
—something has happened. At times, during the Chicago business, the battles in the street during the Democratic National
Convention in Chicago in 1968, I felt that the paper was in
trouble. I felt that my job was to pull it back to the center. This
paper should not be politically discernible." The publisher responded that this was a critical issue and "one that the paper
must discuss" at another meeting. But no such meeting ever
occurred.

Church, State, and Counting House

The issue remained superficially hidden for years, and drew the publisher, Sulzberger, and the editorial page editor, Oakes, into fundamental but largely unexplored conflict. The outside world may have considered that the over-all performance of the newspaper—its handling of Vietnam, the Pentagon Papers, Watergate, the oil crisis, business corruption, and other specific stories, not just the editorial page—revealed a leftward bias. But internally, at the *Times,* concern about such bias focused on Oakes's editorial page.

Oakes, for his part, was concerned about editorializing in the news columns, in violation of *Times'* principles of printing an unbiased news report. In closed meetings and informal conversations, Oakes sometimes criticized stories and "news analysis" pieces for being editorially slanted—to the annoyance but occasionally to the disgruntled agreement of the managing editor, Rosenthal, who expressed no difference in principle with the separation of news reporting from editorializing.

But Rosenthal was no fan of the editorial page; he wondered whether it did the paper any good. He and the publisher were often critical of its tone, which they called "shrill" or "strident," words that intensely annoyed Oakes. From 1961, when he became editor, Oakes had deliberately set out to make the editorial page tougher and more decisive. Before his editorship, *Times* editorials had most often been criticized for their indecisive "on the one hand, on the other hand."

"It's true," says Oakes, "that when I came in, I told everybody that the one phrase I wouldn't want ever to see on the page, *ever,* was 'on the other hand.' I always knocked the phrase out."

Oakes was determined to toughen the editorial page with decisive judgments. "I grew up with the paper," says Oakes, "and for years I thought the editorials were very flabby and never said anything. I was determined that if I made the editorial board, I'd begin writing editorials that said something. For years I felt that our editorials were so damn low-key that no one read them." He felt that the *Times* "had the reputation of being a great paper except for its editorial page."

His effort to change the tone and direction of the editorial page brought Oakes into conflict with Sulzberger, who was particularly concerned that Oakes was "antibusiness." Once, defending himself against that charge, Oakes said that perhaps unfortunate phrases sometimes crept into editorials not because of a "philosophical bias against business" but because of a concern for "the good of the general public as weighed against the special interests." Sulzberger replied that he didn't have any disagreement with Oakes that the paper should focus on the public good, but only objected to editorial positions taken by the paper that he did not agree with.

At a later meeting, Sulzberger wondered about the stance of the paper if the editorial board believed in a policy that was bound to hurt the paper financially. "This is the most difficult one for me," said the publisher. "I don't see how I can stand up and say one thing, and then have the paper come out in another direction." He told Oakes: "I am in agreement with the point of view that the paper should be concerned with straightening out the world. But, when it comes into direct conflict with something that is entirely practical to the business, then I lose the call a hell of a lot faster than you." Oakes replied, "And that is the point that concerns me." And Sulzberger responded, "It's very strange for me to divorce myself—separate myself—from the organization. It may not be strange for you, but it is for me."

The publisher continued to describe his concern when, on several occasions, corporate board members, men whom he respected greatly, had read the paper to find their companies' actions condemned. Oakes said he had never thought of that embarassment but still believed that the correct action for the paper was to condemn the companies even if their chief executive officers were on the board of directors of the New York Times Company. Oakes added, "These businessmen are great human beings, but they have no feelings for the tradition of a great newspaper." Sulzberger answered, "Let us be clear that news and editorial matters are not discussed by these businessmen. But it is still not easy to divorce myself when I know [that we have attacked] someone who sits on our board of directors. . . . None of these men would even think of trying to influence our positions. But they might say, 'You are certainly entitled to print anything you wish, but how on earth did you arrive at such-and-such a position?' "[10]

The three other *Times* executives present supported the idea that the paper must be free to be critical of any corporate policy, including its own; the publisher said he understood that, but still was not completely certain. He wanted to think more about it. The management consultant, Argyris, commented that if he were on the editorial board, he would feel several kinds of insecurities: "On the one hand, I would know that sometimes I would be creating difficulties for the publisher and his business friends. On the other hand, I could never be certain the publisher would stand behind me. I would even wonder if the publisher had the vision of the paper that I had and wished he had."

The other *Times* executives agreed that that was an important point; one said, "I've always been proud of this newspaper because I knew it was free to state the difficult editorial positions —if we thought they were correct—and I always felt absolutely secure that the publisher was going to stand behind me, no matter what the pressures were." Sulzberger said he understood that, and hoped the day would never come when the paper's interests would take precedence over the public interest."

The publisher's concern that the *Times* had come to be regarded by the business community as antibusiness—linked to his concern about the profitability of the paper—was brought to a head by a cover story in *Business Week* magazine of August 30, 1976, headed, "Behind the Profit Squeeze at The New York Times." The article began:

In 1963 when Arthur Ochs "Punch" Sulzberger took over the family business—*The New York Times*—the nation's most prestigious newspaper was riding a wave of prosperity. So the soft-spoken Sulzberger was content to ignore some obvious problems on the paper and let nature take its course, even though Sulzberger bore the titles of publisher of the paper and chief executive of the parent New York Times Co.

Under this loose rein, the paper's pervasive management and marketing shortcomings festered and became much worse. The result is that the financial health of the *Times* has seriously deteriorated. Editorially and politically, the newspaper has also slid precipitously to the left and has become stridently anti-business in tone, ignoring the fact that the *Times* itself is a business—and one with very serious problems.[11]

The piece annoyed and angered Sulzberger; in fact, he was still angry about it three years later. He said: "I understand the piece first came out favorably, and then was sent back for editorial changes. They did a hell of a job on us. It hurt. It was not fair."[12]

Financially, The New York Times Company and the newspaper had already been turned around before the *Business Week* piece appeared. The company's net revenues had nearly doubled from $12.7 million in 1975 to $22.3 million in 1976. Its earnings per share had risen from $1.15 in 1975 to $1.97 in 1976. And the *New York Times* newspaper was doing much better; its contribution to net earnings had risen from 29 cents per share in 1975 to 64 cents in 1976.

All the same, Sulzberger moved to deal with the antibusiness charge. In early 1976, he had decided to consolidate the daily and Sunday departments of the *Times.* That would leave Max Frankel, the Sunday editor, without a job, as Rosenthal took over responsibility for both the Sunday and daily editions.

Sulzberger went to Oakes to persuade him to step down as editor of the editorial page at the end of 1976, to make way for Frankel as his successor; the publisher said that he did not want to lose Frankel. Oakes agreed to become senior editor for the year before his retirement and thereafter would continue to contribute pieces to the Op Ed page.

But what Oakes did not realize was that the publisher planned to make a major change in the editorial board that had served under Oakes, "rotating" more than half its members to other jobs or, in some cases, proposing early retirement. This produced anxiety and anger within the editorial board, and a concern that its integrity was being threatened.

While the editors recognized that the publisher had the right and power to determine the paper's editorial policy, the editorial board had been regarded as a group of experienced and knowledgeable people, who served their consciences as well as the editor or publisher. While the publisher had the ultimate responsibility for what ran in the paper, he had always exercised that responsibility with restraint and in close consultation with the editor. And while the publisher could overrule the editor, the tradition was that this would be done only after careful discussion and, whenever possible, reconciliation of views.

The fear that this tradition was being abandoned intensified on September 10, 1976, a few days before the New York Senatorial primary election. That day *Times* readers read a rollicking endorsement of Daniel Patrick Moynihan, a candidate whom the editorial page had been blasting for months. The editorial sang out:

> We choose Daniel P. Moynihan, that rambunctious child of the sidewalks of New York, profound student and teacher of social affairs, aggressive debater, outrageous flatterer, shrewd adviser—indeed manipulator—of Presidents, accomplished diplomat and heartfelt friend of the poor—poor people, poor cities, poor regions such as ours.

Sulzberger had written notes for the editorial endorsing Moynihan. Max Frankel, who was going to take over the editorial page from John Oakes but had not yet done so, worked on it for the publisher, although he had been leaning toward Bella Abzug.

On the morning of September 9, when Fred Hechinger, the assistant editor of the editorial page, arrived at his desk, he found the Moynihan editorial, with a note from the publisher telling him to run it the next day and saying, "I like it the way it is." Hechinger understood this to mean that it should be run as is. Hechinger called Sulzberger and said he thought he ought to read the editorial to John Oakes, who was at his summer house on Martha's Vineyard. Sulzberger told Hechinger to go ahead and call Oakes.

After Oakes heard the editorial, he called Sulzberger and said he thought the publisher ought to sign the editorial, since it was his piece and not the editorial page editor's or the editorial board's. Sulzberger first agreed to sign the editorial, then changed his mind. He suggested that Oakes could write a dissenting letter to the editor (himself), which would be published the same day the Moynihan endorsement ran.

Oakes had argued that, because the editorial page had been extremely critical of Moynihan in the past, readers deserved an explanation for the sudden switch. Members of the editorial board had been divided in support for Bella Abzug and former Attorney General Ramsey Clark; none was for Moynihan. Oakes had earlier urged that the paper not support any candidate editorially in the Senatorial primary, and thought the publisher had agreed. There had been no discussion about endorsing Moynihan.

Oakes, rushing back to New York, started drafting his letter to the editor on the ferry from Martha's Vineyard. He finished it in a parking lot next to the Aquarium in Woods Hole, and telephoned it to the *Times'* recording room. The letter said, in part: .

> Mr. Moynihan is charming, highly articulate, and certainly intelligent; but so are many other opportunistic showmen. . . . Mr. Moynihan's florid adulation of former President Nixon, expressed when he left the White House to return to Harvard, does not make for . . . confidence. Neither does his solemn assurance, when he quit his post last fall at the United Nations, that he would consider it "dishonorable" if he resigned to run for public office. Neither does his deceptive explanation of the fate of the Family Assistance Plan early in the Nixon Administration. Neither do his manipulative efforts to wheedle press and public, whether in explaining away that infamous phrase "benign neglect" or in defending the Nixon Administration's retreat from its social programs.

On reading Oakes's letter, the publisher decided not to run it. All he would allow Oakes was a one-paragraph statement of disagreement, which, as published, read:

> To the Editor:
> As editor of the editorial page of The Times, I must express disagreement with the endorsement in today's editorial columns of

Church, State, and Counting House

Mr. Moynihan over four other candidates in the New York Democratic primary contest for the United States Senate.

John B. Oakes

Several black members of the *Times* staff were upset about the paper's endorsement of Moynihan. They did not accept his own interpretation of "benign neglect" as designed to have the emphasis on "benign." Some of the blacks on the paper met with Roger Wilkins, the one black member of the editorial board, who wrote a column for the Op Ed page, which was supposed to run on Tuesday, September 12, election day. Under Oakes, the editorial page published a column every Tuesday by some member of the paper's editorial board. In those columns editors could express personal views which might or might not be consistent with the paper's editorial policy; it was regarded as a form of recognition of the editors' freedom of conscience. Wilkins's column, without mentioning the paper's endorsement of Moynihan, stated his opposition to the candidate because of his stand on racial issues. It declared Moynihan's defenders "misinformed and generally quite wrong." But the Wilkins column did not run that Tuesday before election. It was held over and ran Wednesday, after Moynihan had been elected, by less than 1 percent of the vote.

"What happened?" Bella Abzug's campaign manager snapped at a reporter when asked to explain her defeat. "You want it in one word? The New-York-Times."

A *Times* editorial which ran after Moynihan's election said that "Mr. Moynihan will surely be aware that his first task . . . will be to heal the wounds of battle."

Member of The Club

Punch Sulzberger had set out to change the business community's image of the *Times* as a left-leaning, antibusiness paper.

Looking back, Sulzberger acknowledges that that was the basic objective he was trying to achieve: "There was, I felt, an editorial bias that was growing. How can you express it? To say that we were undoubtedly perceived to be against big business, *anti* big business, *antibusiness.* I used to argue with John, and argue with people who claimed that we were antibusiness, that we were *not* antibusiness, because we *are* a business. We have payrolls to meet and all the other things that a business has to do. How can we be against ourselves?

"We were not antibusiness, but indeed we were perceived to be. When you factored into that perception the fact that we were violently anti-Nixon, that we had no alternative but to go for McGovern, because there was no way to go with Nixon, then everybody who felt one way about us added that to it.

"And then Nixon's house of cards began to come apart over Watergate. We were certainly not the leader, unfortunately— *The Washington Post* was that—but we were a pretty good catcher-upper, and then we did some good work on our own."

Did he really think the editorial page had been "left" under Oakes? "What is left?" he says. "What does the word mean? The business community really disliked us. When it all started to unravel with Nixon's collapse, we were perceived even more so as left. I heard it when I went out in the business community.

"We were not, in my judgment, anywhere near guilty of the things we were charged with. I don't think we were any more antibusiness than anybody else. I think that when Max took over as editor of the editorial page we really did not have a very dramatic shift in our editorial policy. Problems often had come up because of a difference in the turn of a phrase, a little turn of a phrase. I think we are far more acceptable today. It is not just the editorial page, but bringing out *Business Day** and improving the quality of our business report. But it takes a terribly long time to change people's image of you. A whole lot of things

---

*The fourth section of the daily *Times,* devoted to economic, business, and financial news.

had happened together. There's no question that we were perceived that way, as antibusiness. Businessmen said, 'We don't understand why you don't like us.' Our business is to report what goes on, and theirs is to hide it. They say: 'Why don't you ever write anything nice about us?' And I say: 'It's not our business. We cover the news.' They don't remember that we cover their increases in profits, write about their investments—but they don't count that."

Is he satisfied with the changes that have been made with the editorial page? "Yes," he says, "I'm satisfied." Were the changes, in his view, only stylistic? "They are stylistic, but they are more than that," he responds. "We're more open-minded. We don't start with the assumption that something is inherently wrong with business.

"I guess that I'm pretty responsible for the change. I myself look at things as a businessman. I don't like taxes better than anybody else, and I'll do everything in my power to make sure the *Times* pays the least possible taxes."

Sulzberger's strongly held position harks back to an old argument between him and Oakes; it would be difficult to find a better illustration of the conflict that goes on within a newspaper between self-interest and the public interest: The editorial page editor told the publisher that he thought the *Times* should endorse a city tax in the public interest even if the paper's profits ultimately suffered.[13]

> *Sulzberger:* I should do about any goddam thing to stop the tax. That's the difference between you and me.
> *Oakes:* But what is more important than any tax or bill is the reputation of the paper. There is no year when you can afford to sacrifice the reputation of the paper. There are no sabbaticals on integrity.
> *Sulzberger:* I understand you, but we have to keep the corporation going, and so we have to perform some very dangerous balancing acts.

The publisher of the *Times* has been worried about the American public's hostile reaction to the press, and "wishes he completely understood it."

"I had a letter this morning," he said one day, early in the summer of 1979, "enclosing a brochure starting out 'Dear Friend,' and asking isn't it time we stopped talking about freedom of the press and started talking about freedom *from* the press. It was signed Frank Sinatra." Sulzberger laughed and said he thought Sinatra, who in the past had occasionally been complimentary about the *Times,* was angry over a series of articles by Seymour Hersh and Jeff Gerth about the questionable affairs of Sidney Korshak, a Hollywood lawyer and financial broker, who was a friend of Sinatra's. Sulzberger said it was easy enough to understand why some people were hostile to the newspaper when their own interests, or their friends', were adversely affected, but he had more trouble understanding the broader public hostility: "Vietnam, Watergate—it's a distrust of institutions. Now nobody believes anything. I suppose it's just too much to expect that the press would not be subject to the same kind of doubts and scrutiny. They want to know why *we* are so pure."

The publisher recognized that the motives of the press were under suspicion—even at the highest levels in society. He said: "Certainly the dislike and distrust of the press by the Chief Justice of the Supreme Court has exacerbated a very uncomfortable situation. We'll continue to have trouble from the courts until time takes care of some of these judges. But, every time I think we have problems, I'm glad I'm not in the power business, the airplane business, or the grain business, or the oil business. Even doctors today are suspect—you don't trust your friendly doctor. They are charged with operating on people for profit and not because you need it." Yet Sulzberger appears to assimilate the role of the newspaper more nearly toward that of other businesses than to the professions, although there are ambiguities in his attitudes. Similarly, he sees the *Times* as inside what he variously calls "the Club" and "the Establishment," but on terms that leave the paper free to play a critical outside role, independent of the club and its leading members.

"I'm not quite sure today what the Establishment is," he says. "I looked around at a dinner party the other night for Jack Javits

Church, State, and Counting House

[Senator Jacob Javits of New York] on his seventy-fifth birthday. Harry Van Arsdale [the New York labor leader] was there. Is Harry in the Establishment? I guess he is, in a way. Is labor in the Establishment? No, I don't think so, but I suppose Harry is. Well, *we* are in the Establishment. That's why they are so surprised when we write against them. They believe in that 'good old boy' kind of stuff. They have a misapprehension, a misunderstanding of what our role is. The biggest example, I suppose, was when Nelson [Rockefeller] died.* They wanted to know: 'Are you in the club or aren't you in the club?'

"We couldn't shirk our responsibility. Did we go further than we should have? That's a perfectly legitimate question. Different judgments can be made. But there are certain things that people read the *Times* for."

Was this news fit to print? The Rockefellers certainly did not think so. But doubts among Rockefellers about the *Times* as an acceptable member of the Establishment go beyond personal to ideological concerns. David Rockefeller says disapprovingly that the paper has become "liberal in the modern sense of that word, suggesting support for the welfare state, which tends to be antibusiness in its general reaction." He says he doesn't notice much change since Frankel replaced Oakes or Sulzberger tried to change the antibusiness image.

"It has long been my impression," says David Rockefeller, "that the *Times* conceives its objective to be on the side of the people versus business. I don't agree with that prejudice, and I think the business community generally feels the *Times* is unsympathetic." Rockefeller does not limit his judgment to the editorial page but believes the paper is antibusiness in its news columns. He has complained to *Times* editors about what he regarded as unfair coverage of the financial performance of the Chase Manhattan Bank.

Asked specifically whether he noticed any change in the paper's allegedly antibusiness bias since Oakes left the editorship of the editorial page, Rockefeller said, "Maybe a little bit

*The *Times* investigated the circumstances of the former Vice-President's death by heart attack, at which a young woman was present.

editorially, but not in the news department." He then complained of columns Oakes had written for the Op Ed page about Chile and Argentina, as being "too far left" and distorting the overall picture of those countries. These columns discussed political prisoners and violations of human rights in those countries.

Sulzberger himself maintains that the changes in the editorial page since the Oakes editorship have been "more in tone than anything else. Everybody on the editorial page is as much in favor of clean air and clean water as John. I think there is greater realism also. John's argument was that it was up to somebody else to compromise. We under no circumstances whatsoever ought to compromise, because if we did it, we would surrender the whole thing. But there is going to be compromise, whether on electric power or anything else. We are more willing to recognize that fact and express that view. Compromising is a fact of life."

Just what was the Oakesian antibusiness sin? A lecture he delivered at Temple Emanu-El, the principal synagogue of New York's most prominent Jews, typified it. He said:

> The corruption of American institutions did not begin or end with Watergate. As we have since learned, some of the most respected—or once-respected—names in American business, including the heads of huge multinational companies, were no more averse to engaging in the subversion of our political system at home by illegal campaign financing than they were to falling in line with the easy immorality of bribing public officials abroad—which they also did on a lavish scale.[14]

Could this perhaps be regarded as an effort to uphold traditional concepts of morality as the foundation of free enterprise and a free society? As one defender of the *Times* wrote to *Business Week:*

> . . . I want to take issue with your statement that the *Times* has become "stridently antibusiness, ignoring the fact that the *Times* itself is a business . . ."
>
> You confuse "antibusiness" with critical of business. The *Times* is often critical of business. So is *Business Week,* even, on occasion,

stridently. But the *Times* is clearly not against business per se. Indeed, it quite consistently supports competitive markets and private enterprise.

I'm sure the editors of *Business Week* would recoil in horror if asked by the business side of the magazine to defend or support some industry or form of business behavior because it might aid the magazine's financial results. As a longtime BW reader, I have the impression the editors seek to remain disinterested in the world they cover.*

Sulzberger insists that there has not been a dramatic shift in the Times' editorial policy: "I think our editorial policy was in many respects misunderstood by the business community. I would like it to be perceived as being, first of all, thoughtful, fair, somewhat liberal, international, not overly regional." He looks back with some regrets at the way the changes on the editorial page were handled. "I don't know how you handle it better, but it wasn't handled *right*. It caused pain for a lot of individuals I liked very much; some suffered real pain and agonies. We made a genuine effort to get people into the right jobs. Shouldn't we be able to move people around?"

While insisting on the power of "ownership" to control editorial policy, he worries about the possibility of takeovers of newspapers by nonpublishing corporations, such as banks or oil companies. "I don't particularly like it as far as the New York Times Company is concerned. Because of the way our stock is set up, it is impossible for anybody to acquire us unless the three trus-

---

*A letter from Chris Welles to *Business Week*, September 27, 1976. Welles, an economic journalist, later became director of the Bagehot Fellows Program in economic journalism at the Columbia University School of Journalism. The Mobil Oil Company protested his appointment by withdrawing its financial support from the program. Interviewed on this matter, Herbert Schmertz, then Mobil's vice-president for public relations, said, "Rightly or wrongly, we concluded that we did not have confidence in the person chosen to run the Bagehot program." Asked whether Mobil gave only to those with whose views they were in sympathy, Schmertz said in an interview with us, "I don't know how to handle that. How do you go along with someone in whom you don't have confidence? It's a dilemma. People said we made a bad public relations decision." (Other oil companies continued to support the Bagehot Fellows Program.) Schmertz added: "Chris Welles and Columbia were not going to be critical of Mobil— that was not the issue. On the other hand, we have never advertised in *The Daily Worker*." Schmertz resigned from Mobil in late 1979 to join the presidential campaign staff of Senator Edward M. Kennedy.

tees agree to sell it, and there's no chance of that happening now or after the trust expires. If my three sisters and I kick the bucket, it binds my children's children all through for something like twenty years after the death of the oldest grandchild living. We're talking about a hundred years; after that it can be somebody else's problem.

"But I don't like it. It worries me. I think somewhere along the line we ought to have some division of our labor. I think steel companies ought to make steel, newspaper companies ought to publish newspapers. It gets very, very fuzzy when a newspaper company such as ours ventures out into buying a filmmaking company, not movie films, or other things like that, right on the edge. You then have to say, look, if you can be a widely dispersed kind of company, what on earth is wrong with an industrial company going the other way and buying newspapers?

"What is wrong, in my judgment, is that one could lose an independent voice and an independent spirit that really is the driving motor of good journalism. I don't really care whether it's conservative, or liberal, just so long as it is independent and feels free to call the shots. And if you are owned by an oil company, I don't care how independent they say you're going to be, there is a chilling effect on what you would be writing. I think that is dangerous and bad."

How can this danger be guarded against? "There is no way to guard against it," says Sulzberger, "except that you would hope the people who run American industry are aware of this danger also. I mean it's not just our liberties and things we're protecting, it's theirs also."

How can an independent newspaper cover business with the same penetration and objectivity that it covers government or labor without provoking the anger of those business leaders on whose support a large commercial newspaper depends?

"I don't think we necessarily have to make them mad," says Sulzberger. "Sure, I get mad myself at times. They want to have only the good news reported, and our job is to report also some of the bad news as well as the good. I'd rather prove our virtues and take the heat and try to work with them, be understanding of their problems, not think that we're so superior that we can sit in some ivory tower and say everything they've done for years and years was stupid and useless, show some degree of understanding and sympathy for their problems, to some degree maybe help them in trying to solve their problems or at least to air them, and give them the ability to respond."

The Business of the Press

Thus the publisher of the *Times* tries to get and stay on reasonably good terms with business while upholding the principle of giving the news "without fear or favor." Though different heirs of the Ochs heritage stress different aspects of his creed, all pay homage to his separation of "church" and "state"—the editorial page, defined as church, and the news department defined as state. And all insist on the separation of both church and state from the counting house—the business side of the paper.

Unfortunately, however, there is no necessary connection between "calling the shots" in reporting and editorials, and making money in the newspaper business. Many excellent newspapers (*The Chicago Daily News* most recently) which once called the shots have perished.

The dilemma is particularly acute for the *Times:* the only truly national general daily; the international if unofficial, voice of the United States; the nearest thing the country now has to a newspaper of record; the setter of the news agenda for other news media; and, at its best, the agenda and conscience for the Establishment and the nation. Yet, to do its job and survive, the *Times* must make money.

Its courage knows no limits where foreign dictators are concerned, or even Presidents of the United States, not to mention mere heads of the CIA and FBI. But the paper is more vulnerable to the hostility or scorn of business.

In a sense, the vulnerability of a newspaper like the *Times* is precisely the same as that of the American Establishment itself, which also needs to preserve the goodwill and support of business. Capitalists inevitably judge the performance of the press, the universities, foundations, and research centers, in terms of their impact on business interests.

As serious a constraint as this may be, especially on the commercial press, it is unquestionably less deadening than the heavy hand of government. For businesses are many and diverse; their interests often diverge and conflict. And business executives need and respect the truth, and usually welcome it—as long as it does not hurt their own company's interest. A good and honest newspaper can survive and develop a strength comparable to that of any other institution in the society, even government itself.

A truly free press—a press that not only enjoys but exercises its freedom—is a crucial component of that third force that serves as a counterpoise in the American society to both business and government. Trying to discover and expose those unpleasant, unwelcome, and sometimes damaging truths about the powerful is a tough job, and can be dangerous for the press itself. It has been the exposure of wrongdoing in high places that has provoked much of the government, business, and public antipathy toward the press. The coverage of the Vietnam War, and just how America got into it, and the exposure and ultimately the pulling down of President Nixon and his men, probably hurt the public standing of newspapers like the *Times* and *The Washington Post* more than they helped it, even though the papers called the shots right and served the public, and traditional American principles, well. True, the messenger was blamed for the bad news. But, more than that, the press had proved its power.

Power is feared in America, even by the Establishment—especially when that independent power lies outside the control of the Establishment. Even a Rockefeller cannot curb an Oakes or a Sulzberger, once he has his dander up. Professor Samuel P.

Huntington of Harvard said, in a paper written for the Trilateral Commission, founded by David Rockefeller:

> In the two most dramatic domestic policy conflicts of the Nixon Administration—the Pentagon Papers and Watergate—organs of the national media challenged and defeated the national executive. The press, indeed, played a leading role in bringing about what no other single institution, group, or combination of institutions had done previously in American history: forcing out of office a president who had been elected less than two years earlier by one of the largest popular majorities in American history. No future president can or will forget that fact.[15]

And the Trilateral Commission concluded that

> . . . the responsibility of the press should be increased to be commensurate with its power; significant measures are required to restore an appropriate balance between the press, the government, and other institutions in society. . . . The increase in media power is not unlike the rise of the industrial corporation to national power at the end of the nineteenth century. Just as the corporations enveloped themselves in the constitutional protection of the due process clause, the media now defend themselves in terms of the First Amendment. In both cases, there obviously are important rights to be protected, but broader interests of society and government are also at stake. In due course, beginning with the Interstate Commerce Act and the Sherman Antitrust Act, measures had to be taken to regulate the new industrial centers of power and to define their relations to the rest of society. Something comparable appears to be now needed with respect to the media.[16]

Such talk is anathema to publishers, reporters, and editors as well. They regard the rights of free speech and free press as in no way comparable to the property rights of corporations; free speech and a free press are rights not just of the "institutional press" but of all citizens, and are vital to a free and democratic society.

But freedom and power may conflict. The issue that the news media cannot avoid is that of their own power, which is growing with the concentration of media ownership. Unless exercised responsibly, that power could jeopardize the ability of minority and dissenting voices to be heard. And it could endanger the professional principles and integrity of those who cover the news and write editorials. If business interests (whether outside or inside the media) come to dominate the news and editorial sides, the press will degenerate and freedom decay.

It is an undeniable fact that the press and the electronic media are big business in America; and, like the rest of big business, they must cope with the political pressures of a society that dislikes and fears concentrations of power as well as with the economic hazards of the marketplace. It will take determination and skill, not only on the part of publishers but of writers and editors, to preserve a truly free and disinterested press in this new environment.

Profit and principle will have to go hand in hand. In recent years, to increase its profitability, the *Times* has flowered forth with a host of new features aimed at serving consumers' interests and catching advertisers' dollars. "It's more than just a newspaper," proclaimed one ad for "The New New York Times."*

What would Adolph S. Ochs think of today's *Times?*

His grandson, Arthur Ochs Sulzberger, says: "I'd have to answer that by telling you what my mother thinks—she's the best transition between her father and myself, and she says she thinks he would have thought it just wonderful. He was a big believer in change and was not at all fearful of trying new things. I think he would have approved of the way the whole company has moved."

But the former editor of the editorial page, John B. Oakes, is dubious. "A. S. O.," he says, still using his Uncle Adolph's initials, "was two people. He was both pragmatic and idealistic. But even from a strictly pragmatic point of view, I do not believe that he would have thought that the only way to save the *Times* would be to load it so heavily with feature-type material

---

The New Yorker registered the arrival of the new *New York Times* with a cartoon: In a posh hotel restaurant, one waiter is saying to another, "What a night! We've got someone from 'Living' in the Tap Room, someone from 'Weekend' in the Grill, someone from 'Home' in the Blue Room and Mimi Sheraton on the Terrace."

as to erode the unique public perception of the *Times* as the one great American newspaper of record. He was a very genuine idealist where the paper was concerned. He felt that the paper had to have a tremendous internal integrity as a purveyor of news and to be resistant to any kind of outside pressure from any quarter."

In the American press, the publisher has the last word. But not the only word. Reporters and editors remain the heart of a great newspaper, and when the Establishment itself shows signs of rot or corruption, their job is to expose and cleanse it.

Chapter 4

Investing in Virtue:

The Ford Foundation

I N HIS brilliant essay *The Protestant Ethic and the Spirit of Capitalism* Max Weber contended that capitalism was the social counterpart of Calvinist theology. He put particular stress on the Calvinist concept of "a calling," which was not the state of life in which the individual had been placed by Heaven (Martin Luther's concept of "calling") but the earthly business he chose for himself, and which he had to pursue with religious fervor and responsibility. Thus the obligation to work hard, to be thrifty and sober, to save money and invest it prudently acquired sanctity.

But Weber held that, although capitalism may have begun as "the practical idealism of the aspiring *bourgeoisie*,"[1] it ended as an orgy of materialism—particularly in the United States, the *reductio ad absurdum* of capitalism:

Where the fulfilment of the calling cannot directly be related to the highest spiritual and cultural values, or when, on the other hand, it need not be felt simply as economic compulsion, the individual generally abandons the attempt to justify it at all. In the field of its highest development, in the United States, the pursuit of wealth, stripped of its religious and ethical meaning, tends to become associated with purely mundane passions, which often actually give it the character of sport.[2]

America's greatest private philanthropy, the Ford Foundation, was the offspring of mundane passion; Henry Ford created it as a tax dodge to enable his family to retain control of the Ford Motor Company after his death. But the Ford Foundation was a latecomer on the philanthropic scene. Set up in 1936 and truly active only after World War II, its career in good works depended on achievements that had taken place long before. Indeed, around 1904, when Weber made his grim assessment of capitalism in the United States, a few American capitalists, similarly disturbed at what their system had wrought, were seeking to reestablish the ties between capitalism and a higher calling. Foremost among them were Andrew Carnegie and John D. Rockefeller. Their efforts were indispensable to the making of the American Establishment.

The Gospel of Carnegie

Andrew Carnegie, who came to the United States as a poor immigrant from Scotland, built the Carnegie Steel Corporation out of whose cash flow, like Aphrodite emerging from the waves, sprang the Carnegie Endowment for International Peace, the Carnegie Institute of Washington, the Carnegie Corporation of New York, the Carnegie Foundation for the Advancement of Teaching, the Carnegie Institute of Technology (which became the Carnegie-Mellon University when joined to another industrial fortune), the Carnegie Hero Fund (to reward heroic deeds by civilians), Carnegie Hall, over two thousand free public libraries and many other benefactions.

This eleemosynary explosion represented no simple super-
stititious effort by Carnegie to buy his way into heaven. He had
given much thought, as his own writings testify, to the social
role of the rich. In 1889, the great steel magnate proclaimed his
"Gospel of Wealth" to the multitudes, with special reference to
his fellow millionaires.

"The problem of our age," he wrote, "is the proper administration of wealth, that the ties of brotherhood may still bind
together the rich and poor in harmonious relationship." Capitalism was a marvelous system, producing a level of material prosperity unknown in human history. But it had a drawback, one
great irregularity. It generated a tremendous "surplus wealth"
for the small number of industrial entrepreneurs who ran it.
Mutual hostility between rich and poor was the result.

Socialism or communism were, as remedies, out of the question for Carnegie. The present economic system, based on "individualism," was the "soil in which society, so far, has produced the best fruit." Scrapping it was not only undesirable but
impossible; that would require altering human nature itself.

One way or another, however, rich men would eventually
have to dispose of their surplus wealth. Carnegie asked them to
live modestly while using the bulk of their fortunes to help the
poor. That was the proper antidote for the unequal distribution
of wealth. The condition of society would improve as year by
year "thoughtful and earnest" millionaires administered the
"trust funds" of the community "far better than it could or
would have done for itself." The masses would appreciate the
benefactions visited upon them. Resentments would cease. Let
the government levy massive estate taxes, Carnegie urged, to
encourage the rich to follow his advice. He warned that if the
millionaires left their fortunes behind them, they would die
"unwept, unhonored, and unsung." Dying rich, they would die
disgraced. That was the true gospel concerning wealth.[3]

But living by this gospel was hard and sometimes thankless
work, requiring patience, delicacy, and judgment. There were
those who wanted no part of what they regarded as ill-gotten
gains. When Carnegie offered Pittsburgh $250,000 to build a

library, the City Council turned up its nose; later it relented and Carnegie, who had a forgiving spirit, came across with a cool million.

Eventually, Carnegie did establish his good name. He was an appealing figure: short, dynamic, a celebrant of his adopted land. But he never forgot his native Scotland or his humble origins; he was as rooted in the poverty, and as mindful of the poor, as, say, Sam Gompers, the labor leader; business heads with socialist hearts. Carnegie could joke—and could take a joke. Mark Twain, a frequent correspondent, sometimes addressed him as Saint Andrew* and wrote him letters that begged and kidded him at the same time:

> You seem to be in prosperity. Could you lend an admirer a dollar & a half to buy a hymn book with? God will bless you. I feel it. I know it. N.B. If there would be another application this one not to count. P.S. Don't send the hymn-book, send the money. I want to make the selection myself.[4]

A philanthropic P. T. Barnum, Carnegie advertised himself and his works unabashedly, and took a puckish glee in saying outrageous things. He was wary of experts, fearing that they would be, even on foundation boards, too precious, too conservative or reactionary, too remote from "the masses"; he wrote to W. M. Frew, secretary of the Carnegie Institute:

> The expert mind is too narrow—the artistic, very narrow. For this reason, painters of the day ridiculed Millet as vulgar; the musicians of the day, Wagner as insane; writers of the day, Shakespeare as bombastic. The future is to laugh at many pictures which experts are extolling today; and art amateurs are buying to be in the fashion, and at many books which are supposed to have the elements of enduring fame. I wish to trust my fund to a committee dominated by able men of affairs, who have within reach the expert element with which they can confer. Besides this, I wish a larger number of officials directly from the people in the commitee, as I am satisfied that unless the institution be kept in touch with the masses, and therefore popular, it cannot be widely useful.[5]

---

*Sometimes Mark Twain addressed him as "Miss Carnegie," as in a begging letter asking him to invest in a company that made a new kind of food out of skim milk.

The Jupiter of Wall Street, J. P. Morgan, who bought Carnegie out of business at the turn of the century for a quarter of a billion dollars, found him impossible. But John D. Rockefeller, building the Standard Oil Company, was an admirer of Carnegie's, despite his agnosticism. "I would that more men of wealth were doing as you are doing with your money," Rockefeller wrote to Carnegie, "but be assured that your example will bear fruits."[6] Rockefeller, taciturn, puritanical, and pious, was Carnegie's principal competitor in good works; indeed, in the establishment of worthy institutions it often seemed as though Carnegie were imitating him. Rockefeller set up the University of Chicago in 1891, nearly a decade before Carnegie founded his university. The Rockefeller Institute for Medical Research, established in 1901, preceded the Carnegie Institute of Washington, which was dedicated to scientific research, by a year. Rockefeller's General Education Board (est. 1902) was three years in advance of the Carnegie Foundation for the Advancement of Teaching. And although Rockefeller's great philanthropic holding company, the Rockefeller Foundation (est. 1913), was two years behind the Carnegie Corporation, that was only because Congress held it up for three years.

Traveling identical paths Rockefeller and Carnegie ended by creating a new kind of institution: the immense multipurpose private foundation. The gospel of wealth, like the Christian one, turned out to require institutional forms, and these foundations became its great churches, where priests—later known as philanthropoids—ministered to the faithful. As these lay churches emerged—respected by some, resented by others—the whole problematic of the Establishment was played out, and nowhere with greater clarity than in the philanthropic odyssey of John D. Rockefeller and the Rockefeller Foundation.

Investing in Virtue: The Ford Foundation

Rockefeller's Baptism

Rockefeller owed his charitable impulses to his deep Baptist faith, but it was not because of superior piety that he was able to steal a march on the religious skeptic Carnegie in building worthy institutions. For this he had to thank a sometime Baptist preacher named Frederick T. Gates.

Gates came to Rockefeller's attention in the late 1880s when, as head of the American Baptist Education Society, he maneuvered Rockefeller into founding the University of Chicago. Rockefeller, who had an eye for talent, invited the energetic young man to come to New York to organize and manage his benevolence. Gates turned out to be the perfect man for the job. He converted Rockefeller's piecemeal and haphazard giving into wholesale philanthropy, by application of what he called "the principles of scientific giving."[7] When Rockefeller's son, John, Jr., came to work in the family offices at 26 Broadway, Gates tutored him in those principles. Junior made philanthropy his life's work, but Gates, as the senior Rockefeller said, was "the guiding genius in all our giving."

Unlike the tight-lipped Rockefellers, Gates was a thunderer. In the style of an ancient Hebrew prophet, he summoned his employer to good works. "Your fortune is rolling up, rolling up like an avalanche! You must distribute it faster than it grows! If you do not, it will crush you, and your children, and your children's children."[8]

But for all his evangelical fervor, Gates was not conventionally religious. Even during his youth in rural New York and Kansas, he had never felt much attraction for the Protestant orthodoxy of his preacher father. The Christian ethic of service, not theology or profound religious experience, led him to the ministry. After going to work for Rockefeller, he succumbed to the teachings of Darwinian science and Biblical text-criticism, and abandoned doctrinal Protestantism altogether. Always a stalwart churchgoer, he continued to call himself a Christian, but by that he simply meant that he was devoted to "the service of humanity in the spirit of Jesus."

Medicine, Gates believed, was the most exalted sacrament of human service. In this he saw eye to eye with Harvard's President Eliot, whose religious views closely approximated his own. Once the two men were walking down Broadway talking about Gates' brainchild, the Rockefeller Institute for Medical Research. The minister remarked that as far as he was concerned, "Nothing is to me so exciting, so fascinating as the work the Institute is doing."

> Dr. Eliot stopped short in the street and turned to me and said, with emphasis and emotion, "I myself feel precisely so. The Rockefeller Institute is to me the most interesting thing in the world."[9]

Gates told the story at the tenth anniversary of the Institute's founding in an address that expressed his sense of the religious character of medical research. The Institute, he said, was "as universal in its scope as the love of God, and . . . as beneficent in its purpose." Health was happiness; disease, the root of all evil. The destruction of evil was the Institute's mission.

> Do not smile if I say that I often think of the Institute as a sort of Theological Seminary. But if there be over us all the Sum of All, and that Sum Conscious—a Conscious, Intelligent Being—and that Being has any favorites on this little planet, I must believe that those favorites are made up of that ever enlarging group of men and women who are most intimately and in every truth studying Him and His ways with men. That is the work of the Institute.[10]

Medical research, Gates expected, would even discover "new moral laws and new social laws—new definitions of what is right and wrong in our relations with one another." When Eliot read a transcript of the speech, he urged Gates to publish it. The Religion of the Future had found another prophet.

Gates did what he could to encourage Rockefeller to adopt a more universal and ecumenical vision. Until 1905, for example, Rockefeller gave money to no religious organizations that were not Baptist, a practice his advisor considered narrow-minded.

Investing in Virtue: The Ford Foundation

That year, Gates successfully interceded with him on behalf of the secretaries of the Congregational Board of Missions in Boston. But the Congregationalists, though delighted with Rockefeller's $100,000 donation, were embarrassed to admit to their role in soliciting the support of the world's wealthiest and most notorious Baptist. They therefore announced the gift in an obscure corner of their monthly periodical with the comment that they had received Mr. Rockefeller's check "with surprise," as though to imply that Rockefeller had unloaded the large sum on another denomination's missionary society for obscure reasons of his own.

The announcement did not escape the notice of the Reverend Washington Gladden, the nation's leading Congregational preacher and longtime scourge of the Standard Oil Trust. Gladden angrily denounced Rockefeller and demanded that the money be returned. It was, he said, "tainted." A huge public outcry followed. For weeks, condemnations of Rockefeller's "tainted money" issued from from press and pulpit, until, under pressure from an infuriated Gates, the secretaries owned up to their role.

The affair was deeply troubling to Gates. "I trembled as I witnessed the unreasoning popular resentment at Mr. Rockefeller's riches, to the mass of the people a national menace."[11] Not that he had any sympathy for this feeling. Only good—more oil at cheaper prices—had come out of Standard Oil as far as he was concerned. But he worried about what was to be done with Rockefeller's ever expanding personal fortune. Rockefeller himself, he suspected, did not fully appreciate its size. The philanthropies undertaken so far had barely dented it. Steps had to be taken. Gates issued a stern lecture to his employer.

Only two courses, said Gates, were open. One was to arrange for permanent corporate philanthropies dedicated to the good of mankind. The other was to keep the wealth within the family, allowing it to "pass into the unknown, like some other great fortunes, with unmeasured and perhaps sinister possibilities."[12] Since the second course was morally indefensible, Gates proposed that Rockefeller establish a series of trusts, each under separate management and each addressing a broad area of human affairs, such as higher education, medical research, agriculture, and fine arts.

> These funds should be so large that to become a trustee of one of them would make a man at once a public character. They should be so large that their administration would be a matter of public concern, public inquiry, and public criticism. They should be so large as to attract the attention and the intelligence of the world, and the administration of each would command the highest expert talent.

Gates was dreaming of a vast Rockefeller Establishment, powerful and immortal, private and professional, which would undertake to look after the wellbeing of mankind. The scope of the giving should equal the scope of the getting, he told Rockefeller. "Nothing less would befit the vastness of your fortune and the universality of its sources."[13]

It did not work out exactly as Gates planned. Rockefeller decided that he wanted greater centralization, a kind of philanthropical Standard Oil Trust, and in 1909 he set aside $50 million worth of Standard Oil stock for a Rockefeller Foundation that would finance and supervise his other institutions. These now included, besides the Institute for Medical Research, the General Education Board (set up in 1902 to foster primary school education in the southern states, but, after 1905, supporting both higher education and farm demonstration), and the newly established Rockefeller Sanitary Commission (about to embark on its remarkable campaign against hookworm disease in the South).

Before going ahead with the Rockefeller Foundation, a charter of incorporation was sought from the United States Congress. This was unnecessary, but not unprecedented. A simple deed of trust would have sufficed; however, Gates felt that the American people ought to have a say in such a powerful institution. Numerous other nonprofit organizations, including the General Education Board, had secured federal charters, and Gates expected no trouble for the Rockefeller Foundation, especially since the most powerful member of the Senate, Nelson

Aldrich of Rhode Island, was John, Jr.'s father-in-law. In March 1910, a bill of incorporation was introduced in the Senate.

The move was a mistake. With exquisitely bad timing, the Rockefeller forces had undertaken to supplicate Congress just when the government's antitrust suit against Standard Oil arrived at the Supreme Court.

The public was aware, as never before, of the malfeasances of the Rockefeller company. Should the people's elected representatives confer their blessing on the Rockefellers' philanthropic scheme? The Taft administration was unsympathetic. Attorney General George W. Wickersham wrote to the President opposing the bill and expressing the irony of the government's position. Was it appropriate, he asked, just when the United States through its courts was seeking "to destroy the great combination of wealth which has been built up by Mr. Rockefeller," for Congress to "assist in the enactment of a law to create and perpetuate in his name an institution to hold and administer a large portion of this vast wealth?" President Taft replied that he agreed with Wickersham's "characterization of the proposed act to incorporate John D. Rockefeller."

Cries of "tainted money" again rang out. Some serious and some not-so-serious questions were raised. What kind of control would the government have over the foundation's holdings? Was it a plot to take control of the nation's charities in the interests of big business? Would the foundation's beneficiaries feel constrained to support its corporate interests? In a balanced essay, Edward T. Devine, the editor of the philanthropic journal *The Survey,* pointed out that charitable institutions had a way of shoring up the status quo:

> The very breadth and liberality of the charter of this new Foundation might conceivably lead to artificial and untimely support for other established institutions which are blocking human progress. Pious foundations for higher education in England have worked that way, and, to cite an instance nearer home, the admirably administered Carnegie Relief Fund is undoubtedly a factor, whether for good or ill depends upon the point of view, in the working out of

the industrial relations between steel workers and the steel corporation.[14]

Devine recommended that the government be given a voice in
choosing the foundation's trustees.

In Congress, some senators bitterly denounced the bill, while
others suggested ways of limiting the foundation's autonomy
and size. The opposition was too large for even Senator Nelson
Aldrich to overcome. The bill was withdrawn for the alleged
purpose of incorporating "constructive criticism" into it. The
Rockefeller high command decided to wait for the Supreme
Court decision on Standard Oil before resubmitting a revised
bill on the Rockefeller Foundation.

In May 1911, the Supreme Court ordered the breakup of the
Standard Oil Company, and in June another unsuccessful attempt was made to get the foundation charter from Congress.
Undaunted, Gates decided that what was needed was an unofficial but more or less full-time lobbyist. John, Jr., arranged with
his father for Jerome Greene to be assigned to the task. Greene,
the protege and former secretary of President Eliot of Harvard
had, after the retirement of his mentor, left his job as secretary
to the Harvard Corporation and signed on as general manager
of the Rockefeller Institute for Medical Research. Greene was
valuable to the Rockefellers because of the independent contacts
he had made when toiling in Harvard's vineyards. As Junior
wrote to his father, "While he would go as employed by you to
put the matter through, at the same time he would not be dependent upon us for introductions but would get access to the right
people through his own connections and friends."[15]

Greene labored long and hard on the foundation's behalf. A
new bill was introduced which, among other things, limited the
size of the foundation to $100 million, required it to have a
diversified investment portfolio, and subjected its choice of trustees to a majority vote of nine officeholders: the President of the
United States, the Chief Justice of the Supreme Court, the President of the Senate, the Speaker of the House of Representatives,
and the presidents of Harvard, Yale, Columbia, Johns Hopkins,

and the University of Chicago. These restrictions succeeded in quieting enough opposition in the House so that, in January 1913, the lower chamber voted the charter through by a large margin. In the Senate, however, a hard core of Southern and Western progressives, led by Robert LaFollette of Wisconsin and Hoke Smith of Georgia, remained unalterably opposed; their delaying tactics killed the bill. After three years of struggle, the Rockefellers had had enough. They went to the New York state legislature, which quickly, unanimously, and almost without public notice, voted the foundation a restriction-free charter "to promote the well-being of mankind throughout the world."

The Ludlow Trauma

The crucial event in the childhood of the Rockefeller Foundation was the Ludlow Massacre, which happened on April 20, 1914, less than a year after the Foundation was incorporated. Six months earlier some 9,000 coal miners had made their way from the camps of the Colorado Fuel and Iron Co., which the Rockefellers owned, to tent colonies erected by the United Mine Workers on leased land. The miners were demanding union recognition, an eight-hour day, abolition of the company store system, payment in cash not company scrip, and enforcement of state mining laws. Three earlier strikes to organize the mines —in 1883, 1893, and 1903—had been broken; in fact, many of the strikers of 1913 were the strikebreakers of 1903.

Ludlow was the largest of the tent colonies, and the CF&I's managers brought in militiamen in early April 1914 to destroy it; they mounted a machine gun on a hill overlooking the town. A battle broke out, though it was never determined who fired the first shot. Forty died and many more were wounded. The militiamen moved in fast, set the tents ablaze, took some strikers prisoner and shot three of them. Two women and eleven children who had tried to hide in a pit below the tents suffocated or burned to death.

President Woodrow Wilson sent in federal cavalry to end the open warfare. But attempts at federal mediation between the union and the operators failed, as the mine operators, apparently with the approval of John D. Rockefeller, Jr., rejected the President's recommendations and ended the strike by breaking the workers' resistance once more.

However, the United States Commission on Industrial Relations made a thorough investigation of the strike, taking testimony from representatives of the mine operators, the strikers, state and local governments, and John D. Rockefeller, Jr.; the result was a devastating exposure of the absentminded cruelty of absentee ownership. John R. Lawson, a strike leader and member of the executive board of the United Mine Workers, testifying on January 29, 1915, declared that Rockefeller had violated his own statement that it was the duty of a director to ascertain labor conditions "as far as he can, and if there are abuses, to right them."

Yet upon the stand, throughout three whole days this week, John D. Rockefeller, Jr., insisted that he was absolutely ignorant of every detail of the strike. He stated that he had not received reports on labor conditions, he could not tell within several thousands how many men worked for him in Colorado, he did not know what wages they received or what rent they paid, he had never considered what the proper length of a working day should be, he did not know what constituted a living wage, and, most amazing of all, he had never even read the list of grievances that the strikers filed with the governor of Colorado and gave to the world through the press. He did not know whether or not fifty percent of his employees worked twelve hours a day, and when asked whether or not he considered twelve hours a day in front of a blast furnace to be a hardship he answered that he was not familiar enough with the work to judge. He did not know how many of his employees worked seven days a week the year around, but judged that it would be a hardship, yet when asked what part of the year could be worked under such conditions without hardship, he refused to approximate an opinion.[16]

Investing in Virtue: The Ford Foundation

The litany of charges against John, Jr.'s ignorance went on and on: Despite being a director of the company for more than ten years, he did not know how much was paid to crippled or mangled workers; he did not know that the company's control of the courts had prevented any damage suit from being filed against it; he did not know anything about collective bargaining, though he declared himself in favor of unions; he did not know anything about the company stores or how much they made; he did not know the company built saloons.

This record of "indifference respecting human life and human happiness," said Lawson, was the cause of industrial discontent and strife—"our lives and liberties passed over as a birthday gift or by will; our energies and futures capitalized by financiers in distant cities; our conditions of labor held of less account than dividends; our masters too often men who have never seen us, who care nothing for us, and will not, or cannot, hear the cry of our despair." But there was another cause of industrial discontent, and this, too, said Lawson, "flows from a Rockefeller source."

> This is the skillful attempt that is being made to substitute philanthropy for justice. There is not one of these foundations now spreading their millions over the world in showy generosity that does not draw those millions from some form of industrial injustice. It is not their money that these lords of commercialized virtue are spending, but the withheld wages of the American working class.
>
> I sat in this room and heard Mr. Rockefeller read the list of activities that his foundation felt calculated "to promote the well-being of mankind"—an international health commission to extend to foreign countries and peoples the work of eradicating the hookworm, ten millions for the promotion of medical education and health in China, $100,000 for the American Academy in Rome, thirty-four millions for the University of Chicago, one million for the Belgians, $20,000 a year for widows' pensions in New York, the investigation of vice conditions in Europe, and thirty-four millions for a general education board. A wave of horror swept over me during that reading, and I say to you that that same wave is now rushing over the entire working class in the United States. Health for China, a refuge for birds, food for the Belgians, pensions for New York widows, university training for the elect, and never a

thought for the many thousands of men, women, and children who starved in Colorado, for the widows robbed of husbands, children of their fathers, by law-violating conditions in the mines, or for the glaring illiteracy of the coal camps. There are thousands of Mr. Rockefeller's ex-employees in Colorado today who wish to God that they were in Belgium to be fed or birds to be cared for tenderly.[17]

But worse lay ahead. Junior testified before the Industrial Commission twice, in January and then in May 1915. Despite Lawson's oratory, Rockefeller came through the first session relatively unscathed, having managed to give the impression of being out of touch with Colorado events. By the second session, however, his correspondence had been subpoenaed and turned over to the Commission. It disclosed a close involvement on his part with decisions made by management at Colorado Fuel and Iron.

The effect was brutal—not only on Junior but on the Rockefeller Foundation. Indeed, the Foundation had been dragged into Ludlow. To help Junior deal with the situation, Jerome Greene, then secretary of the Foundation, and Charles Eliot, its most distinguished trustee, had conceived the idea of hiring the former Labor Minister of Canada, William Lyon Mackenzie King, to study Ludlow as a member of the staff of the Rockefeller Foundation. With the enthusiastic support of Junior, a new Industrial Relations Department was inaugurated at the Foundation with Mackenzie King as head. The move raised some eyebrows, but Greene had felt sure that the public would soon be convinced "both of our disinterestedness and of our strictly scientific method." In due course Mackenzie King issued a report advocating a waffling, middle-of-the-road course: neither collective bargaining between company and independent union, nor industrial dictatorship by the company, but a kind of consultative arrangement between labor and management.

It would not wash; the investigation, arranged more in innocence than anything else—a characteristic exercise in corporate public relations—confirmed the deepest fears of people who suspected that the Rockefeller philanthropy was designed to further Rockefeller business interests. There was no getting around the fact that, as Mackenzie King testified before the Industrial Commission, his work for the Rockefeller Foundation had had the purpose of making the Rockefeller companies "better industries than they had been . . ."

Frank Walsh, the fiery Kansas City lawyer who headed the investigating body, was outraged. He declared that the setting up of scientific or social work foundations would lead to a condition of "loyalty and subserviency" to men of wealth and to their interests "from the whole profession of scientists, social workers and economists." Already, he said, there were "thousands of men in these professions receiving subsidies, either directly or indirectly, from the Rockefeller Estate." Such men had been put in a position where "to take any step toward effective economic, social and industrial reform" would bring them "directly counter to the interests of their benefactor." No sensible person could believe, said Walsh, "that research workers, publicists, and teachers can be subsidized with money obtained from the exploitation of workers without being profoundly influenced in their points of view and in the energy and enthusiasm with which they might otherwise attack economic abuses."[18]

The investigation of the United States Commission on Industrial Relations pushed the Rockefeller Foundation into retreat. No longer would it involve itself directly in controversial issues.

Raymond Fosdick, a protege of Woodrow Wilson's at Princeton and brother of the liberal minister Harry Emerson Fosdick, was brought in by Junior as an advisor. He concluded that the impact of the Ludlow investigation was deeply discouraging to the Foundation, but that "in the long run it proved to be salutary." The Foundation, he said, had learned some important lessons:

> Except for a narrow range of noncontroversial subjects, notably public health, medicine, and agriculture, the Foundation's participation in the areas it wished to assist must be limited to grants to outside agencies competently organized and staffed to carry on the work in question. In other words, the Foundation must become primarily not an operating agency but a fund-dispensing agency. This new policy obviously did not imply that the Foundation would

avoid controversial questions. It meant that its approach to such questions would take the form of grants to agencies independent of Foundation control. In no other way could the objectivity of research be established beyond cavil and the projects freed from suspicion of ulterior interest. This was the new pattern which the Foundation was to follow for many years to come.[19]

In the decade after Ludlow, most of the Foundation's income was spent on the International Health Commission, the China Medical Board, and a third agency, created in 1919, called the Division of Medical Education. One important undertaking during those years was the work of the International Health Commission in trying to stamp out yellow fever; among those who made names for themselves in this work was Walter Reed. The Foundation waged war on malaria in the tropics and made large grants to improve medical instruction and education all over the world. University College, London, received $5 million dollars in one sum, and other grants were made to Edinburgh, Cardiff, Strasbourg, Lyons, Brussels, Sao Paulo, and Beirut. Rockefeller helped Canadian medical schools from Dalhousie in Nova Scotia to the University of British Columbia.

The good name of the Foundation was restored. An editorial in *The Times* of London of September 12, 1921 gives a sense of the goodwill that now prevailed toward it in many countries:

> The United States has no more effective ambassadors than the representatives of the Rockefeller Foundation, who, year after year, afford their guidance and help in the great fight against disease. The Foundation itself . . . is an inspiration. Planned on international lines and possessed of great resources, it has come to occupy a position of universal trust. . . . The Foundation, indeed, is one of the strong places of the new commonwealth of science. In addition it reveals the depth and sincerity of American good will towards ourselves and all peoples. Not with words of comfort only, but with rich and lasting benefits have these emissaries of the New World set out upon their great mission.

Investing in Virtue: The Ford Foundation
The Philanthropoid's Creed

Rockefeller, Carnegie, and the other capitalists who followed their example offered philanthropy as an argument in favor of the system that had made them rich. The institution they invented—the large charitable foundation—worked to shore up the status quo and to co-opt the system's critics. It promised another kind of insulation as well.

The foundation put distance between the donor and his benefactions; the glare of honor and prestige would be focused on it, and only by reflection on himself. Its purposes and interests were distinguishable and separate from his own. An independent board and a staff of disinterested experts were supposed to insure the separation. But that did not always happen; in the case of the Rockefeller Foundation, as we have seen, it became necessary to beat a strategic retreat when the interests of donor and foundation were exposed as the same.

Yet there is no basis for dismissing the foundation as a mere exercise in plutocratic hypocrisy. Among those who had it, the passion for giving was genuine and not self-serving. Most of the rich were not so generous. John D. Rockefeller was the philanthropist he was, because he was a pious Baptist, because he had more money than anyone else, and because he had Frederick T. Gates. Charity was an obligation for Rockefeller, but he was hard pressed to fulfil it on his own.

Before Gates came along, Rockefeller nearly worked himself into a nervous breakdown trying to examine all the requests that came his way. He did not part with money easily and lacked philanthropic vision. He was largely uneducated and had little interest in culture or ideas. Gates, though limited himself, supplied both. His own spiritual odyssey had brought him near to President Eliot of Harvard. But Gates was not the liberal that Eliot was. He was rabidly opposed to labor unions (as was Rockefeller, Sr.) and he harbored the normal late nineteenth-century WASP dosage of racial and anti-Semitic prejudice, as his autobiography testifies. He was inordinately proud of his roots in Puritan New England.

Unlike Eliot but like Andrew Carnegie, Gates was suspicious of experts. Yet, like Carnegie, he needed them. Both wanted to do great things—cure diseases, improve minds, build universities and institutes—and that meant acquiring educated brains; but neither was prepared to relinquish supervision to the experts. The institutes, funds, and foundations they established were corporate bodies, both in the sense of being self-perpetuating corporations and in being subject to boards of businessmen. This followed the traditional form of governance of American colleges and universities. Carnegie said, "Americans do not trust their money to a lot of professors and principals [presidents] who are bound in set ways, and have a class feeling about them which makes it impossible to make reforms. Americans put their money under the control of businessmen at the head of the universities. If I had my own way, I would introduce that system into Scottish universities."[20]

This is the uniqueness of the American Establishment: the bringing together of intellectuals under the benevolent governance of business rather than that of the State, as in Europe. It is a privately endowed Establishment, wary of the State, even antagonistic toward it. The businessmen of the American Establishment do not see the State, as Marxists do, as a creature of, first, the aristocracy, then the bourgeoisie. Rather, the American capitalists regard the State as a creature of the People, or of the Politicians, or of the Bureaucrats, but not their own thing.

This view was shared by the first administrators of the great foundations. Frederick Gates was highly conscious of the importance of keeping the private *Third Sector*, as John D. Rockefeller 3d was later to call it, separate from the government. When the Rockefeller Foundation was set up, he vigorously opposed attempts to get it to fund programs in state universities. His colleagues regarded this as extreme at the time but he, typically, saw it as a matter of principle.

Investing in Virtue: The Ford Foundation

Gates did not favor total independence from government control for the foundations. The application for a federal charter for the Rockefeller Foundation reflected his desire, as well as John, Jr.'s, to insure that, if the Foundation ever fell into evil hands, Congress would be able to do something about it. Still, they sought to keep government off at greater than arm's length; the view of most "leading men" of that time (and perhaps even today) was that elected officials could not be trusted to perform good works.

Henry L. Higginson, a fellow of the Harvard Corporation, exposed this prejudice in a letter written to Jerome Greene during the period when Greene was trying to get the Rockefeller Foundation's charter through Congress. Higginson, who was also a member of the board of the Carnegie Institute of Washington, told Greene:

> In the Carnegie Institution the President of the United States, the President of the Senate and the Speaker of the House were members of the Board, and we all were glad to drop them. When the new Act was made, they were dropped, and the Board is now as independent as can be of any Government influence. It is well that the presidents of the universities should be there, and perhaps also the Chief Justice of the Supreme Court, who is sure to have a longer tenure and be a fine man. You see my invincible dislike to having private matters—as Mr. Rockefeller's matters are—mixed with Government matters, and I feel sure that I should select private men or corporations, and not let anybody connected with the Government, and, therefore, the electorate, have any influence whatsoever. . . . You are working for a private individual, as you have all your days, and I hope that you never will work for the Government.

From that fervent hope Higginson turned to what he knew would interest the former secretary of the Harvard Corporation —a new Corporation fellow of just the right sort:

> I have known him from the time he was ten years old, have seen much of him—as a child, when he was in college, when he was in our office, and since then—and recognize what large experiences he has had. He is as dead in earnest for good work as you

are, and he will give his whole strength and time to doing something which will help the country.[21]

Nothing could better express the Establishment's sense of *private* public service. Serving the nation was best done at private places like Harvard, the Carnegie Institute, or the hoped-for Rockefeller Foundation.

Higginson's views were a bit extreme; for others, the government was not to be utterly despised and ignored, but, like a small child, to be shown the way. In another letter to Greene, Higginson suggested that Rockefeller give $50 million to set up tuberculosis camps around the United States.[22] Greene thought not, because "communities are more and more coming to see as a public duty a field of relief work which only a few years ago was the sole property of a few high-minded, far-seeing persons."[23] The Rockefeller approach was to instruct and inspire government to do what should be done. This approach was worked out by Wickliffe Rose, the one-time philosophy professor who headed the Rockefeller campaign against hookworm disease. Rose was intent on collaborating closely with government health authorities, so that they would eventually take over; he called the approach "priming the pump," a homely metaphor that has become a cliché. Nowadays, foundation officials are more likely to call the approach "looking for a multiplier." This quest is at the heart of the foundation way of life.

Thus the true foundation-person searches for the Word and hopes to spread it among all humankind. In an address on the tenth anniversary of the Rockefeller Institute for Medical Research, Gates said:

> Is there not something within us, an instinct of humanity which cannot be fenced in by the boundaries of a merely national patriotism, a sympathy which transcends national boundaries and finds complete expression only when it identifies us with all humanity?[24]

The passion continued to mount within him and reached a climax in his farewell speech as a trustee of the Rockefeller Foundation in 1923. Raymond Fosdick, who was present, describes Gates's farewell:

Shaking his fist at a somewhat startled, but respectfully attentive Board, he vociferated: "When you die and come to approach the judgment of Almighty God, what do you think He will demand of you? Do you for an instant presume to believe that He will inquire into your petty failures or your trivial virtues? No! He will ask just one question: *'What did you do as a Trustee of the Rockefeller Foundation?'* "[25]

The Coming of Ford

Gates's heavy thunder has long since rolled away. When a latter-day philanthropoid like McGeorge Bundy speaks of his calling, it is to remind fellow foundation officers that for them supporting social improvement "is simply a professional duty."[26] Good works, as Bundy's Puritan ancestors knew, do not procure salvation.

But though the rhetoric is cooler, the sense of a powerfully important mission remains. "We find," wrote Bundy after his first year as president of the Ford Foundation in 1966, "there is no present reason to believe that the world will have less need of a large foundation in 1980 than in 1967; the forces we help to counterbalance are not likely to be smaller—the need for an independent agency not likely to be less."[27] Elsewhere Bundy described his organization's primary purpose as "working against evils."[28] How well has Ford—the country's largest and most important foundation—performed its churchy mission?

In less than fifty years of existence and more than $5 billion of giving, the Ford Foundation has ridden like a roller coaster. Established in 1936, it crept along almost imperceptibly for a decade as the instrument of the Ford family's charitable interests, principally the Henry Ford Hospital and the Edison Institute. The most important beneficiary was to be the family itself, for, above all, Henry Ford intended his foundation as a means of bequeathing control of the Ford Motor Company to his heirs.

When the old man died in 1947, the Foundation acquired nearly 90 percent of the company's stock in the form of nonvoting shares, while the family retained the (voting) balance. Some $300 million in inheritance taxes thus shrank to a few million, and it was arranged for the Foundation to pick up even this modest tab; no FMC stock had to be put up at public auction.

When the Foundation came into its inheritance, however, the long-term value of its paper was hard to picture. Only two years before, the company had been losing $9 million a month, thanks to the incompetence of its senile founder and his corrupt, gun-toting henchman, Harry Bennett. The old regime had been turned out in a palace revolution by Ford's grandson, Henry II; the successor, a Yale dropout still in his twenties, suddenly found himself stuck with the huge task of resuscitating the failing corporation.

Wise enough to recognize his own limitations, young Ford hired the team of youthful management experts from the Harvard Business School who had run a statistical control operation in the U.S. Air Force during the war—the famous "Whiz Kids." It was an inspired move. The company's deficits disappeared almost at once, and profits began piling up within a few years. At the Ford Foundation, sitting on 90 percent of the equity of an unexpectedly prospering industrial giant, serious attention had to be paid to the massive philanthropy that lay ahead.

Ford activated the family charity just the way he had turned the failing family business into the model of a modern corporation—by reaching into the new technocracy. At the advice of MIT Chairman Karl Compton and Harvard Business School Dean Donald David, he agreed to undertake a major survey of the philanthropic needs of the world. Compton's former assistant, Rowan Gaither, a San Francisco attorney who was head of the new RAND Corporation, conducted thousands of interviews and in 1949 presented the Foundation's trustees with a report. Its premise was that the most important problems in the world lay in the relations of man and man, not man and nature, i.e. let the Rockefellers worry about science and health. Five areas required attention: world peace, democracy, the economy, education, and the scientific study of man. The trustees, including Compton, David, Henry Ford, and his younger brother Benson, declared themselves well pleased and the decision was made to go ahead.

The Gaither Report was ambitious, idealistic, and dedicated to the cause of justice, understanding, and prosperity through large infusions of capital—a perfect expression of the current spirit of the Marshall Plan. Appropriately, it was Paul G. Hoffman, President Truman's successful Marshall Plan administrator and the former head of Studebaker, who was recruited for the job of president. Things moved quickly. Two semi-independent educational agencies were established, the Fund for Adult Education and the Fund for the Advancement of Education. These were the brain children of Robert M. Hutchins, the middle-aged *enfant terrible* of American higher education, who left the chancellorship of the University of Chicago to become Hoffman's principal assistant. Hutchins expressed the wish that the FAE would "ultimately result in the reorganization of the educational system." Two other new institutions, which thrive happily to this day, were also established: Resources for the Future, a pioneer in the environmental field, and the Center for Advanced Study in the Behavioral Sciences in Palo Alto, California. On the international front, an economic development program was launched, primarily in the direction of India, as well as a series of grants for Western Europe. The Ford Foundation, reformist and internationalist, looked to be the perfect embodiment of postwar liberalism.

But the political mood was changing fast. Marshall Plan enthusiasm gave way to a sullen and bitter anticommunism across the country; hardly was the new Ford Foundation initiative on its feet than it was attacked by the populist right. McCarthyite commentators and columnists like Westbrook Pegler, George Sokolsky, and Fulton Lewis, Jr., saw the Foundation as a comsymp cabal squandering the hard-earned profits of capitalism (there was no more potent symbol of the American Way than the Ford assembly line) on untrustworthy foreigners and pointy heads. In 1952, a congressional committee under the chairmanship of Eugene Cox, a Democratic representative from Georgia, undertook an investigation into the allegedly subversive activities of American foundations. Meanwhile, within Ford itself, conflicts of personality and philosophy among the staff and between staff and trustees arose and were exacerbated by the frequent absences of Hoffman, who became a close advisor of Dwight D. Eisenhower in the 1952 presidential campaign. To restore internal order and help keep the redbaiters from the door, Henry Ford, with the help of Donald David, instituted a purge of Hoffman and company, and recalled the trusty Gaither to run the Foundation.

The last gasp of the Hoffman-Hutchins experimental phase came in February 1953, shortly after the purge, when the trustees made good on an old promise and granted $15 million to the Fund for the Republic, a new organization intended to stand watch for the civil liberties of Americans. This flew into the teeth of the McCarthyite gale, especially when Hoffman, as chairman of the Fund's board, named Hutchins director. Long a special object of right-wing wrath, Hutchins kept the pot boiling by issuing provocative statements and announcing a study of congressional investigating techniques. In mid-1953, a second, far more demagogic House committee, headed by a former chairman of the Republican National Committee, Brazilla Carroll Reece, began to examine the conspiracy of foundations to bring socialism to the United States.

Self-defense was the preoccupation of Gaither's first two years as president of the Foundation. The effort was not, on the whole, courageous. There was nothing to hide. But, as Waldemar Nielsen, a former Ford staff member and long-time observer of the philanthropical scene, recalled, "Here were men presumably of enormous stature and influence in American society, just terrified by the possibilities that they would be exposed to criticism by guys like McCarthy and Reece as being soft on Communism."[29]

John J. McCloy, who joined the Ford Foundation Board after serving as German High Commissioner, and Boston judge Charles E. Wyzanski, Jr., were, according to Nielsen, among the

Investing in Virtue: The Ford Foundation

faint-hearted: "Jack McCloy chickened out; Charlie Wyzanski chickened out. Anyhow that's my opinion based on the way they acted and reacted at those moments when real decisions had to be made."[30] Wyzanski, for example, advocated dissolving the Fund for the Republic. That the Foundation did not utterly disgrace itself was thanks to the steadfastness of a few staff members and trustees, among whom were the house counsel, Maurice T. ("Tex") Moore of Cravath, Swain & Moore, and Henry Ford himself.

More than anyone else, Ford had reason to be concerned about the Foundation's controversial image. Talk of boycotting Ford automobiles as a way of getting at the Foundation and a stream of angry letters and telephone calls from citizens and Ford dealers suggested to company officials that a real threat to profits was afoot.* One official used to carry around a small box containing choice samples of the intimidating missives. Once, during a worrying session at New York's elegant Links Club, Ford seized the box and hurled it into the blazing fireplace. As the man got down on hands and knees to rescue his precious evidence from the flames, Henry roared, "Goddammit, it just makes me sick, this whole attitude that we've got somehow to shape ourselves to the wishes of these people. We're good Americans and we've got a right to our position."[31]

Despite fears in Dearborn, however, the American people showed little interest in punishing the Ford Motor Company for the alleged un-Americanism of its major stockholder. Sales continued to rise, increasing the worth of the Foundation to about $2.5 billion by 1955. The following year, as a first step in the diversification of its holdings, the philanthropy put one-fifth of its FMC stock (18 percent of total company shares) on the market, the sale of which realized some $643 million.†

As the fortune mounted, it became increasingly clear that the modest and pliant Gaither was not the man to disburse it. He

---

*A secret study conducted by the Foundation at the time showed that most of the complaining dealers were simply having their own business problems.

†Almost two decades later, in 1975, the Foundation finally cut itself completely loose from FMC; in the late seventies, the only automobile stock in its immense portfolio was in a handful of foreign companies—a cold-blooded investment decision.

began to wander off alone at night thinking and worrying about how best to do good, and still he could not decide how to spend the stuff. Finally, a frustrated Donald David told him that unless the staff could come up with a better idea, the trustees were simply going to make a massive grant to American hospitals and be done with it. The threat was only partially averted. In 1956, Ford announced that it was giving away nearly $550 million from its stock sale in three large grants: $198 million to the nation's 3,500 private hospitals, over $90 million to the nation's forty-two privately-sponsored medical schools, and $260 million to 615 private liberal arts colleges and universities, to help raise faculty salaries.

Although the Foundation did not come right out and say so, the purpose of the huge giveaway was unabashedly political. The hospital grants were deliberately arranged so that there would be some Ford money flowing into every congressional district. Given the vast number of checks to be written, the Foundation's staff was sometimes inadequately acquainted with the recipients of Ford largesse. Two $250,000 grants had to be quickly recalled when it was discovered that the institutions in question were not hospitals at all but coyly named whorehouses.

Otherwise, the program worked like a charm. Doctors, educators, and editorial writers joined in a chorus of praise, and even the Foundation's right-wing scourges subsided into grumpy appeasement. Lest politicians miss the point, the Foundation littered them with pamphlets listing its institutional beneficiaries by state and congressional district. Of course, by 1956 there was no need for such a public relations coup. The Reece committee had wound up business in late 1954, having made a laughing-stock of itself through the ineptitude of its investigation. Senator McCarthy, disgraced by the nationally televised Army-McCarthy hearings, was a spent force in American politics. The witch-hunting was over. Nevertheless, the big grants gained Ford a reputation for wholesomeness it would not otherwise have had, and which later proved useful.

According to Waldemar Nielsen, the Ford Foundation's pusillanimity in the early fifties was due to immaturity and to a certain intellectual and moral second-rateness on the part of many of its trustees.[32] It might be added that leaders of the Establishment do not show at their best when confronted with authentic American demagogues—whether Joe McCarthy or his pale shadow, Spiro T. Agnew. It is as if they too harbored doubts about their Americanism. Sensitive to the charge that they have lost touch with the people, they often, while deploring the rhetorical excess, accommodate themselves to what seems the popular will. The young, autocratic Henry Ford 2d had no such inhibition.

Go-Go Years

In 1956, failing health forced Gaither to resign the presidency. To replace him, the trustees chose the strong and independent-minded head of New York University, Henry Heald. A mid-westerner by birth and a civil engineer by training, Heald had made his name in Chicago by building the Illinois Institute of Technology into a healthy and respectable institution. At the Ford Foundation he proved as adept at dispensing funds as he had been at raising them. During his nine-year tenure, annual expenditures rose steadily from about $100 million to well over $300 million. But despite the action, Ford was not a happy ship under Heald.

The staff found him remote and inflexible. And the board, which he expected to act as a rubber stamp, soon came to resent his peremptory treatment. Heald had a quick temper and was not above stalking furiously out of a board meeting when he felt he was being crossed. "He did not," recalled one member, "like trustees."[33] Beyond this, Heald had an outsider's distaste for the smooth-mannered world of Wall Street and the Ivy League in which most staff members and trustees moved comfortably. He hated Harvard, and early in his presidency—by way of counteracting Ford's Establishment image—made an effort to avoid depositing money there. The policy did not last long.

Differences of philanthropic philosophy also existed between Heald and his organization. Heald saw Ford as an essentially educational foundation whose primary interest was the financial well-being of the nation's colleges and universities. Not surprisingly, the largest single set of grants over which he presided gave $252 million in matching funds to twelve universities and fifty-seven colleges. Yet neither staff nor trustees fully shared this zeal on behalf of higher education; they grew increasingly anxious for more varied fare.

Open conflict between Heald and the board broke out in 1961, when, against the president's wishes, the trustees set up their own committee to study the overall operation of the Foundation. The committee, which issued its report in mid-1962, read Heald the riot act, ordaining that he involve the trustees more fully in program development and policy making, and instructing him to move the Foundation forward into a broad range of civil rights issues. The trustees were to be informed of the major programs and policies *rejected* by the president and staff. Heald accommodated himself to the new order and an uneasy truce prevailed for three years. By 1965, however, the trustees decided it was time for a new president.

Board Chairman John J. McCloy's personal choice was McGeorge Bundy. National security advisor to Presidents Kennedy and Johnson for the previous five years, Bundy seemed anxious to disburden himself of the unhappy task of managing the war in Vietnam; he was eager for the job—perhaps too eager. Before a formal offer had been tendered, news of the appointment appeared in *The New York Times* in a piece by James Reston. At the Foundation there was speculation that Bundy had leaked the story himself in order to force the board's hand. Whatever the struggle over the succession, Bundy quickly established close relations with the trustees. He also raised staff morale immeasurably and, as a flexible administrator with a nice personal touch, was able to keep it high.

Bundy made it clear from the beginning that gray and cautious days were over at the Ford Foundation. In his first annual report, he declaimed against the rising tide of "public blandness" in the country. The "organization man," he wrote, was "a growing menace to us all. . . . Foundations ought to stand against this kind of thing." The following year, Bundy opened his report with an essay on the struggle for racial equality which concluded with a stirring affirmation of the Foundation's determination to labor in its behalf.

To the surprise of many, the foreign policy expert scaled down the Foundation's international commitments to devote more attention to domestic affairs. With a convert's enthusiasm —and more valor than discretion—Bundy led Ford into the fray, and succeeded in calling down upon the Foundation's head a stream of vituperation unmatched since the days of McCarthy.

The biggest imbroglio occurred in the Ocean Hill-Brownsville section of Brooklyn. In that black neighborhood, Bundy immersed himself and the Foundation in the efforts of Mayor John V. Lindsay to decentralize the administration of New York City's public schools. Through its support of the new community school boards, the Foundation antagonized the education bureaucracy and earned the lasting enmity of the United Federation of Teachers and its president, Albert Shanker. It provoked the wrath of liberals and conservatives alike by its willingness to tolerate the obscene, racist, and sometimes anti-Semitic rhetoric of the militant blacks it was sponsoring. Whether or not it was, in the end, more sinned against than sinning, the Foundation squandered its good will.

There were other controversial projects as well. A black voter registration drive backed by Ford in Cleveland helped elect that city's first black mayor, and Foundation-funded Chicano organizations in Texas antagonized local Hispanic politicians. After the assassination of Robert Kennedy, Ford stirred congressional ire by making travel and study grants to eight of the late Senator's aides. What political aim lurked behind that philanthropic endeavor?

Through the 1960s, big philanthropy's one consistently vocal critic in Congress was Texas Representative Wright

Patman. A throwback to the Southern populists of yore, Patman was generally regarded as an eccentric; few paid attention to the investigations he conducted into the affairs of the country's large foundations from the House Banking and Currency Committee.

In 1969, however, Wilbur Mills's powerful House Ways and Means Committee took a deep look at foundation behavior in preparing its sweeping revision of the nation's tax laws. At the Committee's hearings, Bundy was given a thorough working over and, in the ensuing legislation, specific provisions seemed directed at Ford. Voter registration of the kind the Foundation had supported in Cleveland was forbidden, and Congress ordered that grants be made on an "objective and nondiscriminatory basis," that is, no more Kennedy staff grants.

But what hurt most was the imposition of a 4 percent tax on net annual investment income and the proscription of "attempts to influence legislation through communications with government personnel who may participate in the formulation of legislation except in the case of technical advice or assistance provided to a governmental body in response to a written request by such body or person." The tax, intended to finance stricter surveillance of foundations but interpreted in philanthropical circles as punitive as well, amounted in Ford's case to about $10 million a year. The rule against influencing legislation called into question the whole range of informal contacts which customarily arose between government officials and the officers of a foundation like Ford, which was deeply involved in issues of public policy.

Bundy was especially bitter about the 4 percent tax, which had come along at a most inopportune time.* In the early sixties, the equity market's go-go years, Ford always spent well in excess of income. Despite the red ink, the market value of Ford's portfolio reached a high of nearly $4.1 billion in fiscal 1964. But when Bundy took office two years later, the figure had sunk by

---

*In 1978, Congress responded to a decade's worth of philanthropic lobbying and cut the tax to 2 percent.

over a billion dollars. Clearly, Ford would have to start living more nearly within its means.

The board decided to do so, but it was easier said than done. Previous commitments kept deficits high, though they were slowly reduced. Meanwhile, the market's poor performance continued to eat into the value of the portfolio. In 1969, after a couple of good years, it fell below $3 billion; on expenditures of $238 million, Ford was $89 million in the red. Thus the impending federal excise tax, which in years of expanding budgets might have been laughed off, became a real burden as the Foundation tried to balance its books.

The worst, though, was still to come. In the recession of 1973 to 1974, nearly $1.4 billion slid away, leaving the portfolio's total market value under $1.7 billion. In a decade, the Ford Foundation had shrunk by well over half, not counting inflation. In real terms, it was perhaps one-fourth as hefty. Buffeted by public opinion, federal legislation, and the economy, Ford could well have turned tail and fled. The wonder is that it did not.

Hard Times

A more circumspect Ford Foundation managed to stay out of hot water during the 1970s. As McGeorge Bundy, reviewing his thirteen years tenure, noted, "We have certainly taken greater pains, since 1969, to avoid the appearance of *hubris*, and here the Trustees have gently instructed their president." But he was happy to report that what the 1969 legislation had threatened— to make "timid trustees . . . shy away from controversial activity"—"did not happen here at all."[34]

Principle did not, as it had in the fifties, take a back seat to public relations. If anything, hard times sharpened it. With the days of huge block grants to symphony orchestras, hospitals, and colleges irretrievably gone, the Foundation needed to be clearer in its social philosophy. In 1975, in an internal memorandum to its trustees committee, the National Affairs Division took a stab at defining the Foundation's purpose.

It was, the memo said, "redress of inequity," that is, seeking "a juster distribution of the material and nonmaterial things that society prizes most." Nothing ideologically off center about this, however. As the memo brightly remarks, the "idea of a more just society" is "a large part of what civilization is all about."

> The issues involved in equity permeate virtually every institution, the smallest university as well as world government and influence the actions of political men in the third world as well as the first. A local tax on gasoline and a major foreign aid loan must both file, so to speak, an equity impact statement, a response to the question, what will it mean for the poor? Choosing the redress of inequalities as a theme gives us at least the comfort of association with something that no one may call transient or trivial.

And indeed, "redressing inequity" is a banner which can be waved over a variety of philosophical approaches to a given problem. The Foundation's Education and Research Division, for example, has addressed inequities in the nation's public school system by sponsoring the work of the Marxist economists Samuel Bowles and Herbert Gintis on one side and, on the other, the libertarian educator John E. Coons, a champion of a "market" solution through vouchers. According to James A. Kelly, the program officer in charge, "It's ethically not right for us to take one approach. But we have *not* funded people who would turn out like George Wallace, or who would have no concern in social justice. The overall issue is equity in the public financing of children's services. We want to get people who can help define what equity means in this area."

Of course, there are limits to the search for equity, as the National Affairs memorandum, with considerable understatement admits. "Given financial and political limitations, it may be over-ambitious to pursue the equity goal on a worldwide scale." Even on a nationwide scale, equity in general is too large

Investing in Virtue: The Ford Foundation

a goal to pursue. "The facts suggest that in the United States race remains one of the most important correlates of inequality and that hostilities engendered by race affect American governance more so than many other kinds of frictions. In giving ascendancy to race we have assurance that we will be acting where a large part of the consequential problems are."

Race was the hallmark of the Bundy regime, but Ford's work in this area antedated Bundy. Even in the years of timidity and conservatism, the Foundation managed to address racial problems in a serious way. Over time, however, the approach has shifted significantly. Ford's current philanthropic orientation can best be seen against the history of its involvement with this greatest of social equity issues in American life.

Responsibility for involving Ford in racial issues during the Heald era belongs to a stubborn Minnesotan named Paul Ylvisaker. The son of a Lutheran pastor, Ylvisaker was a Harvard Ph.D. by way of Bethany Lutheran Junior College, Mankato State, and a Littauer fellowship at Harvard's School of Public Administration. In 1955, he joined the Ford Foundation's small public affairs program to work on problems of municipal organization.

Ylvisaker soon realized that what cried for attention in urban America was not the structure of local government but the social dislocation of the rural blacks (and Puerto Ricans) who were streaming into the country's northern cities. It seemed possible to persuade the Foundation to plunge into the problem. Heald himself was understood to be a little bored with the business of shoveling cash down the insatiable maw of American higher education; certainly the trustees were. But, as Ylvisaker learned, the subject of race was regarded as too hot to handle.

One day he had a visit from Milton Katz, the Harvard Law School professor who had worked at the Foundation during the Hutchins years, and who remained an influential counselor. Katz wanted to find something interesting for Heald and the Foundation to do, but he ruled some causes out of court. "We can't," he said, "obviously deal with race, that's out, that's *ver-*

boten." It was, Ylvisaker later recalled, "the first time I'd heard anybody talk this explicitly."[35] Nevertheless, he was determined to press ahead.

In 1958, he gathered a team of urban experts which included Robert C. Weaver, the Harvard-trained economist then chairman of the NAACP. To avoid controversy, Ylvisaker and Weaver decided not to say that they were going to devote their efforts to "race relations"; instead, they neutrally declared themselves interested in the amelioration of "gray areas," a phrase invented by the economist Raymond Vernon to describe the deteriorating urban neighborhoods between affluent downtown and hopeless slum.

Meanwhile, the emerging urban crisis had cropped up in the Foundation's most powerful bailiwick, the Education program. Its head, Alvin C. Eurich, had devised a large grant package for a league of school superintendents from fourteen major cities, led by Benjamin Willis of Chicago. Because of the influx of blacks and Hispanics, the superintendents had found it increasingly difficult to get bond issues passed; they wanted Ford Foundation money to bail them out. Ylvisaker and Weaver fought the proposal.

"It was just simply," Ylvisaker recalled, "unload the boodle and Ben Willis and his boys would buy off the opposition or try to buy their way out of it. . . . We also knew selfishly that if Education took that big hunk of money to work on those problems, we were out, and there wouldn't be city hall in it, there wouldn't be anything of a more fundamental approach."[36]

Against Weaver's advice, Ylvisaker told Heald that the proposal was no good; he suggested that Public Affairs join Education to do something better. For all his conservatism, Heald knew how serious the problems were; his renovation of Illinois Tech had taken place in the midst of a Chicago ghetto. He had Ylvisaker work out a plan and, after a tremendous confrontation with its in-house competition, Public Affairs got its way.

A "field force," cochaired by Ylvisaker, traveled from city to city, and in each place got the school superintendent to appear before the mayor, community activists, and representatives of the local power structure to say what he planned to do with his Ford Foundation money. A series of "Great Cities" grants then set up programs to help black children from rural backgrounds adjust to their new urban environment.

Helping schools was thoroughly respectable. The Ford trustees were happy, even enthusiastic. They gave permission for a more general attack. The field force went out again, got groups together, and asked mayors what *they* would do if they had some money to work with. The staff decided on Oakland, California, as the first site for a Gray Areas demonstration project. Oakland had a cooperative mayor and a first-class city manager who was admired by Stephen Bechtel, head of San Francisco's Bechtel Corporation and a trustee of the Ford Foundation. With Bechtel's support, the project sailed through.

For Ylvisaker, it was magic. "We hit just right and with Bechtel coming and saying, 'This is a great thing,' with blacks saying, 'The first time the Ford Foundation is relevant,' with the mayor saying, 'We'll do it,' and a city manager who could be 'trusted,' it was just like suddenly the combination fell into place."[37] In Boston, New Haven, Philadelphia, and Washington, D.C. other projects followed.

The Gray Areas projects provided comprehensive services to the poor by building coalitions of politicians, businessmen, and community leaders. In helping existing government agencies develop and administer health, education, employment, and community action programs, they effectively became part of the municipal government. It was a delicate business, and might not have worked at another time. But in 1960, people were eager to solve problems and optimistic about chances of success. And the Ford Foundation, having laid down its blanket of hospital and education grants, was now perceived as a Good Housekeeping Seal of Approval.

Then John F. Kennedy, a respecter of reformist intellectuals, became president. Weaver and a number of public officials who had worked on Gray Areas joined the Kennedy administration. The great desideratum was now in sight: turning Ford's experiments into a federal program. Said Ylvisaker, "It was just one of those perfect sequences. Kennedy made it possible for the Ford Foundation to be a hero."[38]

To be sure, the commitment to heroism within the foundation was incomplete. Heald remained lukewarm to Gray Areas, and gave officers from other programs—always anxious to increase their share of the kitty—full scope for raking Public Affairs proposals over the coals. But the White House loved them. Once W. McNeil Lowry, the powerful head of the Arts and Humanities Division and a leading antagonist of Ylvisaker, returned from Washington and reported, "Paul, the one thing that we get back there is the work that you've been doing. That's what's appreciated."

The pay-off came in 1964. When the Johnson administration began gearing up its Great Society programs, Gray Areas provided the model. This did not happen simply by force of example. In on the first meeting which Sargent Shriver held to plan the Great Society, Ylvisaker drafted the plan for community action, successfully fought to have it adopted, and got Gray Areas people jobs in Washington to keep it on track. A handful of single-digit-million dollar projects gingerly entered into by the Ford Foundation suddenly became a federal program worth hundreds of millions. As the joke of the day had it, all the money was in poverty.

When Bundy bounced into the Foundation in the spring of 1966, he immediately indicated that he intended to strengthen the Foundation's commitment. His first words to Ylvisaker were: "Paul, the only shop that survives as having any relevance is yours."[39] But Bundy wanted the shop to be his own; he removed Ylvisaker and waited a year before replacing him with Mitchell Sviridoff, former head of the Foundation's Gray Areas project in New Haven and later of the federal antipoverty agency there. Sviridoff both knew the ways of Ford and was Bundy's man.

Among the trustees, a new daring took hold. The late Kermit Gordon, President of Brookings and a former employee of the Foundation, was shocked at the change when he attended his first board meeting after becoming a trustee in 1967. One of the first proposals to come up was the controversial grant for black voter registration in Cleveland. "I remember the feeling of . . . bewilderment, that the Ford Foundation was willing to accept a risk, that clear and apparent, in the interest of an important cause. . . . It almost took my breath away particularly since my contrast . . . was with the old Ford Foundation and it seemed to me a daring thing to do; I must say, I thought at the time a somewhat reckless thing to do."[40]

It was not only recklessness, however, that got the Foundation into trouble in the late sixties. Times had changed. The coalitions created by Gray Areas had broken down in bitterness and distrust. Militants deliberately sought to antagonize. While Foundation officials could and did learn to listen to their rhetoric without flinching, white politicians, businessmen, and ordinary citizens simply got angry. It was almost inevitable that the Foundation would get caught in crossfires. The lesson was not only to act more carefully, but also to reconsider the approach. Keeping alive its commitment to the disadvantaged and the poor meant confronting the reasons for the failures of the social programs of the sixties.

Federal programs run by government agencies—most egregiously housing programs—promised too much and were badly planned, insensitive to community needs, and subject to corruption and abuse. But programs like Model Cities and Community Action, which relied on grassroots administration, were poorly managed and also generated more words than deeds. Ford came to believe that the solution lay in organizations that, in the words of the National Affairs memo, "combine the technical and professional skills one might expect from government (minus restrictions of civil service and inflexible regulations) with the decentralized autonomy, street wisdom, motivation and local pride that might be found in a community organization." These were "local intermediaries"—nonprofit corporations set up to promote the economic development of a given community: the Community Development Corporation.

The task of the CDC was to attract businesses, create jobs, and improve housing stock. Philanthropy aims for "leverage"—getting the most for your dollar through programs that call forth additional capital from elsewhere. CDC's leveraged money into their communities from the private as well as the public sector, arranging not only government grants but, more importantly, bank loans and direct commercial investment. They were Chambers of Commerce for the poor, exercises in cooperative welfare capitalism. And they were determinedly noncontroversial.

"CDC's do not conduct sit-ins at city hall," the National Affairs memo pointedly notes. "This emphasis on technique and pragmatism is what distinguishes the Foundation's grantees from other local organizations that may also bear community development or community action labels." Thus, during the 1970s, Ford was able to pour millions of dollars into poor urban (and rural) areas without getting into trouble.

The philosophical shift from Gray Areas to CDC's was fundamental. Gray Areas projects were political animals—"adjuncts" to government—which concerned themselves with shaping and delivering public services to the poor. They pushed for the redistribution of public funds and the redistribution of political power over municipal agencies and bureaucracies. Ford's involvement in New York City's school decentralization was a logical extension of this. The public schools had from the beginning been a primary focus of Gray Areas; local control seemed simply the furthest step on the road to adapting the educational system to the needs of "outsider" communities.

This was not the direction of the CDC. "It is," said Mitchell Sviridoff, "quite different from the adversarial notion of the past, that government had to be confronted. It has an enormous potential. It's a sign of the kind of productive role the Foundation can play, which will not be disruptive. It will not put the Foundation in the position of opening itself up to the charge of usurping the rights of the people."

Investing in Virtue: The Ford Foundation

Thomas of Bed-Sty

Even as it was getting sliced up in Ocean Hill-Brownsville, the Ford Foundation was beginning to pour money into the first of its CDC's, the Bedford-Stuyvesant Restoration Corporation, in a Brooklyn ghetto not far from the Ocean Hill battle zone. In 1979, Franklin Thomas, the black lawyer who made the Bedford-Stuyvesant project a triumph, was chosen by the Ford trustees to succeed Bundy as president of the Foundation. Thomas's appointment signalled that Ford would maintain its commitment to the cause of minority rights and opportunities. (Hardly had it been decided than Paul Ylvisaker, now Dean of the Havard Graduate School of Education, received six calls in quick succession from Foundation officials. "You won," they told him excitedly.) It also testified to the trustees' belief in the CDC approach. It was conservative too.

After ten years in Bedford-Stuyvesant working closely with the Ford Foundation, Thomas had spent a year and a half on its board of trustees. He was also well known in the larger world of big business and big good works. He was a director of Citicorp/Citibank, CBS, Alcoa, Allied Stores, and Cummins Engine; he sat on the boards of Lincoln Center, the Urban Institute, and the Women's Action Alliance; he was a trustee of the J. H. Whitney Foundation and had been a trustee of Columbia, his alma mater; he was a member of the Council on Foreign Relations. No one, including McGeorge Bundy, had ever taken over the reins of a major American foundation with such impeccable and diverse credentials, with such connections to the rich, the powerful, and the well intentioned. Said Alexander Heard, Chancellor of Vanderbilt University and Chairman of the Board at Ford, "I was asked by a friend from Texas, after Frank's election, 'Couldn't you find a good white man?' And I said, 'Not one as good as Mr. Thomas.'"

If Thomas was clasped to the bosom of the Establishment, it was, as he is the first to admit, entirely the result of his successful stewardship of the Bedford-Stuyvesant project. "Everything," he says, "came out of that. It was the most challenging, rewarding experience of my life." The experience itself meant performing—actually helping to create—a new professional role in American life: the Third Sector businessman. At Bed-Sty, Thomas, with the responsibilities of a community leader and a government bureaucrat, was above all a venture capitalist and an entrepreneur.

The Bedford-Stuyvesant project began as a straightforward effort to put New York's financial power structure to work on urban problems. The idea was Bobby Kennedy's. He chose Bed-Sty, a relatively unknown but extremely large ghetto in Brooklyn—the second largest ghetto in the United States—with a population the size of Cincinnati. He rounded up as formidable a collection of bigwigs as ever sat around a boardroom, headed by Andre Meyer, chairman of Lazard Frères, and C. Douglas Dillon of Dillon, Read & Company, a former Treasury Secretary.* In applying for a $7 million grant from the U. S. Department of Labor, project officials announced their desire to test "the proposition that the business and financial elite of New York City, by joining forces with political and neighborhood leaders, can make a significant contribution to the reconstruction of its slums."

The forces were, however, formally joined in almost a caricature of paternalistic philanthropy. Two separate corporations were established, one white and one black, each with its own board, staff, and purposes. The bigwigs, together with Senators Kennedy and Javits, sat on the board of the Development and Services Corporation, whose responsibility was to provide the project with business expertise in entrepreneurship and planning. The Restoration Corporation drew its directors from the

---

*The board also included David E. Lilienthal, chairman of the Development and Resources Corporation and former head of the Atomic Energy Commission and the Tennessee Valley Authority; George S. Moore, chairman of Citibank; James F. Oates, Jr., chairman of Equitable Life; Thomas J. Watson, Jr., chairman of IBM; J. M. Kaplan of the Kaplan Fund; Benno C. Schmidt, managing partner of J. H. Whitney and Company; and Roswell L. Gilpatric, partner in Cravath, Swaine & Moore and former Deputy Secretary of Defense.

local community, and was the project's operational arm. Although Restoration was to set overall plans, it soon became clear that D & S, with control of the purse strings, was really in charge.

The whole enterprise got off to a shaky start. There were conflicts among local leaders and community groups. The dual structure raised suspicions in Bed-Sty and permitted a certain high-handedness among the D & S staff. Into the breach stepped Franklin Thomas.

He had grown up in Bed-Sty, was a local boy made good. He had been a basketball star, a powerful forward strong on defense and tough off the boards; he was team captain at Franklin K. Lane High School and also at Columbia, where he set a single season rebounding record that still stands. He returned to Columbia to get his law degree after four years in the Air Force, and had served short stints as an attorney at the Federal Housing and Home Finance Agency, as Assistant U.S. Attorney for New York State's Southern District, and as New York City's Deputy Police Commissioner for legal affairs. Mayor John Lindsay's civilian complaint review board was his creation.

The calm and commanding Thomas was ideal to head the Restoration Corporation: he had roots and standing in the community, he was a competent professional, and he was trusted by City Hall and knowledgeable in its ways. He also proved an ideal intermediary between Bed-Sty and Wall Street. He immersed himself in the life of the community, earning the respect and support of black militants and moderates alike. He worked tirelessly with the whites as well, putting in long hours in the offices of Cravath, that exemplar of New York corporate law, which undertook the project's legal work. George Moore of Citibank was instrumental in setting up a substantial mortgage pool to finance housing rehabilitation; Thomas and his staff worked out is operational procedures with private bankers and officials of the Federal Housing Authority. They also did the research to persuade IBM and Computer Graphics to locate new plants in Bed-Sty; happily, IBM Chairman Thomas Watson was on the D & S Board.

Some tension did exist between the staffs of Restoration and D & S. Restoration's analysts came to resent D & S supervision in the planning and reviewing of small businesses which, as a kind of venture capital operation, the project was sponsoring. By and large, though, relations were amicable, largely due to the closeness of Thomas and John Doar, the D & S president. In 1973, when Doar went to Washington to head the staff of the House inquiry to impeach President Nixon, the two staffs were merged. The paternalistic character of the project faded away.

Bed-Sty married business methods to traditional social welfare purposes. "We had," says Thomas, "as good an information and accounting system as any middle-sized business, and we applied it to a set of tasks that were not profit-oriented."

The project depended on more than good management, however. Not only did it avoid the characteristic inefficiency of government welfare programs, but it steered carefully away from the city's public infrastructure. "In many respects," Thomas admitted, "Bed-Sty was a leapfrogging over state and local government into the community." It stayed clear of the public schools. It had the blessing of the Lindsay administration, but did not immerse itself in city affairs any more than it had to. It was in the community development business; during Thomas' ten years there, some $63 million of federal and private funds were used to finance 118 businesses, place 7,468 workers in jobs, train and employ 4,000 local youths to renovate the exteriors of 4,000 homes on 100 city blocks, and complete 1,280 new or renovated housing units. Thomas was the man who had made it all happen, an entrepreneur who, in ten years of doing the impossible in Brooklyn, earned a name for himself on Wall Street and became one of the Establishment's prize ornaments.

Here lay the significance of Thomas' choice as president of the Ford Foundation. As a rule, the heads of the leading foundations have come from a range of administrative careers stretching from academe to government. In Ford's case, only one president had had any business experience: Paul Hoffman, who came to the Foundation from Studebaker, by way of the Marshall Plan. Otherwise, there were Gaither from MIT and RAND, Heald from Illinois Tech and NYU, and Bundy from Harvard and the White House—and with reason: the Foundation's program centered on higher education and aimed at bringing the weight of academic learning and research to bear on public policy.

Thomas came from between the worlds of business and public service; his accomplishment was to bring the techniques of business management to bear on the problems of urban decay. He is philosophically committed to that approach, and he will strengthen Ford's commitment to it. "It is," he says, "the obvious way to go. It equips you to approach the job of philanthropy differently." He sees it as part of a broad process in which business and government are drawing together in a coalescence of practice and purpose. "The private sector is being forced to take the public into account as a primary responsibility. Traditional welfare agencies are introducing a result-orientation."

Results, Results

In 1976, Henry Ford 2d resigned from the Board of Trustees of the Ford Foundation. To mark the event he wrote a letter, which read in part:

> The Foundation exists and thrives on the fruits of our economic system. The dividends of competitive enterprise make it all possible. A significant portion of the abundance created by U.S. business enables the Foundation and like institutions to carry on their work. In effect, the Foundation is a creature of capitalism—a statement that, I'm sure, would be shocking to many professional staff people in the field of philanthropy. It is hard to discern recognition of this fact in anything the Foundation does. It is even more difficult to find an understanding of this in many of the institutions, particularly the universities, that are the beneficiaries of the Foundation's grant programs.
>
> I'm not playing the role of the hard-headed tycoon who thinks all philanthropoids are socialists and all university professors are communists. I'm just suggesting to the Trustees and the staff that the system that makes the Foundation possible very probably is worth

preserving. Perhaps it is time for the Trustees and staff to examine the question of our obligations to our economic system and to consider how the Foundation as one of the system's most prominent offspring, might act most wisely to strengthen and improve its progenitor.

Trustees and staff were shocked less by the substance of Ford's parting shot than by the manner in which it was delivered. Ford's decision to retire had itself come as a surprise, the result not of any dust-up over Foundation policy but, so it was thought, of a certain loss of interest on Henry's part. He had been in poor health, and had been having troubles at home and at the company.

In the event, Ford and his fellow trustees agreed to mark his retirement with a joint statement of mutual congratulation. Instead, Henry had written his own letter, the uncongratulatory parts of which are printed above, and had released it to the press, which naturally headlined the negative comments. This was very bad form from the standpoint of an institution which prides itself on smooth surfaces and seamless transitions—an institution which would use a small box on the bottom of page two of its newsletter to announce the choice of its new president.*

Ford's actual complaint tended to be shrugged off, however. Chairman Heard, by his own account Henry Ford's "most sanguine interpreter with my colleagues because I am a great friend and admirer of his," cited the Foundation's massive support for business education as an example of an explicit desire to strengthen the workings of the competitive economy. Bundy, in an interview, agreed that everything the Foundation did could be regarded as "making the world safe for capitalism"—reducing social tensions by helping to comfort the afflicted, provide safety valves for the angry, and improve the functioning of government. Both men emphasized that Ford had been an exemplary trustee, a pillar of strength in times of controversy.

Nevertheless, the issue of "support for the system" has wor-

*As it did when Franklin Thomas was named to succeed Bundy in 1979.

ried Foundation officials. In 1973, Bundy made a speech at the Commonwealth Club of California in which he attacked the industrialist David Packard for advocating that corporations give money to private universities only in ways that serve the direct interests of the corporate world—by supporting business schools, useful research, "the right kind of professors." This, said Bundy, represented "a dangerously narrow view of what is good for free enterprise." There is also disapproval when a research organization like the American Enterprise Institute promotes itself as probusiness. "There is a lot of intellectually artificial polarization," commented Bundy shortly before stepping down as president. "AEI is a perfect example."

Nor has the Foundation cherished its own liberal image. Said one vice-president, "It's too bad that we've managed to produce that picture of ourselves." One way the picture was kept fresh during the seventies was through the support of public interest law firms devoted to protecting the environment—for which the Foundation has been vociferously attacked by, among others, the *Wall Street Journal.* But as environmental advocacy came into increasing conflict with economic interests, Ford began to sponsor programs providing third parties to mediate between environmentalists and their opponents.*

This is, in fact, one token of the growth in appreciation at the Foundation for the business sector—and for the Third Sector as well. "I type myself as an old-fashioned liberal type who thinks that government is important," said Harold Howe, the former U.S. Commissioner of Education who is the Foundation vice-president in charge of education and research. "I and others were naive about the Great Society. I now think more favorably towards the Ford Foundation and what an institution like this can do. I think that the capacity of private funds to move into all kinds of questions without political decisions is very valuable. I doubt the capacity of government to venti-

---

*Who mediates for mediators? In a spoof of its newsletter put together to mark Bundy's retirement, a $60,000 grant was announced "for a pilot program that will use fourth-party intervention techniques to resolve conflicts between disputing parties and third-party mediators."

late the issues as clearly and fairly as the private sector."

Howe's disillusionment with government was echoed by Alexander Heard. In his view, the country's central problem— one which "nobody knows how to tackle"—is the "inability of the United States Government to function effectively in a coherent and understandable way facing the problems we have. We have an abundance of participation, an abundance of democracy, an abundance of representation, an abundance of interest groups. The poor President of the United States spends his time running around relating to the people and we wonder what's happening to the problems."

This attitude has helped produce a greater concern with philanthropic efficiency at Ford, especially among the trustees.*

Marshall Robinson, a Ford vice-president who left in 1979 to become head of the Russell Sage Foundation, said, "I sense that the people on the board sense that the system is getting out of control. Jack McCloy just lived in a more orderly world—before they decided to invent blacks and CETA. Things were macrosolved; the number of describable problems that could trouble your well-being was half what comparable people today perceive. . . . Under these circumstances, there is an impatience with the measured and calm approach. This board is not as interested in uncertainties, it wants to insure results."

The Ford Foundation has rediscovered the corporate ideal which appealed so much to progressive intellectuals and businessmen in the first decades of the century. Perhaps naively, they saw the modern corporation, efficient and fully rational-

---

*Between 1966, when Bundy took over, and 1979, when Thomas did, the board became a good deal more diverse. Previously lily-white, all-male, and exclusively American, it added several foreigners including a representative of the much-granted third-world, Dr. Soedjatmoko of Indonesia, a few blacks, and three women. Henry Ford II had not been happy about the women. His late brother Benson, who spent many years attending the Foundation's board meetings, told an interviewer in 1973: "I know if my brother had his way they wouldn't be on the Board. He doesn't believe in ladies. He made a statement here to somebody once, and I shouldn't be quoting him but he said, 'It's going to be a long time before we have a lady on the Company's Board after seeing the ones on the Foundation.' " (Benson Ford, O.H., p. 22) Marion Sulzberger Heiskill, a director of *The New York Times*, became a member of the Ford Motor Company's board of directors in 1976.

ized, as the perfect model of any social institution—private, public, or otherwise. Through the late 1960s, the Foundation might have been called an institutional welfare agency; in the seventies, as University of Massachusetts professor Dorothy Marshall observed shortly after becoming a Ford trustee, it began to look more like a large-scale community development corporation.

Not only was it preoccupied with getting maximum assured results for its philanthropic dollar, but it became increasingly absorbed in the management of its own finances. It set up what amounted to an in-house investment firm because, as Treasurer Jon Hagler put it, "Superior investment decisions cannot be based upon information widely shared by others." The Foundation also undertook a more businesslike kind of philanthropy. It made program money available in the form of loans, direct investment, and recoverable grants. The beneficiaries of such loans and investments have been not only traditional nonprofit groups but actual for-profit companies—mostly minority businesses. For Ford, the effect has been to blur the distinction between giving and earning.

So the Foundation has in fact been moving in the direction that Henry Ford, in his grumpy farewell letter, wished it to move. It recognizes that its present and future health, like its roots, lie in the capitalist system. At the same time it is trying to keep the moral pressure on the corporate world. Frank Thomas is well suited to that task.*

Although an atypical foundation president, Thomas is still a familiar Establishment type—one of those Ivy League lawyer-doers able to move lightly among the worlds of business, government, and good works. Like John J. McCloy, who also rose from modest beginnings to great things via the law, Thomas is much

---

*A year after Thomas took office, the Foundation announced the creation of the Local Initiatives Support Corporation, an agency for helping Community Development Corporations. Joining the Foundation as financial backers were Prudential Insurance, Aetna Life and Casualty, International Harvester, Levi Strauss, Continental Illinois National Bank, and Atlantic Richfield. As Thomas, hailing "balance—sheet philanthropy" in his first annual report, wrote, "In the years ahead, one of our more useful tasks will be to arrange the packaging and brokering of social investment opportunities."

in demand. In the fall of 1977, he was asked by the Rockefeller Foundation to head a long-range study of American-South African relations, with particular attention to corporate investment and industrial practices. Knowing little about South Africa, Thomas was reluctant, but finally consented to study the feasibility of the project. After a year, he agreed to head it; a comparable study of Latin America by Sol Linowitz, the former chairman of Xerox, became the model.

When Ford tapped him for its presidency, Thomas was strongly inclined to give up the South African study. It would put him in the anomalous position of presiding over Ford while working for Rockefeller. But the people at both foundations wanted him on the study, which they regarded as of deep philosophical importance for big philanthropy. He stayed with it.

The situation had its irony. Here was the Ford Foundation, dedicated to the cause of minority rights, with a black president, making money from apartheid through investments in American companies which ran businesses in South Africa. Ford's moral opposition to apartheid was beyond question; it had even undertaken to establish a public interest law firm in South Africa to represent blacks against the regime. But was it at the same time supporting that regime with its $2 billion portfolio? By the words of its officers, and with its series of Program Related Investments, Ford had made it clear that it did not regard its investments as separable from its good works.

The issues, once again, were "tainted money" and the tendency of even enlightened capitalism to shore up an evil status quo. Could corporations conduct business in South Africa without being implicated in the regime? Did efforts made by them to deal fairly with blacks and coloreds really help to change the system or merely give it a small gloss of respectability? Was it possible for a group of well-connected Americans to devise a principled policy toward South Africa which would not entail supporting revolution, possibly violent revolution?

In venturing into this thicket, Thomas was seeking to sort out, at a profound level, the relations between morality and money-making.

Chapter 5

The Dismal Science of Reform: Brookings

THE BROOKINGS INSTITUTION is a social-science research center in Washington, D.C. Its staff, even its liberals, dislike and disavow its reputation as a "liberal think tank."

Of relatively recent vintage, this reputation was thrust upon it soon after Richard Nixon's accession to the presidency. Nixon was angry with Brookings for harboring his "liberal" political enemies. But this was not the first time a president had been angry with Brookings; Franklin Roosevelt was annoyed at Brookings, ironically enough, for being too conservative and for attacking the New Deal.

Brookings tries to play the critic to whatever administration holds power—and usually does this with the help of some former officials of the preceding administration. When administrations change, a few government officials of scholarly bent usually move over to Brookings to stay in Washington, just as some cast-off Congressmen stay on as lobbyists and some dismissed administration lawyers join influential Washington law firms.

In the late sixties and early seventies, Brookings took on the appearance of a Democratic government-in-exile* as refugees from the Johnson administration found new offices in the Brookings edifice at 1775 Massachusetts Avenue, N. W. The most prominent of these were Arthur Okun, chairman of President Johnson's Council of Economic Advisers (CEA), and Charles L. Schultze, his director of the Bureau of the Budget (now the Office of Management and Budget), who joined such prominent Democratic advisers already at Brookings as Joseph A. Pechman, director of economic studies, and Kermit Gordon, then Brookings' president, who had been a member of President Kennedy's CEA and later served as his budget director. Gordon died in 1977 and was succeeded by a moderately conservative economist, Bruce MacLaury, a former president of the Federal Reserve Bank of Minneapolis.

But there were several other less well-known arrivals at Brookings in the early 1970s who were to worry the Nixon administration even more. One of these was Leslie Gelb who had served as head of Policy Planning in the Pentagon's office of International Security Affairs—and who had acted as director of the Vietnam History Task Force, which produced the Pentagon Papers.†

The notion that Brookings as a whole "stood" for something—something anti-Republican—was enhanced by its publication of a series of annual volumes called *Setting National Priorities*, analyzing the President's budget. This series was the brainchild of Charles Schultze (President Johnson's former budget director, later President Carter's chief economic adviser) who, in 1968, had published a book entitled *Agenda for the Nation*. The *Priorities* volumes became an annual exercise; Brookings scholars evaluated the President's entire pro-

*The theme song one could hear sung in the corridors of Brookings in 1969 was, "Those were the days, my friend, We thought they'd never end . . ."

†Leslie Gelb later joined *The New York Times* as a reporter in its Washington bureau. In 1977 Gelb rejoined the government as director of the State Department's Bureau of Politico-Military Affairs. In 1979 he left to become a Senior Associate of the Carnegie Endowment for International Peace.

gram, presented options, and assessed the probable impact of various alternative courses other than those mapped by the President.

Brookings people deny that their intent is to tell the country what to do. The title, *Setting National Priorities,* however, seems to imply something else. Doesn't it mean "Brookings sets the national priorities"? No, said Joseph Pechman, it simply refers to various staff members' analyses of the priorities presented by the annual budget. Pechman bristles at the popular view. To him it reflects a fundamental misunderstanding of what Brookings is all about. "Our output is all that matters," he insisted. By output Pechman meant the studies undertaken by Brookings' scholars, some of which have rubbed his Democratic friends the wrong way. One of these studies was an analysis of the Social Security system, undertaken during the Johnson administration, which correctly predicted the system's current funding problems; the study, which provoked an angry response from the Johnson administration, was not an isolated example. Nor have the recent Brookings budget studies or other publications been gentle on the Carter administration.

Independent thought is cherished and cultivated at Brookings. To some extent, this is made possible by the professional stature of the senior fellows. In the words of Joseph Minarik, a young research associate at Brookings, "I don't want to sound too much like an institutional propagandist, but it is literally true that most of the people here are so big that they can't be had." He cited Pechman's dissection of the Social Security system and Charles Schultze's criticism of the Democratic liberals' Humphrey-Hawkins bill as examples, and added: "During the Ford administration, Okun appeared on the Martin Agronsky show and someone asked him about the nefariousness of Ford's tax proposals. Okun said that was not true—the proposals were okay." And when President Carter was looking for a sympathetic Democrat to replace Arthur Burns as chairman of the Federal Reserve Board, many thought Okun would make the best choice. "Just because my name is Arthur, because I graduated from Columbia and New Jersey, and am Jewish, some people think I ought to be the next chairman of the Fed. Not me," said Okun.

Senior Fellow Robert Hartman stressed Brookings' effort to help all comers. "It is important to understand that we all get calls from both Democratic and Republican congressional staffs —to read this or that bill. I have actually helped more Republicans than Democrats. I remember one time when Alice Rivlin [former Brookings Senior Fellow, later director of the Congressional Budget Office] and I gave Quie [Albert Quie, Republican of Minnesota] a lot of help on an education bill. I cannot name a Democrat with whom I have worked so closely." Hartman found himself unimpressed with the liberal Democrats on the Hill. While describing himself as a "somewhat unreconstructed New Dealer," he nonetheless took the "old-fashioned New Deal liberals in Congress" to task for not understanding "the notion of limits."

Arthur Okun, who had become the most eminent of the Brookings economists at the time of his sudden death, at age 51, in March 1980, cited his colleague Henry Aaron's book, *Politics and the Professors,* [1] as "a little bit of collective autobiography"— autobiography in the tradition of St. Augustine's self-flagellating *Confessions.* Okun also mentioned Charles Schultze's 1976 Godkin lectures at Harvard, *The Public Use of Private Interest,* [2] as manifesting a deep skepticism toward government's ability to solve social problems. Schultze carried that skepticism back with him into the government in 1977 when he became chairman of President Carter's Council of Economic Advisers.

"I myself," said Okun, "am in a much more sober mood toward what you can get by throwing money at problems, although I was never all that optimistic about the prospects of turning a five-year-old ghetto kid into a model of equal opportunity." Hartman concurred with Okun's opinion: "Everyone who specializes in a particular area is especially skeptical about the ability of government programs to succeed there. Even the defense people are skeptical."

Besides the common malaise over government ineffectuality and hard times, another factor seemed to be at work. It was almost as if, in their sensitivity to accusations of liberal bias, the Brookings economists felt a moral obligation to be tough on their political confreres.

The Policy Network

Above all, Brookings is part of the Washington system. Its purpose is to influence public policy, and to be influential it must have a highly developed sense of the possible and accept the status quo in its essentials. As Hartman put it, "Living in Washington has a conservatizing effect on you. There is little truth in the criticism of Brookings from both the right and the left. The people in this building are very conventional and middle-of-the-road in their approach; their interest is in being influential. Even if a way-out idea is appealing, if it's too far ahead of its time no one here is going to spend any time on it. This tendency to stick fairly close to the possible is not so bad." Like Hartman, Joseph Minarik was satisfied with this orientation. "It is a given that people here accept a fixit, a how-do-we-get-from-here-to-there approach to problems. Although there are people who criticize it for being too status quo, no one here would try to change Brookings."

Arthur Okun was a bit more critical. "Brookings is too Establishment-oriented. We have a tendency to accept all the institutions. We know all the principals. We're too much part of the system. Some day after we get a conservative, I'll get Bruce [MacLaury] to get a radical. It would be a better place for me if I had more people to argue with. We're very establishmentarian in every sense."

This impulse towards conventionality comes partly from the experience of having worked in government agencies—and sometimes from the desire to go on or back to government. There is not a senior fellow in economic studies who has not spent some time working for the federal government. President Bruce MacLaury regards this revolving door phenomenon as the greatest source of Brookings' strength: "In principle it is good to have people moving in and out of the government. This is the advantage which Brookings has over a place like Yale: that people have gotten their hands dirty. If we forswore the opportunity of going into government, we would give up our comparative advantage."

At its most disinterested, the impulse to work for the government reflects the unobjectionable desire to know better how things work. As Minarik says, "There are mundane things which somebody has to know. If I were to spend the rest of my life on taxes, I would have to go to Treasury and get my hands dirty with problems like 'How do we treat timber as opposed to raising cattle?' Here we take the broad view: 'How do we treat capital gains?'" The implication is that without government service, analysis will suffer.

Of course, scholarly purposes are not the only reason for wanting to take government positions. The exercise of power and influence over policy has its appeal, although at Brookings a benign face can even be put on this. "The power thing in government work is overestimated. People here want to influence policy not because they are personally ambitious for power, like Joe Califano or Bob Strauss, but because they have a commitment to truth and want to see the right policies adopted." These are the words of Robert Crandall, who was acting director of the Council on Wage and Price Stability during the Ford administration and then served as acting director in the first year of the Carter administration; Crandall became a senior fellow at Brookings when Barry Bosworth left his senior fellowship at Brookings to take Crandall's place as head of the Wage and Price Council under President Carter. Bosworth, unhappy over lack of sufficient White House support in fighting inflation, has since returned to Brookings.

Without trying to distinguish too finely between the blandishments of power seeking for the sake of truth and power seeking for the sake of power, there can be no doubt of Brookings' commitment to the ideal of objective truth seeking. And that is why the staff resents partisan typecasting. In recent years, such typecasting has been encouraged by the rise of a competitive conservative think tank in Washington, The American Enterprise Institute. Brookings people find that this puts them in an uncomfortable position. Their reaction is typified by Roland Hoover, Brookings' director of publications: "Ideological labelling does neither Brookings nor AEI any good. AEI should get off it." Because truth seeking is not an advocacy process like the legal system or politics, the notion that Brookings as an institution should incorporate an ideological bias is anathema. Nonetheless, a few Brookings people can be found who will admit to one. Hoover, who describes himself as "a conservative by temperament," grants that there is a liberal bias "in the *choice* of topics, though not in the research itself." On a broader philosophical level, he says, "Man is perfectible here; he is fallen over at AEI."

In the 1969 Brookings Annual Report, the late Kermit Gordon discussed how Brookings seeks influence in advancing the social good. Gordon addressed himself to the question, "How do you know that you are really contributing to better decision making in public affairs?" This was not, Gordon wrote, easy to answer. Not only do new ideas in any society suffer from shrouded paternity, but in such a pluralistic society as ours, so various and intricate are the forces that converge to influence policy making that it is extremely difficult to discern a causal nexus between study and decision.

> More characteristically, the findings of policy research are transmitted along the complex network of persons and institutions by whose interactions decisions are ultimately made. Linked together in this communications network are legislators and their staffs; policy makers and policy advisors at all levels of government; reporters, editors, columnists, and editorial writers in print and electronic communications; scholars in and out of universities; and opinion leaders in business and the professions.

Studies, Gordon claimed, were impulses fed into this network. If they were deficient they would expire quickly; if they were strong—on criteria of validity, timeliness, clarity, and practicality—then the ideas would reverberate throughout the network. "In the end," said Gordon, "the initiative may be decisive in inspiring an important policy decision, but it will have been strained through so many filters and combined with so many other ingredients that the causal chain may be untraceable."

Brookings' purpose is to feed its research into the policy network, not to proselytize. What Gordon did not mention, though, was Brookings' importance as a place where the network gathers to do its communicating: over lunch, whether informally in the Brookings cafeteria or at the regular Friday lunch around a great oval table at which the staff and their guests keen over the events of the week like the chorus of an ancient Greek tragedy; through consulting, paid and unpaid, for government or business; at conferences; in the Advanced Studies Program; and, over time, by means of the revolving door of government employment. The Nixon White House was angry at Brookings not because it seemed to be a government-in-exile, but because it seemed to be an actual part of the government over which the President's men had even less control than they did over the bureaucracy. This fear of the influence of a group of private and unaccountable experts on the workings of democratic government goes back to Brookings' origins.

Horatio Alger Goes to Washington

The Brookings Institution was the creation of a progressive midwestern businessman, Robert S. Brookings. Born in rural Maryland in 1850, he grew up in Baltimore in the household of his stepfather, a carpenter and builder. At sixteen, he left home to seek his fortune in St. Louis where his older brother Harry was working in the firm of Cupples and Marston, manufactur-

The Dismal Science of Reform: Brookings

ers and distributors of woodenware and cordage. After a year of clerking, Brookings convinced his gruff employer, Samuel Cupples, to send him as a traveling salesman to the West. Armed with order book, violin, a copy of Plutarch's *Lives,* and a certain moral fastidiousness, Brookings traversed the untamed land, hawking his wares.

At twenty-one he became a partner in Cupples & Marston; Ten years later, he took charge and the company prospered. His fortune was made.

But he was restless and ambitious for the better things of life. He began singing in the St. Louis Choral Society, graced the salons of the provincial aristocracy, and solicited reading lists in literature, history, and economics from the dean of the local college. Then he spent a year in Berlin, studying philosophy and the fiddle. He got to know the great violin virtuoso, Josef Joachim, and bought an Amati as a souvenir of his *Wanderjahr.*

Back in St. Louis, Brookings assumed the responsibilities of a solid citizen. Under his renewed leadership, the firm of Cupples & Marston boomed. Brookings bought a farm on the outskirts of St. Louis and started to breed race horses. Then he sold the farm and bought an estate in the foothills of the Ozarks where he laid out a golf course and stocked the woods with English red-necked pheasants. He hunted, played tennis and informal polo, and gave parties. But the life of a country gentleman, like that of a businessman, left him unfulfilled. He must do good works. In 1896, at the age of forty-six he retired from business to devote his life to higher education. His efforts first focused on Washington University, then a struggling institution with less than a hundred students. Brookings became president of its board of trustees and, over the next twenty years, succeeded in building it into a major university.

As a full-time patron of education, Brookings was drawn into the world of national service and philanthropic enterprise. He became friendly with Andrew Carnegie and served as one of the original trustees of the Carnegie Endowment for International Peace. Just before World War I, he accompanied the steel magnate on a peace mission to Kaiser Wilhelm. At President Taft's request, Brookings became a consultant to the Commission on Economy and Efficiency, which had the mission of discovering how to put the federal administration on a sound business footing.

World War I provided Brookings the opportunity to serve his country more actively. In 1917, he accepted President Wilson's invitation to join the War Industries Board (WIB), which was to have the responsibility of securing and distributing all supplies needed by the armed services. Together with such men as Robert A. Lovett, chairman of Union Pacific Railroad, and the financier Bernard Baruch, Brookings helped run a historic collaborative venture of business and government in support of the war effort. He became chairman of the WIB's Price Fixing Committee (no euphemism was then considered necessary), with the task of negotiating prices for all U.S. goods purchased by the Allied governments.

Though nearly seventy years old at the end of the war, Brookings had no desire to return to the provinces for graceful retirement. Instead, he decided to take the reins of a unique but struggling private organization with which he was associated, the Institute for Government Research, a body founded by the lawyer and economist Frederick A. Cleveland. To launch the research institute, Greene had gathered a steering committee of his influential friends—former colleagues in the government and fellow members of the Century Club. They were, for the most part, New York bankers, businessmen, and corporate lawyers. Two of them, Raymond B. Fosdick and Jerome D. Greene, were close to the Rockefellers. Fosdick, a lawyer, was John D. Rockefeller, Jr.'s principal philanthropic adviser, and Greene, who had come to be known at Harvard as President Eliot's alter ego while serving as secretary to Eliot and to the Harvard Corporation, was now secretary to the newly formed Rockefeller Foundation. These two men sat on a special Rockefeller Foundation committee to supervise the initial studies on how to make government more efficient. The studies were begun under Cleveland's direction and were financed by the Rockefeller Foundation.

This Rockefeller connection posed a threat to the integrity of the new organization. Word of it leaked out shortly after the creation of the Institute was made public. In Congress, Senator Henry F. Ashurst declaimed against "accepting for government use one cent of Rockefeller money." *The Washington Times* persistently referred to the Institute as "a Rockefeller Inquiry." Denials were, of course, issued from all quarters; however, as with the Trilateral Commission sixty years later, many people were prepared to believe that the Institute for Government Research was just a front for the Rockefellers.

The Institute's founders recognized the necessity of turning aside accusations that they were serving any special interest. To be effective, the Institute needed to be accepted simply for what it claimed to be: "An association of citizens for cooperating with public officials in the scientific study of government with a view to promoting efficiency and economy in its operations and advancing the science of administration." The founders realized that the Institute needed a moral authority beyond what the promise of disinterested social science could confer. No fewer than six university presidents were recruited to its board of trustees to assure this proper sense of elevated purpose. An aura of representativeness was supplied by adding to the board business leaders from places other than New York—mainly the Midwest. Among these was Robert S. Brookings. His job as a trustee, Greene told him, would be "to vouch before the public for the integrity of the enterprise and its freedom from the slightest political bias."

The Institute for Government Research, the first national think tank, was a pure product of the Establishment mind at work. Under the sponsorship and encouragement of enlightened men of affairs, a staff of earnest academics and other professionals would serve an unobjectionable cause through scientific investigation and close cooperation with the authorities. To ward off accusations of bias or demagogery, it would issue bland and tedious publications.

When the Institute opened its doors in the fall of 1916, the future looked bright. The opposition had been neutralized. The

New Republic, semiofficial organ of Progressivism, had conferred its blessing. Several government agencies submitted requests for its scholarly help.

But hardly had work begun than World War I intervened. Much of the assembled staff dispersed for posts in the rapidly expanding federal bureaucracy. At the Institute, all research plans were shelved in favor of helping the war effort. By the time the war ended, the Institute was near extinction.

Brookings brought the Institute back to life. Appointed chairman, he set about raising funds by appealing to the self-interest of his friends in the business world. "You see how the government is spending the money it takes from you in taxes. What are you going to do about it? Do you want an intelligent treatment of the matters which lie closest to your personal interests? Or do you want things to go on in the haphazard fashion of the past? Do you want a log-rolling or a scientific tariff? Do you want pork-barrel bills or a budget?"

The line worked. In two months he was able to raise a third of a million dollars from ninety-two corporations and a dozen individuals. Times had changed; the rumblings of discontent which had animated the Progressive Era were stilled. People wanted government to be less important—and more business-like.

Incredibly, the federal government had been operating for a century and half without a budget. The Institute for Government Research set out to give it one, and it succeeded in the first year of the Harding administration, thanks to public concern over the size of the war debt. The Institute's director, William F. Willoughby, wrote and stage-managed the budget bill through Congress. The first budget director, Charles G. Dawes, worked out of the Institute for a time, relying on its staff to develop procedures for his infant Bureau. The Institute was also deeply involved in the civil service reform legislation of 1920 and 1923. All in all, it became a useful and inoffensive fixture on the Washington scene. Robert Brookings brought Republican panjandrums onto its board—Chief Justice Taft, Herbert Hoover, and Elihu Root.

The Dismal Science of Reform: Brookings

When his restoration of the Institute was barely completed, the indefatigable Brookings began charging off elsewhere. Government studies, Brookings felt, were fine as far as they went but the big issues facing society were economic, not administrative. What was needed, he decided, was an institute to subject the economic system to the same kind of scrutiny that the IGR applied to the federal government. The Carnegie Corporation proved willing to support such a venture to the tune of $1,650,000, and in June 1922 the Institute of Economics went into operation. Brookings hoped that the new institute would serve as a corrective to the traditional free enterprise pieties of American business. He worried about the wastefulness and instability of the business cycle, and saw a solution in a kind of institutionalized cooperation, with industrial management acting as a trustee for the joint interest of stockholders, labor, and the general public.

Brookings was troubled by the power exercised by great corporations over workers, and believed the situation would be improved by making every man a species of capitalist—through profit-sharing—and by including labor representatives on boards of directors. In an article written to urge these steps, Brookings included a list of twenty-one railway magnates who "rose from the ranks of employees" to top positions in management. Executive talent persisted among the lowly; the modern corporation must be adapted to permit humble clerks and messenger boys to realize the Horatio Alger dream, as Brookings had done himself. He was groping for something he called "economic democracy," a humane and opportunity-laden system which by moderating the faults of laissez-faire capitalism would serve as "America's answer to socialism and communism." He expected his new institute to serve this end.

Then he launched still a third academic enterprise—the Robert S. Brookings School of Economics and Government. Incorporated in 1924, this school had begun the year before as a Washington, D.C. outpost of Washington University in St. Louis. Brookings' original idea was to enable doctoral students to spend time in the nation's capital, working with the staffs of the

Institute for Government Research and the Institute of Economics. His views shifted, however, after the school was put on an independent footing. What he now wanted was not yet another nursery for academicians but an enterprise in training future government officials. This brought on a knockdown fight with the young graduate school's teachers, students, and outside friends. The result was the effective abolition of the school, accomplished in 1927 by the melding of all three operations into one new organization, called the Brookings Institution.

Big Wind from Chicago

That institution's first president was Harold G. Moulton, the economist Robert Brookings had installed as the first director of the Institute of Economics. Trained at the University of Chicago—then as now a redoubt of laissez-faire economics—Moulton was a good deal more conservative than his patron. Indeed, he regarded Brookings as a naive enthusiast, and had accepted the job with trepidation, only after receiving the old man's assurances that he would not meddle. Now, with Brookings in failing health, Moulton began to put his mark on the Institution. Combative by temperament—he delighted in defeating all comers on the Institution's squash court—he inaugurated a style of hard-nosed criticism increasingly distant from the optimistic and cooperative style of earlier days. The Moulton style did not really become apparent, however, until after 1932, the year Brookings died, Willoughby, the expert on public administration, retired, and Franklin Delano Roosevelt was elected President of the United States.

At first, cordial relations between the Brookings Institution and the new administration promised to last. In the months before his inauguration, Roosevelt had declared his intention of dealing with the Depression by cutting federal expenditures, consolidating bureaus, and eliminating government services. In January, the President wrote to Moulton, "Quite frankly, we need help. Because I know of the splendid work that has been done by you and the Institute, and because of my old friendship for Mr. Brookings, I am hoping that you will be able to give us assistance in the preparation of a fairly definite plan between now and early March."

The Institution responded briskly, but its memoranda were ignored. For, once in office, Roosevelt abandoned the goal of budget balancing and turned instead to "bold, persistent experimentation."

Moulton's Brookings reacted to the New Deal with consternation. Fears were expressed that it signalled the end of the free enterprise system. Moulton's particular bête noire was the National Recovery Administration which involved government and business in price-fixing. Moulton organized a massive—and massively critical—study of that beleaguered operation.

This study brought down the wrath of General Hugh S. Johnson, the NRA administrator. Brookings, he asserted, had become "a pressure bureau to publicize the preconceived ideas of Harold Moulton." It was "one of the most sanctimonious and pontifical rackets in the country." Johnson had worked with Robert Brookings on the War Industries Board two decades before. He expressed the wish that Brookings were still alive, so that he could "go into that Institution that bears his name and drive out with the rope around his robe the men who perverted his ideas."[3] Johnson was doubtless right in believing that the old man would have been a lot more friendly to the New Deal than Moulton was.

To be sure, hostility to the New Deal was not unmitigated at Brookings. Edwin G. Nourse, who would become the first chairman of the new Council of Economic Advisors under President Harry S. Truman, conducted a reasonably sympathetic study of the New Deal's Agricultural Adjustment Administration. And several members of the Brookings' staff accepted posts in the Roosevelt administration. Still the dominant attitude was negative, and there was collaboration with the anti-Roosevelt forces in Congress. Increasingly, Brookings began to be perceived, in the words of FDR's braintruster, Rexford Guy Tugwell, as "a kind of research organ for the conservatives." This image was reinforced by Moulton, who, instead of seeking to placate his foes, publicly denounced them in speeches and pamphlets, while proclaiming the Institution's devotion to even-handedness and nonpartisanship.

Beneath the mutual mudslinging lurked a bona fide conflict of principle. The New Deal, not only in practice but philosophically, posed a challenge to the ideology of economy and efficiency which had animated Brookings from its origins in the IGR. The sprawling new federal agencies violated all traditional canons of good administration. Under Roosevelt, a different conception of the federal government was taking hold: no longer was government seen as a kind of large corporation, providing goods and services within limits prescribed by its income, but as an indispensable mechanism for regulating and balancing the economy as a whole, and for insuring the material well-being of society, regardless of whether its own books were balanced. The role of government was to rescue capitalism from disaster.

A new generation of lawyers and economists, the young New Dealers, carried the banner of this novel creed. Just as FDR was branded "a traitor to his class," so were they, in a sense, traitors to the old guard of experts, pharisaical elders whom they confronted with a startling doctrine of unconstrained charity and economic salvation. "The Brookings," as it used to be called, put up a fight in the name of the old-time religion of balanced budgets and free markets but this amounted to no more than a rear-guard action, for the future was with the New Dealers.

The fight, though inevitable, was conducted in a manner which would have dismayed the Institution's founding fathers. The style they had preferred was one of institutional reticence and quiet, easy cooperation with the administration in power. Moulton's pugnacity and ideological strictness helped bring about the result the founding fathers had most wanted to avoid: a reputation for interested partisanship.

Still, Moulton was not solely to blame. Although another sort of president might have kept the waters calmer, his distress at the New Deal was shared by many of the Establishment lords who sat on his board of trustees. For them, as for Brookings itself, the thirties posed the difficult task of adjusting comfortable old doctrines to unpleasant new realities. For Brookings, as for the Establishment as a whole, it took World War II to achieve rapprochement with the Roosevelt administration.

Making Peace with the New Deal

FDR himself signaled a new spirit of accommodation by appointing Moulton to a place on the War Resources Board in 1939. Earlier, the President had been sufficiently piqued by Moulton's denunciations to veto a place for him on the Committee on Administrative Management.* Now, both men were prepared to set aside their mutual antagonism over domestic policy for

---

*In early 1936, with the New Deal increasingly under attack, FDR set up the Committee on Administrative Management as a means of providing himself with a program for exercising more effective control over the executive branch. Despite considerable disagreement among the three committee members and among the staff, the final report, under pressure from the President himself, represented a departure from the old economy-and-efficiency approach to government reorganization. Its guiding principle was not efficiency as removing waste and saving money, but efficiency as effective management and purposeful planning: "to make our Government an up-to-date, efficient, and effective instrument for carrying out the will of the Nation." The committee's recommendations were defeated in Congress in 1937, in part thanks to a set of Brookings studies, carried out on traditional economy-and-efficiency lines for FDR's foe, Senator Harry F. Byrd of Virginia. In 1939, however, with World War II looming ahead, Congress gave its approval; the Executive Office of the President was created and both the Budget Bureau and the National Resources Planning Board were transferred to it. According to one historian, these measures constituted "the institutionalization in American government of one of Roosevelt's greatest contributions to American politics: the presidency as the moveable weight in the balance of democratic government, providing that rapidly adjustable point which might seek to maintain equilibrium in a rapidly changing world." (Barry Dean Karl, *Executive Reorganization and Reform in the New Deal*, [Cambridge, 1963], pp. 258–9.) By the end of the war, the Brookings people and Senator Byrd himself had acquiesced in this new conception of the presidency.

THE AMERICAN ESTABLISHMENT

the sake of the impending war effort. The Brookings board made amends by adding to their number men on good terms with the White House: Edward R. Stettinius, Jr., the well-traveled business executive who served as first chairman of the War Resources Board, administrator of Lend-Lease, and special assistant to the President; Karl T. Compton, president of MIT and member of the War Resources Board; and, Vannevar Bush, former MIT professor and president of the Carnegie Institute. Compton and Bush were the two men most responsible for the scientific side of the war effort. And the rising Democratic star of the State Department, Dean Acheson, was made vice-chairman of Brookings.

These appointments indicated an important political repositioning. Boards of trustees of institutions like Brookings are above all symbolic bodies. What trustees actually do—and usually it is precious little—is far less significant than what they stand for. Appointments are therefore signposts for the interested public, pointing where the institution is moving, or at least hopes to move. In the early forties, Brookings took pains to show that its interest was in helping, not hindering, the efforts of the Roosevelt administration.

During World War II, Brookings found itself in the same position as the IGR in World War I. As much of its staff fanned out to federal agencies to help with war planning and management, its own work dwindled, and financial support ebbed away. After V-J day, however, a full complement of staff returned and material prosperity was resecured. But relations with the Democratic administration did not relapse into the acrimony of the thirties.

Not that Moulton had reconciled himself to the new economics. On the contrary, he never ceased beating his anti-Keynesian drums, declaiming in pamphlet and book agianst "the new philosophy of public debt." Other Brookings economists, in tune with Moulton's general ideological proclivities, supplied the provisions of the Taft-Hartley Bill to curb the power of labor unions and in other ways did what they could to frustrate the desires of the unions.

The Dismal Science of Reform: Brookings

Brookings' conservatism in domestic matters was, however, combined with a thoroughgoing internationalism in foreign affairs. As it happened, the bulk of Brookings' research output in the immediate postwar period was in the international area. The man responsible for this was Leo Pasvolsky, a longtime staff economist who returned to Brookings in 1946 after having spent the better part of the previous decade working in the State Department as a close advisor and troubleshooter for Secretary Cordell Hull. Pasvolsky brought half a dozen State Department bureaucrats with him and, with funding from the Rockefeller Foundation, the Carnegie Corporation, and the Mellon Trust, set up an International Studies Group, which developed the basic procedures for administering the Marshall Plan to aid European recovery.

Thus, combining domestic conservatism with enlightened but hard-nosed internationalism, Brookings entered the Cold War period breathing comfortably. The symbol of its staunch, respectable internationalism was a new member of the board of trustees, John J. McCloy, President of the World Bank (and Richard Rovere's designated chairman of the American Establishment).

But such respectability was no proof against McCarthyism. Indeed it invited populist McCarthyite attack. Brookings became suspect in right-wing quarters because of its close ties with the State Department, allegedly loaded with Reds, homosexuals, and cookie-pusher internationalists. In 1951, *The Chicago Tribune* reported that Brookings carried on "an elaborate program of training and indoctrination in global thinking" and ominously noted that "most of its scholars wind up as policy makers in the State Department in Washington or in the Foreign Service abroad."

But Brookings' reputation for economic traditionalism kept even that isolationist and McCarthyite "world's greatest newspaper," as it so styled itself, off guard; the *Tribune*'s assessment was that the Brookings Institution represented "an odd mixture of conservatism and globaloney." Before long, however, the *Tribune* had to conclude that the half-okay part of the mixture had been drained away. For Brookings was adapting to new patterns of thought and power in America.

As it became clear that the conservatives were not going to muster enough popular support to reverse New Deal social reforms or the Keynesian revolution in economics, Brookings, like other Establishment bodies, moved to join the liberal mainstream. The president chosen to lead this march toward a new middle-of-the-road position, as soon as Harold Moulton had retired in 1952, was Robert D. Calkins. An economist of far more catholic views than Moulton, Calkins was also more widely experienced: he had been dean of the Columbia Business School, chairman of the economics department at the University of California in Berkeley, a labor mediator for the government during the war, and director of the General Education Board since 1947. He combined a good mediator's evenhandedness and sensitivity with a good administrator's aplomb and willingness to work through others. Calkins respected talent. Where Moulton had not been above rewriting an author's conclusions or consigning them to an appendix if he disagreed with them, Calkins maintained a strictly hands-off policy and resisted the occasional effort of a trustee to obstruct publication of an uncongenial study.

Recognizing the need for improving both the quality and currency of Brookings' economic studies, Calkins augmented Moulton's conservative staff with Walter S. Salant, one of the small group of Harvard graduate students (including his brother William Salant, the future Nobel laureate Paul Samuelson, and David Lusher, the workhorse of the Council of Economic Advisers) who brought Keynesianism to America. Another Calkins recruit was Joseph A. Pechman, a product of City College in New York who had done his graduate work at that bastion of liberalism, the University of Wisconsin, where his closest intellectual friend was Walter W. Heller, later to become the chairman of President John F. Kennedy's Council of Economic Advisers and the outstanding publicist of Keynesian doctrines in America.

But the arrival of men like Pechman and Salant did not mean

The Dismal Science of Reform: Brookings

that Brookings had veered to the left. Its board was searching for a wide middle ground in which sensible conservatives and liberals could live comfortably together. The board also wanted the Institution to embody a genteel, even elegant, style. It found the perfect expression of its hopes in Kermit Gordon, a product of Swarthmore College, Harvard University, Oxford University, Williams College, and the Ford Foundation. Gordon had the further advantage of knowing Washington well from his service in the Kennedy administration. Handsome, patrician in manner and taste (he did not like loud voices and raucous laughter, and once eased out a Brookings scholar because of his country-bumpkin style and braying laugh), Gordon offered a delicate blend of moderate liberalism and enlightened, antispendthrift conservatism. A parfit Establishment knight.

Speaking to a group of business economists in the fall of 1963, Gordon made what could have been his campaign speech for the presidency of Brookings. He emphasized the importance of using fiscal policy, especially through tax cuts, to "achieve and sustain national prosperity." Too many people, he said, have come to associate aggressive fiscal policy and loose budgets, "assuming that commitment to the former implies the latter."

Fiscal policy, he said, turns on the relation between receipts and expenditures, and that relationship can be varied by government policy makers "whether the budget is loose, or tight, or somewhere in between." In the then existing circumstances, he said, "when both human and industrial resources are seriously underutilized" (The Vietnam-born inflation was still to come) fiscal policy called for a cut in tax rates relative to spending levels. This aim could be accomplished either by sharply boosting spending or by cutting taxes; fiscal policy as such, said Gordon, "does not require loose budgets." For his part, he preferred to use planned variations in tax rates to fight business recessions because these would lead to better budgetary policy than "hastily devised improvisations on the expenditure side." The principle that tight budgets are consistent with proper fiscal policy, he said, had been well learned by the conservative governments of Britain, France, and West Germany. "Macmillan, de Gaulle, and Adenauer," said Gordon, "hardly fit the definition of spend-thrift radicals."

A new economic-policy consensus, blending the management of total demand by government fiscal policy with wide latitude for the market to allocate resources, had emerged. Social science's image of objectivity shines brightest in times of consensus, and is most tarnished in times of disagreement, like the present. Such periods present Establishment research institutions with a dilemma because those bodies, committed through inertia and reputation to the earlier consensus, seem like partisans of a debatable (or discredited) ideology, rather than as dispassionate ministers of the common wisdom.

The Plan to Bomb Brookings

To the Nixon administration, Brookings was part of "the enemy." Indeed Brookings was almost the first Watergate. John Caulfield, a former New York City police agent serving in the White House as a "security aide" in the summer of 1971, obtained Brookings' tax return. Caulfield's memo on the tax return noted that Brookings had "a number of large government contracts," and H. R. Haldeman, the President's top aide, scrawled on the memo, "These should be turned off." But the government contracts, a minor part of Brookings' financing, never were cancelled.

The most dramatic episode in the Nixon administration's scheming against Brookings was a plan, conceived by Charles Colson, to explode a fire bomb at Brookings; the idea was to create a cover that would enable the FBI to enter the building and seize certain defense-policy papers in the office of Leslie Gelb, who had been in charge of the Pentagon Papers study at the Defense Department, under Secretary Robert S. McNamara.

The Dismal Science of Reform: Brookings

In early July 1971, Colson obtained a copy of a 1969 Brookings pamphlet announcing a projected two-year study, to be directed by Gelb, of the U. S. involvement in Vietnam. Colson decided that, the two years being up, a new installment of the Pentagon Papers could be expected soon—"by the same authors but doubtless more up to date," he wrote in a memo to John Ehrlichman, Nixon's number two White House aide. Colson called for a prompt investigation of the Gelb study. The President, meanwhile, had grown anxious about what was going on at Brookings. "Ellsberg,"* Nixon wrote, "was not our only worry. From the first there had been rumors of a conspiracy." The earliest report, "later discounted," Nixon says in his memoirs, had centered on "a friend of Ellsberg, a former Defense Department employee, who was then a Fellow of Brookings"—Leslie Gelb.

Nixon remembered Gelb from the early days of his administration when he had asked Haldeman to get him a copy of the Pentagon file on the events leading up to President Johnson's announcement of the bombing halt at the end of the 1968 campaign. Said Nixon:

> I wanted to know what had actually happened; I also wanted the information as potential leverage against those in Johnson's administration who were now trying to undercut my war policy. I was told that a copy of the bombing halt and other secret documents had been taken from the Pentagon to Brookings by the same man. I wanted the documents back, but I was told that one copy of the bombing halt report had already "disappeared"; I was sure that if word got out that we wanted it, the copy at Brookings might disappear as well.[4]

Colson's memo to Nixon confirmed his suspicions that dark forces were at work. What to do? Nixon himself authorized a burglary or surreptitious raid on Brookings, as he himself explains:

> In the aftershock of the Pentagon Papers leak and all the uncertainty and renewed criticism of the war it produced, my interest in

*Daniel Ellsberg, the former RAND researcher, who leaked the Pentagon Papers to *The New York Times.*

the bombing halt file was rekindled. When I was told that it was still at Brookings, I was furious and frustrated. In the midst of a war and with our secrets being spilled through printing presses all over the world, top-secret government reports were out of reach in the hands of a private think tank largely staffed with antiwar Democrats. It seemed absurd. I could not accept that we had lost so much control over the workings of the government we had been elected to run— I saw absolutely no reason for that report to be at Brookings, and I said I wanted it back right now—even if it meant having to get it surreptitiously.[5]

So Colson had his marching orders. He called the White House sleuth, John Caulfield, into his office on July 9, 1971, and told him he had talked to "people" in the White House who felt there was "a high priority need to obtain papers from the office of a gentleman named Leslie Gelb" at Brookings. According to Caulfield, Colson suggested that the fire regulations of the District of Columbia could be changed to permit the FBI "to respond to the scene of any fire in the District and that if there were to be a fire at the Brookings Institute *(sic)* that the FBI could respond and obtain the file in question from Mr. Leslie Gelb's office."[6]

Caulfield felt that the implication was clear; he should start a fire at Brookings. He quickly excused himself and ran to John Dean's office, where he pleaded with Dean to get him out of this "asinine" assignment. Dean later said Caulfield told him that Tony Ulasewicz, another former New York police agent who became briefly famous on television for his Damon Runyon-esque rhetoric, had already "cased" Brookings and had made friendly contact with a security man.

Caulfield said the Brookings security system was "extremely tight," which it certainly was not. Brookings had a single security guard, who was usually posted in the lobby. Anyone could get by him by simply saying he was on his way to see one of the scholars. But Brookings was never fire-bombed. Caulfield apparently turned off the burglary by refusing to play. Leslie Gelb later said: "I'm afraid they would have been pretty disappointed with what they found there: three bookcases full of books on

Vietnam, some card files, and drafts of chapters on Vietnam during the Roosevelt and Truman administrations."

It was John Dean who told Caulfield to do nothing further, and persuaded Ehrlichman that the whole scheme was "insane." Ehrlichman called Colson and told him to cancel it. (Colson later denied the whole story.)

Curiously enough, the Nixon administration considered creating a Republican equivalent of Brookings. Colson thought E. Howard Hunt, later famous as a leader of the Watergate burglary, former CIA operator and author of such works as *Bimini Run, I Came to Kill, Angel Eyes, The Coven,* and *Where Murder Waits,* would make a good director of the new Republican Brookings. The White House thought of calling the new research center the Institute for an Informed America or the Silent Majority Institute.

Colson sent Howard Hunt to talk to Jeb Stuart Magruder, who was coordinating the project, about becoming its director. Magruder was at first impressed with Hunt, but, when Hunt sent him a plan for turning the Institute into a base for covert political activity, Magruder decided that he was not quite right for the job because of his "cloak and dagger orientation."

Conservative Competition: The American Enterprise Institute

The new "Brookings Institution for Republicans" was aborted. But that role was assumed by an already existing research center, the American Enterprise Institute for Public Policy Research.

The American Enterprise Association, as it was first called, was founded in 1943 by Lewis H. Brown, chairman of the board of the Johns-Manville Corporation, to promote free-enterprise ideas. William J. Baroody, Sr., who left the United States Chamber of Commerce in 1954 as a staff member to become executive vice-president of AEA, became its president and guiding figure in 1962. Shortly afterward, the AEA changed its name to the American Enterprise Institute, the governing board having refused to call it the Institute for Public Policy Research, a title lacking identifiable ideology.

The growth of the institute was slow, and it was scarcely known to the general public until 1970, when Joseph Baroody, one of Mr. Baroody's sons, founded a public relations firm, Wagner & Baroody, with AEI as its principal client.

AEI became a family enterprise. William Baroody, Jr., who assumed the presidency after his father, said to William Lanouette of *The National Journal* of his own young son: "He's 15, I'm 40. . . . We may be the first family that hands down a think tank from generation to generation. William 3d—he's the brightest of us all. Once a family gets involved in this sort of thing, there is a tendency for the youngsters to see the excitement and tend to move in that direction, and that's what's happened."

During the Nixon and Ford years, AEI gained much financial support and became a research and recruitment base for the Republican administration. When the Democrats captured the White House in 1976, AEI became even more of a refuge for Republican luminaries than Brookings had been for the Democrats. Among the Nixon or Ford administration officials who signed up with AEI for short or long-term assignments were Herbert Stein, Paul McCracken, William E. Simon, Robert H. Bork, Gen. Leonard F. Chapman, Jr., Carla and Roderick Hills, Paul MacAvoy, L. William Seidman, Lawrence H. Silberman, and, as "The Distinguished Fellow," former President Gerald R. Ford.

William Baroody, Jr., said in an interview that the difference between AEI and Brookings is "primarily a matter of emphasis on the part of the kind of scholars who tend to gravitate to one or the other. . . . In confronting societal problems those who tend to gravitate to the AEI orbit would be inclined to look first for a market-oriented solution to a particular problem, though not exclusively, and only in the last resort would they think of a governmental program; while in the other orbit people have a tendency to look for a governmental solution, then to a private solution. I look at it more in terms of emphasis than polarities. A mix one of our scholars would apply is the same mix, but in reverse order."[7]

Herbert Stein, a former chairman of President Nixon's Council of Economic Advisers, who had been with Brookings before he joined the Nixon administration but moved to AEI when he left it, said, "AEI is a think tank of predominantly conservative people, but who by being conservative may be the wave of the future rather than of the past. I think they reflect a certain disaffection with the prevailing trend of thought of the past thirty or forty years. . . . I knew Brookings in the 1930s when Harold Moulton was its head. Well, it didn't have this character it now has. . . . Then, when Kermit Gordon became its head, it began to acquire that group of people—but also they were 90 percent of economics anyway, so they were the easiest kind to recruit. But I don't think there's any official Brookings doctrine, to which the people there have to conform. I think they're all expressing their own views. If a lot of them happen to be of a similar school, well, that's how people tend to flock together."[8]

Brookings tries to keep a stiff upper lip, sometimes even a smiling one, about AEI, but dislikes the implied ideological competition. Robert V. Roosa, a partner of Brown Brothers Harriman and Company and former Under Secretary of the Treasury, who is chairman of Brookings' board, says, "AEI is selling against Brookings. They don't have to do that—they have a role to fill." Roosa believes that Brookings' reputation is hurt by the way AEI goes about gaining support for itself: "They tell business conservatives, 'You need a spokesman.'" Roosa has no objection to that "as long as they don't denigrate us in the process. We do some things on the conservative side —and more now." But he stresses that Brookings, which gets a relatively small share of its support from corporations, does not intend to get it on the basis that "we're on your side." "I think our definition of our role is like that of the universities," says Roosa. "Scholars do not have to toe the line."

The Professors and Politics

Alan Greenspan, the business economist who served as President Ford's chief economic adviser, once remarked that the most important thing he learned in Washington was that all legislation originates in academia. But, like ball clubs, all academic institutions have their winning streaks and their slumps. Brookings has been in a slump in recent years. Even after the Democrats returned to power, the mood at Brookings remained one of discontent over the failure of its earlier ideas and its inability to break new ground. Henry Aaron's *Politics and the Professors,* [9] a critique of social science cast in the form of a history of the breakup of the liberal consensus of the early and middle sixties, reflects this mood of despond.

Aaron has two principal themes: Social science research reflects prevailing political moods at least as much as it influences them; and, insofar as it exercises some influence on political thinking about important social and economic matters, the new quantitative social science is profoundly conservative. Examining the broad areas of poverty and discrimination, education and jobs, and unemployment and inflation, Aaron shows how the theories and prescriptions widely subscribed to by social scientists in the early sixties have given way in each area to a mass of conflicting opinions.

Responsibility for this intellectual confusion belongs partly to the research and evaluation techniques themselves; falsely concrete, they created a murky basis for policy decisions. The same data became susceptible to a wide variety of interpretations, depending on the hidden assumptions or ideological prejudices of the analyst. Politicians and partisan advocates were able to pick and choose among the welter of conflicting studies for the data and conclusions they found most congenial. This variability gave rise to "forensic" social science, that is, to social science as special pleading.*

Amidst such confusion, when the benefits of a given social program are obscure at best, why spend the taxpayers' money, why should the government act at all? Ironically, the new analytical techniques were developed by liberals as a means of convincing Congress of the effectiveness of liberal domestic programs.

Of course, the new quantitative social science did not appear as liberal but as pragmatic. That ideology prescribing "the end-of-ideology," dominant in the late fifties and early sixties, was a perfect formulation of the social scientist's preferred worldview. A fine expression of that world-view, elevated to the highest political level, is found in some remarks of President Kennedy's, delivered impromptu at the White House on June 11, 1962:

> I would like to also say a word about the difference between myth and reality. Most of us are conditioned for many years to have a political viewpoint, Republican or Democratic—liberal, conservative, moderate. The fact of the matter is that most of the problems, or at at least many of them, that we now face are technical problems, are administrative problems. They are very sophisticated judgments which do not lend themselves to the great sort of passionate movements which have stirred the country so often in the past.

In the light of the passionate ideological currents that swept America in the sixties, those remarks of Kennedy's at the start of the decade seem naive. Nevertheless, long after Vietnam and Woodstock, we now seem to be moving into another "end-of-ideology" phase, but one more conservative in stress than that of twenty years ago. A new consensus of economy and efficiency

---

*Aaron's view of the ambiguities of the new social science techniques differed from that of the masters of Harvard's Kennedy School, who saw them as objective tools for clarifying issues of public policy. See chapter 2, pp. 60–63.

and antigovernment spirit has been blown in by the winds of inflation and high taxation.

This emerging consensus is reflected not only among the large majority of both Democratic and Republican politicians but even in the respective stances of Brookings and AEI. Bruce MacLaury, Brookings' president, says, "Being nonpartisan is part of our charter, and it's the only way we would remain credible. There's nothing more important than that, other than I don't think we need to get the extremes of political or radical economic thought on either side, but I think a broad middle ground is what we certainly are after, and in that respect AEI claims very much the same intention." He concedes a difference of emphasis at Brookings: "I suppose someone on the outside might say we selected our people from a tradition that says government has a viable role and our job is to see how that role can be made most effective, rather than to see how it can be limited the most."

And Herbert Stein, ex-Brookings Senior Fellow and now Senior Fellow at AEI, says: "It's probably true that both are moving to the middle, but the middle is moving to the right."

The Reverend William Paley said that if the dissenters should ever become the majority, the Establishment should go over to the dissenters. Is this what's happening at Brookings? Certainly there is a strong tug in that direction. We have seen that tug to the right at Harvard, the *Times,* the Ford Foundation, and we shall see it again. The Establishment, as Finley Peter Dunne might have said, follows the election returns. It is what economists would call a lagging indicator of the nation's political mood.

Chapter 6

Mission on Sixty-Eighth Street: The Council on Foreign Relations

For CONTEMPORARY mongers of global plots, the headquarters of evil is likely to be an institution formally designated "Council on Foreign Relations, Inc." There, depending on the point of view, a capitalist conspiracy engineers the exploitation of the planet by multinational conglomerates, or the central committee of collectivist world government plans the ongoing communist revolution.

At the heart of darkness itself—the town house on East Sixty-eighth Street and Park Avenue—these equally malignant if mutually exclusive images are well known. Books, pamphlets, and articles, litanies of familiar diatribe and revelation, are greeted with amusement and exasperation, and duly filed away in the Council's archives. Not long ago William Diebold, an economist who has been on the Council's staff for many years, sent around his six-page book report on a recently published German dissertation on the Council. With donnish humor, Diebold traced the standard left-wing line, from which the book deviated only in its conclusion: that the Council's efforts were directed towards preventing the outbreak of World War III—surely no small service. "You didn't," Diebold asked his colleagues, "expect *that* did you?"

In 1977, attacks on the Council by the conspiracy-minded provoked Zygmunt Nagorski, then head of the Council's Meetings Program, to take to the pages of *The National Review* with a ringing assertion of the disinterested purposes and benign conduct of his organization. The Council, he emphasized, was not a conspiracy, but a service organization for persons professionally involved in foreign relations—whether businessmen, government officials, or scholars. It never took, nor would it ever take, an official position. In its meetings and studies programs, as in its journal, *Foreign Affairs,* its aim was to provide a forum for opposing views. It was, in short and in the words of *Washington Post* columnist Joseph Kraft, "an incubator of men and ideas." Nothing more. But also nothing less.

There is no way for an apologist like Nagorski to convince its dedicated antagonists of this. For them, the Council has only two alternatives: to own up to its nefarious activities; or, like any other self-respecting conspiracy, to deny that it is one. The conclusion is indestructible. Perhaps because he recognizes the futility of trying to lay the ghost, Winston Lord, the Council's youthful president, likes to say that he welcomes being thought of as a conspiracy. "It means that people think we're more important than we are."

But however misinformed or paranoid their musings, latter-day Cobbetts of the left and right are not entirely mistaken in their underlying intuition. In the United States, if The THING is to be located in its purest form, then the Council on Foreign Relations is the place. Even at the Council this is occasionally acknowledged. In late 1978, a special dinner was held to mark the retirement of John C. Campbell, a Senior Fellow who first joined the Council staff in the thirties. Campbell, in his incisive and entertaining remarks, reflected on the changes of the previous forty years. "I have," he said, "spanned the transition from the rather rigid formality of the era of John W. Davis and Russell Leffingwell, when we wore black tie to every evening meeting, even study groups, to the breezy, sport shirt and blue jeans, bisexual informality of the era of Bayless Manning and Winston Lord. It has been Establishment all the way, but certainly not static."

Indeed, with its roster of scholars and men of affairs (and a small but growing number of women of affairs), its wood-paneled elegance and standards of civility, and its private scrutiny of that most far-reaching national business, foreign policy, the Council is the embodiment of the Establishment style in American society. And within the Council all the tensions of the American Establishment are present: between institutional elitism and democratic instinct, between Eastern parochialism and national, even international, vision, and between disinterested openness to all views and commitment to the "responsible" ones. As Campbell says, it has been this way all the way.

Home from Versailles

The Council of Foreign Relations was a child of World War I, that mammoth exercise of international bloodletting in which the United States emerged for the first time as the most powerful nation on earth. Arising out of the hopeful idealism of the Paris Peace Conference, the Council came into being just at the time when the country, like a maiden vainly seeking to recover her lost honor, was fleeing from entanglement with the League of Nations. From the outset, the Council's founding fathers had to reconcile their own strong anti-isolationist prejudices with their desire to have a nonpartisan organization. Given the times, and the circumstances of the Council's birth, this was not easy.

On June 17, 1919, less than two weeks before the signing of the Versailles Treaty, a large number of the British and American negotiators established a private, bilateral organization called

The Institute for International Affairs. The Institute was animated by internationalist enthusiasms which found voice in the preamble to its founding document.

> Until recent years it was usual to assume that in foreign affairs each government must think mainly, if not entirely, of the interests of its own people. In founding the League of Nations, the Allied Powers have now recognized that national policies ought to be framed with an eye to the welfare of Society at large.

But a cautionary note was sounded: "The proceedings at Paris have shown how necessary it is to create some organization for studying the relation of this principle to practical questions as they arise." With separate branches in the United Kingdom and the United States, the new organization proposed to keep its members in touch with the evolving international situation.

After the Peace Conference, the British moved quickly to set up their branch of the Institute. In America, however, the project languished. Confusion and embarrassment resulting from the Senate's refusal to ratify the Peace Treaty and the League of Nations Covenant had something to do with this, but there were other reasons. The American members of the Institute fell into two camps. On one side were the official negotiators: Commissioners Tasker H. Bliss and Edward M. House, advisors Herbert Hoover and Thomas W. Lamont, and their aides. On the other side was a body of twelve scholars who had served the American delegation in an advisory capacity. These scholars had been assembled in the fall of 1917 by Colonel House, President Wilson's chief advisor, to make preparations for the inevitable postwar peace conference. Known as "The Inquiry," they had squirreled themselves away with books and maps in the American Geographical Society, conducting historical researches and writing position papers. Transported *en masse* to Paris after the conclusion of hostilities, they were quickly put to work negotiating practical solutions to the problems they had studied.

When the two groups of Americans returned home, they were unsure how to proceed. The scholars scattered to their respective universities, mostly Harvard, Yale, and Columbia. The others also dispersed, and grew busy with other matters. Meanwhile, New York, the intended site of the Institute, had gained two apparently similar bodies, the Foreign Policy Association and a Council on Foreign Relations, both established in 1918. Was a third needed?

In 1921, after a series of negotiations, the Institute took flesh by merging with the Council on Foreign Relations, assuming its name, and severing its British connection. The original Council was an organization of New York businessmen and lawyers who, from June 1918 until April 1919, held a succession of dinner-forums on international subjects of common concern. According to Whitney Shepardson, first secretary of the Institute and author of an early history of the Council, this concern was with the effects of the war, and the expected peace, on postwar business. Shepardson noted, with mild disdain, that the membership list "shows the names of the companies displayed as prominently as the names of the individuals."[1]

In the spring of 1919 interest again lagged and, without disolving, the Council lapsed into inactivity. Sporadic attempts to revive it were unavailing and in due course its leaders invited the Institute people to make an overhaul. This task was entrusted to a committee headed by the former U.S. Attorney General, George Wickersham; by the fall of 1921 the new Council was a going concern. It wore its nonpartisanship on its sleeve, with Elihu Root, the Republican elder statesman, serving as honorary president and John W. Davis, former Ambassador to Great Britain and later the 1924 Democratic presidential canditate, as the Council's president. The preponderance of its members—97 in 1921, 210 in 1922—came from the New York business community, but the academics and government officials provided enough of a counterbalance to prevent its being just a Wall Street gentlemen's club.

The Council's principal business remained the dinner-forum, at which the members, convened in general meeting, heard the formal address of a leading statesman—the American Secretary of State, perhaps, or a foreign dignitary like Clemenceau of

France, General Smuts of South Africa, or Canada's Ramsay MacDonald. In addition, however, there were smaller evening discussions, always strictly off the record, where the distinguished guest engaged two or three dozen selected Council members in more informal discussion. Finally, there were study groups, consisting of small groups of members with particular expertise in a given area, which met periodically to examine such issues as "Japan's Economic Development," "Hungary and the Little Entente," "American Naval Policy," or "Inter-Allied Debt and Reparation." This tiered approach to matters of substance made it possible to bring into contact business knowledge and concern, government policy and policy making, and scholarly investigation and analysis. The basic Council mechanism has changed little over the years.

Pursuing their aim to make the Council as serious a place as possible, the founding fathers decided early on that it ought to publish a journal. The prime mover was Edwin F. Gay, editor of *The New York Evening Post,* sometime government official, and once and future Harvard professor. Arguing that "the Council must publish or perish," Gay persuaded *The Journal of International Relations,* a likely competitor, to bow out in favor of the Council's *Foreign Affairs.* He prevailed on Professor Archibald Cary Coolidge of Harvard to undertake the editorship of the new quarterly. He arranged for Coolidge to take on, as managing editor, a young Princetonian who was his European reporter, Hamilton Fish Armstrong. Armstrong, who became editor after Coolidge's death in 1928, remained at the helm until 1972.

Foreign Affairs was an immediate success, and rapidly became the leading journal of its kind. Its first issue, which appeared in 1922, contained articles by André Tardieu, Clemenceau's closest confidant; Eduard Benes, Prime Minister of Czechoslovakia; Elihu Root; Charles Eliot; and a young lawyer by the name of John Foster Dulles. It opened with a statement by Coolidge enunciating his editorial creed. *Foreign Affairs,* he said, would not support any one cause, "however worthy"; it would tolerate "wide differences of opinion" and its articles would present no "consensus of beliefs." All that was required was that they be "competent and well informed, representing honest opinions seriously held and convincingly expressed." The magazine, it was claimed, could "do more to guide American public opinion by a broad hospitality to divergent ideas" than it could "by identifying itself with one school."

It was a fair principle, and Coolidge tried to live by it. He liked being provoked himself, and wanted to be provoking. Once, Armstrong sent for his approval an article by W. E. B. DuBois called "Worlds of Color," in which the black leader reported on race relations in colonial Africa and warned of coming disasters. Coolidge readily gave his assent, not only, he told Armstrong, because the article would raise controversy but also because "many who object to it will do so because the thoughts it suggests make them feel uncomfortable, as in my own case."[2]

Even the appearance of partiality troubled Coolidge. During the 1924 presidential campaign, in which his distant cousin, Calvin Coolidge, was running against John Davis, the Council president, Armstrong became moderately involved in politics on the Democratic side. As Armstrong later recalled:

> Coolidge warned me humorously that if I became identified with Democratic politics he would take to the stump for the Republicans regardless of his personal opinions in order to maintain the review's neutrality. I replied that he need not worry; such desperate measures would not be necessary.[3]

But, despite the best intentions of the editors, an image of strict nonpartisanship was not easy to establish. What made life difficult was the hard-core isolationism of the Republican party. In Armstrong's words:

> The problem was to find representative Republican spokesmen. We did not espouse specific policies but we did assume that the United States had interests and responsibilities which were worldwide. This was contrary to current Republican party doctrine. Republican isolationists said haughtily that their defeat of Wilson's policies had closed the debate not only about future relations with the League of Nations, but about the general relationship of the United States to Europe. Those Republicans who had favored the League

and argued for a Senate compromise, and then had voted for Harding in the hope that eventually he would propose some form of participation in the League, felt rebuffed and betrayed. Some of these were disinclined to pursue a lost cause; others who fought on were not representative enough of current Republican thinking to provide the needed balance to the many Democratic spokesmen ready to be heard.[4]

Republicans who would write were not representative; Republicans who were representative would not write. Beyond that, however, the editors clearly felt that an isolationism which denied that the United States had interests and responsibilities abroad almost *ipso facto* deserved no space in the magazine: it was surely misinformed, if not actually incompetent or dishonest. The real shame was not the lack of spokesmen, but the Republican position.

Men of All Faiths

The same issue confronted the Council as a whole, where nonpartisanship was also embraced, though somewhat less fervently than at *Foreign Affairs*. In late 1922, the enterprising Armstrong, in his capacity as General Manager of the Council, extended an invitation to address the Council to Senator Smith W. Brookhart of Iowa, one of those representative Republicans whose views he found so hard to stomach. Armstrong's purpose in doing this was not simply to expose the membership to a broader spectrum of opinion. "As you know," he wrote to R. C. Leffingwell, one of the Council's leading lights, "Brookhart is a western radical who is 'agin' everything Washington might do in the foreign field. . . . It is important to take this opportunity to educate him and refute some of his views." Leffingwell did not think it a good idea. "These farmer radicals," he told Armstrong, "have seen a great light in the last few months. . . . My advice is, let them alone for a little while. Do not subject them to too much lecturing from Wall Street."

Other reaction was less temperate. Paul Warburg, one of the Council's directors, wrote to say that he got the "cold shivers" when he saw who had been invited to address the next general meeting. He also enclosed a copy of a letter he had received from another Council member, whose name he did not reveal, stating that Brookhart should not be heard and that the author would withdraw from membership in the Council if such people were going to be invited to speak. Armstrong wrote back reiterating the Council's policy of giving a hearing to all views, and stating "Apart from anything else, we are bringing Senator Brookhart to New York in order to educate him." The Senator might be "bumptious and aggressive, but I think that we will do him more good than he does us harm." Warburg replied that while he believed that a variety of opinions ought to be heard, he did not think the privilege of addressing the Council should be extended to a mere demagogue. He was particularly perturbed to hear that the Senator had been bragging around Washington about his invitation to speak to a "Wall Street Club."

Armstrong took the precaution of looking over Brookhart's speech beforehand. One emendation proved necessary. Instead of asking "this Council" to support his position he should ask "you," inasmuch as the Council as such did not take stands. As it turned out, Brookhart's appearance was a great success. Afterward, Armstrong sent copies of his correspondence with Warburg to several of the Council's directors, and received letters supporting his position from Whitney Shepardson and Isaiah Bowman, Director of the American Geographical Society and a member of the Editorial Advisory Board of *Foreign Affairs*. Bowman's letter is one of those pure expressions of the Establishment mind.

> Nothing could be sillier than the attitude of the correspondent who wrote Warburg. It fills one with despair to see the same sort of people ducking the same old issues. It was thus from the foundation of the world. What has Wall Street to gain by refusing to hear even

a demagogue? Certainly if he is a dangerous demagogue we ought all the more to hear him in order to discover why he is dangerous and just how dangerous he is. The correspondent's views are just the sort that the liberals everywhere are so terribly anxious to obtain for exploitation. It is the way they think conservative capitalists behave. Well, here we see that they do behave that way! . . .

Now as a matter of fact and as it turned out, Brookhart is intensely interesting. I could not stay for the discussion of his paper, but all about me I heard the warmest expressions of satisfaction on account of the clearness of his thought and the vigor of his expression. Moreover, I personally have just as much faith in his plan as he has. In a sense the whole world is in revolt all the time. All that we care about is that it shall be a thoughtful revolt and a *gradual* one. In that sense, I am

Always revolutionarily yours,
Isaiah Bowman

Whether Brookhart was as enthusiastic about the Council as the Council was about Brookhart is not known. In any event, at the Council the policy of the open door remained intact.[5]

Through the triumph of this policy, or because controversial foreigners were easier to take, no one seems to have raised a fuss when a dinner was given for a delegation of five high-ranking Soviet officials. This was in early 1929, four years before the U.S. government saw fit to recognize the communist regime. The Soviets, visiting the country to obtain economic assistance in the form of investment and trading relationships, had reason to think that they might receive a reasonably sympathetic reception at the Council.

Coolidge, the country's leading expert on the Soviet Union, had visited Russia shortly after the revolution, and had, under the anonymous designation "K", written an article which appeared in the first issue of *Foreign Affairs*, urging U.S. recognition of the Soviet government. "Shall we refuse to sell sorely needed farm instruments to the Russian peasants because we dislike the Moscow Soviet? To recognize the government of a country does not imply that we admire it, it is merely to take note of an existing fact." The article did not escape the notice of the Soviet authorities. The Council today has in its possession their copy, with a number of passages, including the above, marked in Lenin's own hand.

Whatever the members of the Soviet delegation expected from their meeting at the Council, they soon found that they had ventured into a capitalists' lions' den. According to a letter written by the Council's Executive Director, Walter H. Mallory, to Isaiah Bowman, who had not been able to attend,

> We had a most interesting, free and frank discussion of the history, progress, and plans of the present Russian government. Many embarrassing questions were asked, and a sincere effort was made to answer them. This was not an easy task for our Russian friends, who found it difficult to square principles with practice.

Council members pressed the Soviets on their views of private property and world revolution, and the repudiation of the obligations of previous Russian governments. "Since all the guests were avowed communists," Mallory wrote, "you can readily see that an answer to these questions which would entirely satisfy an American banking audience, would inevitably discredit them at home." Without hedging Marxist principles, the guests urged the audience to focus on the acts, not the words, of their government. No amount of propaganda, they emphasized, would cause revolution if the workers were contented, as they were in the United States. "I carried away a feeling," Mallory concluded, "that practice is swinging away from principle; but this may be due to the peculiar mission of our guests, who, while still advocating Marxian doctrine, come to the leading capitalist country to get help. Obviously, if they get it, it must be on the terms of capitalism."[6]

However much the Soviets managed to allay their hosts' fears, the effort did not go unappreciated at the Council. The following year, at ceremonies inaugurating the Council's new home on East Sixty-Fifth Street,* President Davis spoke of an increasing recognition of global interdependence, citing as hopeful evi-

---

*In 1945, the Council moved into its third, and present, home, the former Harold Pratt mansion at 58 East 68th Street.

dence the mutual consultations of business and government leaders from all countries, "Soviet Russia included."

"The growth of this attitude of taking counsel together," Davis said, explained the existence of the Council. The members ("men of all political faiths, men of all professions") were drawn together "in search of the facts, often hard to get at, which underlie international situations." That independent quest for the facts, in no way related to official government policy making, was "the inevitable accompaniment of the influence which public opinion now exerts on foreign policy."

The Council on Foreign Relations arose in the wake of a war of incredible devastation whose causes were obscure. Rulers and politicians, machinating behind the scenes and orating in front of them, seemed to bear sole responsibility; private citizens and institutions had simply suffered. The animating hope of the Council was that organizations like itself, conducting, in Davis's words, "scientific study outside of the chancelleries," could counteract the tendency of national governments to embroil society in such senseless wars. This hope was expressed in *The New York Times* by reporter P. W. Wilson, in an article marking the 1930 dedication ceremonies. The Council, Wilson noted, was a fact-finding and fact-interpreting organization, not a peace society.

> But it is a fair comment that if there had been such a network of organizations as these before the war, working with a League of Nations, the history of mankind would have been very different from what it became. The mere fact that specialists are watching events at first hand, not excluding intrigues wherever these are attempted, is in itself a certain safeguard against the secret fermenting of a perilous crisis. *It means that finance and industry, the universities and the churches, all the agencies that depend upon and advocate stability of foreign relations, are, as it were, on the inside, not on the doorstep only, of executive authority.* (italics added)

Bucking Isolationism

In the Council's second decade of existence, with war brewing in Europe, American isolationism remained the principal preoccupation. As John Campbell recalled in his retirement speech, "The generation which came to maturity in the 1930s had a Versailles complex and later a Munich complex and was locked in a battle with isolationism." Early in the decade, with the world in deep depression, the issue was posed in economic terms: whether a healthy economy could be achieved through liberal trade policies or through seeking national self-sufficiency, as implied in the restrictive Smoot-Hawley tariff of 1930. The rise of European fascism provoked a more general attack at the Council on the isolationist threat. "You have," Campbell pointed out, "only to look at the books being published by the Council on Foreign Relations in those years. This was a nonpartisan organization, but the leading lights of the Council were certainly taking a stand. 'Can We Be Neutral?' by Allen W. Dulles and Hamilton Fish Armstrong. Answer: No. 'We or They?' by Hamilton Fish Armstrong. Answer: We, but if we don't watch out, it might be they."

The Council pursued its mission by extending its activities in a variety of directions. It published more books and pamphlets, and it undertook a modest studies program complete with fellowships for promising young scholars. It also began running seminars for junior executives, a program which lapsed during World War II, but was revived in 1953 as a useful fund-raising tool. The most interesting of the Council's new endeavors, however, was the establishment of "Committees on Foreign Relations" around the country.

The idea arose from discussions, in 1937, between the Council's Executive Director, Walter Mallory, and Frederick P. Keppel, the energetic head of the Carnegie Corporation. The two agreed that the Council, with Carnegie's financial backing, would establish a number of mini-Councils to promote, in Mallory's words, "the serious discussion of international affairs by leading citizens in widely separated communities."[7] Like the Council, these committees would be devoted solely to the education of their members, that is, no lobbying; they would also be autonomous bodies, independent of their New York progenitor.

Committees were initially set up in Cleveland, Detroit, Denver, Des Moines, Houston, Louisville, St. Louis, and Portland, Oregon. They held periodic meetings at which a distinguished visitor, dispatched by the Council, would hold forth on topics of international importance. Early riders of the Committee circuit included such Council bigwigs as John W. Davis, Isaiah Bowman, Whitney Shepardson, Hanson Baldwin of *The New York Times,* and Allen and John Foster Dulles. Among the topics addressed were "The Tradition of American Political Isolationism vis-a-vis Europe," "The Closing Door in the Far East," "America's Overseas Trade and Investment," "The Desire of the American People to Keep out of War and in Case of War Abroad to Remain Neutral," and "World Rearmament."

The establishment of the Committees was a natural expression of the Council's sense of itself as more than a local body with more than local perspectives and responsibilities. Back at the time of the Brookhart affair, Armstrong had invited Governor Frank Lowden of Illinois to New York for the Senator's address. "We are," wrote Armstrong, "particularly anxious to have you accept our invitation because the Council on Foreign Relations aims to be not merely a New York organization, but one exercising a country-wide influence on matters of American foreign policy." From the first, the Council had included "nonresident" members from other parts of the country; in 1936, there were 250 of them, as against 400 resident members. The Committees were an ideal mechanism for projecting its voice, and extending its approach, across the land.

Some wanted no part of the voice. The Chicago Committee collapsed when its influential chairman, General Robert E. Wood, became a leading America Firster. Others did not appreciate the subtleties of the approach. In 1940, at the second annual conference held in New York for Committee representatives, there was strong feeling that the time for talking was over. As

Percy Bidwell, the Council's Director of Studies, observed, "These groups, judging by the remarks of their representatives, are in the mood to go ahead and do something, and they are looking to the Council for leadership in a program."[8] The idea of presiding in any formal way over an interventionist propaganda machine dismayed Council leaders, and they quickly persuaded their guests to abandon the notion.

After Pearl Harbor, however, there was hope that the Committees would help avert a revival of the isolationist spirit of the interwar period. Wrote Bidwell, "These Committees, and others that the Council may be able to establish, are fitting themselves to give much-needed leadership to popular discussion. No such groups of well-informed, representative citizens, keenly interested in our foreign relations, were in existence in 1918. This time we shall be better prepared to 'win the peace.' "[9] But winning the peace required more than the Committees.

Hardly had war broken out in Europe in 1939 than Mallory and Armstrong hurried down to Washington to propose that the Council undertake on behalf of the State Department an investigation into the likely effects of the war, and subsequent peace settlement, on U.S. interests and policy. The Council had always been on good terms with the Roosevelt administration. President Roosevelt personally shared the Council's view of the world, and its cultural milieu was his own; indeed, the Council's headquarters on Sixty-fifth street were next door to the town house Roosevelt lived in when Governor of New York. Less than a year into his presidency, Roosevelt had two of his chief officials—Henry Wallace, the Secretary of Agriculture, and Lewis Douglas, Director of the Budget Bureau—participate in the Council's study group on national self-sufficiency, out of which emerged the trade-liberalizing Export-Import Bank and Trade Agreements Act of 1934. Thus, it was hardly surprising that the State Department, lacking the necessary funds and personnel, should have accepted the Council's offer to do its planning. What *is* striking, in retrospect, is the poverty of the Department's own resources. Policy planning staffs, not to mention the national intelligence agencies, were things of the future.

It was to be "The Inquiry" all over again, only on a grander scale. Funds for "War and Peace Studies" were obtained from the Rockefeller Foundation, and the work divided into five areas: (1) economic and financial problems; (2) strategic and security planning; (3) territorial problems; (4) political problems; and (5) peace aims. By war's end, one hundred people would have participated in the production of 682 classified memoranda for the government. At first, the Studies groups pretty much set their own course as they examined such issues as Japanese expansionism and what to do about Greenland when the Germans took over Denmark. After the United States entered the war, however, the administration set up an interagency Advisory Committee on Postwar Foreign Policy to manage the research program. The Council was thus effectively mobilized into the government. Early each week the study groups would meet in New York; their research secretaries would then travel down to Washington to report to the Advisory Committee, and receive advice and instruction. There was some resentment of the Council's role within the State Department, but since several of the Council's biggest fish—including Armstrong and Bowman —had themselves taken wartime jobs at State, it was ineffectual.

Although the Council's founding fathers could not be sure of it, the long-awaited day was dawning: when America would assume the full burden of its international role. So hoped Bowman in a letter written to Armstrong a week after the United States entered the war. "To the degree that the United States is the arsenal of the Democracies, it will be the final arsenal at the moment of victory. It cannot throw the contents of that arsenal away. *It must accept world responsibility.* The measure of our victory will be the measure of our domination after victory."[10]

Waging the Cold War

As the war drew to a close, Council members—in study groups and within the government—played leading roles in planning the architecture of the postwar world: the reconstruction of Germany and Japan, the founding of the United Nations, the establishment of the International Monetary Fund and the World Bank. There was no grand design. As John Campbell recalled, "Policy grew from events rather than blueprints." If there was a single overriding concern, it was to avoid the mistakes of the Versailles Treaty, which had laid such a heavy material and psychological burden on the defeated powers of World War I. The task was exciting. For young men like Campbell, "this was something of a heroic period, and the heroes were Truman, Acheson, Marshall, Lovett, Harriman, McCloy."

What made it all possible was the enlistment of the bulk of the Republican party on the side of the internationalist angels. This was achieved through the conversion, in 1945, of Senator Arthur K. Vandenberg, one of the leading Republican isolationists, to the cause of internationalism. With the zeal of the recently enlightened, Vandenberg toured the country urging support for a powerful United Nations. After the 1946 elections, he was instrumental in getting a Republican-controlled Congress to bless the whole range of Truman foreign policies: a British loan package, aid to Greece and Turkey, the Marshall Plan, the NATO treaty. The era of bipartisanship in foreign policy had begun and, for the nonpartisan Council on Foreign Relations, nothing could have been finer.

Senator Joseph McCarthy brought the heroic period to a sour end. All manifestations of "internationalism" in American life became suspect. As the backlash grew, the Council became increasingly concerned about resurgent isolationism. After the 1950 elections, it behaved more intimately with the federal government than propriety should have allowed by undertaking a private poll for the administration of fifty of its leading Committee members across the country, asking them to assess the attitudes of the citizens in their states towards American foreign policy.

But a new isolationism did not take hold. McCarthyism was in many respects a phenomenon of Republican party politics: a rearguard action against the party's repositioning on foreign policy. And for all the havoc wreaked by McCarthy and his allies both inside and outside the government, the broad course of policy was not changed. In fact, the McCarthyites were not in a position to reverse the trend. Although their anger was directed against the traditional enemies of isolation—Wall Street, Eastern fancypants, and intellectuals—the specific sins charged were sins of insufficient intervention, not the opposite: the "losses" of China and Eastern Europe to communism.

Put simply, the two currents of American opinion on foreign policy—America First nativism and prointerdependence globalism—now flowed together. This was partly the result of the country's enormous strength following the war. The United States could enter the community of nations while at the same time remaining indisputably "first." Assuming international responsibilities did not, as it had after World War I, seem excessively to menace American autonomy.

Above all, there was the Communist threat. Resistance to the more humanitarian forms of foreign aid gave way before the ready argument that this was designed to hold off the Russians. Indeed, in many quarters this was the only argument that worked. As one member of the Seattle Committee on Foreign Relations told Per Jacobssen, economic advisor to the Bank for International Settlements, at a 1947 meeting, "You are a curious person. You try to sell the Marshall Plan on its merits instead of talking about defense against Communism."[11]

Stopping communism was equally important in the Council's own purlieus. In 1947, George Kennan, (writing anonymously as "X") articulated the U.S. policy of containment in perhaps the most influential article ever to appear in *Foreign Affairs*. Council members were deeply involved in the original Committee on the Present Danger, which lobbied heavily for increased military preparedness just prior to the Korean conflict. Such men regarded the McCarthyite witch hunting as a misguided distraction from the real business at hand. The Communist danger was to be found not at home but abroad, and the country had to face up to the task of fighting it there.

The Council itself, remarkably enough, came through the McCarthy period relatively unmarked. Whether through oversight, because he was warned away, or for some other reason, Senator McCarthy leveled no attacks against it, although he could hardly miss hitting a number of its members. The Council thus fared better than many of its fellow Establishment institutions.

And if anything, the episode only strengthened the kind of approach to foreign policy making most congenial to the Council. As Arthur Schlesinger, Jr., has pointed out, the ultimate effect of the McCarthyite assault was to discredit Congress as an active participant in foreign policy; "bipartisanship" became the watchword of a Congressional rubber stamp on the initiatives of an increasingly imperial presidency. With foreign policy substantially removed from the arena of partisan combat, the Council was free to pursue its nonpartisan course without fear that the views of its members were at odds with those of the country at large. It could also expect that such enlightenment as it might summon would readily be translated into policy by friendly, familiar, and politically unfettered government officials.

The heady days of the war and the immediate postwar period were, of course, irrecoverable, and the Council resumed business as usual, holding meetings with distinguished guests, unofficially worrying the problems of the moment. It also expanded its studies program, with $1.5 million from the Ford Foundation, and half a million each from Rockefeller and Carnegie. It became, at least according to one observer, "the most important single private agency conducting research in foreign affairs."[12] And its importance did not stop there. As a membership organization with many of its own working for the government, the Council came to serve as a recruiting center for

middle and upper level positions in the new and expanded foreign policy institutions of the postwar world, from transnational enterprises like the World Bank and NATO to the bur-
geoning apparatus of national agencies concerned with
diplomacy, defense, and intelligence. "Whenever we needed a
man," John McCloy once said, "we thumbed through the roll of
Council members and put through a call to New York." When
President Kennedy took office, he had at hand a list of prospec-
tive State Department officials; sixty-three of the first eighty-
two names belonged to members of the Council.

To be sure, the experts did not always agree; consensus, like
other forms of social harmony, is always more perceptible in
retrospect than at the time. In 1957, the Council published the
young Henry Kissinger's *Nuclear Weapons and Foreign Policy,* a
broad-gaged critique of "massive retaliation"—the strategic policy of the Eisenhower administration. Kissinger's book created
a stir, but the debate was essentially in-house, as between friends
who share a common perspective. After all, John Foster Dulles,
Eisenhower's Secretary of State and longtime Council eminence, had enunciated the doctrine of massive retaliation in an
on-the-record speech at the Council in 1954. And *Nuclear Weapons
and Foreign Policy* was the product of Kissinger's two-year stay
at the Council as resident scholar in charge of a study group
devoted to the subject.

There was no disagreement about the monolithic nature of
the Communist world or about America's obligation fully to
confront its immediate and omnipresent threat. The dispute
was over tactics, not principles, a question of nuance compared
with the deep philosophical confrontation between internationalism and isolationism of earlier decades. Foreign policy seemed
to have come down to such nuances, however important, and in
the view of many Council members the democratic process was
badly equipped to handle them. The aging ex-Progressive Walter Lippmann, for example, had taken to disparaging public
opinion as an instrument of foreign policy, while George Kennan, the former ambassador to the Soviet Union, argued that it
should be left in the hands of trained diplomats.

This elitism was not universally shared. Henry Wriston, president of Brown University and president of the Council from 1951 to 1964, defended democratic decision making in *Diplomacy in a Democracy,* a book he privately subtitled "The hell with George Kennan" and "The hell with Walter Lippmann." Wriston asserted that the people could be convinced, and trusted, on the big issues. The question was already decided, however, for in the late fifties and early sixties the people and the foreign policy elite were of one mind. The fruit of this consensus, and the agent of its demise, was Vietnam, the bitter climax of America's postwar foreign policy. That war shook the Council as it had never been shaken before, and it is still recovering from the effects.

The Era of Bad Feeling

It would have been too much to expect the Council to take any sort of lead in mobilizing opposition to, or even raising questions about, the Vietnam war. The Council's disposition had always been to impress upon the country its international responsibilities, and Vietnam certainly seemed one of them; opposition to the war looked at first like only isolationist irresponsibility *redux.* Moreover, so many past and present prosecutors of the war—the brothers Bundy and Rostow, General Maxwell Taylor, Ambassador Henry Cabot Lodge, Secretary of State Dean Rusk—were active and prominent Council members who showed up regularly in New York to give pep talks on the progress of the fighting. In 1965, when a national "Committee for an Effective and Durable Peace in Asia" was formed to support President Johnson's Vietnam policy, its members included Council director Arthur Dean (as chairman) and Council Chairman John McCloy, Vice-President David Rockefeller, and Treasurer Gabriel Hauge.

Doubts did not begin to be heard until 1967. At a December meeting, George Ball, who had been a voice murmuring in the wilderness before and after his resignation from the Johnson administration in 1965, spoke out in a gentlemanly way against U.S. involvement. But for the Council, as for American society at large, serious disaffection set in only after the Tet offensive of early 1968. Now it began to be clear that the war was going nowhere.

Hamilton Armstrong wrote critically of the war in *Foreign Affairs*. With President Johnson's announcement of de-escalation (along with his decision not to run for another term) at the end of March, a negotiated settlement became the order of the day; in meetings and study groups, the Council began to conjure seriously with the problems of Vietnam. But the Council's mannerly way of life, with its unspoken assumptions about the good will and good faith of all members, was ill suited to the passions and deep divisions which Vietnam provoked. Even within its boardroom, the postwar consensus was breaking apart. And in the world outside—on campuses and in Congress—voices were being raised which the Council did not care to ignore. Retaining civility without losing touch was a tough act.

From 1969 to 1970 the Council tried to stay in touch by running a series of meetings on dissent. One of the speakers, the organizer of the Vietnam Moratorium Committee, Sam Brown, disarmed his jumpy audience by noting at the outset of his address that half the faces he saw in front of him belonged to people he had picketed.

In addition, a thoroughgoing attempt was made to infuse the membership with new blood. Younger men and more blacks were hustled through the rather intricate election process; in 1970, against the bitter resistance of some of the old guard, the Council opened its doors to women. All this reflected the broad imperatives of reform the 1960s impressed on most American institutions. At the Council, it had the effect of bringing in both active critics of U.S. Vietnam policy like Daniel Ellsberg and

David Halberstam, and numerous others unburdened with the policies and preconceptions of the past.

Finally, the Council tightened ship by combining into one office the positions of executive director and (previously unsalaried) president. Bayless Manning, a fresh face from the West, left the Deanship of the Stanford Law School to become the Council's first full-time president. Manning was known to be unsympathetic to U.S. involvement in Vietnam.

Under the new dispensation, the Council became a less clubby, less genteel place. A certain testiness developed between hawks and doves; expressions of outright hostility were occasionally directed at apologists for the war. But to a number of the livelier and newer members the change in atmosphere amounted to little. Stanley Hoffmann, a Harvard government professor, told an interviewer in 1971, "Discussion is bland. They're polite but unresponsive. It's like punching an eiderdown."[13] That same year John Kenneth Galbraith resigned "out of boredom." Dissatisfaction with the Council's stuffiness extended to its periodical. In 1970, in order to counter the ponderous *Foreign Affairs*, Hoffmann and several younger Council members helped found a more upbeat journal in the field, *Foreign Policy*, issued under the auspices of the Carnegie Endowment for International Peace.

As it happened, the biggest internal fight at the Council concerned the choice of a new editor for *Foreign Affairs*. In 1971, the directors announced the selection of William P. Bundy to succeed Hamilton Fish Armstrong, who was due to retire the following year after rounding out his half-century with the magazine. The announcement angered several of the Council's young doves; Bundy, as Assistant Secretary of State for East Asian and Pacific Affairs during the Johnson administration, had been deeply involved in planning the escalation of the war in Vietnam. Professor Richard Falk of Princeton and Richard Barnet of the Institute for Policy Studies quickly mounted a protest. Meetings were held and letters written.

The charge against Bundy was immorality—in prosecuting

and defending an immoral war while in office, and in refusing to admit the error of his ways afterwards; and the Council's directors were themselves morally obtuse in making the appointment. More fundamentally, the dissidents felt that the whole business was the result of the Council's refusal to abandon its old-boy style. Bundy, with his Brahmin roots and Groton/Yale schooling, seemed to symbolize all that was wrong with the best and the brightest. It also turned out that David Rockefeller, the new Chairman, had offered him the job at the 1970 Harvard-Yale game—tentatively but without authorization. What really counted were connections. As Rockefeller remarked, "Why, I know all the Bundys, and they're a fine, upright family."[14]

The tempest took the directors by surprise. With liberal academics lining up against Bundy, there was the disturbing prospect of a mass professorial defection from the Council's ranks. But then pro-Bundy forces in academe began to materialize. "McCarthyism of the left" was charged. Resignations were threatened if the Board backed down. In the end, it stuck to its guns and reaffirmed the decision. No mass resignations occurred. The Bundy affair subsided, less important in itself than as a symptom of the personal and political strains which the Vietnam period inflicted on the country's foreign policy community.

Not only internally did the strains begin to tell. With Vietnam, foreign policy became a subject of partisan conflict in a way that it had not been since before World War II, and this made some of the Council's more sensitive leaders leery of continuing the postwar pattern of easy familiarity with the national administration. In 1972, for example, Hamilton Armstrong decided to boycott the gala dinner held in September to celebrate the Council's fiftieth anniversary—at which he was to be specially honored. Armstrong, the most gentlemanly of men, objected to the dinner's being held at the Americana Hotel, now the Sheraton Center; it was, he said in a letter to Bayless Manning, "a shoddy and commercialized place," unworthy of the Council. His decision not to show up, however, was based on the scheduling of Secretary of State William Rogers as principal speaker.

> The idea of involving the Council in a spectacular affair like this in the middle of what will be an intensely bitter campaign, and with the country split on a number of crucial issues, is most unfortunate. Rogers himself will not add intellectual distinction to the occasion, and he is known, in addition, to be without much influence on policy. To become involved with the Nixon Administration at this time seems to me to be bad judgment.

Armstrong's particular concern was, as it had always been, to maintain the purity of his journal. "The Council organization may not feel that it matters if it identifies itself with the Nixon administration in the middle of an electoral campaign; in my opinion it matters a great deal, and I would not want 'Foreign Affairs' to be involved."

A certain uneasiness did characterize the Council's relations with the White House. An observer, in 1969, might not have expected this. After all, Nixon himself had aired his views on foreign policy two years previously in a lead article in *Foreign Affairs*. And the President had chosen as his national security advisor Henry Kissinger, the Harvard professor whose career had been launched in the Council's bosom.

But Nixon hated the world of the Council, with its smooth patrician manner and aura of inherited wealth and status. Throughout his life, he had suffered under its real and imagined slights. On becoming president, Nixon apparently decided that there would be no more occasions for slighting him. Thus, while he offered high government positions to the right big shots, he refused to give them the opportunity to bargain directly, or to turn him down to his face. Twice, at the beginning of each term, he offered the Treasury secretaryship to David Rockefeller, but was never, said Rockefeller in an interview, "willing to talk to me about it unless I first agreed. . . . He didn't want to have that direct discussion. To me it was a very strange way of employing a person for a major job in the country." To the David Rockefellers, Richard Nixon remained as he had always been: an aloof outsider, a strange bird.

Kissinger himself stayed away from the Council during his years in office. No doubt this was partly a calculated effort to demonstrate his loyalty to Richard Nixon. Kissinger was distrusted at the White House for having been the protege, tutor, and confidant of Nelson Rockefeller; the Council was Rockefeller territory, and Kissinger had every reason to avoid emphasizing the connection. But there was more to it than that; for, even after Nixon's resignation, when with Nobel Prize in hand he dominated the cabinet of an administration which had Rockefeller as vice-president, Kissinger did not choose to darken the Council's door.

The Secretary of State was angry at the Council for what he regarded as breach of support. According to David Rockefeller, always Kissinger's most sanguine interpreter, the problem had to do with "some very vocal and vitriolic members of the Council" who made no secret of their hostility to Kissingerian foreign policy. "I think when he thought of the Council, therefore, he thought of those who had created problems for him, rather than a very large group who supported him and his views. I certainly was one of them and think if you would ask him, he would agree that that was the case. But I think that he was piqued by the fact that there were several prominent members of the Council who took very strong positions against him." Among the opponents was Council Pooh-bah and long-time Treasurer, the crusty and intellectual commercial banker Gabriel Hauge.

Vice-President John Temple Swing did not entirely agree with David Rockefeller. "Henry never knew how many people here disagreed with what he was doing." And there was pique on both sides, and feelings of ingratitude. "Kissinger owed his career to the Council, but he never set foot here the whole time he was in office.* He is, as you know, extremely arrogant."

Swing believed that Kissinger, despite his long association with the Council, never really appreciated the Council's role of providing a forum for criticism of government policies. Just as he was bitter at being criticized by former colleagues in the

*Not quite true. In 1969, Kissinger showed up at a black-tie dinner to explain White House policy.

academic world, so he fumed at the Council for failing to provide the backing he felt he was owed. Kissinger had always
subscribed to a "Great Man" theory of diplomacy. In his book
on nuclear strategy he attacked the American proclivity for
putting foreign policy in the hands of businessmen and lawyers.
Businessmen, he argued, were too devoted to mere good management; lawyers, to compromise. A truly first-class foreign
policy, he seemed to think, could only be created by a brilliant
and tough statesman. When such a one came along, he should
be given as free a hand as possible. If they wished to be useful,
lesser mortals—and agencies like the Council—should offer
their support.

The great man carried grudges. In 1975, the head of the Council's Meetings Program, Zygmunt Nagorski, angered Kissinger
by inviting Sergio Segre, the Italian Communist party's leading
foreign policy spokesman, to attend a Council conference on
Italian-American relations. U.S. law required that members of
Communist parties receive a special waiver from the State Department before being permitted to enter the country. Nagorski
had not checked with State before inviting Segre. Rather, he had
made the case publicly—in an interview with an Italian journal
and in an op-ed piece for *The New York Times*—for opening U.S.
borders and establishing contact with Western Euro-Commu-
nists. Nagorski's efforts created a furor in Italy and received
considerable attention elsewhere, both at home and abroad. The
suspicion was widespread that Nagorski was quasi-officially
(What, after all, was the Council but a quasi-official arm of the
government?) signaling a softer U.S. line towards the Italian
Communists.

Nothing could have been further from the truth. The Secretary of State was busily beating the drums to warn of a Euro-
Communist threat, and issuing apocalyptic predictions about
what would happen if the Italian Communist party joined—as
it later, and rather uneventfully, did—a coalition government.
Kissinger was furious at the Council for, as he thought, undermining his position. He permitted no State Department waiver
to be issued. Even more, he tried to get David Rockefeller, the

Council chairman, to fire Nagorski. This Rockefeller refused to do, although he felt it had been "unwise" to invite Segre without first checking with State. While, in his view, the Council should "be encouraged to invite anybody they want to speak," it should not create problems for the government.

After leaving office, Kissinger, with pique intact, took to remarking that he had been the first Secretary of State never to have been invited to address the Council—a gratuitous fib which greatly irked Council staffers. Throughout his term at the State Department, he always, with one excuse or another, begged out of repeated invitations. Only once did he agree to speak and then, with 700 members signed up to attend, had backed out at the last minute. For all this, Kissinger liked to suggest, even to those who knew better, that he had been ostracized at the Council during his government service. "It really is strange," said David Rockefeller, "that he sometimes still implies that."

In Search of a New Consensus

In 1971, shortly after taking over as president of the Council, Bayless Manning told a reporter, "We're moving into a period when we don't have any idea what we're doing in foreign relations. Vietnam was the last spasm of one way of looking at the world. The Council's role, as I envision it, will be to help the country evolve a new consensus."[15]

Institutions often try to forge ahead by looking to recapture a glorious past. Having discovered what seemed a turning point in American foreign policy, the Council, hearkening back to its War and Peace Studies of World War II (which in turn hearkened back to The Inquiry), decided to undertake another feat of postwar planning. The new endeavor, called "The 1980s Project," emerged out of a Council working group on International Order which met from 1971 to 1973 under the direction of Miriam

Camps, Senior Research Fellow and former vice-chairman of the State Department's Policy Planning Council.

Camps set the stage for the project by turning the working group's discussions into a monograph, "The Management of Interdependence."[16] Her feeling was that the search for a new foreign policy consensus ("now underway") was best pursued by focussing on "the kind of international system toward which we should be seeking to nudge things." She contrasted this approach to one which tried to chart the future simply by looking at America's *national* interests.

Overall, Camps argued for a world whose increased interdependencies would be managed not by a handful of great powers or by a single world government, but by a flexible set of regional associations, international processes of consultation, and transnational organizations. No longer willing to serve as the world's policeman and unable to exercise the economic hegemony of the postwar period, the United States had to join with its industrial allies to lead the way to this promised land, not in order to recover an irretrievable dominance, but simply to insure the health and survival of a global community whose fate was inseparable from its own.

Current American foreign policy met with her disapproval. The goal of Nixon, Kissinger, and Treasury Secretary John Connally was not, she thought, to steer the world towards a more harmonious form of collective management but to free the United States to be the tough "manager" and "manipulator" of a new balance of power. This was shortsighted and destabilizing at a time when interdependence was leaching away the autonomy of the major industrial nations.

By the time "The Management of Interdependence" appeared, in 1974, the Council's 1980s Project was already off the ground. With Richard H. Ullman, director of the Studies Program, in charge, staff was enlarged, working groups organized, papers farmed out, and funds raised. (In due course, $1.3 million was supplied by the Ford, Lilly, Mellon, and Rockefeller Foundations.) Manning had announced the Project with considerable fanfare in the fall of 1973, and the following year he devoted the bulk of his annual report to it. A new international system was, he said, hard upon us, and the time was ripe for a systematic study of what it portended and what it might best become. Alluding to the Council's earlier War and Peace Studies, he warned that the public was not as disposed to rethink the world order as it had been at the close of World War II, but concluded, hopefully, that it "should not require the catastrophe of world war to provide the impetus for reevaluation."

Ullman aimed at promoting fresh and broader thinking about the world's problems. He sought out as authors younger scholars less habituated than their teachers to looking at the world in terms of American dominance. To insure a catholic perspective, he arranged for foreigners to write 20 percent of the Project's papers. Chairing the working groups, at which the papers were discussed and criticized were some of the leading lights of the liberal center: among others, Cyrus Vance, in between jobs at the State Department; Leslie Gelb, who directed the compilation of the Pentagon Papers; Father Hesburgh of Notre Dame; Harvard Professors Joseph Nye and Roger Fisher. The titles alone of some of the volumes which eventually appeared sufficiently indicate the Project's disposition: *Reducing Global Inequities, Sharing Global Resources, Enhancing Global Human Rights.*

All in all, the 1980s Project was the vehicle of that segment of the foreign policy community which Stanley Hoffman has described as wanting to return to the internationalist ideal which had been perverted by cold war "realism" and neglected by Kissingerian *realpolitik.* Hoffmann, one of the Project's most active participants, gave the following self-portrait.

It is a chorus of moderate activists, without hegemonic pretenses, eager to draw on the reservoir of American moralism on behalf of international cooperation. Like the progressives, these voices insist on the the importance of transnational and international forces, an old liberal dream; on the importance of the common problems of mankind, an old inclination to apolitical thinking; on the need for the United States no longer to confuse conservatism and stability, anti-Communism and democracy, again, the critique of American support to tyrannies, as in Kissinger's Chilean policy; on the need not to mistake the defense of capitalism and political democracy.[17]

Hoffmann's 1978 book, *Primacy or World Order,* was a kind of summary "white paper" of the 1980s Project.* The title named the alternatives for U.S. foreign policy. Hoffmann wanted world order, and led off with an attack on the recent Republican administrations—and Henry Kissinger, his former colleague, in particular—for pursuing primacy, with a stridently nationalistic tone to boot.

Interdependence was a fact of life; there was no way to avoid reliance on international institutions. The only sensible course was to accept the inevitability of "creeping globalism" and to adopt a "world order policy." The most that Hoffmann could bring himself to hope for, however, was a regime of "moderation plus": doing whatever possible within the current international system to minimize disruption while seizing such small opportunities as presented themselves to build up the world community. Throughout, Hoffmann emphasized the blocks and pitfalls impeding progress towards a more just and orderly world. By comparison even with Camps' small optimism, the book is the glummest of internationalist briefs.

But even Hoffmann was more hopeful than he should have been about the prospects for an American world order policy. Writing in the first year of the Carter administration, he saw the world out there as the chief impediment; American policy makers, he felt, had their priorities in order. "At home, most of our leaders and experts and what is left of our foreign policy elite agree on the main outlines of our action in the world."[18] But what seemed to him like an emergent consensus of enlightened internationalism was actually a pseudoconsensus on the verge of dissolution. On home turf itself, at the Council, it had not even been able to prevail.

---

*Hoffmann, in his preface, called the book "an illegitimate offspring" of the Project. The Council tried to get McGraw-Hill, publisher of both Hoffmann and the Project, to designate the separately contracted book as part of the Project, but the company refused, thinking this would hurt sales. So much for the public value of the Council's imprimatur.

Bundy vs. Kissinger

When Jimmy Carter was elected president, a number of the 1980s Project's strongest supporters on the Council's Board—Cyrus Vance, Michael Blumenthal, Marshall Shulman, Paul Warnke—left to join the new administration. (By long-standing rule, an official of the federal government cannot serve as a director of the Council.) Of the seven new directors who took office in 1977, only one had had any contact with the Project and several were downright unsympathetic to its approach to life. Foremost among those was Henry Kissinger, himself in many ways the Project's *bête noire*. David Rockefeller had entertained hopes of arranging for the former Secretary of State to take his place as chairman of the board, but hostility to Kissinger dissuaded him from making a direct proposal. Kissinger could not, however, be denied a place on the Board and, as an incoming director, he quickly took steps to make the Council more congenial to himself.

In the Council's upper reaches a certain unhappiness had arisen regarding Manning's performance as president. Word was out that he was a mediocre administrator, a poor fund-raiser (at a time when foundation support was drying up), an enthusiast who promised more than he delivered. Gently, Manning was shown the gate. By leaning heavily on David Rockefeller and his brother Nelson, Kissinger was able to get the succession to fall to one of his former aides, Winston Lord.

Lord, a Pillsbury heir, had been a Washington-based Foreign Service Officer and Defense Department analyst before being picked by Kissinger in 1969 to serve on the staff of the National Security Council. Hardworking and loyal, he was the only one of the group of five "house doves," as they were called, who stayed with Kissinger after the U.S. invasion of Cambodia in the spring of 1970.* After becoming Secretary of State, Kissinger

---

*The others were William Watts, Roger Morris, Anthony Lake, and Lawrence Lynn. See William Shawcross, *Sideshow* (New York, 1979), pp. 141–2.

made Lord director of the Department's Policy Planning Staff. Lord's ideological complexion was, like Manning's, broadly centrist, but there was a discernible difference between the two. In the words of a former Council staffer, "Bay was more interested in institutional change while Lord is a cruder cold warrior. Some of Kissinger has rubbed off on Win."

Thus, when the first of the Project's volumes began to appear in 1977, the Council found itself drifting away from the vision of world order which had inspired them. And, as publication proceeded through the next couple of years, there was growing disenchantment with the Project. Some of the criticism was well founded, and readily granted by those most intimately involved. The quality of the work, it was agreed, was uneven. Richard Ullman, who some felt had not helped matters by leaving the Project in 1976 to write editorials for *The New York Times*, believed that relying so heavily on outside authors had been a mistake. In his view, the Project's greatest shortcoming was its relative inattention to "multiple impacts"—the interrelationships among issues. A larger in-house staff, doing all the writing itself, could have had a better go at this most difficult of intellectual enterprises.

Part of the trouble, though, was that the Project had been oversold by Manning. The Council's Board felt let down when the studies failed to have the promised impact. The directors wanted to see a greater return on what had been a substantial investment. In the event, the product was anything but splashy. Prose tended toward the dull and academic; conclusions, toward the inconclusive. "All our authors," said Catherine Gwin, the Project's final director, "are very cautious and qualified." No grand design had been advertised, but people expected one anyway. What they got instead were incrementalist suggestions and hopes, creeping globalism. And that, finally, was not good enough. A visitor to the Council in the summer of 1979 would hear that the Project, then winding up, had been "naive," "too abstract," "too academic," and "insufficiently grounded in political realities." Those comments really indicated that the Project's time had passed.

Designed to peer ahead hopefully at an interdependent future, the 1980s Project closed its books with the future at hand —no closer to the projected goals, and in important respects further from them, than when it had begun. For all the multivalent assertiveness of the Third World, fifties-style bipolarism was on the rise. The hoped-for consensus had failed to materialize with a vengeance, and in some quarters, that hope was abandoned. James Chace, the managing editor of *Foreign Affairs*, wrote a lead article for the journal's Fall, 1978 number entitled "Is a Foreign Policy Consensus Possible?" Chace, a Francophile given to Gallic skepticism, argued that it was not. Never more than lukewarm about the 1980s Project anyway, he made a possible virtue of apparent necessity by asserting that a "disorderly world need not also be a more dangerous one."[19]

But it was harder to be sanguine about the actual dissensus that had developed. Inflation and energy shortage, the actual decline in U.S. economic power, and the widely perceived decline in U.S. prestige combined to invigorate the jingo strain in the American polity. As usual, the strain ran strongest within the Republican party. The growing strength of hard-line sentiment exerted a gravitational force on the princes of the Establishment. Here is David Rockefeller on the inadequacy of President Carter's foreign policy: "I think in part it is because some of his ideological objectives have been in conflict with . . . national objectives, particularly human rights versus basic national interests. And I think that where they come in conflict the resolution has differences from case to case . . . and the results have not always been good. Internationally it has led to a feeling that we didn't really have a foreign policy . . . and that we were not a very reliable party." The key phrase here is "national interests." In the stately progress of the Establishment mind, the movement was away from the accommodating, world-order approach of the 1980s Project and towards a more vigorous, self-interested assertion of American power.

So far, however, the movement was partial, troubled, and contested. David Rockefeller himself remained a staunch supporter of SALT II and, in the summer of 1979, was deeply critical of Senator Howard Baker for, as he thought, playing politics with the treaty. If he was not prepared to tax Henry Kissinger with the same sin, there were others who were.

"An intellectual disgrace" was Richard Ullman's private estimate of Kissinger's on-again, off-again support of the SALT treaty he had himself substantially negotiated, and this view was shared by other prominent figures. McGeorge Bundy, after leaving the Ford Foundation, went after Kissinger in a speech delivered in Switzerland at a conference of the London-based International Institute of Strategic Studies. As reported by Flora Lewis in *The New York Times,* Bundy, emphasizing the strength of the U.S. nuclear deterrent, took special care to point up recent Kissingerian flipflops on questions of weapons policy. Not that these had come as a surprise to him. Months earlier, before the former Secretary of State had addressed the subject publicly, Bundy remarked in private, "If I know Henry, he'll find three reasons why he can't support SALT now." Similarly his brother William went on the offensive; in the lead article of *Foreign Affairs'* Fall, 1979 issue, the editor took Kissinger to task by name and by implication no fewer than seven times for a variety of past and present positions.

As the 1980 presidential campaign loomed into view, Kissinger became a kind of focal point for the liberal Establishmentarian resistance, not only because of his ambivalent posture as chief Republican kibbitzer of SALT but also thanks to William Shawcross's book on U.S. policy in Cambodia, *Sideshow,* from which Kissinger emerged as chief villain. It depicted Kissinger as a snake nurtured at the breast of the Establishment, a man cynical enough to bomb small countries into oblivion just to give the B–52s something to do; to recommend from the sidelines exactly the limitation of presidential prerogative which, in office, he had hysterically opposed; to help bring on a brutish and destructive national debate on the conduct of U.S. foreign policy.

Kissinger did not exactly fall all over himself in an effort to correct the impression. Defending himself against Shawcross's account in a letter to *The Economist,* he denied wanting "to propagate a 'stab-in-the-back' thesis or launch a 'who-lost-Indo-china?' campaign"—then did exactly that: "Those whose pressures rigidly restricted American assistance to Cambodia, who cut off all American military action to help resist the Khmer Rouge, and who finally succeeded in throttling all aid to a still resisting country in 1975, cannot escape their responsibility by rewriting history."

Neither did the appearance of Kissinger's book of memoirs, *White House Years*, in the fall of 1979 do anything to still the troubled waters, certainly not as far as McGeorge Bundy was concerned. Among its numerous thumbnail sketches of famous people was an unflattering portrait of the man who had been Professor of Government and Dean of the Harvard Faculty when Kissinger was just a lowly graduate student and assistant professor, the man who had been a predecessor of his in the post of National Security Advisor:

> I admired his brilliance even when he put it, too frequently, at the service of ideas that were more fashionable than substantial. . . . He tended to treat me with the combination of politeness and sub-conscious condescension that upper-class Bostonians reserve for people of, by New England standards, exotic backgrounds and excessively intense personal style. . . . He was perpetually finding himself on the fashionable side, but at the very moment that fashion began to wane. A hawk on Vietnam, he was baffled by the demoralization of the Establishment whose maxims had produced the war; at heart he was a conservative whose previous associations had driven him into causes for which, ultimately, he had no passion.[20]

Perhaps smarting under these not so subtle suggestions of anti-Semitism and intellectual trendiness, Bundy summoned up his passion for a gloves-off attack on Kissinger in *Foreign Affairs*. Kissinger had claimed that the Nixon administration had made clear to the American people private assurances it had given President Thieu regarding U.S. enforcement of the 1973 Paris peace accords. Was this true? asked Bundy. The answer was no. Citing chapter and verse of available sources, Bundy concluded that "the public record and the private assurances are poles apart."[21]

Mission on Sixty-Eighth Street

What about another of the former Secretary of State's "remarkable claims": that his Vietnam policy would have succeeded "but for the collapse of executive authority as a result of Watergate." Kissinger was again dissembling. Congress was in full revolt before Watergate broke. "The simple truth is that the Cambodian bombing, not Watergate, quite literally *forced* the Administration to explain itself, and that the lameness of its explanation made congressional action inevitable."[22] The true meaning of Kissinger's apologia? "What we are left with is contempt for the clear opinion of the Congress, and ultimately for democracy itself."[23]

Meanwhile, William Bundy's *Foreign Affairs* article, a remarkable piece of Establishment adjuration, tried to hold off the recriminatory campaign that Kissinger was helping to stir up. Entitled "Who Lost Patagonia? Foreign Policy in the 1980 Campaign," it sought to set bounds for the expected Republican assaults on President Carter's foreign policy. Specifically, Bundy was concerned to protect Carter from the charge that he had "lost" Iran and Nicaragua. Not that U.S. policy towards either of those countries was beyond the reach of serious, responsible debate, but Bundy wanted at all costs to avoid a repetition of the Republican "Who lost China?" war cry of the early 1950s. And, "the gravest consequence of all, for the long term, could be the impact of a heated and intemperate debate in 1980 on the whole American approach to changes in the Third World."[24]

In effect, Bundy aimed at preventing the last phase of America's familiar twentieth-century cycle of war, immediate postwar idealism, and perfervid anti-Sovietism combined with domestic recrimination of less than hard-line Americans. Parallels with the period after World War II were striking. The idealism attending the establishment of the United Nations and the Marshall Plan was mirrored in the world-order sentiment which spawned the 1980s Project, as well as in the relatively accommodating foreign policy of the first three years of the Carter administration. Where once alliance with the Soviets had given way to cold war, now it was detente which was doing the same.

The call to rearm sounded by the original Committee on the Present Danger was repeated by its latter day reincarnation. McCarthyite denunciation of professors and bureaucrats found echo in the animadversions of old and new conservatives against a "new class" of intellectuals and professionals charged with undermining the American system by a virtually treasonous uncommitment to capitalism. The leap of the Red Army into Afghanistan—and the cautious response of many intellectuals and bureaucrats—seemed to signal that the cycle was complete.

But 1980 was not 1950. The world was manifestly more complicated. Vietnam had been a real lesson for Americans. Moreover, the memory of McCarthyism stood as a powerful roadblock to blacklisting and Redbaiting. As the new decade dawned, Henry Kissinger himself appeared to be moving away from political polemic. "I've made my own criticisms," he told the *Times'* James Reston, "and I may make them again on a philosophical level, but I think that if the Administration wanted to put together a really nonpartisan consensus and stop playing Mickey Mouse games with the Republicans, they'd have an obligation to cooperate . . . and so far as I have any influence, I would support such an effort."[25]

Still, all was not rosy at the Council. A small shiver went up its spine when George Bush, the Yankee patrician who had made his fortune and political career in Texas, resigned his membership and seat on the Board, claiming that the organization was too liberal. The former congressman and CIA director, whose failed run for the Republican presidential nomination had received the substantial blessing of Establishment Republicans, apparently found it too risky politically to be associated with a body which featured Henry Kissinger, stalwart Republican fundraiser, as a director, Kissinger's protégé Lord as president, and included among its members such lions of the hard line as William F. Buckley, Jr., Paul Nitze, the Rostow brothers Walt and Eugene, Irving Kristol, Norman Podhoretz, Patrick Moynihan, and Richard Pipes. This was an ominous sign. Had a rising tide of right-wing populism placed the Council, with its internationalist traditions, its dedication to reasoned discussion, and its hospitality to a wide range of views, beyond the Republican party's pale of acceptability?

Going Public

Under Winston Lord, the Council has sought a more prominent place for itself. "I am," says Lord, "anxious to influence the public debate." There have been some initiatives in public education: paperback editions (for use in schools) of *Foreign Affairs'* year-end summary issues, television programming, even press coverage of some Council meetings. "I am appalled at the lack of intelligent reporting of foreign affairs issues," laments vice-president John Swing. He and Lord would like to reach beyond the 100,000 readers of *Foreign Affairs* to the five million citizens who could, in their view, reasonably be expected to contribute to the public discussion of foreign policy.

The Council's principal concern, of course, is with the smaller elites which lie closer to hand. Lord regards the far-flung Committees, 70 percent of whose speakers are dispatched by the Council, as "our biggest asset," and he has made efforts to establish even closer ties with them. He has disseminated more information to the Council's own nonresident members and has urged them to come to New York more frequently. He has also moved his mountain to provincial Muhammads by arranging Council conferences in San Francisco and Boston, as well as by expanding the activities of the Council's Washington, D.C., office. The establishment of the latter by Manning in the last years of the Vietnam war really marked the beginning of the Council's current push for a higher profile.

The push has not had the unanimous support of Council insiders. In 1972, Hamilton Fish Armstrong's secretary was approached by the head of the new Washington outpost, offering to do promotional work for *Foreign Affairs.* This brought the office to the eminent editor's attention for the first time, and he was not at all pleased. He wanted no help with promotion, he testily wrote Manning. "I don't know the man's name, nor his knowledge of *Foreign Affairs,* nor his experience in dealing with newspaper editors. Many of these are friends of mine, and I prefer dealing with them myself." As far as the office itself was concerned, Armstrong felt sure that it would become known as a lobby; this was just the sort of "entanglement" in the "Washington political jungle" that he and his colleagues had, he claimed, been fighting for years. "I simply do not want the prestige and character of *Foreign Affairs* mixed up with anything that can be called political."

More recently, Zygmunt Nagorski has complained of the Council's growing proclivity for "the spectacular and the public relations." Nagorski, who retired as head of the Council's Meetings Program in 1978, feels that the Council best serves the country not as a public platform, of which there are many, but as a discreet forum where leaders can communicate with each other in a freer and more confidential way than they can in public view. Putting talks on the record is anathema to him.

But if it wants influence, the Council may no longer be able to rely on the closeted habits of the past. The growth of foreign policy study—in think tanks, universities, and government planning bodies—has created a cacophony of learned analysis and advice vying for the ear of policy makers. Moreover, the country as a whole has a far greater economic stake in foreign policy than it used to, from midwestern grain farmers to southwestern oilmen to farwestern high technologists. All this, together with the distrust of presidential leadership created by Vietnam and Watergate, has made foreign policy making as confused and congested a political activity as domestic policy making has always been. The bounds of Ham Armstrong's small and familiar world are burst. As John Campbell told his colleagues, "It makes you yearn for the good old days of the elitist system."

But, as Campbell went on, "you can't go home again." The Council's present leadership is prepared, at any rate, to act on the proposition. Lord wants to have working groups issue reports and take stands (!) on the issues they study. Efforts are under way to bring publications out more quickly and to promote them better. For Lord, the long-time bureaucrat, the fundamental question about a piece of Council work is, "Does this belong in the in-box of so-and-so in Washington?" This has meant turning the Studies Program away from the more distant horizons of the 1980s Project towards greater "policy relevance."

In former days, the Council's ability to achieve a more than regional perspective was a result less of the reality of national representativeness than of the aspiration to it. Now, after nearly a decade's worth of close attention to criteria of age, sex, race, ideological bent, and geography, the 1800 members of the Council really do constitute something like a national cross section. With only moderate exaggeration do its officers claim that the Council has transformed itself from an intellectual gentlemen's club to the select professional association of the country's foreign policy community.* Today, no policy implications can possibly be drawn merely from an observation that most of a given administration's top foreign policy appointees are members of the Council. Only the discovery that most were *not* members would be worthy of note. It would mean that the nation's foreign policy was in the hands of amateurs or neophytes.

The current trend is not out of line with a Paleyan mission; an established church ought to be both visible and inclusive. But there are dangers too. Publicity seeking and proportional representativeness have both tended to make the Council more like the political arena, with constituencies fighting it out for position. Growing politicization has another source as well.

That is the rise, within the foreign policy community, of forensic scholarship, in which professorial champions engage each other in partisan political battle. The emergence of the academician-politician (along with the actor-politician) is a token of this; the most notable manifestations are Henry Kiss-

---

*There remain members, some of recent vintage, who have no discernible professional involvement in foreign affairs. Good connections, or simply being an important person, can still do the trick.

inger and Senators Moynihan and Hayakawa. No one would deny professors the right to enter politics; in Europe a professorship is a normal route to high public office, and in America, academe has provided such distinguished public servants as Woodrow Wilson and the late Senator Paul Douglas of Illinois. But forensic scholarship, if it gets out of hand, can be an ugly and subversive game.

In the fall of 1979, with hard-line attacks on American foreign policy reaching new heights of acrimony, Leslie Gelb warned the readers of *The New York Times* that the right wing was in the process of destroying "the political center that used to provide the ballast for United States foreign policy." To support his proposition he cited, among other things, the following small incident.

> A few weeks ago at a conference of foreign-policy experts in Europe, one of these right-wing experts was asked to summarize the afternoon's discussion, which he proceeded to do with a total disregard for what was said. When challenged about these misrepresentations, he looked up and simply responded, *"C'est la guerre."*[26]

An institution like the Council cannot survive a war of that kind.

Hamilton Fish Armstrong, more than anyone else in the Council's history, understood that, for the Council as for his beloved *Foreign Affairs,* the appearance of disinterestedness was almost as important as the thing itself. Institutionally, both are threatened by the partisan machinations of experts. The institution is even more threatened when self-interest is seen to be lurking behind the arras.

In 1979 the Council was ill served when its chairman, David Rockefeller, together with Henry Kissinger, put public and private pressure on the Carter administration to allow the deposed Shah of Iran into the country, assertedly for both humanitarian reasons and reasons of state, although their efforts on behalf of the Shah appeared to have much to do with their personal friendship and Rockefeller's role as the Shah's banker. The redoubtable John J. McCloy, public servant and a former chairman of the Chase Manhattan Bank, added his weight to the campaign to persuade the President to admit the Shah. Joseph V. Reed, close personal aide to David Rockefeller and advance man for his business trips abroad, relayed the Shah's medical reports to the State Department.[27] And in November 1979, President Carter admitted the Shah to the United States for medical treatment—precipitating the seizure of the American Embassy in Teheran and the taking of fifty-three hostages.

It was a tragic blunder on the part of the President and his advisers. The Rockefeller-Kissinger-McCloy involvement seemed anything but disinterested.[28] It was the sort of thing about which Isaiah Bowman had warned—establishmentarians would play into the hands of people "terribly anxious" to expose their exalted pretensions. "It is the way they think conservative capitalists behave," said Bowman. "Well, here we see that they do behave that way."

Chapter 7

Big Business and

the Establishment

WHEN David Rockefeller arrives in Moscow, Budapest, or Belgrade, the local ruling elite turns out and lines up to meet him as though the true Prince of Capitalism had come, and not some mere politician. The Marxists believe that, when all is said and done, big business *is* the American Establishment.

But the actual relationship of big business to the Establishment in America is far more complex than the Marxists suppose. Most businessmen are in no sense members of the Establishment. What they are concerned about overwhelmingly is their own business. They are wary and suspicious of Washington, its politicians and bureaucrats; they shrink from government planning or regulation, and celebrate the market and the free-enterprise system. They distrust academic intellectuals and what they like to call "the media," which they accuse of being "antibusiness."[1] Charged by their critics with possessing too much power, businessmen complain of their *lack* of power to control not only the broad society but even their own businesses; they regularly insist that, on the contrary, they themselves are excessively controlled by government regulations and public pressures.[2]

At the turn of the century Henry Demarest Lloyd, the muckraker, warned that "this era is but a passing phase" in the evolution of "corporate Caesars."[3] But the closest thing this nation has known to corporate Caesars was that initial generation of tycoons, robber barons, and master builders that Lloyd knew, and we are left with largely unknown "managers," who enjoy a fairly short tour of duty at the top of their corporate bureaucracies and are soon gone into retirement. A lifetime spent in working one's way up the greasy corporate pole is usually a narrowing experience; it leaves the typical corporate chairman little time or energy to master the social, economic, and political problems of the nation or the world, which are the meat and drink of the Establishment. Indeed, to the extent that most American businessmen think about the Establishment at all, they doubtless regard themselves as anti-Establishment, anti-snob, anti-do-gooder, anti-Eastern, anti-double-dome: practical men attentive to their own business affairs.*

Obviously, however, this is not true of all American businessmen or financiers. There is a select group of business leaders who, in America, play the role which in Britain and other ancient European societies is performed by the aristocracy: they endow the Establishment with their prestige, power, grace, and money.

America's corporate aristos may be even more money minded, however, than their feudal counterparts abroad. The industrialists and big bankers of the American Establishment openly proclaim—and urge their more benighted colleagues to

---

*This is by no means a peculiarly American phenomenon among businessmen. Take this British example: "Believe me, my darling, there's nothing complicated about my viewpoint or any other sensible banker's, maligned as we always are. Horse-sense is what we need, horse-sense is what we admire, and horse-sense is what we have. Enough, thank you, consistently, to keep off you with your hearts too big for your heads and all those liberal young men . . . with guilty sociological consciences, Oxford accents, and economic theorists' doubtful rules of thumb." James Kennaway, *The Bells of Shoreditch* (London, 1963), p. 173.

recognize—the principle that corporate profits and growth are bound up with the health and growth of the nation (and "vice versa," as Engine Charlie Wilson of General Motors pointed out.)

Where, in these democratic times, the European nobles modestly imply that their benevolent social behavior is an obligation of their high birth and rank, American business executives customarily make explicit the doctrine that the doing of social good can be justified only if it is joined to their self-interest. Alexis de Tocqueville pointed out a century and a half ago that the American national philosophy is what he called "the doctrine of self-interest."

Americans need no instruction in that doctrine; it is considered common sense. Few feel any embarrassment in expressing the religion of self-interest. In 1926, one disciple of the creed, William Feather (publishing executive and contributor to *Nation's Business*) stated it plainly and unforgettably: "It is inconceivable to a one-hundred percent American that anyone except a nut would give something for nothing."[4]

Creed of Big Business

Such plain declarations of self-interest are too coarse for true establishmentarians. They prefer a more orotund tone. More important, they regard narrowly focused or cynical statements of self-interest as inimical to an appreciation of the interdependence of the public and private sectors. It is David Rockefeller himself who has described business as a public mission. A few years ago, he advised his fellow businessmen to accept their "social accountability" with pride, to regard it as an integral part of corporate conduct rather than a "philanthropic add-on." Only by doing so, he said, can business assure that it will "move forward within an acceptable framework of public purpose," and "only in that way will corporations assure the healthy social climate vital to their own future economic prosperity."

> If we are to come up with feasible and effective programs, we must do much more to develop cooperative undertakings that bring the enormously diverse talents of the business community to bear on the problems of our society. Problems such as pollution abatement, provision of good housing, and the need to supply adequate sources of energy are exceedingly complex and require concerted and dedicated action. Unless business takes a leadership role in creating workable solutions, it will only suffer with its environment. It will also abdicate to government and others much of its potential for a more positive position in our society.[5]

He called upon businessmen to "press forward on the national level to create broader and more viable long-range goals, to assess what business can and cannot do to meet those goals, and to set more comprehensive strategies to combine the strengths of public and private resources."[6] He declared that combining social responsibility with "the inherent strength of capitalism" would help Americans "to move toward our common objectives of economic viability, social progress, and personal fulfillment."

Such talk may seem vague to most businessmen. Skeptics in the corporate world insist that the crucial issue is how to achieve business's own interests and stave off public criticism. They ask: is the public interest really superior to private interests? If inefficiency and low profitability were deemed essential to the public interest, should business comply? How will the public be better served if businesses decay? Should government not promote and aid American businesses (as foreign governments help their enterprises) instead of regulating them to death?

Indeed, a David Rockefeller asks the same questions. The social-responsibilities creed is not taken to mean a lessening of concern for profit. On this point, the traditional free-enterprise creed and the modern social-responsibilities creed are harmonious. The universal business creed argues that higher profits *serve* the public interest, rather than conflict with it. Profits provide the funds for research and development and for investment in productivity-raising new plant and equipment. They enable the corporation to behave as a good citizen, creating more jobs and higher income, accelerating national economic growth, and strengthening the nation's security.

Certainly, some businessmen emphasize the importance of focusing on long-run, rather than short-run, profit. Good deeds paid for at the expense of immediate profits, they say, may sometimes be worth the short-run cost if they strengthen the corporation's long-term growth and public image. And they may extend this reasoning to corporate actions that sacrifice immediate gains for the sake of the national or the international economy (and ultimately expand their own markets.) But such sacrifices frequently prove to be mere rhetoric. Simon Ramo, a founder of Thompson Ramo Wooldridge (now TRW), remarked, "All businessmen on the make aim at maximizing short-run profits. They have no choice, given the day-to-day pressures they face. But when they have risen in the world, they start to talk about long-run profit maximization. They talk like statesmen. But the real secret that a businessman will tell only his best friend or his wife in bed is that he is still aiming at short-run profit maximization."

American businessmen, whether in or out of the Establishment, are determined not to seem soft on profits—or soft on foreign policy or anything else. The business culture is one that approves of toughness, executive boldness, and two-fistedness; this is why so many big businessmen at first favored John B. Connally for the Presidency in 1980.

Businessmen tend to take aggressive, nationalistic positions on foreign policy, even when they are heads of multinational corporations. They usually favor big defense budgets—an exception to their general opposition to big government spending. Even when they speak of their "social responsibilities," they usually deny that they intend to behave altruistically. In this respect, they have changed scarcely at all since the early days of the Republic. Tocqueville said the doctrine of self-interest found such universal praise among Americans that they often failed to do themselves justice. Like people everywhere, he thought, Americans sometimes gave way to "those disinterested and spontaneous impulses that are natural to men." But Americans would seldom "admit that they yield to emotions of this kind; they are more anxious to do honor to their philosophy than to themselves."[7]

A century later, when Americans—with a businessman, Paul Hoffman, in charge—moved to rescue a war-devastated Europe, they still insisted that they were only protecting their self-interest or, at best, their "mutual" interests with the Europeans. Ironically, many of these same hard-headed Americans were later outraged by the failure of the Europeans to show more gratitude for America's professedly nonaltruistic behavior.

Despite its wounded *amour propre*, however, the American Establishment recognized that its business interests were not only national but international, and did not retreat to isolationism.

Croly Rescues Hamilton

Industrialism after the Civil War helped bring the modern American Establishment into being by making business interests national and international, rather than only regional or local. In the 1880s, when Senator Sherman was campaigning for his antitrust act, he warned that society "is now disturbed by forces never felt before—the powerful forces of industrial growth and national integration." If Congress refused to safeguard competition, he said, there would soon be "a trust for every production and a master to fix the price for every necessity of life."

But Andrew Carnegie, that master builder of industry and the Establishment, considered vain the effort to preserve old atomistic and highly competitive market structures; if successful, they would be destructive of national interests. He said mass production involved heavy fixed charges on capital, and that a chaotic market would wreck huge industries, waste and deplete capital, and prevent national industrial development. The days of Adam Smith, said Carnegie, were dead and gone.

James B. Dill, the lawyer who brought Carnegie together with J. P. Morgan, the great financier, to form the United States Steel Corporation, declared: "Trusts are natural, inevitable growths out of our social and economic conditions. You cannot stop them by force, with laws. They will sweep down like glaciers upon your police, courts, and States and wash them into flowing rivers. I am clearing the way for them."[8]

As the corporations grew in size and national scope, politics and business grew closer together. To some observers (such as the cartoonist Thomas Nast and the muckrakers Ida Tarbell, Joseph Stannard Baker, and Lincoln Steffens), the essential story spoke of scandal and corruption. But not all liberals and progressives saw the growing affinity between politicians and big businessmen as undesirable.

Herbert Croly, the founder of *The New Republic*, and a powerful influence on President Theodore Roosevelt's New Nationalism, saw the career of the Republican political boss Mark Hanna as an effort to fuse business and government interests for the sake of the public welfare. As a politician, said Croly, Hanna could not help representing business because business was a part of himself—"because business was in his eyes not simply money-making but the most necessary kind of social labor." Hanna, Croly asserted, saw no evil in what he was trying to do; rather he sought to keep alive "in his own policy and behavior the traditional association between business and politics, between private and public interest, which was gradually being shattered by the actual and irresistible development of American business and political life." Hanna, in Croly's view, saw the essential harmony between the interests of business and those of the whole community and sought to develop it.

How could this be done? How could one avoid the danger that the uniting of public and business interests would come at the expense of the "common people?" This, as Croly saw it, had been the central issue in American politics from the beginning, starting with the classic debate between Alexander Hamilton and Thomas Jefferson. In *The Promise of American Life*, Croly chose Hamilton, the proponent of a strong central government, founded on the combination of business and state interests, as his hero and Jefferson, the advocate of weak central government and of a wide and equal dispersion of power among farmers, laborers, and all individuals in the society, as his villain:

> . . . Hamilton's political philosophy was much more clearly thought out than that of Jefferson. He has been accused by his opponents of being the enemy of liberty; whereas in point of fact, he wished, like the Englishman he was, to protect and encourage liberty, just as far as such encouragement was compatible with good order, because he realized that genuine liberty would inevitably issue in fruitful social and economic inequalities. But he also realized that genuine liberty was not merely a matter of a constitutional declaration of rights. It could be protected only by an energetic and clear-sighted central government, and it could be fertilized only by the efficient national organization of American activities. For national organization demands in relation to individuals a certain amount of selection, and a certain classification of these individuals according to their abilities and deserts. It is just this kind of effect of liberty which Jefferson and his followers have always disliked and discouraged. They have been loud in their praise of legally constituted rights; but they have shown an instinctive and implacable distrust of intellectual and moral independence, and have always sought to suppress it in favor of intellectual and moral conformity.[9]

American business overwhelmingly adopted the Jeffersonian creed, transmuting it into an ideology with a strong antigovernment animus, a hostility toward other organized groups (especially labor unions), and an emphasis on "rugged individualism," meaning the rugged individualism of business executives, sometimes heading organizations with tens or hundreds of thousands of employees. To critics of the Jeffersonian business ideology, such principles came to seem utterly inappropriate in a society increasingly dominated by huge corporations, and a threat not only to efficient operation of the economic system but to the liberty of the individual in the new age of industrialism.

The Progressive Tycoon

The social responsibilities creed, which emerged early in the twentieth century and led some big businessmen to associate themselves with the Progressive movement, represented a return to Hamiltonian principles. Some business leaders, centered in the Northeast, were coming around to the logic of the southern statesman, Benjamin Watkins Leigh, who early in the nineteenth century warned that "power and property may be separated for a time by force or fraud—but divorced, never. For so soon as the pang of separation is felt . . . property will purchase power, or power will take over property."

But the American society had become far more complex than it was in Leigh's day, and there was no longer a simple dualism between power (meaning political authority) and property (meaning business interests.) With the rise of the great corporation, the concept of property had itself been drastically modified, with a widening diffusion of ownership and control both through stock ownership and through the political process and governmental rules and regulations. The huge corporations called into being other bodies, including labor unions, farm organizations, and civic groups contending for power to influence the course of American life.

From around the turn of the century, a few leading business executives, such as Elbert Gary, chairman of the board of U.S. Steel; George W. Perkins, "Secretary of State" for the House of Morgan; the formidable J. P. Morgan himself, and Frank A. Vanderlip of the National City Bank of New York, began to stress the importance for business of working more closely with government and the political leadership, as well as with other organized groups in the community, rather than imperiling the corporations' position by standing in endless opposition to them.

These corporate magnates and financial moguls of the Northeast felt that mustering greater political support would be vital if big business were to avoid being hamstrung or even destroyed by politicians representing smaller banks, businesses, farmers, and regional interests in other parts of the country. Those southern and western businessmen, farmers, manufacturers, and bankers were hostile to the railroads, the oil companies, "Wall Street," and the great New York and Boston banks as a menace to their own interests. "The effete East wishes to enrich itself at the expense of the rough and rugged West," declaimed T. R. Frentz, an Oshkosh, Wisconsin banker. "Beware, Mr. Morgan, Mr. Kenne and you Standard Oil crowd! You may form steel trusts and other kinds of trusts, but you cannot lick the cream off Mr. Frentz' own saucers in his own home."[10]

The eastern tycoons and financiers sought to recast themselves as civic benefactors, as corporate builders with a conscience, as practical fellows who believed in social and economic reform and could make reform work. If they could not lick the Progressive movement, which supported antitrust laws, the regulation of business, the rights of organized labor, relief for the poor, and civic reform, they would join it. They would help a Frederick Howe to translate a yearning for community service into an effective industrial democracy. They would support a Jane Addams in rescuing and educating the poor. And by cooperating with some Progressive political leaders, such as Theodore Roosevelt of New York, they would moderate and contain the threat to the existence of the "trusts."

With Theodore Roosevelt in the White House, big business had good cause to worry. Roosevelt had made cautious but reassuring statements to the corporate leaders who had come to visit him, but then he had vigorously prosecuted the Northern Securities Company, the Standard Oil Company, the meat packers and other trusts. Clearly big business needed a closer working relationship with Roosevelt; how could it be effected? The House of Morgan developed a technique; J. P. Morgan in 1902 had himself suggested man-to-man understandings between the corporations and the President, but it was Elbert Gary who negotiated comprehensive agreements with the Roosevelt administration, carefully articulating the case for bigness for the sake of efficiency and national growth, and price stability as a necessary condition for prosperity. The threat of widespread mayhem to the corporations was contained, not by fighting the White House tooth and nail but by "civilizing" government regulation of industry.

Small businessmen of the South and West had sought to use the Government's Bureau of Corporations to destroy their big business competitors everywhere, but big business parried the attack by itself supporting the Bureau of Corporations. This was chiefly the work of George Perkins, a life insurance executive and Morgan partner (called "Footfalls" in the secret code of the House), who had enjoyed friendly relations with Roosevelt since his days as Governor of New York.

Some big businessmen even joined conservative labor leaders, led by Samuel Gompers, president of the American Federation of Labor, and civic reformers such as President Seth Low of Columbia University, in supporting peaceful and cooperative labor-management relations. This brought down on those big business leaders the wrath of the vast majority of American businessmen, organized in such bodies as the National Association of Manufacturers, the National Founders Association, and the American Cotton Manufacturers' Association, who were utterly unwilling to accept labor unions or work with their leaders and other civic reformers. They branded the National Civic Federation as part and parcel of the American Federation of Labor and denounced it as an exponent of "the most virulent form of socialism, closed shop unionism." The presidents of the National Association of Manufacturers denounced the big business members of the National Civic Federation as "industrial doughfaces" and carried on a secret war of spying and political intrigue against it.[11]

The attack by the NAM on the NCF was based on more than a difference over relations with organized labor. The smaller and regional businessmen of the NAM feared the threat of a corporate state, dominated by big business, which they thought would transform the American economic and political system and inflict grave damage on their own businesses. They were horrified by the possibility of "socialized industry"—big business and big labor combined—leading to what John Kenneth Galbraith in a later age would call "the new industrial state." Thus they saw the National Civic Federation as a conspiracy of magnates and unionists directed against themselves.

Yet, with all their anxiety about the perceived threat to small business, the officers of the NAM were ambivalent toward the tycoons whom, with all their wealth and power, they both feared and admired. While still criticizing Wall Street and "bigness," NAM leaders pleaded with big businessmen to support their open-shop drive against the unions. On their side, many big corporate executives were torn between the need to work within the emerging industrial state and their desire to stay free of entangling alliances with labor or the government in Washington.

Big business—really, big banking—made its most important and lasting national contribution during the Progressive era by its role in creating the Federal Reserve System. As early as 1906, Frank A. Vanderlip of the National City Bank had converted a number of leading New York businessmen and bankers to the idea of a banker-controlled central bank—an institution capable of serving as the bulwark of the nation's entire financial system and acting as a "lender of last resort" for hard-pressed private banks. Before the Federal Reserve System it was the House of Morgan that played that role, a kind of private central bank, with J. P. Morgan as chairman of the board, or rather autocrat of the system. The panic of 1907, which threatened to shake the system to its foundations, alarmed even Morgan himself, and it became evident to the bankers that they must have a central bank whose resources would far exceed those of Morgan or any other private banking institution.

So the Establishment came together after the panic to draw up a plan. One day in the fall of 1910, Frank Vanderlip, Henry P. Davidson of the House of Morgan, Assistant Secretary of the Treasury Abram Piatt Andrew, and Paul M. Warburg of the Jewish investment banking house of Kuhn, Loeb met on a dreary railroad platform in Jersey City; they were soon joined by the man who had called them to meet there—Senator Nelson W. Aldrich (father-in-law of John D. Rockefeller, Jr., and grand-father-to-be of his namesake, Nelson A. Rockefeller.) Aldrich, the most powerful man in the Senate, swore the four others to secrecy about the mission on which he was taking them, made them promise to use only first names, and then herded them onto a private railroad car which rolled off to Georgia.[12] They ended their journey by being rowed out to Jekyll Island, a hidea-way resort of the rich purchased in 1883 by a group that included J. P. Morgan, Cyrus McCormick, William Rockefeller (John D. Rockefeller's brother), William K. Vanderbilt, and George F. Baker (who founded the Harvard Business School with a gift of $5 million dollars). There on Jekyll Island, with only one day off for shooting, the five men drew up a plan for what, in 1914, became the Federal Reserve System.

There was nothing starry-eyed about the business reformers of the Progressive era. Although regulation has more recently become a dirty word among most businessmen, it was bankers who campaigned for and defended the Federal Reserve System; shippers, the Interstate Commerce Commission; merchants and manufacturers, the Federal Trade Commission; and interna-tional traders who pressed for tariff reform. They linked self-interest to national interest; as Wiebe put it, they put reform "on a business basis." They represented, in Richard Hofstadter's phrase, "the hard side of progressivism."

As the Progressive era passed and the menace of antitrust faded, big business began to work more closely with its small-business and medium-business opponents in the National Asso-ciation of Manufacturers and in other antilabor, antigovern-ment business associations. World War I solidified this alliance among business groups. Though, on one side, the war repre-sented the fulfillment of the vision of some Progressive tycoons of an effective alliance between business and government, on the other side the war liberated big business from the guilt, in-security, and apprehension of a political assault by the com-bined forces of small business, labor, agriculture, and social reformers that had hung over it at the end of the nineteenth century and the first decade and a half of the twentieth century.

After World War I, in the heady atmosphere of boom, boost-erism, and a spreading get-rich-quick fever, the corporate mag-nates, with rare exceptions, reverted to the traditional business creed with its strong bias against government and the unions. To be sure, some businesses still saw that a sympathetic govern-ment had its uses, for instance, to keep out labor unions or to bar foreign competition. But the twenties were a heyday of rugged business individualism—and business dominance.

The great crash of 1929 shattered that environment, and the coming of the New Deal meant that big government would counterbalance big business in the American society. The New Deal probably saved the nation from more radical change; 1933, the year Roosevelt took over the White House, was the year that Hitler took power in Germany. In the United States, as in Germany, the cruel irony of joblessness and hunger in the midst of potential prosperity and idle factories, posed a genuine threat to the continuation of democracy and individual liberty.

Overwhelmingly, big businessmen and financiers did not ac-cept or appreciate the New Deal's transformation of the Ameri-can system. They saw it, not as the rescue, but as the ruination of all they held dear; they called Roosevelt "a traitor to his class." With rare exceptions, they opposed public works programs, Social Security, the Securities and Exchange Commission, the Fair Labor Standards act establishing minimum wages, and, perhaps most of all, the National Labor Relations Act establish-ing the right of labor to organize and bargain collectively. Fear-ing that Roosevelt's intentions were socialistic, most business-men were unwilling to help his government undertake the mammoth task of economic reconstruction. As a result of busi-ness hostility to reform—and to the depression itself, for which business was blamed—the respect and admiration once ac-corded to business enterprise gave way to a sense of distrust and betrayal by many common citizens who had seen the American dream become a nightmare.

Birth of the CED

Not every businessman rejected the idea that big business had helped cause the Great Depression of the 1930s by acting irresponsibly and with unconcern for the wellbeing of the national economy and its workers and ordinary citizens. One man who felt that way strongly was Paul Gray Hoffman, president of the Studebaker Company and a trustee of the University of Chicago, John D. Rockefeller's brainchild, his rival to Harvard. Hoffman, though he had started his career as an auto salesman, was establishmentarian in his every instinct. He felt that business, having helped to destroy prosperity, was obligated to work toward restoring the economy to health and prosperity.

He envisioned an organization of businessmen and academics to uncover the reasons behind the economy's failure. He hoped to bring the American business community back into the position of leadership and respect it had abdicated in the 1920s. But Hoffman did not assume, as so many businessmen did, that he already knew how to construct a stronger economy; he believed that economic practice and theory had become so widely separated that the best brains in the country, including trained economic minds at the universities, needed to be brought into the process of planning the nation's future.[13]

The war in Europe—a war into which America almost surely would soon be drawn—was liquidating the depression. But when the war ended, Hoffman feared, America and the other industrial democracies could well be back where they were in the 1930s, if no advance thinking and planning were done.

On an early spring day in 1941, Hoffman went to the campus of the University of Chicago to discuss his ideas with two young men—Robert Maynard Hutchins, president of the University, and William Benton, its vice-president. Hutchins, an educator who had demonstrated his daring by abolishing the football team as inappropriate to a serious intellectual venture, had been acting dean of the Yale Law School at twenty-eight and president of the University of Chicago since 1929 when he was thirty. Benton, who had cofounded the advertising agency, Benton & Bowles, in 1929, when he was twenty-nine, had just sold his share in the Madison Avenue firm to devote his life to higher learning and public service.

Hoffman told Hutchins and Benton: "As a trustee of the university I think it's high time the university played a more active role in trying to do something about the state of the nation. The University of Chicago has economists and other scholars. These men have the knowledge, but their knowledge is not being applied to the good of the country. What can we do about it?"

Hoffman called for a study on "what is the matter with democracy—an analysis of practices of business which are harmful to democracy; of education; of the church; of labor." To do the study he proposed to set up a group of about twenty or twenty-five people, not just businessmen but labor leaders, churchmen, and others, with a full-time researcher from the university to work with the group. Hutchins and Benton responded warmly; they and Hoffman promptly began organizing what they called the American Policy Commission. Along the way they decided to combine it with another group, set up by *Fortune* magazine in 1939, called the Fortune Round Table. The Round Table had brought together Professor Sumner Slichter of Harvard, an economist well-regarded by businessmen, the heads of New Jersey Bell Telephone Company, Detroit Edison, and several other businessmen, as well as a Federal judge from Georgia and a farmer from Iowa.

Somewhere along the way, Hoffman's original idea of bringing businessmen together with labor leaders evaporated; members of the business leadership are always torn by the problem of how to relate to labor. The true establishmentarians (as was true of those business members of the National Civic Federation) think it makes good sense to sit down with labor, but the more characteristic businessmen regard labor if not as The Enemy then as beyond the pale and likely to be too antagonistic, too clannish, too close-minded, and unsympathetic to what the businessmen think and say. In any event, the Hoffman-Hutchins-Benton team decided to leave labor out, as well as the farmers and churchmen, leaving only the businessmen ("literate" businessmen, they said) to work with chosen academics.

The men they recruited (this was in the not very distant days when no one would have thought of recruiting a woman for such a group) included Ralph McCabe, head of the Scott Paper Company; Henry Luce, the editor-in-chief and cofounder of *Time, Life,* and *Fortune;* Ralph Flanders, a Vermont toolmaker and Boston banker; Marshall Field, the Chicago merchant and newspaper publisher; Clarence Francis, head of General Foods; Ray Rubicam, an advertising man; and Beardsley Ruml, treasurer of Macy's in New York and the former dean of social sciences at the University of Chicago.

It was Ruml, a remarkable businessman-scholar (the American version of Plato's philosopher-king), who turned out to be the star of the show, the idea man whose conceptions proved not merely brilliant but *practical.* Ruml had always blamed his hatred of physical labor for his intellectual accomplishments. At high school in Cedar Rapids, Iowa, he attacked his work furiously one year with the hope of getting a year ahead so he could relax. At Dartmouth College he wrote poetry and plays. At the University of Chicago he took a doctorate in intelligence-measuring. At the age of twenty-seven he was given the job of thinking up ways to spend the $74 million which John D. Rockefeller, Jr., had put into the Laura Spelman Rockefeller Memorial Fund. There he pushed for and won the first large grants to social science research, causing Robert Maynard Hutchins to call Ruml "the founder of social sciences in America." In 1930, Hutchins named him dean of social sciences at the University of Chicago. Four years later, the intellectually restless Ruml moved into business to become treasurer of Macy's. (Hutchins cracked that Ruml had given up ideas for notions.) As an Iowa product, he had never lost interest in the farmers; before he moved to Macy's he had thought up a domestic allotment plan to aid the depression-stricken farmers; President Roosevelt used Ruml's plan as the basis for the Agricultural Adjustment Act. At Macy's, although he had never studied accounting, Ruml set up a new system of accounting to help management make decisions; it worked. He dismissed his business success as an example of his imaginative ignorance.

Word about Ruml got around quickly in New York; he was named a director, then chairman, of the Federal Reserve Bank of New York. When the call came from Paul Hoffman and William Benton, "B" Ruml, as he was called, was keen to put his imagination to work on national economic planning, to assure that the nation would preserve its prosperity after the war. Meanwhile, with America now engaged in World War II—and the problem of how to pay for the war without causing rapid inflation—Ruml thought up the idea of "pay as you go" taxation, with employers required to make weekly deductions from their employees' paychecks. Ruml ran a one-man campaign for, and won, what has become the permanent system of payroll deductions. (Blessing or curse, it has plucked the geese of more feathers with fewer squawks.)

Of course, businessmen like Ruml, Hoffman, and Benton were not the only ones who, in the midst of war, were worrying about how to preserve prosperity after the war ended. At the Commerce Department, a small postwar planning unit had been set up. Indeed, only a month after Pearl Harbor, Arthur R. Upgren, the head of the unit, and his associate, Richard M. Bissell, a young Ph.D. from Yale, submitted their first report, *A Program of Postwar Planning*. During the war, some economic planners became involved in intelligence operations. Bissell stayed on in intelligence long after the war—and, as deputy director for plans of the Central Intelligence Agency, took the fall for the Bay of Pigs fiasco early in the Kennedy administration. During World War II, the intelligence function was suffused with high purpose; the OSS, predecessor to the CIA, was regarded as the province of the most brilliant and dedicated people, the stomping ground of the fully engaged intellectuals of the Establishment. Long afterward, the CIA had not shed all of its establishmentarian origins.

Upgren and Bissell based their postwar planning report largely on work being done at the General Electric Company.

The report urged two steps for business: first, each company should forecast as well as possible the demand for consumer goods and private investment, on the assumption that the level of national income would be maintained; second, each company would begin at once to plan the adjustments and capital spending it would make, based on those forecasts. The aim was to develop a "shelf of *private* projects, which can be initiated when the situation demands."

The Commerce group sought to push this concept with the business community, but found only one ardent supporter— Marion B. Folsom, a Georgian who had gone from the Harvard Business School to Eastman Kodak Company, and, by the time World War II broke out, had become Kodak's treasurer. Folsom had set up the Eastman pension plan and the Rochester Unemployment Plan, and was one of those able, energetic, restless businessmen (like Hoffman, Benton, and Ruml) who never seem fully happy or content unless involved in larger social affairs. Working with President Roosevelt, Folsom, while still at Kodak, had helped build the Social Security system, possibly the New Deal's greatest accomplishment.

When America entered the war, the Secretary of Commerce was Jesse Jones, a tough Texas businessman. Other businessmen regarded Jones as one who had "sold out" to the New Deal, but New Dealers often regarded him as an ultraconservative Trojan Horse from business. Jones was indeed conservative, but, when it was put on his desk, he liked what the Upgren-Bissell report proposed, particularly the idea for an organization of businessmen to engage in postwar planning, and decided to push it.

Without knowing what was on his mind, Paul Hoffman and William Benton sought a meeting with Secretary Jones to try to sell him their idea for an "American Policy Commission." Expecting to be turned down, Hoffman quickly spelled out for Jones a plan for a group that would analyze, criticize, and challenge the thinking and policies of business, labor, agriculture, and government which, he feared, "would work against the attainment of high levels of employment and production." Jones heard Hoffman out and asked him and Benton, "Well, boys, what would you study?" Hoffman gave some concrete examples, stressing the impact federal tax laws. "All right," said Jones, "it sounds practical to me."

Jones got on the phone in the weeks that followed and recruited his own team of business planners. He drew on the suggestions of Hoffman and Benton, who had given him their list for the American Policy Committee, but, for reasons unstated, rejected several, notably Henry Luce and Marshall Field; Jones may have been averse to publishers, or perhaps only to Luce and Field on personal grounds. However, he did accept B. Ruml and most of the others.

The Hoffman-Benton group agreed to work quietly and privately while public attention was focused on winning the war. Its financing would come from private corporations and foundations. Hoffman was elected chairman, Benton vice-chairman; they would be attacked, Jesse Jones warned them, by "liberal" publications as self-seeking tycoons.*

What to call themselves? They pored over lists of suggested names, including the "Organization for the Public Good" and dozens of plays on "the American System" and "the American Way of Life." Some unknown hand had written down, "The Committee for Economic Development through Commerce and Industry." The last four words were dropped, and on September 3, 1942, the Committee for Economic Development—the CED—was formally named and incorporated in the District of Columbia.

The next day, at the first official meeting of the CED trustees, Paul Hoffman read its formal purpose from the certificate of incorporation: "To foster, promote, conduct, encourage, and finance scientific research, education, training and publication in the broad field of economics in order that industry and commerce may be in a position in the postwar period to make their full contribution to high and secure standards of living for people in all walks of life through maximum employment and high

---

*In fact, they were attacked in *The New Republic* and *The Nation*. The charge was that the business planners were linked to the National Association of Manufacturers and would give postwar planning an isolationist cast.

productivity in our domestic economy; to promote and carry out these objects, purposes and principles in a free society without regard to and independently of the special interests of any group in the body politic, either political, social or economic."

The social responsibilities creed of the Progressive Era was back in business.

The Mission Abroad

From the beginning, CED took an international perspective of business's, and the nation's, responsibilities. One of the first and most important of its international ventures was a report called "International Trade and Domestic Employment," written, in 1944, by Professor Calvin B. Hoover of Duke University.[14] In his preface, Professor Hoover quietly noted that "in the course of this study I was fortunate enough to be able to spend some weeks in both London and Stockholm. The opportunity to consult with British and Swedish industrialists and economists and to view our foreign trade from a different angle was very useful." What Professor Hoover did not mention, until years later, was that the study he undertook for the CED was also the cover for intelligence activities in which he was engaged for the OSS; in fact, he was the head of the OSS in Northern Europe, and his flights between London and Scandinavia were made in the belly-gun bubble of a B-17. Hoover's network, based in Stockholm, was considered the hottest and most professional of all U.S. intelligence operations. Among other jobs, it pinpointed the location of German synthetic oil plants; in knocking them out, Allied bombers effectively grounded the Luftwaffe during the Normandy invasion. Hoover's Stockholm group acquired many national secret codes. It reported, as early as May 7, 1945, on Japanese peace feelers. It got advance warning of the attempt on Hitler's life, and might have started negotiations to end the war in the summer of 1943 if Washington's position had not frozen on unconditional surrender. For his wartime activities, Hoover was awarded the Medal of Freedom.[15]

The most conscientious of men, Hoover worked hard on his economic report, which he had been commissioned to do by Professor Theodore Yntema,* on leave from the University of Chicago to head the CED research staff. Hoover's report was anything but a routine piece of "cover" for his spy activities. Far from urging, as CED's liberal critics had feared, an isolationist course for American business after the war, the Hoover report recommended American participation in a program for the expansion of international trade and for freeing this trade from the more constricting and objectionable forms of national control. The report helped muster business support for United States participation in the International Monetary Fund that had been blueprinted at the Bretton Woods conference (in which the chief negotiators were Harry Dexter White for the United States and John Maynard Keynes for Great Britain). To restore world production and trade, the Hoover report also urged business support for the International Bank for Reconstruction and Development—the World Bank.

Liberal trade would be crucial in rebuilding the world economy, and the Hoover report recommended securing international agreements for eliminating international cartels, "among the most objectionable barriers to trade," as well as "lowering our protective tariff in a substantial degree in return for reciprocal action by other countries, and refraining from using the tariff as a means of fending off foreign competition for our war-born industries." This helped build American business backing for what ultimately emerged as the General Agreement on Trade and Tariffs.

Thus, while the war continued, the report helped win business cooperation in constructing the three fundamental pillars

---

*Professor Yntema later became the senior financial officer of the Ford Motor Company—and one of those key advisers who helped young Henry Ford II transform the image of the company from a crabbed, anti-Semitic, antilabor institution into a modern, sophisticated, progressive company.

of the postwar world economy—the International Monetary Fund, the World Bank, and GATT.

American business leaders demonstrated they had not only been converted to internationalism, politically as well as economically, but they were prepared to be generous toward former enemies as well as allies in the interests of peace and economic development. They had learned the lessons of Versailles that John Maynard Keynes had sought and failed to teach in time in his *Economic Consequences of the Peace.*

After the war ended, Calvin B. Hoover, on leave from his deanship at Duke University, working with Paul Hoffman, was one of the principal initiators and developers of the Marshall Plan. He opposed the line that Germany should be kept as a "goat pasture," and instead advocated the position Keynes had taken after World War I that a "Carthaginian peace would be unstable and dangerous." Oddly enough, Keynes himself declined to help Professor Hoover in his efforts to resist the so-called Morgenthau line (led by Roosevelt's Secretary of the Treasury, Henry Morgenthau) which sought to prevent German reconstruction to a position of power. Keynes said he was too heavily engaged in the effort to rebuild the world monetary system.

But Hoover moved to a devastated Berlin in 1945 and, under General Lucius Clay and General William Draper, both men with backgrounds in business and investment banking, designed the basic plan for restoring the German economy. Hoover's plan produced an explosion when Raymond Daniell of *The New York Times* broke the story. Official Washington, still so close to the newly discovered horrors of Nazi concentration camps, was outraged; and Moscow, which had felt the full impact of the Nazi armies and the S.S., was even more furious. Hoover, characteristically, made no complaint about Daniell's story; he had admired and worked closely with newspapermen throughout his career, especially in Stalin's Russia and prewar Hitler Germany. On the contrary, he wrote: "The basic statistics of our Report were given quite accurately . . . [and] the connection between the need for exports to pay for necessary imports, and the provision for an increased population in addition to the costs of the Armies of Occupation, were set forth very competently."

Even though the general tone of the *Times*'s story was hostile to the report—its headline on October 8, 1945, read: "U.S. Experts Urge Reich Export Rise; Russians Suspicious"—Hoover concluded it was all for the best that it came out; he had an old-fashioned religious faith that the truth was mighty and would prevail.

Nevertheless, the United States and its leaders faced an agonizing moral problem in coming to terms with those German industrialists who had willingly done business with the Nazis and who were now just as willing to do business with the Americans in the reconstruction of Germany. The problem was dramatized when those German industrialists who had been convicted of war crimes at Nuremburg were all released from Landsberg prison in early 1951, their sentences commuted by the American High Commissioner, John J. McCloy. Eleanor Roosevelt, Telford Taylor, the chief American prosecutor at Nuremburg, and a number of other distinguished Americans severely criticized the McCloy decision as politically motivated—a means of strengthening the United States-German alliance during the cold war. Whatever the motivation, the blanket release of the convicted industrialists was taken within Germany—and by them—as a sign that businessmen were not to be seriously blamed for their involvement in matters for which others were hanged or suffered long imprisonment.[16]

Business Bootlegs Keynes

At the end of World War II, the economic doctrine of John Maynard Keynes that government could, by manipulating total demand through its budget and tax policies, cure unemployment, was, with only rare exceptions, anathema to the American business community. To educate American businessmen to an understanding and acceptance of modern countercyclical fiscal policy required that an "inside job" be done by fellow business-men whom they would respect. The job was done by several economists, including Theodore Yntema, Lloyd Mints, A. G. Hart, Henry Simons, Herbert Stein, and most of all, Beardsley Ruml, all of whom had associations with the University of Chi-cago. (It is somewhat ironic that it was Chicago, nowadays thought of as the bastion of anti-Keynesian thought, that brought the Keynesian revolution to the business community in America.)

Ruml had earlier made the Keynesian revolution palatable for President Roosevelt—something Keynes himself had failed to do. In the spring of 1938, when the nation had slid back into recession so deep that it appeared the Depression was back in all its fury, Ruml, on a train headed south to visit Macy's Atlanta store, bumped into two New Dealers. The economist, Leon Henderson, and the WPA deputy administrator, Aubrey Wil-liams, were on their way to Pine Mountain Valley, near Warm Springs, Georgia, where they were going to help Harry Hop-kins shape a fiscal program for Roosevelt. Henderson and Wil-liams persuaded Ruml to go with them to Pine Mountain Camp; there they drafted several memoranda for Hopkins, who shut-tled them over to Roosevelt. In the most crucial memorandum, Ruml wrote:

> Within recent months and particularly within recent weeks, a number of observers in reflecting on the present crisis in production have drawn together certain lines of thought which have not ordi-narily been associated. As a result there appears in broad outline an appreciation of the system which, if correct in the main, should have a profound effect on current policy.
>
> The problem centers on the role of national government in eco-nomic stabilization or economic advancement.[17]

The memo then set forth some simple arithmetic. A national income of $88 billion was needed if the country were to regain reasonably full employment; but national income was then running at only $56 billion. "If money invested or spent turns over two or three times a year," wrote Ruml, "it would require between 7 and 10 billion per year of *additional* investment or spending, public or private, to get reasonable full employment."

Deficit spending by government would be necessary to make up the gap, but Roosevelt and his Treasury Secretary Morgenthau regarded that (believe it or not) with as much horror as did business. Ruml, the persuader, put the problem into historical perspective:

> ... The whole course of American economic advancement had been accompanied and permitted by the alienation of the national domain to create purchasing power for the growing national product. First the gold under the ground had been turned into money—national domain into purchasing power in one step. Then the public lands had been alienated, given to railroads and homesteaders, who borrowed on the lands from the banks and in the process created money —national domain into purchasing power in two steps. Then franchises, public grants of right to engage in certain kinds of business, had been given to corporations, which established enterprises, which borrowed on the strength of their prospective earnings and thus generated money—national domain into purchasing power in three steps.[18]

Now it was necessary to continue the process one step further: it was necessary to use a small part of the federal government's claim on future tax income as the basis for borrowing to create purchasing power and stimulate the national economy. The government had two choices: it could try to push production directly by business or it could push consumption, which in turn would generate more production; the latter was the democratic way. Roosevelt was impressed and convinced; it was part of an ongoing historical process, and Ruml had offered him a democratic solution, not a surrender to business.

But when B. Ruml turned his persuasive talents on behalf of the Keynesian revolution to converting business, he had to use a rather different approach, shifting the emphasis from the spending side of the budget to the tax side. For tax reduction, by strengthening consumption and production, could be as effective as expenditure increases, and far more harmonious with business's antigovernment predilections. Furthermore, business's aversion to swelling government debt could be handled by proposing a fiscal policy that, over the longer run, would reduce the Federal debt. The CED statement on taxes in 1944 accepted the Ruml position: "The Committee deems it wise that the tax structure and the budget should be so drawn as to make possible substantial reduction of the Federal debt at a high level of employment. As much debt should then be retired as is consistent with maintaining high levels of employment and production."

The CED tried to make modern fiscal policy as respectable for Republicans as for Democrats. But it took until January 1971, for a Republican president to declare: "I am now a Keynesian."

Inflation and Reaction: The Business Roundtable

Just as some leading businessmen had made regulation respectable during the Progressive era early in the twentieth century, so their successors legitimated Keynesian fiscal policy after World War II. President Nixon had put the Republican seal on what had started out as a Democratic policy. He was adding insult to the injury of his political foes, much as the fictional politician described by Anthony Trollope had done in *Phineas Redux* (1873): "This man, this audacious Cagliostro among statesmen, this destructive leader of all declared Conservatives, had come forward without a moment's warning, and pretended that he would do the thing out of hand!"

The conservatives of the business world were enraged. Inflation was the cardinal sin of the Keynesians, Republican or Democratic. Inflation was undermining the stability of the nation, and its moral fiber. It was destroying the value of the dollar, at home and abroad. It was weakening the ability of the nation to keep up with other countries. It would end by wrecking the entire world economy.

And, after the long era of postwar good (or at least relatively good) feeling between business and labor, business and the intellectuals, business and the liberals, business and government, business and the blacks and other social groups, an era of business defensiveness mixed with hostility emerged in the seventies. This hostile mood of business was a response to these events: the Watergate scandals, in which over two hundred business corporations were involved through illegal campaign contributions; improper corporate payments abroad, which came to light as a result of the establishmentarian citizens' lobby Common Cause (headed by a former head of the Carnegie Corporation and Secretary of Health, Education and Welfare John Gardner) investigation of the Watergate-linked corporate slush funds; and the oil crisis following the Arab oil embargo during the Yom Kippur War of October 1973. Business anger flared at what it construed to be a media attack on the oil companies and business in general.

The combination of worsening inflation and the most severe recession of the postwar period from 1973 to 1975 had indeed helped to undermine public confidence in business, as poll after poll showed, much as the Great Depression of the 1930s had done. Corporate executives felt put upon—by organized labor, liberals, blacks, environmentalists, women, and other critical public-interest groups and their lawyers, and perhaps most of all by the rise of new and costly forms of government regulation in such areas as occupational health and safety, air and water pollution, and equal employment rules.

Rather than accept such public criticism and regulation as a just and necessary corrective for wrongdoing, businessmen generally regarded the attacks as exaggerated, unfair, a threat (deliberate or unconscious) to the very existence of the free enterprise system. Business suffered from an acute feeling that its enemies were closing in on it. As Hershel Sarbin, executive vice-president of Ziff-Davis, observed: "Business is suffering from a siege mentality. . . . Corporate managers feel self-protective. They report to people with gigantic vested interests. They must show that they are not weakening or departing from the line that the system is being threatened by groups that would undermine it. Their attitude toward academics, writers, and other members of the intelligentsia is one of superiority and often disdain. This stems from their feeling that they pay them, and they are not behaving responsibly."

To implement its new mood of aggressiveness, big business formed a new, militant organization, the Business Roundtable: top corporate executives would be their own braintrust and would do direct lobbying in support of business interests; enough of establishmentarian shilly-shallying and dependence on moralistic academics to tell them what to think. The Roundtable was first brought to wide public notice by a November 16, 1975, page-one story in *The New York Times*, written by Eileen Shanahan and headlined: "Antitrust Bill Stopped by a Business Lobby," which began:

> A carefully organized lobbying effort, chiefly directed by a little-known organization whose members are all giant corporations, has succeeded in killing a proposed major amendment to the antitrust laws. Similar efforts against other legislation are in process and planned.
>
> The organization is the Business Roundtable, whose 158 corporate members range, alphabetically, from the Allis-Chalmers Corporation to Xerox Corporation. Its members include the three largest automobile manufacturers, the three largest banks, seven of the largest oil companies, the largest steel companies, major retailing organizations and many of the largest utilities, including American Telephone and Telegraph Company.

By December 1976, *Business Week* had caught up with the story and called the Business Roundtable "Business' most powerful lobby in Washington." "After several years of near-clandestine existence," the *Business Week* story began, "the Roundtable had emerged as the most powerful voice of business . . ."

President-elect Carter, the piece said, was "openly courting the business community through the Roundtable." His staff was working closely with Irving S. Shapiro, chairman both of the Roundtable and DuPont, and with another Roundtable leader, General Electric chairman Reginald H. Jones. *Business Week* thought the Roundtable would have "the same access to the White House under Carter that it did under Presidents Nixon and Ford.

"The guts of the Roundtable," said Chairman Shapiro, "is the fact that the chief executive officer is the man who participates" —and who does the lobbying. This had given the Roundtable clout that had already eclipsed the lobbying powers of such old-line groups as the U.S. Chamber of Commerce and the National Association of Manufacturers. The Roundtable was putting its top-level lobbyists to work on such major legislative issues as tax reform, proposed indexation of the minimum wage (which they opposed), amendments to the Clean Air Act, policies to increase employment by providing incentives for capital formation, opposition to the Humphrey-Hawkins "full employment" bill, and opposition to labor legislation favored by the AFL-CIO.

To be sure, as *Business Week* acknowledged, some critics thought that the Roundtable's influence, and its acceptance by top government officials extended too far. One critic recalled that in the fall of 1975 Vice-President Nelson A. Rockefeller had held a private briefing for Roundtable members on a proposed report by the staff of the National Commission on Water Quality; the report was critical of the progress of federal water quality programs. "Without notifying the nonbusiness members of the commission," said a commission source, "Rockefeller called a meeting of eight or ten Roundtable members in the Executive Office Building where the draft report was outlined to them. The business group, which included representatives from Texaco, Du Pont, Kennecott, and Weyerhaeuser, then offered alternative proposals which later were adopted word for word as the recommendations of the commission."

The impetus for the formation of the Roundtable had come from the Duquesne Club in Pittsburgh, the exclusive hangout of that city's business elite. Roger Blough, the retired chairman of U.S. Steel and chairman of what was called, by its members, "Roger's Roundtable," Donald C. Burnham, the former chairman of Westinghouse, and John D. Harper, the chairman of Alcoa, were key figures in its founding. The broad Business Roundtable really was an outgrowth of the Construction Users Anti-Inflation Roundtable founded in 1969, with Blough as its head, for the purpose of uniting construction customers behind building contractors in their battle with the building trades unions.[19] This group merged with the Labor Law Study Committee and other business groups in 1972 to form the Roundtable. Its thinking was closer to the traditional ruggedly individualistic free-enterprise creed than to the social responsibilities creed favored by the businessmen of the Establishment.

But the Roundtable, created at a time when businessmen were drawing their wagons together in a circle, collected many businessmen who were normally social responsibilities thinkers and, indeed, members of the CED. Some, like James Ferguson, board chairman of General Foods, and a member of both the Roundtable and the CED, tried to exercise a moderating influence on hard-line Roundtable thinking. In the fall of 1978 he urged an independent and objective study of "consumerism" (a bugbear of many Roundtable members), and how consumer interests *could* best be protected and served. "I thought the Business Roundtable ought to be concerned with that issue," said Ferguson, "not just oppose efforts to protect consumer interests, as with the Consumer Protection Agency [which business lobbying, including by the Roundtable, had helped to defeat in the 95th Congress]. My proposition was that we ought to study the roots of the problem, and I recommended two sources to study consumerism. The Roundtable rejected the Harvard Business School, which was one of them, and it will probably reject the Conference Board, the other, because it cannot control the results and publication. They were suspicious of the guys at Harvard, even at the Business School." Ferguson said he was worried about "lowest-common denominator thinking" at the Roundtable.

In its lobbying efforts, the Roundtable defeated a proposal

by the Commerce Department for measuring corporate social performance and a bill to finance congressional campaigns out of the U. S. Treasury. It eliminated language that it thought might open the way to national economic planning from legislation creating the new Department of Energy. It defeated a measure to set ceilings on hospital charges. It overturned a commitment of Labor Secretary John Dunlop to permit common-site picketing by construction labor, thereby causing his resignation. And it blocked a labor-law reform bill that the AFL-CIO urgently wanted, leading, in the summer of 1978 to the breakup of a high-level labor-management advisory group which Dunlop had formed after returning to Harvard.

"My own feeling," said Ferguson of General Foods, "is that what is perceived as a rightward shift on the part of business and an effort by business to dominate the society is that business has found its voice and discovered that it has power to a somewhat greater degree than it thought it had, and it is using that power. My perception is that business was getting kicked around compared to labor, consumers, and other groups, and the constant cry within the business community was, 'How come we can't get together and make our voices heard?' It's been something of a revelation to them, through various efforts, such as the Business Roundtable, how much business could get accomplished. Maybe in the course of that change, if and as business finds its ability to get things done and realizes its power, it may begin to take a more dispassionate look at some issues than it's doing right now."

In fact, the Business Roundtable began looking for opportunities to make positive contributions to solving national problems, rather than taking negative stands on all government actions. For instance, Irving Shapiro, chairman of DuPont, along with the heads of Exxon, Mobil, General Motors, General Electric, Chase Manhattan Bank, Bechtel, FMC, and Federation Department Stores met with the Anti-Defamation League of B'nai B'rith, the Jewish civil rights organization, at the behest of the government, in an effort to devise compromise antiboycott legislation that would be acceptable to American corporations doing business with Arab countries and to American Jewry.

Through the first half of 1977 lawyers of the Roundtable and ADL laboriously worked out an agreement: in return for measures to prevent discrimination against Jews as individuals and against corporations refusing to trade with Israel, businesses gained the right to obey Arab laws when doing business in Arab countries. American corporations could usually abide by Arab orders specifying the American or foreign companies (that is, "non-Zionist" companies) from which they would buy spare parts and subcontracting services, but could *not* continue to discriminate against Israeli and Jewish customers or employees in their wider commercial relations.[20]

President Carter thanked the Roundtable and ADL for their work. In early May 1977 the Senate passed the antiboycott bill by an overwhelming vote of 70 to 1.

Byrom's Synthesis

The American business community, at the start of the 1980s, had still not recovered from its anxious and defensive mood. It remained hostile toward public groups that it believed endangered business's effectiveness and even threatened its survival.

This posed a problem for the business establishmentarians: how to attack public groups harassing business without seeming to abandon their concern about the broad public interest.

One business leader caught in that dilemma was Fletcher Byrom, who, as chairman of the Committee for Economic Development, was the heir of men like Paul Hoffman, William Benton, and Beardsley Ruml. Byrom was also, however, a Pittsburgher in good standing at the Duquesne Club, the chairman of the Koppers Company, a metallurgist by education, a product of Penn State, and a member of the top Policy Committee of the

Business Roundtable. He was an individualist, a stormy petrel, an intellectual among businessmen, a feisty capitalist who enjoyed arguing with socialists.

In an interview in the fall of 1979, Byrom said business was still aggressive, worried, and anxious over its position in the American society: "We have a highly educated society that has very little comprehension of the economic functioning of that society. I do not believe that there is a well-seeded perception that industry, as I represent it, is a positive contributor to the wellbeing of society. Now I happen to believe that it is. I happen to believe that in any society there needs to be the assignment of the wealth-creating function, and I don't care how a society is organized, somewhere there has to be a wealth-creating function. In our system, it is in the private enterprise area, or has been.

"I think there's a lot of people who honestly believe that you can repeal fundamental economic principles by popular referendum, and therefore I do believe that a lot of characters like me find ourselves in a state of siege. This isn't a defensive posture for Byrom per se. I've got four years to go before I retire. You know, from a financial standpoint I'm a fool to be working. So that my concern fundamentally is a societal concern, not one of trying to defend a personal vested interest."

Byrom saw no philosophical contradiction but only a functional difference between the CED and the Business Roundtable: "I happen to be on the Policy Committee of the Roundtable as well as being Chairman of the CED. You know, I've been asked how can you be a Christian and be a chief executive officer. I don't find the two contradictory, and I don't find this position contradictory. . . . The Roundtable is taking a very pragmatic, short-term approach to specific legislation at the present time. The CED, through the trustees and its Research Advisory Board, is trying to understand the external issues that are going to impact on society. I think one of the great problems is that we have become such a single-interest political society that, on the short term issues, you do get forced into a non-conciliatory, adversary position."

Corporate law, he complained, is still fundamentally personal property law, "and I don't think the corporation is in the same context as my personal property. I horrified somebody the other day at the Stock Exchange Advisory Committee meeting by saying that I was not at all sure that my stockholders had first priority in the decision making process in our company, or deserved it. Once a stockholder has received a level of return on his investment that is sufficient to cause him to make the investment, does society gain by his receiving any more?"

"If present trends continue," Byrom stressed, "we will have so deteriorated the capital base of capital-intensive industry that there will be a very significant movement toward state ownership or significant state subsidy to the point where an effective state will have major control. I don't think that's the end of the world. . . . We're just going to be less free and much poorer."

His conviction is that, in America, it is essential to base industrial decisions on economic, not political or social considerations: "My view is that the economic entities should be run efficiently, and then society should use the wealth that's created as they see fit. . . . And I don't object to that at all. But I think that to deny the most efficient processing of natural resources is a foolish maneuver. And I think that's what's going to happen."

He thought the system's inability to provide enough jobs for people was moving it toward state control. "As we move toward higher and higher technology in our industry," Byrom said, "we have really less and less need for people. As highly educated people come in with the work force and find no place in industry, they are still going to try to find a place in society. These are smart, ambitious young people who want to have something to say about what's going on. And I think there's an awful lot of these people working to take over industry, if you will. Not because they're against the system, but because the system didn't have any room for them, and they want to be in control."

He is torn between his antipathy toward state control and his recognition of the need for state intervention. "I have a seminar in our company that I run. Last night we were doing Robert

Heilbroner's decline of business civilization. I said, forget the semantics of what Bob says. Let's talk about the dysfunctions within the system. Let's face it. There is no way that you could improve the quality of the environment except by some form of intervention by society. The market system, per se, without imposed standards of performance would never have achieved what we want to do, because it doesn't work on the basis of altruistic efforts to improve the quality of the human condition."

Unimpressed with the power of business—he cited as example its inability to press Congress into controlling inflation— Byrom saw a loss of power and control over the American society. "The pluralism of our whole system is now, in my book, chaos approaching anarchy, and I suspect that we will reach anarchy and not violent anarchy.

"The Presidency today is not very important. The proof is that since about 1963 we have almost been without a President. The last days of Nixon, he wasn't acting as President, when you read the tapes. Ford, you know, was not there long enough to be in, and Carter has not been effective as a President. In all fairness, I'm not at all sure that anybody can be . . .

"But one kind of President might be effective, in my opinion, and I'm frightened of this because other societies have moved to this and ended up with Hitler and Mussolini. But the one kind of President would be a charismatic soul who can get the nation behind him, to the point where Congress is forced to go along with the President not because he has convinced the Congress that he is right but because he has convinced the nation he is right.

"I think this nation is at the point where the only chance that the present political system will work will be that we get that kind of a leader. And I'm frightened of what it might mean. But I am really at the point where I don't think the system is going to work unless we get that. I will maybe upset you but I have come out very early, as a lot of other businessmen have and that may be very bad, for John Connally.

"The only reason I have come out for Connally at this point, very frankly, is that I have been told that Reagan has the convention locked up, and I am absolutely appalled at the idea as I perceive Reagan and his people to be extremists to the right, and I'm frightened by what that means. I don't want any part of it. I feel that Connally is the only guy who might be able to lick Reagan if enough of us get on his bandwagon soon. One thing about John Connally that bothers me is that I really think he is pretty hard. Once in a while he shoots from the hip. Whether he is the best man or not may not be very important. You know, I don't think Bush can get nominated and Bush may well be the best man, I don't know, in the Republican party. I look at politicians as they go. . . . I consider Carter completely ineffective and I have no support for him.*

"Margaret Mead once said to me—I introduced her at a Conference Board meeting one time, it was the best experience I ever had because I had an hour with her alone—she said, 'Mr. Byrom, the world is in a state of chaos moving toward anarchy,' and that's where I got that line. Sidney Harris, in one of his columns years ago, said the human being is not very capable of doing things from a positive, constructive motivation. He reacts to crisis with heroism. And Pogo says we have met the enemy and they is us. You put those three things together and that's where we are."

*This interview was conducted September 12, 1979. By the late winter of 1980, it was clear that Connally was going nowhere in the presidential race. The great majority of Republican voters were evidently even more frightened than Byrom by the kind of charismatic leadership Connally was offering. He withdrew on March 9, 1980 and threw his support to Ronald Reagan, who presented a gentler image. Connally's reputation as a big time wheeler-dealer also proved unattractive to the masses of small businessmen, farmers, and other "Middle Americans" of the Republican party—Reagan's natural constituency. (See chapter 9.)

Big Business and the Establishment

The Struggle Within

Dragged hither and yon by conflicting pressures and his own inner tensions, the American big businessman distrusts the State but knows he plays a crucial role in the polity. He needs and respects trained intellects but is suspicious of, even hostile to, intellectuals. This makes him an easy target for those friendly intellectuals who warn him against the bid for power of a "New Class." As Thomas A. Murphy, chairman of General Motors, told the Downtown Kiwanis Luncheon in Birmingham, Alabama on October 4, 1977, "This New Class has ready access to our leading editorial writers and TV journalists. They do not like what they call the 'materialism' of our society—and they certainly do not like the automobile. They tend to look upon most of the achievements of our society as childish and foolish. They don't like the idea that the individual American can exercise his freedom of choice, fully and freely—to live where he wants to live, to spend his money and his time as he chooses."

Mr. Murphy vigorously rejected the assertion of Professor Charles Lindblom of Yale that large corporations are a "threat to democracy." "There is nothing undemocratic," Mr. Murphy wrote, "about the connection between public appetites and business' ability to distribute rewards. If I am able to provide products or services that other people are willing to pay for, I may be handsomely rewarded, and if I can combine with a lot of other people to provide these things on a large scale there will be a lot of rewards to go around. I suppose the public does accept this as the 'natural order of things,' but then I had always thought it was a fundamental part of our democratic vision."[21]

And the chairman of General Motors regarded the statement that the "business of America is business" as "just another way of saying that ours is a society which caters to consumers' choices, in all their diversity and individuality. This kind of easygoing tolerance is hardly a 'threat to democracy'; it is only a barrier against the imposition of more disciplined regimes which people like Professor Lindblom admire—invariably from afar." (Certainly an unwarranted accusation in the case of Mr. Lindblom, an ardent foe of totalitarianism.)

Business leaders, while routinely praising democracy "from afar," seem extremely dubious about many of its concrete political manifestations. By and large, American business leaders do not see themselves nearly as powerful as their critics do. On the contrary, they commonly contend that they are dominated by other forces, including public interest groups, labor unions, consumers, the news media, even the academics, and most of all by government. Business blames all of these for undermining its efficiency, and the press particularly for its fall in public esteem. Unquestionably, business legitimacy has suffered a sharp decline over the past decade. In its relations with government, business is sorely troubled by the changing conditions of the "social contract"; it feels that the power of government has been strengthened at the expense of its own rights of "consent."

As a defense mechanism, business feels more compelled than ever to intervene in the political process to insure that public policies and actions are not contrary to its own interests. This new militancy accords awkwardly with the Establishmentarian impulses toward conciliation and accommodation of some big business leaders.

Yet business feels more patriotic than self-interested in striking out in its own defense. The dictum that what is good for business is good for America remains a deeply abiding principle. Thus business profits are a vital social good, though misunderstood and maligned by the intellectuals and hence by much of the public. And the belief that accumulating capital best serves public interests remains an article of faith, crucial not just to the corporation but to the nation. Business leaders see themselves as the trustees of capitalism and, ultimately, of the American way of life; and, when challenged, they must be prepared to fight for it against other groups in the society. The militant businessman sees not merely personal insult to himself or a commercial threat to his business, but treachery and treason on the part of those who would transform or tear down the free-enterprise system.

This makes typical businessmen rather a different kettle of fish from the professionals of the Establishment—professors, journalists, philanthropoids—whose religion is disinterestedness.

Disinterestedness, however, is not a feature of the capitalist ethos. Fletcher Byrom to the contrary notwithstanding, it has been, ever since Adam Smith, the pursuit of self-interest that capitalism celebrates as productive of the greatest social good. The clergy of the Establishment have long assumed the mission of persuading businessmen that the benefits of capitalism, though substantial and much appreciated, are insufficient to assure a healthy society—and that more is needed.

In this mission, the professional clergy has, from time to time, been remarkably successful. Just as the Unitarian moralists were able to "civilize" their commercial patrons, and the Brahmins and associated seaboard elites were able, during the Progressive era, to enlist the help of industrial magnates in making government regulation acceptable and respectable, so the business-oriented intellectuals like Beardsley Ruml and Calvin Bryce Hoover (and unusual businessmen themselves like Paul Hoffman and William Benton) were able to convert a generation of American big business leaders to the cause of promoting national and international peace and prosperity.

Yet, despite the hopes of a Croly, a Lippmann, or even a John Kenneth Galbraith, this effort to civilize American business thinking remains unconsummated. The ancient capitalist creed has not succumbed to Establishment morality, nor to Keynesian economics, scientific management, nor updated technocracy. In the gray North as well as in the blooming Sunbelt, the devotees of capital remain uncomfortable with the ministers of the Establishment.

Our designated chairman of the Establishment, David Rockefeller, says, "Well, personally, this term Establishment has always interested, and to some extent troubled me." Rockefeller insists, "It certainly is not anything that has any organized reality, and I suspect it means different things to different people. But to the extent that it signifies a certain group of the thought leaders and formers, people who have influence, I suppose that at any given moment in time there is such a group that can be described in those terms."

Whether it is an *Eastern* Establishment, he seriously doubts: "It started out Eastern because of the country's history, but gradually moved across the country." This, Rockefeller says, is true in many spheres, including the financial: "Philadelphia was really the first financial center, and then it moved to New York, and has pretty much stayed here ever since, as the principal financial center of the country. But since World War II the preeminence of New York declined in relative terms as regional banks grew. In fact, the largest bank in the country is the Bank of America, not even based in New York, and there are many other banks of major importance in centers such as San Francisco, Dallas, Houston, Boston, Atlanta, and so on."

The same diffusion, says Rockefeller, has occurred academically: "When you look at the University of Chicago, Stanford, and other institutions of that calibre, certainly the Northeast is not the predominant academic area. As a loyal Harvardian, I guess I still think Harvard probably is, by almost any measure, at the top of the heap, but that doesn't mean there aren't others that are very close by and have certain fields superior to Harvard."

Rockefeller says that people who use the term Establishment usually use it in a pejorative sense, but he prefers to think of it as a private group of people and institutions concerned about the public good. On that basis, he ventures to name "Jack" McCloy, who, Rockefeller says, "I would think almost everybody would agree would be viewed as a member of the Establishment, if defined almost any way. He likes to tell the story that, as a young law student, he had tried to get a job as a tutor in our family and was turned away from the door by the butler. This was in Seal Harbor in Maine in the summer, and I suppose that quite a few people came to the door. He has told the story many times. It has made considerable impact. I mention it only because certainly at that time he was very far from being a member of the Establishment."

Have the intellectual and business wings of the Establishment been pulling apart in recent years? In the bland style for which he is famous, Rockefeller replies: "There has always been a traditional difference between 'town and gown' in the academic community. There have always been differences between academics and the business world, and yet they have necessarily worked together through boards of trustees and otherwise in major academic institutions. I wouldn't think that the cleavage is significantly greater today than it has been."

In the elegant office high in Chase Manhattan Plaza, late in the afternoon of a warm August day, all is still. Mr. Rockefeller is ready to leave for Seal Harbor.

Chapter 8

The Establishment

in the Political Ring

LIKE Artemus Ward, the Establishment practices a politics of "a exceedin accommodatin character." It embraces the spectrum of moderation from reasonable right to responsible left.

Two opposing urges work to keep the institutions of the Establishment in politically centrist equilibrium. One is the desire to be influential; this drives institutions toward any president who happens to be in office. As Winston Lord of the Council on Foreign Relations says, "I want to help every administration."

The opposite urge is to be critical; a change of the guard in Washington inevitably pulls to the new president those prominent establishmentarians most friendly to his aims, while pushing their counterparts from the previous administration back onto the staffs and boards of the Establishment's private institutions. (These institutions usually have rules forbidding government officials from governing *them.*) Thus, when Carter replaced Ford, the Council on Foreign Relations traded directors Michael Blumenthal, Cyrus Vance, Marshall Shulman, Paul Warnke, and Zbigniew Brzezinski for Henry Kissinger, Winston Lord, Marina Whitman, and—until he decided to play out his Council option—George Bush. A similar shift occurred among Brookings senior fellows. Such transfers temper the institutional urge to cozy up to the White House with the dissents, grumbles, and kibbitzing of the recently dispossessed. In this way, honor and disinterest may be maintained.

But successful centrism requires being on good terms with both major political parties, and this the Establishment has never quite been able to manage. Despite, or perhaps because of, its Republican roots and the preponderant Republicanism of its leading princes, the Establishment has long found the GOP more nettlesome than its Democratic rival. The trouble dates from the presidential election of 1912, when Theodore Roosevelt's third-party candidacy put an end to the GOP's career as the party of national reform.

The original Establishment impulse throbbed strongest in the hearts of reform-minded upper-class Easterners, from gentle philanthropists like John D. Rockefeller, Jr., to fiery crusaders like Taft's trust-busting attorney general, George Wickersham. Most of them were Republicans. Some joined T. R.'s Progressives in 1912; others refused to break from GOP ranks. But the effect was to leave the party machinery firmly in the hands of the standpatters. Those Bull Moosers who returned to the fold were regarded as pariahs; their friends the Progressive nondefectors were also suspect. The Republican schism of 1912, which turned the White House over to the Democrats, left the Grand Old Party with an enduring sense of the perfidiousness of patrician do-gooders within its midst. Meanwhile, the spirit of Progressive reform now descended on the Democratic party. As a result, many of the do-gooders found themselves in a kind of political limbo. Spurned by the GOP yet unwilling to join the Democrats' great unwashed hordes, they put the best face they could on things; "rising above" domestic politics they would henceforth serve the public weal as appointive officials and disinterested citizens—and through private institutions of their own devising.

A Puritan in Politics

The political history of the Establishment in the first half of the twentieth century is perfectly embodied in the career of one man: the many-termed cabinet officer and public official Henry L. Stimson. Stimson, a New Yorker of Puritan Yankee stock, was one of those old-family gentlemen whose public-spiritedness gave Eastern Progressivism—and the Establishment itself —its special character. Born in Manhattan in 1867 and educated at Andover, Yale, and the Harvard Law School, Stimson joined, in 1891, the firm of Elihu Root (future Secretary of War, Secretary of State, U.S. Senator from New York, and ultimately the Republican elder statesman par excellence). In 1892, the young lawyer broke with traditions of family and firm to vote for Grover Cleveland, who had expressed an interest in reducing the tariff. Such mugwumpery was anything but unconventional for Eastern Republicans of a reformist bent; they were distressed, as they would be distressed in 1912, at seeing the GOP as the party of the special interests, with log-rolling and high protective tariffs its most cherished legislative stock-in-trade. But, for men of Stimson's stripe, the Democratic party was even worse, embracing as it did wild-eyed Western populists, Southern Bourbons, and, closest to hand, urban bossism, corruption, and polyglot ethnicity. Too repelled by Tammany Hall actually to become a Democrat, Stimson joined the Republican party and immediately took a leading role in the successful reform of its corrupt Manhattan organization. This put him in touch with the up-and-coming politician Theodore Roosevelt, who became his friend and patron. In 1906, after he was well into the presidential term he had won in his own right, Roosevelt appointed Stimson U.S. Attorney for New York's Southern District.

The appointment brought Stimson out of a professional malaise seemingly inspired by the example of his revered father. Lewis Stimson had given up a lucrative career in banking to study medicine, ultimately earning a modest living as a hospital surgeon and professor. His son likewise came to regard the pursuit of private gain as less than fulfilling life's work. As he told his Yale classmates at their twentieth reunion, "The profession of the law was never thoroughly satisfactory to me, simply because the life of the ordinary New York lawyer is primarily and essentially devoted to the making of money. . . ." Just as his father had largely forsworn private practice in order to minister to the needs of the poor, so Stimson was able to apply his professional skills where they were needed most.

> Whenever a great public question has come up, in which there has been a rich corporation on one side and only the people on the other, it has seemed to me that the former always had the ablest and most successful lawyer to defend it, and very often the side of the people seemed to go almost by default. I have found comparatively few successful lawyers, in modern times, putting their shoulders to the public wheel.

Switching professionally from the side of the corporation to the side of the people had, Stimson said, gotten him "out of the dark places where I had been wandering all my life, and . . . out where I could see the stars and get my bearings once more."[1]

Stimson spent more than three years pursuing corporate malefactors as U.S. Attorney, then followed his patron into retirement in the spring of 1909 to refeather his nest at Winthrop & Stimson; but before long he was back under the stars again. In 1910, he ran for Governor of New York as Roosevelt's hand-picked candidate to succeed the popular and progressive Charles Evans Hughes, who was leaving the state house for the more exalted purlieus of the U.S. Supreme Court. The unsuccessful campaign foreshadowed 1912, for Stimson's defeat was due not only to the efforts of Tammany but also to lack of support from regular Republicans hostile to progressives generally and to Roosevelt in particular.

The following year, President Taft, in a vain effort to repair the breach between his administration and the Roosevelt wing of the party, made Stimson Secretary of War. The job put Stimson, for all his devotion to the cause of party unity, in a supremely uncomfortable position. He owed his public career to Roosevelt; his official loyalty now belonged to Taft, a man he liked and respected but whose tariff and conservation policies he opposed. As 1912 rolled around, Stimson made futile attempts to persuade T. R. not to challenge Taft. The burden of Stimson's plea can be found in a letter written to Roosevelt back in 1910. The following passage, urging the hero of San Juan Hill to resist leading his followers out of the party under the banner of the New Nationalism, is one of the most revealing expressions of the spirit of combined noblesse oblige and enlightened self-interest which animated Progressive reform.

> The only thing I wished to say particularly is that it seems to me vitally important that the reform should go in the way of a regeneration of the Republican party and not by the formation of a new party. To me it seems vitally important that the Republican party, which contains, generally speaking, the richer and more intelligent citizens of the country, should take the lead in reform and not drift into a reactionary position. If, instead, the leadership should fall into the hands of either an independent party or a party composed, like the Democrats, largely of foreign elements and the classes which will immediately benefit by the reform, and if the solid business Republicans should drift into new obstruction, I fear the necessary changes could hardly be accomplished without much excitement and possibly violence.[2]

Philosophically, Stimson subscribed to the Progressive thinking of Herbert Croly and Woodrow Wilson, which altered the course of American liberalism by shifting its defense of individual freedom from reliance on greater democracy and decentralized governmental authority to support of strong executive control over powerful and exploitative private interests. But

Stimson was constitutionally unable to follow his convictions out of the Republican party, even as it rushed to take up the reactionary stance he feared. He had a miserable time of it in the 1912 campaign; his public support of Taft succeeded only in alienating him for several years from the affections of T. R.

After the election Stimson returned to New York where, in a final bout with domestic politics, he spent a few years failing to clean up the state GOP and get a reformed state constitution adopted. Then, when war broke out in Europe, he turned to lobbying first for American preparedness and then for the United States to declare war on Germany. When this finally occurred, he turned down a high civilian post in the Democratic party's first great experiment in bipartisan war administration. Stimson was set on practicing what he had been preaching and, in 1917, enlisted in the army, eventually becoming, at the age of fifty, a colonel of artillery.

Before the war, Stimson had been in general sympathy with President Wilson's moderately progressive domestic policy. Then, he gave his partisan impulses expression by attacking Wilson for what he regarded as an isolationist posture. His distress may therefore be imagined when, after 1918, his own party repudiated its internationalist past. Vainly, Stimson tried to rally Republican support for the League of Nations. And although he often blamed Wilsonian intransigence for the Senate's failure to ratify the Treaty of Versailles, he recognized that ultimate responsibility for the United States' failure to assume its international responsibilities lay with the irreconcilables of his own party.

Nonetheless, even after the nomination of Harding sealed the League's fate, Stimson could not bring himself to follow his long-time friend and colleague in Republican reform, Herbert Parsons, in leaving the implacably isolationist GOP. On the contrary, he signed the notorious Statement of Thirty-One Republicans, which sought pro-League voters by arguing that the election of Harding would be the best way into the League. That move, which Stimson later characterized as "a blunder," did not even advance his own public career. After the election, as his memoirs curtly note, he "shared the oblivion which over-took most of the younger Eastern Republicans during the early 1920's."[3]

The Republican restoration of 1920 brought cold comfort to Establishment hearts. It quickly became clear that nothing would be done to bring about U.S. participation in the League. Moreover, the new administration's ideal of normalcy seemed the unreconstructed Republicanism of McKinley's day; there was little enthusiasm for reform and less for reformers. How-ever much the fires of reform had cooled in their own breasts, the old Eastern progressive Republicans had no desire to see the clock turned back to the Gilded Age, especially if it involved the sort of political scandal, reminiscent of Grant's presidency, which defaced the Harding administration.

For his part, Stimson spent this period of oblivion making himself rich through the practice of law. He kept in touch with foreign affairs by joining the new Council on Foreign Relations. His "favorite reform," on whose behalf he lobbied and testified in both New York and Washington, was that most conservative item on the Progressive agenda—and the animating cause of the young Brookings Institution—the executive budget.[4]

The rise of nationally-oriented Establishment institutions be-tween 1912 and the Great Depression reflected the political dis-enfranchisement of many of their leading lights. Spurned by the Republicans and often ill-at-ease with the Democrats, these men turned to such organizations as Brookings, the National Civic Federation, the great foundations, and the Council on Foreign Relations to pursue their goal of responsible social amelioration.

Stimson, bored with money making and eager for action, began serving Presidents again in 1927, when Coolidge sent him to Central America to mediate the civil war in Nicaragua. He spent the final year of the Coolidge administration as Governor General of the Philippines. Then, with Hoover's accession, he returned to the big time. After the 1928 election Stimson re-ceived word in Manila that the President-elect wanted to ap-point him to a cabinet post and, after replying that he would only be interested in the State Department, he got it. He had

The Establishment in the Political Ring

high hopes for Hoover, a distinguished engineer who had been a model of probity as Secretary of Commerce under Harding and Coolidge, was hardworking and intelligent, and valued the services of progressive Republicans.

Although Stimson's term as Secretary of State began well enough, it ended in unhappiness. Stimson became increasingly distressed at his government's refusal to apply anything more than moral pressure against Japanese aggression in the Far East. He found idiotic the unwillingness of the United States to bind itself by treaty to consult with its former European allies in case war threatened. He felt that American insistence on the repayment of war debts only served to deepen the world-wide economic crisis, as did the latest version of his old bugaboo, the notoriously protectionist (Republican) Smoot-Hawley tariff, which Hoover signed—and which seriously aggravated the Depression. While Stimson recognized that these misguided policies were rooted in the hardening nationalistic and isolationist mood of the country as a whole, he was prepared to place some of the blame on the President. In Stimson's view, Hoover was, for all his virtues, too weak a leader and, in following his Quaker lights, too much the pacific isolationist.

The final indignity came during the 1932 election campaign, when Stimson was called upon to make speeches defending the tariff and attacking the Democratic candidate. Although he had no qualms about supporting Hoover, Stimson was affronted at having to voice anything that smacked of *ad hominem* assault: "To use the great office of Secretary of State to launch a purely personal attack on Roosevelt is quite inconsistent with my dignity and that of the office."[5] Eight years later, he was delighted when, as Roosevelt's "non-partisan Republican" Secretary of War, he was placed under no obligation to campaign for, or even publicly to support, his chief.

While FDR was one of their own (Groton, Harvard, New York society), the upper crust of the Establishment found him hard to swallow. He had his cousin Teddy's knack for inspiring intense antagonism and, among them, the antagonism rose as the New Deal entered its second phase. His trump, however,

275

was foreign policy; no Republican president could have come close to the internationalist stance which he maintained. As war approached, his patrician peers, not without his solicitation, began to line up behind him. Like World War I only more so, World War II became a great love feast between the Establishment and a Democratic administration.

During the thirties, Stimson viewed Roosevelt with the ambivalence of his class. Early in 1933 he had come away from conversations with the President-elect convinced that Roosevelt would handle foreign policy well, and he found no reason to doubt that judgment later. But he was suspicious of Roosevelt's domestic advisors and, as the decade wore on, became an increasingly vocal critic of the New Deal. By 1940, however, Stimson's overriding concern was with the war in Europe. It was after a Yale commencement speech urging abandonment of neutrality and institution of universal compulsory military service that Stimson was offered the War Department by FDR.

Announcement of the appointment (together with that of another prominent Republican, Frank Knox, as Secretary of the Navy) came on the eve of the Republican nominating convention and predictably stirred the wrath of the GOP. The chairman of the Republican National Committee read both men out of the party. Later, at his Senate Confirmation hearings, Stimson was deeply offended when Senator Robert Taft, rising above family feeling, directed hostile questions—though perfectly appropriate ones for a good isolationist—at the man who had served his father loyally in the identical post. At the end of the presidential campaign, Stimson, having kept his own counsel, voted for Roosevelt, rejoiced at the election results, and got down to the business of preparing the nation for war. He got along well with Democratic leaders, finding "as always in his political life . . . that once the central issue of partisan opposition is removed, there are few roses so sweet as those that grow over the party wall."[6]

It was a welcome climax to Stimson's long career. The "baneful influence of politics" was finally removed. There was also, "the best staff he ever had": as Undersecretary, Robert P. Patterson, former federal appeals judge; as Assistant Secretaries, Robert A. Lovett, on-leave partner at Brown Brothers Harriman, and John J. McCloy, partner at Cravath; and as special assistant, Harvey Hollister Bundy, Boston lawyer and Assistant Secretary of State under Stimson during the Hoover years. These men—three Republicans and a Democrat, but all nonpolitical— were just the sort that Stimson had always wanted: "private citizens of standing and ability" willing to undertake "the labor of disinterested public service, and the financial sacrifice which it involved"[7] in order to help their country. At the State Department, Stimson had had great difficulty attracting such men; the Depression had imposed as large a financial sacrifice as they cared to endure, thank you, and Stimson could appeal to them with "neither the crusading spirit of Theodore Roosevelt's day nor the overriding appeal of national defense."[8] World War II provided both.

Once the war was over, Stimson's aides did not simply shuffle back to private life. Patterson succeeded his boss as Secretary of War. McCloy, after a year at Milbank, Tweed, became president of the World Bank and then U.S. High Commissioner to Germany, before taking over as head of the Chase Manhattan Bank. Lovett became Undersecretary of State and, after a year back at Brown Brothers, Deputy Secretary and Secretary of Defense under Truman. Only Bundy did not take another government post—though he did, during the fifties, do service as Chairman of the Carnegie Endowment for International Peace and President of the World Peace Foundation; he also contributed his sons, William and McGeorge, to public service.

These men, through Stimson, were the lineal descendents of the New Nationalism's progressive right wing. (After the war, McGeorge Bundy helped lay out their inheritance as coauthor of Stimson's memoirs.) By mingling with public servants who had imbibed the crusading spirit of the other Roosevelt's day, they helped reconstitute, during the war and in the immediate postwar period, the Eastern progressive consensus of wealth, brains, and good breeding which had broken apart in 1912. Some old progressives, men like Harold Ickes, Henry Wallace, and

Dean Acheson, had signed aboard the New Deal when it first shipped out. There were also the scores of young New Dealers —lawyers and economists—reminiscent of the bright young men who had gone into government with reform in their hearts in the early years of the century. What drew the conservatives in was not simply the war, though this was the proximate cause; beneath the surface was a common philosophy of government. All believed in a strong role for the federal government and— against Congress's nineteenth-century predominance—in having a strong executive in command.

This was the revised liberalism on which T. R.'s crusaders had cut their teeth; once the radical haze of the New Deal had cleared, formerly critical excrusaders emerged ready to acknowledge their portion in it. Stimson, for example, had originally opposed the Tennessee Valley Authority as a transgression against private enterprise. But by 1947 "he was prepared to admit—perhaps even to claim—what he had denied in 1935, that the principle of TVA, as an adventure in the effective use of national resources, was a direct outgrowth of the position he and other conservationists had taken back in 1912."[9]

If there was anyone who stood for the association of conservative aristocrats of service and young New Dealers it was Felix Frankfurter. Back in 1906, Frankfurter, after a brilliant showing at the Harvard Law School, was hired by Stimson to work in the U.S. Attorney's office in New York. There he became Stimson's devoted friend and protege, following him into his private practice in 1909, advising and writing speeches for him during his 1910 gubernatorial campaign, serving under him in the War Department during the Taft administration. For all his closeness to Stimson, however, Frankfurter parted ways with him politically and became a Bull Mooser in 1912. Subsequently he supported Wilson in 1916, Cox in 1920, the Progressive Robert M. LaFollette in 1924, and Al Smith in 1928, before attaching his star to Franklin Roosevelt. Between 1912 and 1932 he was, like many liberals, a man in search of a party; only after 1932 was it certain that the party was the Democratic one.

With time out for work in the War Department during World

The Establishment in the Political Ring

War I, Frankfurter spent the years between 1914 and his 1939 appointment to the Supreme Court as a professor of law at Harvard. Yankeedom held a special appeal for this Jewish immigrant and graduate of New York's City College. He married the daughter of a Massachusetts Congregationalist minister and, among his students, his favorites were not only the exceptionally brilliant but also, as Joseph Lash has pointed out, "the boys of old and wealthy families."[10] The young men he sent down to Washington to clerk for Justices Holmes, Brandeis, and Cardozo were the original amalgam of Harvard's "best and brightest."

Frankfurter's susceptibility to WASP culture also manifested itself in a deep anglophilia (or "anglomania," as his friend, the British Marxist Harold Laski, called it). It was the British—and Brahmin—ideal of public service which particularly inspired him; he had England's elite and broadly educated civil service in mind when he arranged for Harvard to establish its school of public administration. During the Hoover administration, Frankfurter had helped Stimson find able assistants to work in the State Department. Later, he served FDR as chief Harvard recruiter for the New Deal. As he wrote to his old boss and patron,

> Of course there are some things we can no longer afford—above all we can no longer afford to do without a highly trained, disinterested government personnel. What this Administration has had to do is to create something like the English civil service over night. And few things have been more shocking to me than all the silly and partisan and unworthy prattling on the part of many a responsible public man about the 'brains trust.' The term is silly enough, but wickeder is the implication that somehow or other brains, the brains of men who have given their lives to the study of governmental and economic problems, are either dangerous or unworthy of service to the state.[11]

Such missives helped keep Stimson from drifting too far into opposition to the Roosevelt administration. Back in 1933, Frankfurter had been responsible for setting up the initial meeting between FDR and the outgoing Secretary of State. When Stimson became Secretary of War seven years later, it was Frankfurter who, from the sanctity of the Supreme Court, acted as his advisor and discreet advocate within the administration's inner circles.

The young men whom Frankfurter sponsored and served shared more than a view of the role of the federal government. They were eager for public office but were for the most part inclined, or compelled, to seek it by means other than the political process—through business, the law, or the philanthropical and intellectual institutions so dear to their hearts. Frankfurter himself had meditated on these options as a young man. In a memorandum written to himself on the pros and cons of going to teach at Harvard, he noted that, although Stimson and T. R. had advised him to become a "citizen-lawyer" in New York, "I am not sure that Harvard isn't as good a ticket to draw in the lottery of chances for office as the other routes . . ."[12]

Out of the various nonpolitical routes to office emerged the Establishment as it came to be thought of in the postwar period. Opposition did not come from the Democratic party, which found it useful, ideologically congenial, and politically unthreatening, but from within the GOP, where an anti-intellectual, anti-elitist, and often reactionary populism had taken deep root. There the "unelected" fancypants and pointyheads in and out of government were lumped together as a collective, and collectivist, enemy.

Modern Republicanism

Between the World Wars, the most important change in the Republican party was the shift of Eastern financial interests away from the Old Guard and toward the party's more moderate and pragmatic wing.[13] This shift was a reflection of the traditional antipathy between Wall Street and the small businessmen of the American heartland, a division which expressed itself institutionally in the temperate, Establishment-oriented U.S. Chamber of Commerce on the one hand and the shrill, anti-Eastern National Association of Manufacturers on the other. Thus, in the age-old battle between New York and Ohio for mastery of the GOP, the New Yorkers, who liked to think of themselves as the "citizen wing" of the party, assumed the mantle of ideological compromise and enlightened self-interest, as against the strict laissez-faire Republicanism of the heartland. What they had going for them within the party was money and, after the Depression hit, the force of circumstance. In 1936 and 1940, the evident failure of conventional economics helped them secure the Republican presidential nomination for two moderates of their own choosing: Alfred M. Landon, the governor of Kansas, and Wendell L. Willkie, a Wall Street lawyer from Indiana.* In 1944 and 1948, hot and cold war internationalism became the lever of moderation; both times Governor Thomas E. Dewey of New York gained the Republican nomination against a host of more conservative men, of whom the most prominent was Senator Robert Taft of Ohio.

In 1952, the keepers of the faith, determined to put up one of their own, coalesced around Taft, but the citizen wing would have none of it. Unabashed at the signal failures of the past four elections, it chose as its champion the NATO commander and liberator of Europe, Dwight Eisenhower. As before, Taft was sabotaged by the taint of isolationism. Within the party Ike not only had the support of people such as Paul Hoffman, the president of the Ford Foundation and recent head of the Marshall Plan, but also young legislators like Gerald Ford and Richard Nixon, World War II veterans who felt that Taft could not be depended upon to maintain a sufficiently engaged role in the world for the United States. Once again the New Yorkers had their way, only this time, thanks to Eisenhower's personal popularity, the candidate won.

From his sponsors' standpoint, Eisenhower's job was to make the Republican party respectable again, both numerically and

---

*Harold L. Ickes, FDR's salty Secretary of the Interior, called Willkie "a poor, barefoot Wall Street lawyer."

philosophically. Ike himself, in the course of his presidency, came to regard this as the great desideratum. The enemy was the Republican right wing which, he once said, held so little appeal for the country at large that it could not even elect "a man who was committed to giving away $20 gold pieces to every citizen of the United States for each day of the calendar year."[14] Eisenhower's goal was therefore "to build up a strong progressive Republican Party" capable of dominating the center of the political road. To express his wishful conviction that his was "the party of progress," he floated such tepid slogans as "dynamic conservatism," "moderate progressivism," and "modern Republicanism."[15]

But the kite would not fly. Eisenhower was unable to extend his personal popularity to the GOP as a whole; the Democrats controlled both houses of Congress in all but the first two of his eight years in office. Right-wingers, who never forgave him for snatching the nomination in 1952, took the recurrent electoral setbacks merely as further indications of the bankruptcy of the Eisenhower brand of progressivism. Even the Establishment was unenthusiastic about it.

Part of the trouble was stylistic. Ike's fumble-tongued oratory stirred no pulses—nothing there to summon rough riders from Wall Street and academe to Rooseveltian crusade. More important, however, the Eisenhower administration was simply too conservative, too stand-pat—in a word, too Republican—for the postwar Establishment. Its economic policies betrayed scant recognition of the usefulness of Keynesian macroeconomics in keeping the country safe for capitalism. Inside the administration, the chief sympathizer with the New Economics was the chairman of the President's Council of Economic Advisors, Arthur Burns. His moderate views, however, could not prevail against the entrenched conservatism of Treasury Secretary George Humphrey. Burns' return to Columbia at the end of Eisenhower's first term left the administration uniformly devoted to the principle of balanced budgets and firmly opposed to the use of fiscal policy as a means of lifting the economy out of recession.

The Establishment in the Political Ring

On civil rights, Eisenhower, for all his dispatch of troops to Little Rock, waffled. Unenthusiastic about the Supreme Court's 1954 school desegregation decision, Ike communicated this lack of enthusiasm through equivocal public statements emphasizing the limited nature of the government's capacity to foster racial equality.

Finally, Eisenhower seemed a little complaisant about the great Manichaean struggle between freedom and communism. Sputnik left him relatively unmoved; no massive federal program was needed, he felt, to stem any precipitous decline in American technological know-how. Nor, in the last years of his presidency, did he share fears of a developing "missile gap" between the United States and the Soviet Union or of an overall weakening of American military might.

On each of these counts, the Establishment found Eisenhower wanting. The document which best preserves its state of mind is the famous "Compact of Fifth Avenue," an artifact of Nelson Rockefeller's eleventh hour attempt to dictate the 1960 Republican platform.

Arriving in Chicago for their July convention, Republicans already knew that the candidate would be Richard Nixon, a man broadly acceptable to the party as a whole and, for the right wing, the first nominee in forty years capable of generating wholehearted support. The old ideological conflict therefore came to focus on issues, not candidates. The Republican platform, already written, was a careful compromise worked out by the then president of Bell & Howell, Charles H. Percy. (Percy had become chairman of the Platform Committee after serving as head of the Committee on Program and Progress, an Eisenhower enterprise in defining "modern Republicanism.") As the convention prepared to convene, however, Percy found himself confronted with a committee of conservative true believers and a Rockefeller determined to have his liberal way. With the threat of utter philosophical disarray looming over Chicago, Nixon, in one of his typical "bold strokes," flew to New York and, in the Rockefeller triplex overlooking Central Park, accepted his antagonist's terms.

They were the Establishment's terms, the product of Rockefeller's consultations with the staff of advisors he had gathered
a year before to further his own presidential aspirations. The
text of the "agreement" released to the public on June 23 included a Wilsonian fourteen points, evenly divided between
foreign policy/national defense and domestic affairs. The foreign policy section was filled with alarums. "New political
creativity" was vitally needed to combat "the growing vigor and
aggressiveness of communism." The "swiftness of the technological revolution" (remember Sputnik) required "new efforts"
to insure our "survival" against "Soviet aggressiveness." (Yes,
Virginia, there is a missile gap.) The "imperatives of national
security" included "more and improved bombers, airborne
alert, speeded production of missiles and Polaris submarines,"
etc. Also, in accord with the thinking of Rockefeller's young
advisor, Henry Kissinger, the Compact called for "a modern,
flexible and balanced military establishment with forces capable
of deterring or meeting any local aggression." In short, "there
must be no price ceiling on America's security."

On the domestic side, a finger was crooked at the New Economics: "the rate of our economic growth must, as promptly as
possible, be accelerated by policies and programs stimulating
our free enterprise system . . ." Concerning civil rights, the call
was for "aggressive action" to combat segregation and discrimination in voting, housing, schools, and jobs. In addition, the
Compact advocated federal programs for school construction
and health care for the aged—both of which the Eisenhower
administration had opposed.

Eisenhower was, of course, outraged at this bland repudiation
of his administration. He particularly resented the implicit
charge that he, the military man, was guilty of shortchanging
the national defense. The missile gap, he knew, was utterly
spurious. Who was behind it? In the famous warning against a
"military-industrial complex" in his farewell address to the nation, Eisenhower seemed to hearken back to his agrarian populist roots, seeing the fine hand of Wall Street's war merchants
at work in the alarmist rhetoric of the Compact of Fifth Avenue.

The Establishment in the Political Ring

At the Republican convention the attempted coup did not fully succeed. Amidst conservative cries of betrayal, a stronger civil rights plank was written in and some tougher language on military posture added. Further than that an embittered Platform committee—and an angry Ike, on the phone from Newport, Rhode Island—would not go. Rockefeller declared himself satisfied.

Theodore H. White, whose *Making of the President, 1960* preserves the episode for history, notes how the Compact of Fifth Avenue confirmed regular Republicans in their long-held belief "that some mysterious Eastern conspiracy was always and permanently at work to frustrate both them and the Party from an expression of true faith."[16] But if the workings of the conspiracy were mysterious, the Compact's terms were anything but. Rockefeller had merely put forward, in his usual heavy-handed way, the familiar liberal agenda, an agenda towards which the country was increasingly well-disposed.

Eisenhower himself paid backhanded tribute to the strength of the emergent consensus by his wishful search for a modern Republicanism to appeal to the voters. The Compact of Fifth Avenue was, in fact, simply Rockefeller's version of that elusive creed. Its only shortcoming for Republicans was that, in 1960, it could have served perfectly well as the Democratic platform. After the election, management of the new consensus devolved on the Democratic party, with John F. Kennedy as vigorous standard bearer. Establishmentarians, feeling at one with the populace as never before in peacetime, rushed to join the crusade. The old Stimsonians McCloy and Lovett took up posts as senior advisors. McGeorge Bundy, the new national security advisor, led troops down from Cambridge. Douglas Dillon, the Republican investment banker from New York, took over at Treasury. Dean Rusk, old State Department hand and president of the Rockefeller Foundation, became Secretary of State. "Just about everyone now agrees," began Richard Rovere in his 1961 essay, "that there is an Establishment in America." After years in the shadows, the American Establishment had finally emerged to face the bright light of day.

That emergence shifted the drama of national politics away from the traditional contest of entrenched antagonists—the two major parties—towards wars of the periphery against the center. A logical outcome of the Establishment's strategy of bipartisan consensus, the results were not pleasant. The Establishment itself became the locus of discontent.

For all that the 1964 presidential election was a stunning defeat of conservative Republicanism, the lasting significance of Barry Goldwater's candidacy was in initiating the anti-Establishment style that became the salient feature of national political campaigns for the next decade and more. The brutal treatment of Republican moderates and liberals at the Cow Palace in San Francisco was not only revenge for past indignities but also the manifestation of a powerful desire to break with the whole impulse towards national consensus. Goldwater, unlike the accommodating Easterners, offered "a choice, not an echo." By invoking a slogan which exalted extremism over moderation, the candidate deliberately assumed the role of a crusader from the periphery off to lay waste the slack and unprincipled center.

Goldwater's real alternative was to the Johnson administration's domestic policies. On national defense and prosecution of the young Vietnam war, what he offered was more resounding echo than choice. Four years later, objectors to the international side of the liberal program took up arms against the Establishment from within the Democratic party. Eugene McCarthy and, in his own way, Robert Kennedy articulated the challenge. Hubert Humphrey's subsequent defeat was as much as anything else due to the lukewarm support of the then peripheral antiwar Democrats. Humphrey, they asserted, offered "no choice" on the war. In 1972, the antiwar anti-Establishment had its way within the Democratic party when it secured the nomination for George McGovern. And in 1976, another peripheral figure became the Democratic nominee. Jimmy Carter was pure periphery; his claim to the presidency rested not on a different approach to issues, but simply on the fact that he was from "out there."

But, in the dialectic of Establishment and anti-Establishment which characterized so much of American politics in the sixties and seventies, Richard Nixon was the star performer. No leading politician, perhaps, understood the conflict as well as he did; certainly none felt it so deeply. He was in a sense the conflict's embodiment: the Red-baiter who became Ike's loyal soldier, the signer of the Compact of Fifth Avenue whose heart belonged with the regulars. "I won the 1968 election as a Washington insider, but with an outsider's prejudices," he writes in his memoirs.[17] Those prejudices succeeded in making Establishment politics for the first time the central preoccupation of a sitting administration.

The Best of Enemies

Richard Nixon, arriving at the White House in 1968, had spent his life tilting with establishments. It had always been Nixon the outsider: taking on the smart set at Whittier College; turned down, after law school, by John Foster Dulles' Wall Street firm; getting elected to Congress by defeating the wealthy, ex-radical Yalie, Jerry Voorhis; making his name by bringing down Alger Hiss, fair-haired scion of the New Deal; enduring, as Vice-President, Eisenhower's indifference and the slights of the White House staff; suffering defeat at the hands of a glamour boy from Harvard; then, after the disastrous California gubernatorial candidacy, cold-shouldered in New York by Nelson Rockefeller.

Unlike Barry Goldwater or George Wallace, however, Nixon was not a heroic adversary, a free lance doing battle with the Eastern host. The wounds he suffered during his early public career were those, rather, of an unappreciated servant. So he presents himself. He had supported the Marshall Plan and the United Nations, opposed outlawing the American Communist party, and favored Eisenhower over Taft. Yet, because he had endeared himself to the McCarthyite right by prosecuting Hiss, his job as Ike's running mate was to do the political dirty work of denunciation and rabble-rousing. Eisenhower could take the high road while Nixon kept the right wing happy. "In a sense, the hero needed a point-man."[18]

After the election, Nixon was the one to maintain party unity and keep McCarthy at bay—while Ike golfed. When McCarthy went after the army: "Once again I seemed to be the only person with enough credibility in both camps to suggest a compromise. Eisenhower was away on a golfing vacation, and I wanted to keep the situation from spilling over into a public brawl."[19] McCarthy refused to compromise; while Nixon helped White House staffers draft a response, the now returned President, "probably to relieve the tremendous anger he felt, practiced chip shots on the South Lawn."[20]* Nixon sums up service in Eisenhower's court by disclosing a confidence of Ike's World War II chief of staff, General Walter Bedell Smith.

> He was very tired, and he uncharacteristically began showing his emotions. Tears began to stream down his cheeks, and he blurted out his pent-up feelings. "I was just Ike's prat boy," he said. "Ike always had to have a prat boy, someone who'd do the dirty work for him. He always had to have someone else who could do the firing, or the reprimanding, or give any orders which he knew people would find unpleasant to carry out. Ike always had to be the nice guy. That's the way it is in the White House, and the way it will always be in any kind of an organization that Ike runs.[21]

In the White House, Nixon suggests, the prat boy was himself.

Eisenhower repaid Nixon badly for services rendered. During the "Nixon Fund" crisis of the 1952 campaign—when Nixon was accused of maintaining a secret and illegal slush fund—Ike's support for his running mate was lukewarm at best. In 1956, Ike also played around with the idea of dropping Nixon from the

---

*During the crisis which followed revelations that Sherman Adams, the austere White House chief of staff, had accepted gifts and favors from a New England industrialist, Ike was "hitting 5-irons on the South Lawn." Meanwhile Nixon, the president who would fire his own chief of staff personally, was busy, he says, pressuring Adams to resign. Ibid., p. 196.

ticket.* And four years later, he often seemed unenthusiastic about his Vice-President's presidential candidacy. When asked by a reporter what major ideas Nixon had contributed to his administration, Ike responded, "If you give me a week, I might think of one." More harmfully, he refused to use fiscal policy to bring the economy out of recession in time for the election—action which would probably have resulted in Nixon's victory.

But behind the ambivalent Eisenhower, Nixon discerned a far more hostile force: "the Eastern liberal establishment,"[22] which had saddled the GOP with Ike in the first place. Party stalwarts, according to Nixon, did not resent Eisenhower so much as the men around him, "particularly the Eastern liberal faction that had managed his nomination, symbolized by Cabot Lodge, Sherman Adams, and Tom Dewey."[23] Eisenhower's establishmentarians, Nixon felt, were always against him, urging that he be dropped from the ticket in 1952 and 1956, and gravitating to Nelson Rockefeller in 1960. Nonetheless, he was, or sees himself as having been, their prat boy as well as Ike's.

When it came to policy, Nixon was always closer to Eastern liberals than to Midwestern conservatives. The Compact of Fifth Avenue represented no renunciation of principles for him; however, he and not Nelson Rockefeller had had the dirty work of selling it to the convention. Moreover, on an individual basis, Nixon claims credit for protecting the Establishment from McCarthy. McCarthy had wanted to launch an attack from the Senate floor against the nomination of Harvard's President Conant as U.S. High Commissioner for Germany. "Getting wind of his plan, I managed to talk him out of it."[24]

In the summer of 1953, McCarthy discovered that William Bundy, "one of (CIA Director) Allen Dulles's brightest young men," had contributed money to the legal defense fund of Alger Hiss. When the Senator made known his intention of investigating not only Bundy but also the entire CIA, Dulles asked Nixon

*Nixon quotes Charles Jones, the president of Richfield Oil, as having told the President, "Ike, what in the hell does a man have to do to get your support? Dick Nixon has done everything you asked him to do. He has taken on the hard jobs that many of your other associates have run away from. For you not to support him now would be the most ungrateful thing that I can possibly think of."

to intervene. Bundy seemed to be a loyal American, Nixon told McCarthy. The Hiss contribution? " 'Joe,' I said, 'you have to understand how those people up in Cambridge think. Bundy graduated from the Harvard Law School, and Hiss was one of its most famous graduates. I think he probably just got on the bandwagon without giving any thought to where the band-wagon was heading.' "[25] McCarthy called off his dogs.

But if Nixon—and even McCarthy!—were capable of making allowances for the old school tie, no reciprocal forebearance, Nixon thought, could be expected from the Eastern liberals. The Hiss case was his great triumph, and trauma. As he noted in his 1962 volume of memoirs, *Six Crises:*

> Hiss was clearly the symbol of a considerable number of perfectly loyal citizens whose theaters of operation are the nation's mass media and the universities, its scholarly foundations, and its govern-ment bureaucracies. This group likes to throw a cloak of liberalism around all its beliefs. . . . as soon as the Hiss case broke and well before a full bill of particulars was even available, much less open to criticism, [it] leaped to the defense of Alger Hiss—and to a counterattack of unparalleled venom and irrational fury on his ac-cusers.[26]

Here was the enemy which Nixon, when he finally achieved the presidency in 1968, sought to overthrow.

He pressured his first Cabinet officers to hire only Republi-cans and urged them "to resist the Washington habit of recruit-ing their staffs solely from Eastern schools and companies and instead to branch out and get new blood from the South, the West, and the Midwest."[27] The Cabinet officers themselves, he claims, were subject to the same criteria. David Kennedy, the Chicago banker who became Secretary of the Treasury, "met my requirement that my Secretary of the Treasury not be part of the New York-Boston banking establishment that had domi-nated the department for too long."[28]*

---

*This suggests that the job had been offered in bad faith to David Rockefeller, who would have taken it under different circumstances; Nixon must have known that the head of the Chase would never join his administration lackey-like, without speaking with him directly. See Chapter 7.

The Establishment in the Political Ring

Throughout Nixon's term in office, amid all the struggles with the federal bureaucracy, the news media, and the Democrats, the Establishment remained his principal demon. He could not exorcise it. Even after his landslide reelection, before Watergate broke in upon him, "Congress, the bureaucracy, and the media were still working in concert to maintain the ideas and ideology of the traditional Eastern liberal establishment that had come down to 1973 through the New Deal, the New Frontier, and the Great Society."[29]

It was Nixon's fortune to be president at a time when the enemy most resembled his prejudiced image of it. In the late sixties and early seventies the Establishment was far from the brave and bellicose assemblage of the New Frontier. It had become, like the country itself, divided and demoralized over the war in Vietnam and, for the first time in its history, was beginning to think in terms of the limits, rather than the limitless possibilities, of American power. Here, for Nixon, was just that failure of nerve, misplaced idealism, and lack of patriotism which he had always discerned in those people.

In both his books, Nixon gives the same moral to the Hiss affair.

> Since 1917 Moscow had been successful in convincing all too many of our best educated citizens of the superiority of Communism and caused them to abandon Western ideals and values for the chimera of Soviet "idealism" which unconsciously became their moral standard.[30]

The problem of postwar America was how to "instill in brilliant young Americans the same dedication to the philosophy of freedom that the Communists seemed to be able to instill in people like Hiss."[31] The best educated citizens, brilliant young Americans, people like Hiss—these were the culprits. From their ranks had come the Communists and fellow travelers of McCarthy's day and the doves of McGovern's, symbols for Nixon of the decadence of the country's privileged class.

Communist countries had no such problem. Nixon envied China its "leader class"; in comparison with the elite of Maoist society, ours seemed feckless and demoralized. When he returned from his presidential journey to the Middle Kingdom, Nixon informed his Cabinet: "Whatever the failures of their system, there is in their leader class a spirit that makes them formidable. . . . The leader class in the U.S. sometimes lacks the backbone, the strength, that they have. History tells us that as nations become better educated they tend to soften."[32]

Nixon had come into office "anxious to defend the 'square' virtues" and identifying himself with "unabashed patriotism."[33] His goal as president was to unfurl the old banners, to reinspire the country with the American Way. This meant dissociating his administration as clearly as possible from America's soft and overeducated leader class. The Establishment felt that patriotism should be expressed discreetly; flaunt American flag lapel pins. The Establishment believed in keeping religion out of sight: bring Billy Graham into the White House for prayer breakfasts. The Establishment thought of its institutions as beyond all but the most sympathetic criticism: have Agnew roast the universities and the media. The Establishment disported itself in sophisticated and elegant circles: keep the White House staff out of Georgetown.

Nixon admired the fervor of the Chinese leaders; he may also have admired their philosophical commitment to live and work among the peasants. Although he was anything but a folksy, backslapping politico, Nixon prided himself on his closeness to ordinary citizens. As he confided to his diary shortly before the 1972 election,

> The American leader class has really had it in terms of their ability to lead. It's really sickening to have to receive them at the White House as I often do and to hear them whine and whimper and that's one of the reasons why I enjoy very much more receiving labor leaders and people from middle America who still have character and guts and a bit of patriotism.

The passage concludes with the hope that the labor leaders will not, after the election, become partisan Democrats again. "Frankly, I have more in common with them from a personal standpoint than does McGovern or the intellectuals generally. They like labor as a mass. I like them individually. The same can be said of all other groups or classes, including young, black, Mexicans, etc."[34]

Incapable of leadership and out of touch with the common man, the Establishment was, for all its power in Washington, on the edge of extinction. Watergate was simply its death rattle. So Nixon thought on March 13, 1973, when the dimensions of his Watergate problem were beginning to dawn upon him. As he remarked to John Dean,

> They are, they're, they're going to Watergate around in this town, not so much our opponents, but basically it's the media, uh, I mean, it's the Establishment. The Establishment is dying, and so they've got to show that after some rather significant successes we've had in foreign policy and in the election, they've got to show, "Well, it just is wrong because this is—because of this." In other words, they're trying to use this to smear the whole thing.[35]

When, on April 23, H. R. Haldeman, the White House chief of staff, heard that his resignation had been decided upon, he vainly tried to avert the evil decree by arguing, "This would be the first real victory of the Establishment against Nixon."[36]

Nixon saw himself as a world-shaker. His revenue-sharing programs, which turned federal funds over to states and localities for use at their own discretion, represented "no less than the New American Revolution."[37] In 1972, after reelection he redoubled his efforts to "break the Eastern stranglehold on the executive branch and the federal government."[38] All political appointees in the executive branch had to submit their resignations; henceforth the White House would control all high-level hiring. Nixon's aim was, by 1976, to have given the country "the beginning of a new leadership class whose values and aspirations were more truly reflective of the rest of the country."[39] In a memo written to himself at the outset of his second term, Nixon listed "New Establishment" among his political goals. The phrase came just below "New Majority." Nixon hoped to supervise the realignment in American politics which had been postulated by Kevin Phillips in his 1969 book, *The Emerging Republican Majority.*[40]

The New Majority

Phillips, the lawyer who served the 1968 Nixon campaign as resident expert on ethnic voting patterns, saw a new populist movement sweeping the land. Like earlier populist movements, this was directed against an Eastern Establishment; unlike them, it was conservative.

Phillips understood political behavior as a function of the mutual animosities of "voting streams," a kind of class analysis he once described to Garry Wills as "knowing who hates who."[41] Prejudice determines political affiliation. The political division of the American heartland traced to the Civil War; a solidly Democratic South faced a more or less Republican Midwest. But this animosity (mainly of Southern whites for the Republican party) was ending. Phillips predicted that the South would become the bastion of a new Republican party which was middle class, staunchly conservative, and dominant everywhere but in the Northeast and Northwest. Only in those corners of the country was the GOP likely to lose members, as, indeed, it had been for some time. This prospect did not trouble Phillips; it simply signified the consolidation of the Establishment within the Democratic camp.

In Phillips' view, the old, pre-New Deal Establishment of financiers and industrialists had become liberal by somehow falling under the influence of "the rising clique of Roosevelt-era entrants into the publishing houses, universities, government agencies and the arts."[42] It was now embodied in and shaped by "the research directors, associate professors, social workers, educational consultants, urbanologists, development planners, journalists, brotherhood executives, foundation staffers, communication specialists, culture vendors, pornography merchants, poverty theorists and so forth." Phillips saw these unsavory types as representing "a new collectivity of research, scientific, consulting, internationalist and social interests which, benefiting from the expenditures and activities of big government, propagated an ideology which promoted big government."[43]

Of course, the benefits of big government were hardly confined to Phillips' Establishment and its alleged clients, the urban poor. Indeed, if anyone had a stake in federal munificence it was farmers dependent on agricultural subsidies and businessmen with government contracts, not journalists, culture vendors, and social scientists. Phillips admitted, though *sotto voce*, that there were businessmen susceptible to the ministrations of big government, as well as "an increasing number of private sector employees [who] were technicians and specialists more akin to government planners than to the small entrepreneur of Horatio Alger legend and old-line Republican sympathy."[44] But for Phillips the crucial issue was moral rather than economic: "Horatio Alger" versus "pornography," "planners," and "internationalist . . . interests." The economics was mythic, grounded in the hoary image of the self-making American who only needs to be free of government interference in order to succeed.

Phillips' ideas helped shape the Southern strategy of the 1968 Republican presidential campaign. But to Nixon, the moral crusade was at least as important as the electoral tactic. Phillips offered the prospect of recapturing the country from just those dark forces which Nixon believed dominated it. As far as Nixon was concerned, the New Majority did not even have to be Republican. He and his staff spent several days after the 1972 election discussing the idea of galvanizing it with a new political party.[45] The important thing was to seize the moral initiative.

My fears about the American leadership classes had been confirmed and deepened by what I had seen and experienced during my first four years as President. In politics, academics and the arts, and even in the business community and the churches, there was a successful and fashionable negativism which, in my judgment, reflected an underlying loss of will, an estrangement from traditional American outlooks and attitudes. The Vietnam war had completed the alienation for this group by undermining the traditional concept of patriotism.[46]

At another time Nixon might, on policy grounds, have had second thoughts about rushing into a hard-shell conservative coalition. But the Nixon administration was dominated by Vietnam, and it was over the war that its domestic battle lines were inevitably drawn. The New Majority really comprised those Americans, or those types of Americans, who, in Nixon's eyes, preferred "peace with honor" to war guilt.

The principal artifact left from Nixon's intended moral revolution is the notorious White House "enemies list." That list, or rather, the bundle of lists and other documents which John Dean had collected in a file entitled "Opponents List and Political Enemies Project," must be seen against the background of Vietnam and the special compulsion to overturn the Establishment which the war created in Nixon.

The enemies project was part of the White House response to Daniel Ellsberg's leaking of the Pentagon Papers, the massive secret history of U.S. involvement in Vietnam compiled in the Defense Department towards the end of the Johnson administration. On June 24, 1971, eleven days after *The New York Times* published its first account of the Papers, the first listing of enemies circulated through the White House. A covering memo for John Dean and press aides Van Shumway and Jerry Warren stated innocuously, "Attached is the list of opponents which we have compiled. I thought it would be useful to you from time to time." It was signed by George Bell, a member of the staff of Charles Colson, White House counsel and chief political hardballer.

Like the Plumbers, the news leak-plugging team which went into operation two weeks later, the enemies project reflected the White House's conviction that now, with the Pentagon Papers, its opponents inside and outside of government were finally coming out of the woodwork for a full-scale assault on the Nixon presidency. There was a refusal to believe that Ellsberg had acted independently. David Young, the Plumber in charge of stage-managing the House Armed Services Committee's investigation into the Pentagon Papers affair, reported to his superiors that others were involved: Morton Halperin and Leslie

Gelb, the directors of the study; Paul Warnke, their boss at the Defense Department; officials of the RAND Corporation, where Halperin, Gelb, and Ellsberg had worked after leaving the government. "Furthermore, the whole distribution network may be the work of still another and even larger network . . . "[47] Circles within circles.

The initial opponents list had some two hundred entries grouped under various headings: "Politicos," "Media," "Business," "Labor," "Academics," "Celebrities," and "Organizations." The set is similar to the list Nixon put under "New Establishment," in the memo he wrote to himself at the outset of his second term: "Press," "Intellectuals," "Business," "Social," "Arts." The new Establishment of Nixon's imagining was to be conservative, patriotic, New Majoritarian. The old Establishment was liberal, dovish, pro-Democratic, and its "successful and fashionable negativism" was insidiously prevalent throughout society. The list of two hundred presents a more or less coherent image of negativism's nattering nabobs, a kind of White House fantasy of the ultimate network for disseminating Ellsbergism across the land. Scattered through the list were all of the supposed principals in the Pentagon Papers affair, including the head of RAND, Henry Rowen, and World Bank president Robert McNamara, who, as LBJ's Secretary of Defense, had ordered the study in the first place. Among fifty-six inimical reporters, columnists, and media executives, three newspapers which had a hand in publishing the Papers—the *Times*, *The Washington Post*, and *The St. Louis Post-Dispatch*—were designated as Nixon opponents in themselves.

In his memoirs, Nixon, rather more courteous than some of his apologists, presents Watergate as the reaction of the Establishment to his assaults against it. Seeking on behalf of America's "Silent Majority" to "give the Eastern liberal elite a run for its money for control of the nation's key institutions,"[48] he had, after the 1972 election, "thrown down a gauntlet to Congress, the bureaucracy, the media, and the Washington establishment and challenged them to engage in epic battle." Watergate was not a minor incident blown out of proportion but "a cavernous weakness in my ranks" which his enemies could legitimately exploit, all being fair in war.

The scenario is too grandiose, however. It depends on the questionable claim that Nixon's enemies hated him more in the spring of 1973 than they did during the 1972 campaign, in which Watergate played an insignificant role. It was not Nixon's gauntlet which made Watergate the issue it became, but the judicial process. Watergate burglar James McCord spoke up when threatened with a heavy prison sentence; John Dean began to talk when faced with the likelihood of criminal prosecution. No administration could have escaped wholesale denunciation for what became known about the Nixon White House in March and April of 1973: how it had conspired to obstruct justice.

Richard Nixon was one of those rare possessors of paranoid fears whom fate permits to bring fantasy to life. The Establishment of his nightmares never existed as a coherent body unified against him until he supplied Watergate. Dean's file played its own small part in the unification; even some staunch supporters of Nixon among the "Eastern elite" began to drift over to the enemy camp when they saw the contents.

William F. Buckley, Jr., was particularly bothered by a memo of Dean's urging that "the available federal machinery" be used "to screw our political enemies." That, said Buckley, was "an act of proto-fascism . . . far and away the most hideous document to have come out of the Watergate investigation." He called on the President to denounce it. *Fortune,* also concerned about the memo, warned readers that, whatever the wrongs of some government regulation of business, "it would be an evil of different magnitude if regulatory powers were wielded—or suspected of being wielded—for partisan political ends."

Samuel Lambert of the National Education Association was outraged. "If I were an enemy of the President, heaven help the real enemies," he said. "I voted for Mr. Nixon and so did the majority of the members of the organization I headed. This is unbelievable." The columnist Joseph Alsop, calling the lists "poisonously silly," gave thanks that the operation had not been in abler hands. That "would have been genuinely dangerous to all we care for."

Perhaps the supreme indignity of Watergate for Nixon lay in seeing the Establishment grab the initiative back from him. He seems, somehow, to have had a premonition of it. "I had a rather curious dream," reads a diary entry from the 1972 campaign, "of speaking at some sort of a rally and going a bit too long and Rockefeller standing up in the middle and taking over the microphone on an applause line. Of course, this is always something that worries a person when he is making speeches, as to whether he is going on too long. It is a subconscious reaction. It is interesting."[49]

Hardly had Nixon achieved his greatest electoral triumph than the Establishment took the platform of moral leadership away. In the end, no one would listen to him. He resigned and many of his New Majoritarians went to jail. His last contribution to the polity was to talk his successor, Gerald Ford, into making Nelson Rockefeller the new Vice-President.[50]

Trilateralism: Rise and Fall

How much was Watergate a triumph for the Establishment, the Establishment of our conception rather than the prepotent thing which Richard Nixon believed to dominate the federal government and the nation's cultural life? Certainly the institutions we have examined had ample reason to be happy to see Nixon go. The administration had not liked any of them. Harvard was the living symbol of the enemy, and the source of Archibald Cox and his special Watergate prosecutors. Brookings was the object of special White House antagonism. The Ford Foundation stood for do-goodism in all its elitist glory. The Council on Foreign Relations was the heart of Rockefeller country. *The New York Times* perpetrated the Pentagon Papers.

Watergate was, moreover, tailor-made for Establishment morality. The White House had in the most sordid and partisan way undermined public trust in the presidency, the nation's great unifying institution. National cohesion was the Establishment's big business. Against the White House's flagrant self-interestedness, it posed its creed of disinterested service; against the obscenity of the tapes, its good manners; against Nixonian hypocrisy, its honorable patriotism. If Watergate was a great victory for the American system, it was also a great victory for the cherished values of the Establishment. But for all that, it did little for the Establishment's political fortunes.

Gerald Ford set up a kind of right-wing-of-the-Establishment administration, somewhat similar to Eisenhower's. It worked even less well than Eisenhower's did as far as the Republican party was concerned. Despite a conservative domestic policy and a foreign policy tending towards the jingoistic, the GOP did not take kindly to its good-natured president.

Nixon's political demise turned out, in the end, a personal disgrace, not a disgrace for the forces of right-wing populism he did so much to rally. Thus, although Nixon regarded his defeat as Nelson Rockefeller's victory, many Republican right-wingers saw no need to go along. They wanted no part of Rocky, and made enough noise to force him off the 1976 presidential ticket. Having done that, they abandoned President Ford for one of their own, the ex-Governor of California Ronald Reagan, and came within a whisker of depriving Ford of the nomination. It was business as usual within the GOP: let friends of the Establishment beware.

Within its own houses of worship, meanwhile, the Establishment was taking stock and not having a very good time of it. The economic shocks of the 1970s were disastrous for the Third Sector generally. At Harvard, Brookings, and Ford, money problems helped encourage philosophical review; likewise at the *Times*, the editorial line and the bottom line showed a new sensitivity to each other. Overall, the Establishment had begun a stuttering adjustment rightwards, but what it wanted was anything but clear. Nelson Rockefeller, hoping quixotically for the 1976 GOP nomination, set up a Commission on Critical Choices to pack him a new, more conservative briefcase.

On the domestic side, the Establishment's agenda was confused by the conflicting pulls of slow growth and steady inflation, by the desire to increase productivity and at the same time maintain environmental, consumer protection, and occupational safety standards. In foreign policy there were opposing currents too. How to adjust to the post-Vietnam world? The Council on Foreign Relations' 1980s Project represented one approach to the problem. Another approach, more significant for American politics, was the Trilateral Commission, founded by David Rockefeller. Its chief academics were Zbigniew Brzezinski, then a professor at Columbia, and Henry Owen of the Brookings Institution.

In 1971, Brzezinski had persuaded Huntington Harris, a wealthy Washington businessman and trustee of the Brookings Institution who had been a chief agent of the OSS during World War II and won the Medal of Freedom, to fund a series of studies on a subject dear to his heart and Henry Owen's: the common economic and political interests of Western Europe, Japan, and the United States. Owen was a tenant of David Rockefeller's at one of the Rockefeller summer houses at Seal Harbor, Maine, where he delighted in talking trilateralism with Rockefeller and Brzezinski, another Mount Desert Island summer dweller. All three were growing increasingly worried, as the Nixon-Kissinger foreign policy unfolded, over deteriorating relations among the United States and its principal allies.

The Nixon foreign policy was based on a concept called "Pentagonalism," according to which the world was viewed as divided among five great powers: the United States, the Soviet Union, China, Japan, and Western Europe. Under Pentagonalism, the United States would be free to play a tough, independent, and self-centered strategy against the other four. It could enter into temporary coalitions with one or more of the others, but would be free to shift alliances and play one bloc off against another. The substance was nationalistic, the style self-righteous, and the execution secretive and sudden.

Pentagonalism produced "Nixon shocks" to Western Europe and Japan; Treasury Secretary John B. Connally used high-pressure tactics on trade and monetary issues, while Henry Kissinger negotiated deals with the Soviets and the Chinese that stunned the Japanese and the Europeans. Trilateralism, a reaction to Pentagonalism, was more comfortable with the traditional postwar American bipolar view of the world as divided into capitalist and Communist spheres. The Trilateralists advocated, both for the sake of economic growth and national security, that the United States work as closely as possible—and at the highest level—with the other industrial powers. They feared that the very existence of the postwar alliance was at stake, threatened not only by Nixon's adventurist foreign policy but also by resurgent economic nationalism.

In 1972, David Rockefeller decided to launch the Trilateral Commission after returning from a Bilderberg Conference in Holland—an annual closed meeting among prominent Western business leaders, presided over for years by Prince Bernhard of the Netherlands until he was disgraced by the exposure of his involvement in the Lockheed Aircraft bribery scandals.

Owen and Brzezinski helped Rockefeller to choose the American members of the new Commission. The European chairman, Max Kohnstamm, principal of the European University Institute in Florence, Italy, and the Japanese chairman, Takeshi Watanabe, head of Trident International Finance, Inc., and former president of the Asian Development Bank, picked their own representatives. In all, 145 "commissioners" were recruited from the Trilateral countries—bankers, industrialists, labor leaders, lawyers, politicans, and academics. Among the ten U.S. commissioners who were active politicians was James E. Carter, Jr. (as he was called in the first Trilateral Commission membership list). The then Governor of Georgia was welcomed as an enlightened representative of the New South; in that guise he had been awarded, in 1971, a cover on *Time* magazine.

The Establishment in the Political Ring

The Commission held biannual meetings in one or another of the Trilateral countries. At their seances, scholarly studies were presented, then published and disseminated under the Commission's auspices. When some measure of consensus evolved, Commission members would set their recommendations before government officials in the respective countries. American commissioners did not have much influence on policy; Henry Kissinger did not appreciate meddling. But they did help in the education of Jimmy Carter. Here is the testimonial from his 1976 campaign autobiography, *Why Not The Best?*

> In order to insure the continuing opportunity for penetrating analyses of complicated, important, and timely foreign policy questions, there is in operation an organization known as the Trilateral Commission. A group of leaders from the three democratic developed areas of the world meet every six months to discuss ideas of current interest to Japan, North America and Europe. Subjects like the world monetary system, economic relations between rich and poor nations, world trade, energy, the future of the seas, aid to less developed countries, and other possibilities for international understanding and cooperation are first studied by scholars, then debated by members of the commission, and finally analyses are published and distributed to world leaders. Membership on this commission has provided me with a splendid learning opportunity, and many of the other members have helped me in my study of foreign affairs.[51]

After his election, President Carter made his thanks for the help manifest. He chose from among the Trilateralists his Vice-President, Secretary of State, Under Secretary of State for Security Affairs, Under Secretary of State for Economic Affairs, Secretary of the Treasury, Under Secretary of the Treasury for Monetary Affairs, Secretary of Defense, National Security Advisor, Deputy Director of Central Intelligence, Ambassador to the United Nations, Ambassador to Italy, Ambassador in charge of the Panama Canal Treaty, Ambassador-at-Large for the Law of the Sea, Ambassador-at-Large for Nonproliferation Matters, Representative (later Ambassador) to the People's Republic of China, Chief Disarmament Negotiator, Ambassador for arranging summit conferences among the leaders of the Trilateral powers, and a few others. There were only a few others left. In all, some 40 percent of the American members of the Trilateral Commission joined the Carter administration.

It was little wonder, then, that some outsiders should have come to regard the Trilateral Commission as nothing more nor less than a conspiracy to take over control of the United States or (with the collaboration of its foreign commissioners) the world. Writing in that nonestablishment journal of views, *Penthouse*, Robert A. Manning claimed that the Commission was an antidemocratic, elitist cabal composed of "the most powerful people in the world," who had for several years been grooming Carter for the American presidency. "There can be no doubt today," Manning concluded in September 1977, "that David Rockefeller and his Trilateral Commission have succeeded in seizing control of America's foreign policy." In the less fevered *Atlantic*, Jeremiah Novak was inclined to regard it as a liberal internationalist fraternity, allied with the public interest groups Common Cause and New Directions, whose purpose was to "fashion a new world order." It had now achieved its "vital political objective," said Novak, "to gain control of the American Presidency."

Such fears were laid to rest soon enough. National Security Affairs advisor Brzezinski and his aide Samuel Huntington were shortly feuding with Secretary of State Cyrus Vance and SALT negotiator Paul Warnke over arms control, the SALT talks, and a host of other issues. Trilateralist Andrew Young, the Ambassador to the United Nations, fell afoul of both sides and in due course had to resign for speaking on the sly with a representative of the Palestine Liberation Organization.

International monetary policy remained uncoordinated and the dollar sank against the German mark, the Swiss franc, the Japanese yen, and gold. U.S. energy policy floundered. The Western Europeans were crossed up by the decision to cancel the neutron bomb. Arms sales proceeded apace. Congress slashed the size of U.S. contributions to the International Monetary Fund. In brief, the Trilateral program was in shreds. Many wondered whether the administration had any foreign policy at all. Some conspiracy.

There had never been a conspiracy in the first place. The Trilateral Commission, typical of institutions of its kind, had contained the usual ideological range of respectable foreign policy positions and, after the Carter administration took office, the several viewpoints flowered forth. Still, Carter's Trilateral connection was worth pondering, because so much of the confusion of the Carter presidency lay in the ambiguous relations of the outsider in the White House and the Establishment which had spawned the Commission.

Inside Looking Out: Carter

When Jimmy Carter set out in quest of the presidency as a little known Georgia politician, his persistent theme was anti-Establishment. In February 1976, he declared:

> I can tell you that there is a major and fundamental issue taking shape in this election year. That issue is the division between the "insiders" and the "outsiders." . . . The people of this country know from bitter experience that we are not going to get these changed merely by shifting around the same group of insiders. . . . The insiders have had their chance and they have not delivered. And their time has run out. The time has come for the great majority of Americans—those who have for too long been on the outside looking in—to have a President who will turn the government of this country inside out.

Those closest to him were the Georgian outsiders: such men as Bert Lance, Charles Kirbo, Jody Powell, and Hamilton Jordan. After Carter defeated Ford, Jordan, his chief political operative, announced: "If, after the inauguration, you find Cy Vance as Secretary of State and Zbigniew Brzezinski as head of national security, then I would say we have failed."

THE AMERICAN ESTABLISHMENT

By those standards, they failed. Jordan had apparently hoped to separate his boss from the Establishmentarians with whom he had been associating on the Trilateral Commission. But although the press had a good deal of fun with the injudicious remark, Jordan remained Carter's most important aide and Carter himself retained his outsider's prejudices. He felt that "Washington" distrusted him, and warned his staff to expect to be held up to contempt and ridicule. After a couple of years in office, he remarked in an interview, nearly all of them had— "all," he said, "except Stu Eizenstat."

For its part, Washington was inclined to regard Carter as a bush leaguer, a bright and hard-working performer perhaps, but one who had been brought along too fast. The Georgians in the White House seemed all thumbs and stubborn; their good-old-boy style and self-assurance were jarring to the Establishment. But the Georgians gave no quarter to the Eastern big shots who joined the Carter administration. They preferred a folksier, humbler, regional powerhouse like Robert S. Strauss of Texas. He was regarded as the wise old man, the role model, for the young White House aides. Steering clear of the salons of Georgetown, the Georgians reminded some Washingtonians of the Nixon men.

But Carter was no Nixon. In the summer of 1979, when he was far down in the polls and had just shaken national confidence by dismissing his Treasury Secretary, Blumenthal, his HEW Secretary, Califano, and his Energy Secretary, Schlesinger, Carter turned to the Establishment for help. He offered David Rockefeller first the Treasury secretaryship, and later the post of chairman of the Federal Reserve Board. Rockefeller declined both times. In his view, what the economy needed was a tough hand willing to fight inflation, even at the cost of generating a slump. David Rockefeller did not, he told us in an interview, think it would do the President much good to have a Rockefeller at the Fed, responsible for forcing people into unemployment; the symbolism would be awful. Instead, Carter got a major Rockefeller ally and former employee, Paul A. Volcker, president of the New York

The Establishment in the Political Ring

Federal Reserve Bank, as his new Federal Reserve chairman.

And Carter was able to recruit to his White House staff two earls of the Establishment: the Washington lawyer Lloyd Cutler as his senior counsel and Hedley Donovan, the just retired Editor-in-chief of Time, Inc., as a jack-of-undefined-trades. Trilateralists both and card-carrying members of strings of Establishment institutions, they helped Carter bail out his leaking ship. When a tempest blew up over the discovery of a brigade of Soviet troops in Cuba, elder statesmen from previous administrations lent a hand in pouring oil on the troubled waters. Among these was McGeorge Bundy, who some months before had been contemptuous of the administration's internal disarray over foreign policy, especially the feuding between Brzezinski and Vance. Now, rushing to the rescue, Bundy took to the pages of the *Times* to say that the Soviet troops in Cuba had arrived during his own tenure as national security adviser nearly twenty years earlier; he pooh-poohed their importance. Bundy also, in *Foreign Affairs*, pointedly contrasted Carter's respect for constitutional processes in the conduct of foreign policy to the disregard shown by Nixon and Kissinger. In return, President Carter dispatched the First Lady as a dove of peace to the Establishment. Late in the year, Mrs. Carter went to the Council on Foreign Relations to describe her visit to the Cambodian refugee camps along the Thai border.

Thus, even before the seizure of the American embassy in Teheran and the Soviet invasion of Afghanistan rallied the veteran troops, the Establishment was willing, even if more skeptically than the first time around, to lend support to its sometime protege, Jimmy Carter. Some of its liberal members were keeping their options open on the last of the current generation of Kennedys, Edward. But they regarded Jerry Brown, explorer of the new politics, California-style, as beyond the pale. So did the Democratic voters.

On the Republican side, old patterns of hostility toward the Establishment still existed. On the stump, Ronald Reagan attacked Carter for being under the thumb of the Trilateral Commission. Pointing at the Commissioners within the administra-

307

tion, Reagan's issues adviser, Edwin Meese 3d said, "All of these people come out of an international economic-industrial organization with a pattern of thinking on world affairs." Their influence, he said, had led to a "softening of defense," because the Trilateralists believed that "trade and business should transcend, perhaps, the national defense."

Reagan also used the issue of the Establishment and the Trilateral Commission against his Republican rival, George Bush, in the primaries. In New Hampshire Reagan's supporters presented their candidate as the champion of Middle America, the harassed taxpayer, the inflation-shocked forgotten man of 1980 —and assailed Bush as the affluent candidate of the bluestocking Yankee Republican establishment. "Mr. Bush is the candidate of the self-appointed elite of this country," said William Loeb, the powerful publisher of *The Manchester Union Leader*, which had made Bush its main target. "It's old school tie and inherited influence against the working middle-class Americans, the first-generation college people," said Gerald Carmen, Reagan's New Hampshire campaign manager. "We're really running against the preppy, old-school-tie establishment."

In the Florida primary, Bush, who had resigned from the Council on Foreign Relations because, he said, it was "too liberal," was dogged by the Reagan supporters' charge that he was an agent of the Trilateral Commission, from which he had neglected to resign. The true Establishmentarian usually has more memberships than he can keep track of.

Whether Reagan himself was actually the scourge of the Establishment he seemed was uncertain. His campaign staff whispered to Eastern newsmen that Reagan was looking for "a good Harvard professor"—not Kissinger—for a top advisory post.* "Reagan is not antagonistic toward the Establish-

---

*But Kissinger, for his part, was willing to serve Reagan, and not so easy to put off. On March 29, 1980 Kissinger told an audience at Loyola College in Baltimore that he would be prepared to return to government service if Reagan were elected President. "I have made it a policy not to refuse Presidents," he said. "I think if one is asked to serve as Secretary of State, one has an obligation to the President—to take that seriously." Earlier, however, Kissinger had endorsed Gerald R. Ford, Reagan's foe. Ford, after declaring that, in his opinion, Reagan could not be elected,

ment," said Jude Wanniski, one of his economic advisers. The Reagan juggernaut seemed unstoppable, and the Establishment Republicans were prepared to get aboard—if they were invited.

On the Democratic side, many establishmentarians were still keeping their options open on Jimmy Carter—especially since he and his family appeared disposed to make peace with them. Even Billy Carter, the First Brother, said in the springtime of 1980 that he himself had altered his low opinion of Northerners. He told a New York television audience that until recently "I never did think there was such a thing as a good Yankee." When Secretary of State Cyrus Vance resigned in protest following the President's aborted military effort to rescue the hostages in Iran, Carter replaced him with a Northeasterner, Senator Edmund Muskie of Maine, a move intended to reassure the nation and the Establishment.

For those establishmentarians unwilling to go with either major party candidate, John Anderson, the smart, principled, independent-minded Republican congressman from Illinois, offered an alternative—but one that looked like the longest of long shots.

Free at Last

In 1980 Americans finally appeared to be losing their illusion that political outsiders would do better than insiders. If so, the Establishment stood to gain, with its own traditions of insiderdom and professionalism. Free of the false enthusiasms of Came-

---

subsequently took himself out of the race and said he would support the Republican candidate, whoever he was. Kissinger then sent forth his message to the Reagan camp in his Baltimore speech: "I have not consulted with his campaign, but I met on seven or eight occasions before the primaries started with Governor Reagan, and have had rather extensive conversations about the substance of foreign policy. And I was impressed with my meetings with him."

lot, the incubus of Vietnam, and the wallows of Watergate, it was ready to give its help to any competent President of either party. It wanted to be serviceable to government but to stay at arm's length from politics—to carry on its disinterested work, unloved but no longer despised and vilified.

Somehow it takes an exceptional national leader to bring the Establishment fully alive and to make it as useful as it can be. Henry Stimson searched for such a leader all his life, thought he had found him first in Theodore Roosevelt, then in Herbert Hoover, and believed he had him at last in Franklin Roosevelt in time of war. A generation later, a whole host of Trilateralists looked hopefully to Jimmy Carter, and, when he failed to provide the strong and consistent leadership they needed, they too stumbled. Politic, cautious, and meticulous, the Establishment can be useful to a strong leader, but rarely can it lead.

Chapter 9

The Prospects of
the Establishment

SINCE the earliest days of the Republic, central forces of power, political or financial, have been the targets of a series of withering attacks from different directions. Early in the nineteenth century, some postrevolutionary politicians discovered that they could succeed in life by refighting the War of Independence. They sought to make their own new coalitions of power legitimate, as David Brion Davis has put it, "by picturing their opponents as heirs of the British and Tories—as an un-American elite whose systematic encroachments demanded, on the model of the Declaration of Independence, a proclamation of grievances proving 'a long train of abuses and usurpations.'"[1]

The Anti-Establishment Habit

Over the years, while the revolution faded from view, the anti-Establishment habit remained, a potent and noisy weapon of democratic righteousness. A favorite target has been Wall Street, the black beast of William Jennings Bryan and his followers. In the 1930s, Franklin Roosevelt played on this hostility by inviting public scorn upon the "economic royalists."

The most vitriolic—and sincere—attacks on the Establishment have come from the extreme left and the extreme right— from the Communists on one side and from such home-grown fascist groups as the Ku Klux Klan, the John Birch Society, and the American Nazi Party on the other. A weird current example of anti-Establishment vitriol is the U.S. Labor Party, which, at the will of its founder and leader, Lyndon LaRouche, Jr., has leaped from extreme left to extreme right without losing its paranoia; its monsters have remained Wall Street, the Rockefellers, the Council on Foreign Relations, and that most traditional of foreign devils, Great Britain.[2]

What all these extremist anti-Establishment groups have in common is their inconsequentiality. They have lacked appeal to the vast majority of the American people, and their threat to the Establishment or the American polity as a whole has been trivial, even when social and economic breakdown loom, as in the Great Depression. As a constant reminder of the blessings of freedom and sanity, however, they remain useful.

The democratic left in America has been nonrevolutionary. Although a new social order is a formal part of their long-range agenda, they have been chiefly interested in near-term, achievable social reforms; commonly, they have sought support from the Establishment itself, and have often got it—under the Establishment's principles of tolerance to dissenters and sympathy for social idealism and constructive change. Moderate Marxists and Social Democrats can be found at the Century Club and the Ford Foundation, and even at the Harvard Faculty Club. Their rhetoric is often anti-Establishment, but they live within the gates.

There are times, however, when the American left roars. In times of national crisis, when the Establishment behaves with unusual insensitivity, lethargy, or stupidity, the left may enhance perception and speed action. Such was the case with the social and industrial reforms of the 1930s and the anti-Vietnam crusade of the late 1960s and early 1970s; much of the Establishment itself ultimately joined those causes. But the threat of radical change to the system, or to the Establishment, from the left has evaporated whenever the immediate crisis passed.

This is not to say, however, that there are no serious challenges to the Establishment, with its aspiration of playing a mediating and guiding role between the contending forces of democracy and capitalism. One of these challenges is a manifestation of popular democracy. The other derives from the primordial spirit of capitalism.

The Populist Attack

The sources of populist hostility toward the Establishment are cultural, regional, and economic. The populist assault traces back to the early nineteenth century when it took the form of a rural and Western revolt against the economic and political dominance of Eastern commerce and finance. Late in the century, the torch of Thomas Jefferson and Andrew Jackson was raised high by William Jennings Bryan, who, as the champion of Southern and Western farmers and miners, vainly assailed the citadels of Eastern capitalism and irreligion. The Democratic coalition which triumphed in the presidential elections of the 1930s and 1940s depended on the old Bryan wing of the party, but after World War II the voice of American populism expressed itself mostly on behalf of political reaction, especially in the South and within the increasingly dominant right wing of the Republican party.

Both Senator Joe McCarthy of Wisconsin and Governor George Wallace of Alabama made national careers by using their own flaming versions of 100 percent Americanism to arouse traditional anti-Eastern and anti-Establishment emotions and suspicions. In less malignant ways, Barry Goldwater, Richard Nixon, and Ronald Reagan have done the same, casting themselves as Middle American warriors against the effete and the elite.

Nixon's presidency was remarkable for carrying the old populist antipathy into the White House and making it a primary shaper of national policy; his New American Revolution was to be a fulfilment of populist dreams and nightmares. Watergate and the downfall of Nixon did not, however, signal a grand national rejection of Nixonian populism. On the contrary, its pulse beat with renewed vigor after Nixon was gone: in Ronald Reagan's nearly successful attempt to seize the 1976 GOP nomination from Gerald Ford, in the emergence of the tax-cutting enthusiasm symbolized by California's Proposition 13, and in the revival of America-First nationalism as it expressed itself in the Congressional debates on the Panama Canal and SALT II treaties.

In recent years, the populist revival has fed upon a new regionalist theory of power in America. Some Republican strategists and politicians have interpreted recent history as the struggle of an increasingly prosperous and populous Sunbelt to wrest national leadership from a declining Northeast. The Sunbelt, the southern rim of states stretching across the country from Carolina to California, is the domain of rugged individualism, old-fashioned mores and prejudices, and aggressive patriotism. Its denizens, the "Cowboys", mighty with oil, agribusiness, and other economic body builders, are more and more asserting themselves over their decadent Yankee opponents.

But the battle has not gone all one way. Kirkpatrick Sale, whose book, *Power Shift*, appeared in 1975, treats Watergate as a

The Prospects of the Establishment

Yankee counterattack. But this reversal of fortunes, he concluded with ominous portent, was unlikely to last. "Indeed, it seems most probable, given the populational and economic verities of the Southern Rim, that the forces of the Sunbelt will enjoy another period of national resurgence, and not too many years away. Perhaps they will then be more constrained, perhaps ameliorated by time and fertilization, but their basic characteristics are almost certain to be intact.[3] The Sunbelt's "challenge to the Eastern Establishment" (as the book is subtitled) cannot be denied.

With all its current vitality, however, the populist threat to the Establishment can easily be exaggerated. Whatever the importance of its new regional strength, the populist appeal has, at least since the Civil War, always been to political outsiders. During the years of Republican preeminence in the late nineteenth and early twentieth centuries, it found a home within the Democratic party, then turned to the GOP when the Democrats, with the New Deal, became the national governing party. Populist enthusiasm in America springs from disgruntlement at the powers that be; once attached to power itself, it becomes embroiled in contradiction, an enemy of itself. This, as Garry Wills foresaw so brilliantly in his 1969 volume, *Nixon Agonistes*, was Richard Nixon's problem as President. As the lifelong outsider and populist warrior, he could not come to terms with the power he had won.

In a way, Nixon himself understood the dilemma, at least as far as his own party was concerned. He flirted with the idea of starting a new political party because, as he says in his memoirs, the Republicans did not know how to think like a majority party.[4] There were, he believed, plenty of Republicans intelligent and committed enough to govern; but somehow they were uncomfortable with the business of wielding power. Populism had to be transformed into an instrument of power. Thus, Nixon was excited by John Connally's "Democrats for Nixon" organization in 1972, and especially by Connally himself, his first choice to succeed Spiro Agnew as Vice-President in 1973, as well as his preferred GOP presidential candidate for 1976. No discomfort with power there.

But Connally was no real candidate to head the "New Establishment" which Nixon, rather pathetically, wanted to summon forth. Connally was happy to go up to New York to try to convince *The New York Times* editorial board that he was a reasonable fellow. (Talking to the *Times'* editorial board was just what Nixon was not prepared to do.) Connally was also happy to speak at the Council on Foreign Relations (on the record, as he insisted) and to deliver the prestigious Pollack lectures at Harvard's Kennedy School of Government in 1978. In short, as populist true belivers by and large appeared to realize in 1980, Connally the would-be GOP candidate was not one of them— no crusading outsider he, rather an insider with the insider's proclivities, a man prepared to deal with the Establishment on its own terms.

The problem with Nixon's "New Establishment" was not, however, that Connally was a false messiah. For the new body Nixon hoped for was a phantom, even more evanescent than Chairman Mao's own "leader class." For true populists, no Establishment is acceptable, since Establishments are the enemy. Even as it triumphs, the populist impulse is already sliding away, back into its habitual opposition. With no substitute to offer, its threat to the hated Establishment remains empty. Indeed, as Nixon's behavior showed, it tends to *reinforce* the Establishment, building the villain up to justify its own antagonism and to validate the importance of its own existence. Nixon is inconceivable without the Harvards, the Councils, the Hisses (not enough of them), and the Rockefellers (a few too many). They are the yang to his yin. And they, in turn, batten on him, and build him up in his villainy.

The Prospects of the Establishment

The "Free-Enterprise" Challenge

An even more serious challenge to the Establishment originates from a somewhat different, though closely related, source: the challenge of the unreconstructed, ideological free-enterprisers. The free-enterprise creed* posits that the only successful way to run a business—or a society—is for business to concentrate strictly on maximizing profits, within rules of the game set by law and with the government as "umpire," except for national defense virtually its only proper function. This free-enterprise ideology opposes itself to the social responsibilities creed of the corporate Establishment, as expressed, as we have seen, by a David Rockefeller. In the words of an apostle of the counter-creed, Milton Friedman:

> Few trends could so thoroughly undermine the very foundation of our free society as the acceptance by corporate officials of a social responsibility other than to make as much money for their stock-holders as possible. This is a fundamentally subversive doctrine. If businessmen do have a social responsibility other than making maxi-mum profits for stockholders, how are they to know what it is? Can self-selected private individuals decide what the social interest is? Can they decide how great a burden they are justified in placing on themselves or their stockholders to serve that social interest? Is it tolerable that these public functions of taxation, expenditure, and control be exercised by the people who happen at the moment to be in charge of particular enterprises, chosen for those posts by strictly private groups? If businessmen are civil servants rather than the employees of their stockholders then in a democracy they will, sooner or later, be chosen by the public techniques of election and appointment.
>
> And long before this occurs, their decision-making power will have been taken away from them.[5]

The free-enterprise challenge, unlike the populist, is subversive of the Establishment rather than in a state of permanent

*For a thorough exposition of the traditional "free-enterprise" ideology, see Francis X. Sutton et al., *The American Business Creed* (New York, 1949).

opposition. The tempting creed it offers, that the only public service incumbent on businessmen is to make as much money as possible, was just the creed that the Establishment was formed to moderate. Since the Progressive era, its claim has been that capitalism was not enough. Society, of course, was capitalist, but it was more than that; and the prudent and well-intentioned businessman had to look beyond the success of his own corporation if he wanted the society—and a capitalist economic system—to endure. The polity had other interests and forces which demanded notice and accommodation. The way to attend to them was by supporting a Third Sector of private and independent institutions concerned with the public good.

The free-enterprise ideology received its severest setback during the Great Depression, when its deficiencies became painfully obvious. After World War II, the institutions of the Establishment were in a position to bring the lessons home to business. To ease the burdens of the business cycle, to safeguard capitalism itself, the federal government had to have a discretionary hand in managing the national economy. Labor unions were not socialism's shock troops. Business itself had social responsibilities beyond the balance sheet. The system benefited from free and freely critical universities and research organizations, and even from its reasonably well-behaved dissidents.

But despite the hope of postwar liberalism that old ideological categories would be transcended and the "mixed economy" gain universal acceptance, the free-enterprise ethic did not wither away. In the late 1960s, partly because of the overselling of the Great Society and partly because of the resuscitation of the intellectual left in academia, it began a wholesale revival.

Businessmen finally rebelled against the familiar postwar preaching of their social responsibilities. "By God, why should we worry about the plight of welfare cheats and subsidize the Marxist rhetoric of professors who call us war criminals?" they asked. Of course, conservative businessmen, unreconciled to the new dispensation, had never ceased to exist. Now, however, they began to be joined by the previously enlightened. The capitalist-philanthropist David Packard, chairman of Hewlett-

Packard and a former Deputy Secretary of Defense, was not alone in calling upon the business community in 1973 to give only to academic enterprises that directly serve corporate interests.

In the 1970s, a growing number of intellectuals undertook to encourage this natural inclination of businessmen. Most prominent among these intellectuals were the so-called "neo-conservatives,"[6] a mixed bag of former liberals and leftists who, at the end of their respective ideological odysseys, had discovered the Market. They embraced it with nearly as much old-time religious fervor as the older generation of celebrants of laissez faire. And they discovered that, while the free market was in trouble in the West, the market for libertarian apologetics was booming.

In print, public lecture, and private consultation, the neoconservatives encouraged their new-found corporate patrons to think well of themselves and their works, and to proselytize aggressively for the economic values which they held, or were supposed to hold, dear. The free-enterprising businessmen were less consistent than their intellectual counsellors. When in deep distress, they were likely to rush to government for corporate bailout, protective tariff, quota or trigger price, subsidy or other succor.

But, since the neoconservatives were extolling the virtues of immediate self-interest, they found an attentive audience among businessmen. Especially as economic conditions worsened, businessmen were pleased to assert that their activities could no longer be denigrated or taken for granted, that what they did best they should be freer to do better—for the good of society.

Among the most outspoken of the free-enterprise warriors in recent years has been former Treasury Secretary William E. Simon, whose book, *A Time for Truth*, was on the best-seller lists for the better part of 1978. A harsh dualism governs Simon's world, in which a small but enlightened troop of champions of capitalism and freedom are beleagured by the immense hosts of liberal darkness.

To save the Republic, Simon calls on the business community

to support the raising of a (Republican) "counterintelligentsia."[7] "Multimillions" must be given to those philanthropical foundations "imbued with the philosophy of freedom."[8] There must be no more "mindless subsidizing of colleges and universities whose departments of economics, government, politics and history are hostile to capitalism. . . ."[9] Those news media which serve as "megaphones for anticapitalist opinion" must get no more money from business; rather, it must go to media which are either "procapitalist"* or "at least professionally capable of a fair and accurate treatment of procapitalist ideas, values and arguments. The judgment of this fairness is to be made by businessmen alone."[10]

Thanks to the insidious designs of the designated anticapitalist enemy, fairness need only be a one-way street.

> Those capitalists who, in the interests of "fairness," have financed the intellectual opposition have seen their foundations literally taken over. The textbook case of such infiltration was dramatized recently when Henry Ford III [sic] resigned from the Ford Foundation. I called Mr. Ford on reading of this in the newspapers and asked him to explain how this had happened. He answered: "I tried for 30 years to change it from within but couldn't."[11]

Mr. Ford must have been misremembering; only in the late 1970s did it occur to him that "his" foundation might be insufficiently attentive to the needs of capitalism. To Simon, however, the lesson is clear: once the opposition passes the gates, it cannot be dislodged. Thus, "this absurd financing of one's philosophical enemies must not be tolerated in the new foundations."[12]

It is somewhat surprising that Simon, a hardheaded multimillionaire financial executive and bond salesman, who had made a fortune pragmatically helping New York City market its rapidly growing mountain of debt, should put so much stock in the battles of intellectuals; he urged that "non-egalitarian schol-

---

*In 1977 Mr. Simon tried to launch a "procapitalist" newspaper in New York, called the *Trib*, but was forced out by the paper's other entrepreneurs, who charged that he wanted to use it to further his own political ambitions. The paper promptly folded.

ars and writers" be given "grants, grants, and more grants in exchange for books, books, and more books." American capitalists have always understood the value of advertising, but there is more to it than that. Without the help of professional ideologists, businessmen cannot, in his view, be trusted to look out for their own interests. This Simon makes clear in his account of New York City's 1975 to 1976 financial crisis, the most personal and revealing chapter in his book.

As President Ford's Secretary of the Treasury, Simon had opposed using federal funds to bail out New York's sinking ship. In his campaign to force the city to declare its bankruptcy, he naturally expected the opposition of local politicians, labor leaders, and the liberal intelligentsia. What shocked him was the behavior of his former Wall Street colleagues. Foremost among these was David Rockefeller, who "rushed about frantically warning financial leaders all over the world that the entire international financial system would disintegrate if New York defaulted."[13] This, Simon asserts, was laughably untrue. Yet other leading bankers, even the most sober and responsible, ultimately added their voices to that of David Rockefeller's. "It was one of the saddest days of my life when financial giants like Pat Patterson of Morgan Guaranty and Walter Wriston [of Citibank], who had been steadfast for so long, caved in and finally joined the others in asking Washington for federal aid."[14]

The bankers no doubt were thinking about the New York paper they were holding. (The Chase had more than anyone.) But that, according to Simon, was not the true explanation. "The banks were not really afraid of going broke."[15] No, "as much as anything, the bankers' fear was *moral.*" That was the real issue. As usual, the liberals had been able to "orchestrate a nationwide uproar over good versus evil."[16] The evildoers were those, like Simon, who wanted New York's creditors to foreclose. But the potential foreclosers were not up to the job. It had always been so.

Businessmen and bankers, who seem to value respectability more than their lives, are incapable of tolerating this moral abuse. Invariably they collapse psychologically. And whatever they may think and say in private, in public they either go mute or stumble frantically over their own feet as they rush to join the moral bandwagon.[17]

As he makes clear, however, Simon did not oppose the bailout because he thought that bankruptcy was the most efficient and least costly solution to New York's problems. He was engaged in his own moral countercrusade to teach the city—and the country—a lesson. New York had been the source of the liberal philosophy "that has ruled our nation for forty years."[18] It was "America in microcosm—America in its most culturally concentrated form."[19] Thus, while the failure of New York would not have had serious economic effects on the rest of the nation, the aborting of that failure was disastrous to its moral condition. ("What is happening to New York, therefore, is overwhelmingly important to all Americans, and it is imperative that they understand it.")[20]

The compromise solution which has enabled the city to go on without serious disruption was so displeasing to Simon precisely because of its moral indeterminacy: "On the most fundamental philosophical level, little had changed."[21] All those nonegalitarian books were needed to strengthen the backbones of the "gutless financiers"[22] who had refused to support their secretary of the treasury in his hour of near-heroism. Never again should they be browbeaten into thinking that "to question liberalism was to be a reactionary blackguard."[23]

Beyond the business community lay bigger game: the American people generally. They had to be made to realize that their true interests lay with unfettered capitalism. Putting this message across was a considerable task, since the people's normal impulse was to ask the government for what they wanted. And it was, in the end, their government which made the rules. "Ultimately, of course, it is in the political arena that we must definitely solve these problems. The difficulties will be great because Congress today, much of the judiciary, and for the moment the executive are dominated by a coercive, redistributionist, and collectivist philosophy."[24]

The Prospects of the Establishment

During the 1970s, the capitalist forces sought to turn the country around by, among other things, unabashedly pressuring the Third Sector. They were, of course, pushing with the tide, for the country at large—Third Sector included—was moving to the right on its own. As we have seen, this was broadly true even among the Establishment institutions which lie at the Third Sector's heart. The question is how much further they, under right-wing goading, will allow themselves to be pushed.

Establishment institutions have found it difficult to resist this pressure from the right precisely because part of its business is to accommodate new interests and impulses in society. Rather than pick up the gauntlet flung at its feet by the counterinstitutions of the right, the Establishment has walked gracefully (to the right) around it, hoping to co-opt the would-be foes.

That the Establishment will proceed as far as the free-enterprise ideologists want, however, is unlikely. Only if the nation becomes locked in the embrace of the new (old) business ideology—and if that turns out to be the answer to its problems, from inflation and unemployment to a cleaner environment and a healthier population (in the literal not metaphorical sense)—will the Establishment, in accordance with Paleyan principles for its own survival, go along. But if, as we believe, the free market is not the philosopher's stone of a crowded, chaotic, polluted, and combative industrial society, then the Establishment can be expected to continue along its mediating path. It will still try to bring order to a nation where highly organized economic and social groups—corporations, labor unions, farm organizations, and government itself—lustily compete for power, and, in that struggle, neglect and endanger the broad public interest.

Liberty, Now and Then

Thomas Jefferson's was the sweet voice of liberty, and it is no wonder that his song appealed not only to businessmen but to farmers and laborers and most of the rest of a young nation, born in a battle for freedom. But Jefferson thought the way to ensure the United States would remain a nation of free people was to keep the economy essentially agrarian. "The mobs of great cities," he said, "are like sores on the human body." If Americans were "piled upon one another in large cities, as in Europe . . . they shall become corrupt, as in Europe." Even in Europe, they heard his song. The poet William Blake wrote:

> Why should I care for the men of Thames
> And the cheating waters of chartered streams
> Or shrink at the little blasts of fear
> That the hireling blows into mine ear?
>
> Though born on the cheating banks of Thames—
> Though his waters bathed my infant limbs—
> The Ohio shall wash his stains from me;
> I was born a slave, but I go to be free.

A century after Blake wrote, one would have to be mad to bathe an infant in the Ohio. Factories spewed their wastes into the river. Along the Ohio, beside the Great Lakes, down the Mississippi, down the Atlantic and Pacific coasts, even in the Lone Star state, the cities sprawled—cities that vastly out-reached those European cities of Jefferson's day. And the United States had become a nation of hirelings; employers blew whistles of fear into their hirelings' ears. So the hirelings organized against them, and fought them.

It was out of that environment of industrialization and industrial conflict that the modern American Establishment emerged. The hope of its most dedicated leaders was to build a private source of public good, to join the knowledge and moral authority of a nonsectarian sect to the interests of a ruling class, in an effort to preserve liberty in a mass-industrial society. They recognized, as the philosopher John Dewey put it, that the United States had moved "from an earlier pioneer individualism to a condition of dominant corporateness." If liberty were to survive under the new industrial and social conditions, it could not do so on the basis of the Jeffersonian creed of agrarianism, minimal government, and unbridled individualism—not only for flesh and blood people, but for those artificial persons, the great corporations.

Nor could liberty be protected simply by aggrandizing the power of the State. That would be (to quote the late Soviet leader, Nikita Khrushchev) like setting the goat to guard the cabbage patch.

A third force was needed: the Establishment.

Thus, in our conception, there are three great forces in the American polity. Two are what Benjamin Watkins Leigh called "Power" (political power) and "Property" (material wealth), and the third is this mysterious institution called the "Establishment." Where Power in America derives from popular democracy, and Property, in the modern sense, overwhelmingly from corporate capitalism, the Establishment has roots that trace back to civilizations which knew neither of these. Although the origins of the Establishment are ecclesiastical and aristocratic, in America it is firmly joined to both democratic and capitalist institutions. But its ambitions go beyond: it seeks to protect and advance social, moral, and aesthetic values that transcend the interests of any single person, economic group, or political constituency or organization; it affects to be a harmonizer, an arbiter, a wise instructor of the nation—and particularly of its political and business leaders.

Power, Property, and the Establishment have different means of shaping social outcomes: politicians by garnering votes, enacting laws, collecting money and redistributing it, passing out rewards and punishments; business executives by raising capital, controlling stock, building corporate structures, creating jobs, creating new technologies; but the Establishment (without direct support of the electorate or vast sums of money of its own) can prevail only by impressing politicians, business-men, and whatever part of the public is willing to listen and show some respect for its knowledge, experience, and moral principles.

Morality (a term less used today) may be most crucial of all. The turning point in the downfall of Senator Joseph McCarthy came when the Boston lawyer, Joseph Welch, invoked moral principle against him for threatening to destroy the career of a young lawyer in his firm. It was moral outrage, excited by the press and then picked up by the courts, over Watergate and the White House coverup, that destroyed Richard Nixon.

Prestige counts. An echo chamber seems to exist out there in the country for what the Establishment says. Whether right or wrong, it matters.

For the Establishment is more than a collection of worthy and visible institutions: it is a spirit, a ghost, a force which draws others to it, especially in times of national crisis.

But the Establishment is influential not just because of its prestige or knowledge or moral principle, but because it, too, is "political." It listens to what the nation wants and it reacts, adapts, to meet changing national demands. Indeed the hallmark of the Establishment is its adaptability. This has enabled it to survive great lurches in public opinion and revolutions in economic and social conditions.

Adaptability, however, can also be a vice. The danger is that one day the Establishment might adapt itself out of existence, lose a secure sense of its moral and leadership role, see its institutions abridge their special character and become mere forums, or chameleons for every shifting color in the political jungle.

Should that happen, the Establishment would lose its strength as a unifying national force: as mediator between rich and poor, black and white, management and labor, industrialists and environmentalists, hawks and doves.

The Establishment can play such a mediating role only if it preserves its disinterestedness, devotes itself to finding truth and "calling the shots," insists upon and practices civility, enunciates an ethic that puts the public interest above special interests or any one political interest (including its own).

These are great aims and difficult for anyone or any institution, to attain. When an Establishment institution, or some prominent Establishment figure, falls short of its or his or her own proclaimed ideals, the world takes note, expressing anger and contempt, as it should.

Has the Establishment a future? The institutions of the Establishment are, for the most part, well-situated, flexible, resourceful—and survival is what they seek. But that should not be the major goal. Better that an institution that has lost its heart and spirit and principles vanish, and let another more vital and dedicated take its place. What matters is that the *idea* behind the institutions live; and, as Conrad put it, the unselfish belief in the idea. In America that idea, from the beginning, has been liberty and service to the common good.

How well has the American Establishment lived up to that idea? That is what we have tried to discover. It would be presumptuous of us to try to hand down verdicts: Harvard, guilty; the Ford Foundation, not guilty; *The New York Times*, the jury is still out, etc. The readers will have to judge, the nation will judge, and the members of the institutions themselves will judge. In general, we think we would render a Scotch verdict: we approve of some things the Establishment has done and disapprove of others. While we wish it would behave better— more courageously, with a quicker sense of justice and a stronger will to right social wrongs—we are on the whole glad it exists.

Does it? Having worked through all these pages and the researches and interviews that lie behind them, we are reasonably sure that it does. But, assuming that it does, as we do, we think it works best as a truly secret organization, secret even from its own membership.

Let it fade back into the shadows it came from. Let its institutions forget that they are part of it; let them worry about their own institutional integrity, their own work. Let them not be puffed up with pride or part of a vast cabal. Let it be a spirit, a ghost borne on the wind, an American thing, a myth.

NOTES

Chapter 1

1. Interview with Sol W. Sanders, "How to Beat the Reds in Southeast Asia," *U.S. News & World Report*, (February 18, 1963); see also Bernard B. Fall, *The Two Viet-Nams*, 2nd revised ed. (New York, 1963, 1964, 1967) pp. 246–253.

2. Reprinted in A. J. P. Taylor, *Essays in English History* (London, 1976) pp. 49–54.

3. Hugh Thomas, ed., *The Establishment* (London, 1959) p. 20.

4. Richard Rovere, *The American Establishment and Other Reports, Opinions, and Speculations* (New York, 1962).

5. Daniel Walker Howe, *The Unitarian Conscience* (Cambridge, 1970) p. 140.

6. Ibid., p. 182.

7. Ibid., p. 181; Cf. E. Digby Baltzell, *Puritan Boston and Quaker Philadelphia: Two Protestant Ethics and the Spirit of Class Authority and Leadership* (New York, 1979).

8. Henry James, *Charles William Eliot*, (Boston, 1930) vol. I, p. 34.

9. Barrett Wendell, "De Praeside Magnifico," *The Harvard Graduates Magazine* 1909–10, p. 16.

10. Charles W. Eliot "The Religion of the Future," *Harvard Theological Review*, October 1909, pp. 389–407.

11. Walter Lippmann, *A Preface to Morals* (New York, 1929) p. 65.

12. Ibid., p. 239.

13. Ibid., p. 272.

14. Ibid., p. 283.

Chapter 2

1. Samuel Eliot Morison, *Three Centuries of Harvard* (Cambridge, 1936) p. 61.
2. John Le Boutellier, *Harvard Hates America: The Odyssey of a Born-Again American* (South Bend, 1978).
3. Ibid., p. 44.
4. Ibid., p. 157.
5. See Christopher Lasch, "The Moral and Intellectual Rehabilitation of the Ruling Class," in *The World of Nations* (New York, 1973).
6. William James, "The True Harvard," *The Harvard Graduates Magazine*, 12, 1903–4, pp. 5–8.
7. Henry Aaron Yeomans, *Abbott Lawrence Lowell* (Cambridge, 1948) p. 169.
8. Harvard Class of 1923, *25th Anniversary Report.* (Cambridge, 1948) pp. 792–93.
9. Yeomans, *Abbott*, pp. 215–16.
10. Samuel Eliot Morison "The Harvard Presidency," *The New England Quarterly*, XXXI, No. 4, December 1958, p. 445.
11. Nathan M. Pusey, "A Faith for These Times," *The Age of the Scholar* (Cambridge, 1963) pp. 1–8.
12. The *New York Review*, July 14, 1977.
13. McGeorge Bundy, "Were Those the Days?" *Daedalus*, Summer 1970, p. 551.
14. See Leonard Silk, *The Economists* (New York, 1976) pp. 13–15.
15. Daniel Bell, *The Reforming of General Education* (New York, 1966) p. 87.
16. A.B. and D.C. Stone, "Early Development of Education in Public Administration," Frederick C. Mosher, ed., *American Public Administration*, (Alabama, 1975) p. 37.
17. Paul Herzog, "A Study of the Graduate School of Public Administration, Harvard University," (unpub. 1957) p. 29.

Chapter 3

1. Myer Berger, *The Story of The New York Times, 1851–1951* (New York, 1951) pp. 242–43.
2. The *Times*, July 22, 1975.
3. Richard Nixon, *RN: The Memoirs of Richard Nixon* (New York, 1978) p. 684.
4. See Sanford J. Ungar, *The Paper & The Papers: An Account of the Legal and Political Battle Over the Pentagon Papers* (New York, 1972).
5. Neil Sheehan, ed., *The Pentagon Papers*, as published by *The New York Times*, (New York, 1971).
6. Nixon, *Memoirs*, p. 509.
7. Ungar, *The Papers*, p. 234.
8. Chris Argyris, *Behind the Front Page: Organizational Self-Renewal in a Metropolitan Newspaper* (San Francisco, 1974).
9. Ibid., p. 157.
10. Argyris, *Behind the Front Page*, p. 176.
11. " Beyond the Profit Squeeze of *The New York Times*," *Business Week*, August 30, 1976, p. 42.
12. Interview, June 25, 1979.
13. Argyris, *Behind the Front Page*, p. 172.

14. John B. Oakes, "The United States of America: Two Hundred Years Later." For the Bicentennial Lecture Series at Temple Emanu-El, New York, November 2, 1975.

15. *The Crisis of Democracy, Report on the Governability of Democracies to the Trilateral Commission* (New York, 1977) pp. 99–100.

16. Ibid.

Chapter 4

1. Max Weber, *The Protestant Ethic and the Spirit of Capitalism*, Forward by R. H. Tawney, (New York, 1958) p. 3.

2. Ibid., pp. 181–82.

3. Andrew Carnegie, "The Gospel of Wealth," *The Gospel of Wealth and Other Timely Essays*, Edward C. Kirkland, ed., (Cambridge, 1962) pp. 14–29.

4. Joseph Frazier Wall, *Andrew Carnegie* (New York, 1970) p. 825.

5. Ibid., p. 834.

6. Burton J. Hendrick, *The Life of Andrew Carnegie*, (London, 1933) vol. I, p. 349.

7. Frederick Taylor Gates, *Chapters In My Life* (New York, 1977), p. 161.

8. Ibid. p. 285.

9. Ibid., p. 184.

10. Ibid., pp. 182–88.

11. Ibid., p. 206.

12. Ibid., p. 208.

13. Ibid., p. 209.

14. *The Survey*, March 12, 1910, p. 205.

15. Letter of November 10, 1911. Rockefeller Archive.

16. U.S. Congress, Senate, Final Report and Testimony Submitted to Congress by the Commission on Industrial Relations, 64th Congress, 1st Session, Senate Doc. 415 (Washington, D. C.: Government Printing Office, 1916), VIII, 8004–8006.

17. Ibid., pp. 8006–8008.

18. James Weinstein, *The Corporate Ideal in the Liberal State: 1900–1918* (Boston, 1968), p. 205.

19. H. R. Fosdick, *The Rockefeller Foundation* (New York, 1952) pp. 27–28.

20. Wall, *Carnegie*, p. 834.

21. Letter of January 23, 1912. Rockefeller Archive.

22. Letter of January 22, 1912. Rockefeller Archive.

23. Letter of January 24, 1912. Rockefeller Archive.

24. Gates, *Chapters In My Life*, p. 185.

25. Fosdick, *The Rockefeller Foundation*, p. 1.

26. Ford Foundation 1967 Annual Report, p. 3.

27. Ford Foundation 1966 Annual Report, p. iv.

28. Ford Foundation 1975 Annual Report, p. vi.

29. Ford Foundation Oral History Project. Nielsen interview, p. 11. [Hereafter "O.H."]

30. O. H., p. 12.

31. Nielsen interview, O. H., p. 14.

32. See W. Nielsen, *The Big Foundations* (New York, 1972) pp. 85–86.

33. Bethuel Webster, O. H., p. 10.

34. Ford Foundation Annual Report, 1978, p. viii.

35. Paul Ylvisaker, O.H., p. 20.

36. Ibid., pp. 24–25.

37. Ibid., p. 28.

38. Ibid., p. 20.
39. Ibid., p. 40.
40. Kermit Gordon, O. H., pp. 43–44.

Chapter 5

1. Henry J. Aaron, *Politics and the Professors* (Washington, D.C., 1978).
2. Charles Schultze, *The Public Use of Private Interest* (Washington, D.C., 1977).
3. Charles B. Saunders, *The Brookings Institution: A Fifty-Year History* (Washington, D.C., 1966).
4. Richard Nixon, *RN: The Memoirs of Richard Nixon* (New York, 1978), p. 512.
5. Ibid., p. 512.
6. J. A. Lukas, *Nightmare—the Underside of the Nixon Years* (New York, 1977) pp. 78–79.
7. Interview with William Lanouette, 1978.
8. Ibid.
9. Aaron, *Politics.*

Chapter 6

1. Whitney H. Shepardson, *Early History of the Council on Foreign Relations* (New York, 1960) p. 11.
2. Hamilton Fish Armstrong, *Peace and Counterpeace* (New York, 1971) p. 225.
3. Ibid., p. 276.
4. Ibid., p. 226.
5. Series of letters of January, 1923. Council Archives.
6. Letter of January 14, 1929. Council Archives.
7. Joseph Barber, *These Are the Committees* (New York, 1963) p. 5.
8. Ibid., p. 25.
9. Ibid., p. 34.
10. Lawrence H. Shoup and William Minter, *The Imperial Brain Trust* (New York, 1977) p. 163.
11. Barber, *Committees,* pp. 51–52.
12. Elisabeth Jakab, "The Council on Foreign Relations," *Book Forum,* vol. III, no. 4, 1978 p. 444.
13. J. Anthony Lukas, "The Council on Foreign Relations," *The New York Times Magazine,* November 21, 1971, p. 128.
14. Ibid., p. 138.
15. Ibid., p. 142.
16. New York, 1974, p. 7.
17. Stanley Hoffmann, *Primacy and World Order* (New York, 1978) p. 95.
18. Ibid., p. 320.
19. James Chace, "Is a Foreign Policy Consensus Possible?" *Foreign Affairs,* Fall 1978, p. 16.

20. Henry Kissinger, *White House Years* (Boston, 1979) pp. 13–14.

21. McGeorge Bundy, "Vietnam, Watergate, and Presidential Powers," *Foreign Affairs*, Winter 1979–80, p. 402.

22. Ibid., 403.

23. Ibid., 404.

24. William Bundy, "Who Lost Patagonia?" *Foreign Affairs*, Fall 1979, p. 20.

25. *The New York Times*, January 4, 1980.

26. *The New York Times*, September 26, 1979.

27. *The New York Times*, November 18, 1979.

28. See "Chase Bank and Others Court Challenges On Huge Loans to Iran," *Wall Street Journal*, March 28, 1980, p. 1.

Chapter 7

1. See Rawleigh Warner, Jr., and Leonard Silk, *Ideals in Collision: The Relationship between Business and the News Media*, The 1978 Benjamin F. Fairless Memorial Lectures (Pittsburgh 1979).

2. Leonard Silk and David Vogel, *Ethics and Profits: The Crisis of Confidence in American Business* (New York, 1976).

3. Henry Demarest Lloyd, *Wealth Against Commonwealth* (New York, 1899) pp. 9–10.

4. James W. Prothro, *The Dollar Decade* (Baton Rouge, Louisiana, 1954) p. 43.

5. David Rockefeller, "The Essential Quest for the Middle Way," in Leonard Silk, *Capitalism: The Moving Target* (New York, 1974) p. 98.

6. *Ibid.*, p. 98.

7. Alexis de Tocqueville, *Democracy in America*, (New York, 1836) vol. II, pp. 130–31.

8. Lincoln Steffens, *Autobiography* (New York, 1931) p. 196.

9. Herbert Croly, *The Promise of American Life* (New York, 1909) p. 44.

10. T.R. Frentz, *Financial Age* (New York, 1902); quoted by Robert H. Wiebe, *Businessmen and Reform: A Study of the Progressive Movement* (Cambridge, 1962). p. 12.

11. Wiebe, *Businessmen and Reform*, p. 31.

12. Kit Konlogie and Frederica Konlogie, *The Power of Their Glory: America's Ruling Class: The Episcopalians* (New York, 1978) pp. 80–81.

13. Karl Schriftgiesser, *Business Comes of Age* (New York, 1960).

14. Calvin B. Hoover, *International Trade and Domestic Employment* (New York, 1945).

15. Calvin B. Hoover, *Memoirs of Capitalism, Communism, and Nazism* (Durham, N.C., 1965) pp. 218–220.

16. See Benjamin B. Ferencz, *Less Than Slaves: Jewish Forced Slaves and the Quest for Compensation* (Cambridge, 1980).

17. Ruml Papers, University of Chicago Library, Chicago, Ill.; quoted by Herbert Stein, *The Fiscal Revolution in America* (Chicago, 1969) p. 110.

18. Herbert Stein, *The Fiscal Revolution in America*, p. 110.

19. Kim McQuaid, "The Gray Eminences: Big Business and Contemporary American Public Policy," unpublished manuscript (Lake Erie College, Painesville, Ohio, 1979).

20. Ibid.

21. Letter, T.A. Murphy to L. Silk, Detroit, Michigan, June 21, 1978.

Chapter 8

1. Henry L. Stimson and McGeorge Bundy, *On Active Service in Peace and War* (New York, 1948) p. 17.

2. Ibid., p. 22.

3. Ibid., p. 107.

4. Ibid., p. 107.

5. Ibid., pp. 284–85.

6. Ibid., p. 337.

7. Ibid., pp. 194–95.

8. Ibid., p. 195.

9. Ibid., pp. 43–44.

10. Felix Frankfurter, *From the Diaries of Felix Frankfurter*, with a biographical essay and notes by Joseph P. Lash, assisted by Jonathan Lash (New York, 1975) p. 35.

11. Lash, *From the Diaries*, p. 35.

12. Harlan B. Phillips, *Felix Frankfurter Reminisces* (New York, 1960) p. 84.

13. See Milton Viorst, *Fall From Grace* (New York, 1968) pp. 173ff.

14. Elmo Richardson, *The Presidency of Dwight D. Eisenhower* (Lawrence, Kansas, 1979) p. 85.

15. Ibid., pp. 59, 85, 190.

16. Theodore H. White, *Making of the President, 1960* (New York, 1961) p. 239.

17. Nixon, *RN: The Memoirs of Richard Nixon* (New York, 1978) p. 351.

18. Ibid., p. 88.

19. Ibid., p. 141.

20. Ibid., p. 142.

21. Ibid., p. 198.

22. Ibid., p. 88.

23. Ibid., p. 90.

24. Ibid., p. 139.

25. Ibid., pp. 139–40.

26. Richard Nixon, *Six Crises* (Garden City, 1962) p. 67.

27. Nixon, *Memoirs*, p. 352.

28. Ibid, pp. 339–40.

29. Ibid., p. 761.

30. Nixon, *Six Crises*, pp. 68–69.

31. Nixon, *Memoirs*, p. 71.

32. William Safire, *Before the Fall* (New York, 1975) p. 412.

33. Nixon, *Memoirs*, p. 354.

34. Ibid., p. 670.

35. "Transcript of March 13, 1973 Meeting," *Statement of Information: Hearings Before the Committee on the Judiciary*, Book III, part 2 (Washington, 1974) p. 873.

36. Nixon, *Memoirs*, p. 768.

37. Ibid.

38. Ibid., p. 769.

39. Ibid., p. 762.

40. Kevin Phillips, *The Emerging Republican Majority* (New Rochelle, New York, 1969).

41. Garry Wills, *Nixon Agonistes* (New York, 1970) p. 247.

42. Ibid., p. 85.

43. Ibid., p. 88.

44. Ibid., p. 85.

45. Nixon, *Memoirs*, p. 769.

46. Ibid., pp. 762–63.

47. Peter Schrag, *Test of Loyalty* (New York, 1974) pp. 117–18.

48. Nixon, *Memoirs,* p. 764.
49. Ibid., p. 686.
50. See Gerald Ford, *A Time to Heal* (New York, 1979) p. 29.
51. Jimmy Carter, *Why Not the Best?* (New York, 1976) pp. 145–46.

Chapter 9

1. "Patricide in the House Divided," *The New York Review of Books,* October 25, 1979, p. 26.
2. See the two-part series on the U.S. Labor Party by Howard Blum and Paul Montgomery, *The New York Times,* October 7 and 8, 1979.
3. Kirkpatrick Sale, *Power Shift* (New York, 1975) p. 310.
4. Richard Nixon, *RN: The Memoirs of Richard Nixon* (New York, 1978) p. 769.
5. Milton Friedman, *Capitalism and Freedom* (Chicago, 1962) pp. 133–34.
6. See Peter Steinfels, *The Neoconservatives* (New York, 1979.)
7. William E. Simon, *A Time for Truth,* 2nd ed., (New York, 1979) p. 255.
8. Ibid., p. 246.
9. Ibid., p. 248.
10. Ibid., p. 249.
11. Ibid., p. 247.
12. Ibid.
13. Ibid., p. 173.
14. Ibid., p. 171.
15. Ibid., p. 170.
16. Ibid.
17. Ibid.
18. Ibid., p. 137.
19. Ibid., p. 193.
20. Ibid.
21. Ibid., p. 190.
22. Ibid., p. 171.
23. Ibid., p. 141.
24. Ibid., p. 255.

INDEX

Aaron, Henry, *Politics and the Professors*, 156, 180
ABC, 78
Abzug, Bella, 89, 90, 91
Acheson, Dean, 170, 199, 278
Adams, John Quincy, 56
Adams, Sherman, 288n, 289
Addams, Jane, 232
Adenauer, Konrad, 174
Adler, Julius Ochs "Julie," 78
Advisory Committee on Postwar Foreign Policy, 198
Aetna Life and Casualty, 151n
Afghanistan, 220, 307
AFL-CIO, 251
Agnew, Spiro T., 77, 131, 292, 316
Agricultural Adjustment Administration, 167, 242
Agronsky, Martin, 155
Aiken, Henry, 47
Alcoa, 143, 256
Aldrich, Nelson, 112–13, 114, 238
Alger, Horatio, 295
Alliance for Progress, 62
Allied Stores, 143
Allis-Chalmers Corporation, 254
Allison, Graham T., 24, 64; *Essence of Decision*, 62
Alsop, Joseph, 298–99
America First Committee, 196, 200
American Academy (Rome), 117
American Baptist Education Society, 109
American Cotton Manufacturers' Association, 236
American Enterprise Association; *see* American Enterprise Institute for Public Policy Research
American Enterprise Institute for Public Policy Research, 149, 159, 177–80
American Federation of Labor, 236; AFL-CIO, 251
American Geographical Society, 186, 191
American Nazi party, 312
American Policy Commission, 241, 244–45;

see also Committee for Economic Development
American Revolution, 28, 29
American Telephone and Telegraph Company, 254
Anderson, John, 309
Andover (Phillips Academy, Andover), 12, 39, 270
Andrew, Abram Piatt, 237
Angell, James B., 33
Anglican establishment (U.S.), 12, 29
anglophilism, 29, 39, 57, 279
Anti-Defamation League, 257–58
anti-Semitism, 48, 77–78, 121, 218; in corporate world, 40, 79, 247n, 257–58; and university quotas, 38–41; *see also* Jews
apartheid, 23, 24, 25, 152
Arabs, 253, 258
ARCO Forum of Public Affairs (JFK School of Government), 23n
Argentina, 96
Argyris, Chris, 84, 87
Armstrong, Hamilton Fish, 188, 189, 190–91, 195, 196, 197, 198, 204, 205, 206–7, 221–22, 224
Ashurst, Henry F., 163
Asian Development Bank, 302
Atlantic, The, 304
Atlantic Richfield, 151n
Atomic Energy Commission, 144n

Bagehot, Walter, 6
Bagehot Fellows program, 97n
Baker, George F., 238
Baker, Howard, 217
Baker, Joseph Stannard, 232
"balance-sheet philanthropy," 151n
Baldwin, Hanson, 196
Bancroft, Harding, 80
Bank for International Settlements, 200
Bank of America, 266
Barnet, Richard, 205
Baroody, Joseph, 178
Baroody, William, 178
Baroody, William, Jr., 178–79

337

Baroody, William 3d, 178
Bartley, William W. 3d, 44–45, 44n, 46
Baruch, Bernard, 162
Bay of Pigs invasion, 243
Bechtel, Stephen, 138
Bechtel Corporation, 138, 257
Bedford-Stuyvesant Development and Services Corporation, 144–46
Bedford-Stuyvesant Restoration Corporation, 143–46
Beer, Samuel, 46, 47
Belgium, 117, 118
Bell, Daniel, 51
Bell, David, 59
Bell, George, 296
Bell & Howell, 283
Belmont, August, 68
Benes, Eduard, 188
Bennett, Harry, 126
Benton, William, 240, 241, 242, 243, 244–45, 258, 265
Benton & Bowles, 241
Berenson, Bernard, 43
Berger, Myer, Story of The New York Times 1851–1951, The, 70n
Berkeley (University of California), 64, 172
Bernhard (prince of Netherlands), 302
Bethany Lutheran Junior College, 137
Bidwell, Percy, 197
Bilderberg Conference, 302
Bissell, Richard M., 243; and Upgren, Arthur R., Program of Postwar Planning, A, 243–44
Black, Hugo, 83
blacklisting; see McCarthy, McCarthyism
blacks, 26, 40, 91, 137–39, 141, 150, 152, 189, 204, 253, 293; see also specific people and projects
Blaine, James G., 34n
Blake, William, 324
Bliss, Tasker H., 186
Blough, Roger, 255–56
Blumenthal, W. Michael, 214, 269, 306
B'nai B'rith, 257–58
Bok, Derek Curtis, 23, 24–25, 52–54, 58, 60–61, 62, 63, 64
Bork, Robert H., 178
Boston Athenaeum, 14
Boston City Council, 39
Boston Latin School, 37
Boston Post, 30
Bosworth, Barry, 158
Bowen, Francis, 13
Bowles, Samuel, 136
Bowman, Isaiah, 191–92, 193, 196, 198, 225
"brains trust," 379

Brandeis, Louis Dembitz, 279
Brazil, 59
Bretton Woods conference, 247
Brookhart, Smith W., 190, 191, 192, 196
Brookings, Harry, 160
Brookings, Robert S., 160–62, 163, 164–66, 167
Brookings Institution, 18, 140, 153–82, 269, 274, 299, 300, 301; Advanced Studies Program, 160; annual reports, 159–60; bipartisanship of, 155, 156; bomb plot, 174–77; conservative challenge to, 177–80; formation of, 160–66; as government critic, 154–55, 163, 164, 166–69; International Studies Group, 171; in policy network, 157–60; Setting National Priorities, 154–55; staff quality, 154–56
Brookings School of Economics and Government, 165–66; see also Brookings Institution
Brown, Jerry, 307
Brown, Lewis H., 178
Brown, Sam, 204
Brown Brothers Harriman and Company, 179, 277
Brown v. Board of Education, 283
Brownell, Herbert, 80
Bruner, Jerome, 47
Bryan, William Jennings, 312, 313
Brzezinski, Zbigniew, 269, 301, 302, 304, 305, 307
Buckley, William F., Jr., 220, 298; God and Man at Yale, 31
Bull Moosers, 269, 278
Bundy, Harvey Hollister, 277
Bundy, McGeorge, 23, 49, 50, 52, 59, 125, 132–33, 134–35, 137, 140, 143, 147, 148, 148n, 149, 149n, 150, 203, 217, 218–19, 277, 285, 307
Bundy, William P., 203, 205–06, 217, 277, 289–90; "Who Lost Patagonia? Foreign Policy in the 1980 Campaign," 219
Bureau of Corporations, 236
Bureau of the Budget, 59, 154; see also Office of Management and Budget
Burger, Warren C., 83–84, 94
Burnham, Donald C., 256
Burns, Arthur F., 155, 282
Bush, George, 220, 262, 269, 308, 308n, 309
Bush, Vannevar, 170
Business Roundtable, 254–58; Policy Committee, 258–59
Business Week, 87–88, 97, 97n, 254–55
Buttrick, George, 44, 45
Byrd, Harry F., 169n
Byrne, James, 40
Byrom, Fletcher, 258–62, 265

Califano, Joseph, 158, 306
Calkins, Robert D., 172
Calvin, John, 16, 27
Calvinism, 12, 13, 28, 30, 104
Cambodia, 214, 218, 307
Cambridge University, 55
campaign financing: illegal contributions, 96, 253, 288
Campbell, John C., 184-85, 195, 199, 222-23
Camps, Miriam, 210-11
Canada, 188
capital gains, 158
capitalism, 6, 9, 14, 30, 31, 33, 51, 104-5, 122, 127, 147, 148, 165, 168, 183, 192, 193, 212, 225, 226-67, 313, 318; see also Free enterprise
Cardozo, Benjamin Nathan, 279
Carmen, Gerald, 308
Carnegie, Andrew, 105-7, 108, 122, 161, 231-32
Carnegie Corporation of New York, 58, 105, 108, 165, 171, 195, 253
Carnegie Endowment for International Peace, 18, 105, 154n, 161, 205, 277
Carnegie Foundation for the Advancement of Teaching, 105, 108
Carnegie Hall, 105
Carnegie Hero Fund, 105
Carnegie Institute of Technology (Carnegie Mellon University), 105
Carnegie Institute of Washington, 105, 107, 108, 123, 124, 170, 201
Carnegie libraries, 105, 106-7
Carnegie Relief Fund, 113-14
Carnegie Steel Corporation, 105
Carter, Billy, 309
Carter, James E. Jr. (Jimmy), xi, 11, 154, 155, 213, 214, 216, 219, 220, 224-25, 254-55, 258, 261, 262, 268-69, 286, 307, 309; and Trilateral Commission, 302-04, 305-06, 307-08; Why Not the Best?, 303
Carter, Rosalynn, 307
Catholics, 40, 51
Catledge, Turner, 78
Caulfield, John, 174, 176-77
CBS, 78, 143
Center for Advanced Study in the Behavioral Sciences, 127
Central Housing Council, 59
Central Intelligence Agency, 9, 75, 100, 177, 220, 243, 289
Century Association, 18; see Century Club
Century Club, 3, 4, 18, 162, 312
CETA, 150
Chace, James, "Is a Foreign Policy Consensus Possible?," 216
Channing, E. T., 13
Chapman, Leonard F., Jr., 178

Chase Manhattan Bank, 96, 225, 257, 277, 290n, 321
Chattanooga Times, 68
Chicago Daily News, 99
Chicago Tribune, 171-72
Chile, 96, 212
China, 200, 219
China, People's Republic of, 73, 74, 291-92, 301, 302, 303
China Medical Board, 117, 120
Christianity, 29, 31, 42-43, 44, 259; see also specific denominations
Church of England, xii, 8; see also Established church
Citicorp/Citibank, 143, 144n, 145, 321
Citizen's lobby (Common Cause), 253, 304
City College of New York, 38, 172, 279
civil liberties, civil rights, 51, 128, 133, 283, 313; see also Racism
civil service, 164, 279; see also Public administration
Civil Service Commission, 55
Civil War, 29, 67-68, 231, 294, 315
Clark, Ramsey, 90
Clay, Lucius, 248
Clean Air Act, 255
Clemenceau, Georges, 187-88
Cleveland, Frederick A., 162
Cleveland, Grover, 34n, 270
Cleveland voter-registration drive, 133, 134
Cobbett, William, 6-7, 184
Cohen, I B., 47
Cold War, 171, 199-203, 212, 219-20, 249, 281
Colorado Fuel and Iron Company, 115, 116, 117-18; see also Ludlow Massacre
Colson, Charles, 174-76, 177, 296
Columbia Business School, 172
Columbia University, 18, 38, 40-41, 60, 77, 114, 143, 145, 187, 236, 282, 301; School of Journalism, 97n
Commission on Critical Choices, 301
Commission on Economy and Efficiency, 162
Committee for an Effective and Durable Peace in Asia, 203
Committee for Economic Development, 18, 245-48, 256, 258, 259; Research Advisory Board, 259
Committee on Administrative Management, 169, 169n
Committee on the Present Danger, 220
Common Cause, 253, 304
Commonwealth Club, 149
communism, 106, 165, 183, 193, 283, 284; in foreign countries, 4, 7, 48, 71, 72, 200, 201, 202; in United States, 30, 41, 48, 127-28, 201, 312; see also Euro-Communism;

INDEX

communism (continued)
McCarthyism; Marshall Plan; United States foreign policy; specific parties and countries
Communist party (Italy), 209
Communist party, Communists (United States), 30, 49, 287, 291, 312
Community Action programs, 141
Community Development Corporation programs, 141–42, 143, 151n see also Bedford-Stuyvesant Development Corporation
"Compact of Fifth Avenue," 283, 284, 285, 287, 289
Compton, Karl, 126, 127, 170
Computer Graphics, 145
Conant, James Bryant, 41, 42, 43–44, 45, 49, 57, 58, 289
Congregational Board of Missions, 111
Congregationalist establishment, 12, 14–15, 29
Connally, John B., 211, 230, 261–62, 262n, 302, 315–16
Conrad, Joseph, 327
conservationists; see Environmentalism
conservatism, conservatives, 20, 64, 79, 137, 153, 157, 159, 168, 171–72, 173–74, 179–80, 181, 182, 192, 212, 220–21, 225, 252, 278, 281, 282, 294, 297, 300; "neoconservatives," 319
Construction Users Anti-Inflation Roundtable, 256
"consumerism," 256, 257, 301
Consumer Protection Agency, 256
"containment doctrine," 71, 200
Continental Illinois National Bank, 151n
Coolidge, Archibald Cary, 188–89, 192
Coolidge, Calvin, 274, 275
Coons, John E., 136
Cornell University, 33
Council of Economic Advisers, 154, 156, 167, 172, 179, 282
Council on Foreign Relations, 18, 34, 49, 143, 183–225, 268, 269, 274, 299, 301; Enhancing Global Human Rights, 212; International Order group, 210–11; Meetings Program, 184, 222; 1980s Project, 210–11, 212–13, 213n, 214, 215–16, 219, 223, 301; origin, 185–90; Reducing Global Inequities, 212; Sharing Global Resources, 212; Studies Program, 211, 223; "War and Peace Studies," 198, 210, 212; see also Internationalism; Isolationism; specific leaders
Council on Wage and Price Stability, 158
Cox, Archibald, 32, 59, 299
Cox, Eugene, 128
Cox, James Middleton, 278
Crandall, Robert, 158

Cravath, Swain & Moore, 129, 144n, 145, 277
Croly, Herbert, 232–33, 265, 272; Promise of American Life, The, 233
Cuba, 51, 62, 243, 307
Cummins Engine, 143
Cutler, Lloyd, 307
Czechoslovakia, 188

Daily News (New York), 79
Dalhousie Medical School, 120
Daniel, Clifton, 78
Daniell, Raymond, 248
Dartmouth College, 242
Darwin, Charles, Darwinians, 109
David, Donald, 126, 127, 128, 130
Davidson, Henry P., 237
Davis, David Brion, "Patricide in the House Divided," 311
Davis, John W., 184–85, 187, 189, 193–94, 196
Dean, Arthur, 203
Dean, John, 176, 177, 293, 296, 298
de Gaulle, Charles, 174
de Montaigne, Michel, 37
Deism, 13
democracy, 6, 7, 29, 32, 33, 56, 72, 126, 198, 212, 239, 263, 264, 312
Democratic National Convention (1968), 84
Democratic party, 34n, 75, 79, 154, 155, 156, 189, 269, 280, 282, 315; factionalism in, 286; see also specific politicians
Democrats for Nixon, 315
Depew, Chauncey M., 70
Depression; see Great Depression
Detroit Edison Company, 241
Devine, Edward T., 113–14
Dewey, John, 325
Dewey, Thomas E., 281, 289
Diebold, William, 183–84
Dienbienphu, 72
Dill, James P., 232
Dillon, C. Douglas, 144, 285
Dillon, Read & Company, 144
disinterestedness, 14, 17, 19, 67, 68, 102, 163, 184, 230–31, 265, 279, 300, 326
Division of Medical Education, 120
Doar, John, 146
Donovan, Hedley, 307
Douglas, Helen Gahagan, 76
Douglas, Lewis, 197
Douglas, Paul, 224
Douglas, William O., 83
Douglass, Frederick, 26–27
Draper, William, 248
DuBois, W. E. B., "Worlds of Color," 189
Duke University, 64, 246, 248

Dulles, Allen W., 195, 196
Dulles, John Foster, 49, 188, 196, 202, 287
Dunlop, John, 61, 63, 257
Dunne, Finley Peter, 182
DuPont Corporation, 255, 257
Duquesne Club, 255, 258

Eastern Europe, 200; see also specific countries
Eastman Kodak Company, 244
École Nationale d'Administration, 55
economics; see specific leaders and issues
Economist, The, 218
Edison Institute, 125
egalitarianism, 29, 32, 49, 223, 321, 322
Ehrlichman, John, 175, 177
Eisenhower, Dwight D., 44, 76, 80, 128, 202, 281–83, 284, 285, 287, 288–89, 300, 309
Eizenstat, Stuart, 306
Eliot, Charles W., 15–16, 33–35, 36, 46, 51, 71, 110, 114, 118, 121, 122, 162, 188; "Religion of the Future, The," 16, 42–43, 45
elitism, 7, 14, 20, 21, 28, 29, 30, 31, 32, 33, 55, 202–03, 223n, 275, 277, 280, 314
Ellsberg, Daniel, 80, 175, 175n, 204, 296–97
Emerson, Ralph Waldo, 36
energy shortages, 216, 253
Engelhard, Charles, 23–24, 26
Engelhard Foundation, 23
Engelhard Library (JFK School of Government), 23, 24, 26, 27
Enlightenment, 13
environmentalism, 96, 127, 149, 183, 253, 254, 261, 272, 278, 301, 323, 324
Episcopalianism, 29
Equitable Life, 144n
Erhard, Werner, 44n
Espionage Law, 82
established church, 7, 8, 9, 10–12
Establishment, 185; antagonism toward, xi–xii, 5–6; centrism of, 268–69; characteristics of, 8–9, 275, 277; democratic nature of, 10, 19; as mediator, 6; prospects of, 311–28; style of, 173, 206; see also Egalitarianism; Elitism; specific people and institutions
Eurich, Alvin C., 138
Euro-Communism, 209
European University Institute, 302
Executive Office of the President, 169n
Exeter, (Phillips Exeter Academy), 39
Export-Import Bank, 197
Exxon Corporation, 257–58

Fairlie, Henry, 7
Falk, Richard, 205
Family Assistance Plan, 90
fascism, 195, 298, 312; see also Hitler, Adolf; Mussolini, Benito; World War II
FBI, 75, 100, 174, 176
Feather, William, 228
Federal Housing and Home Finance Agency, 145
Federal Housing Authority, 145
Federalists, 29
Federal Reserve System, 154, 155–56, 237–38, 243, 306
Federal Trade Commission, 238
Federated Department Stores, 257–58
Fiedler, Arthur, 23
Field, Marshall, 242, 245
Finley, John, 46, 47, 78
Fisher, Roger, 212
Flanders, Ralph, 242
Flint, Charles R., 68
Folsom, Marion B., 244
Ford, Benson, 127, 150n
Ford, Gerald R., 155, 158, 178, 180, 255, 261, 269, 281, 299, 300, 305, 308n, 309, 309n, 321
Ford, Henry, 105, 125–26
Ford, Henry II, 126, 127, 129, 131, 147–48, 150n, 151, 247n, 320
Ford Foundation, 18, 50, 59, 63–64, 105, 125–43, 146–52, 173, 182, 201, 211, 281, 299, 300; disbursements of, 126, 128, 129, 130, 132; interests of, 126–27, 136–42, 149, 151; portfolio value of, 134–35; right-wing attacks on, 127–29; success of, 125–26; see also specific members, institutions, programs
Ford (Henry) Hospital, 125
Ford Motor Company, 60, 105, 125–26, 129, 129n, 247n, 257–58
Foreign Affairs, 71, 184, 188–90, 191, 192, 200, 204, 205, 216, 217, 218, 221, 222, 224, 257–58, 307
foreign exchange, 304
Foreign Policy, 205
Foreign Policy Association, 187
Fortune, 241, 242, 298
Fortune Round Table, 241
Fosdick, Harry Emerson, 119
Fosdick, Raymond B., 119–20, 124–25, 162
France, 72, 174, 188
Francis, Clarence, 242
Frankel, Max, 81, 88, 89, 92, 95
Frankfurter, Felix, 56–57, 59, 278–80
Franklin, Benjamin, 28
free enterprise, 28, 51, 65, 96–97, 147, 148, 149, 165, 166, 168, 174, 178, 179, 226–67, 281, 295, 317–23, 324, 325; see also Capitalism
Frentz, T. R., 235
Frew, W. M., 107

Friedman, Milton, *Capitalism and Freedom,* 318

Fund for Adult Education, 127

Fund for the Advancement of Education, 127

Fund for the Republic, 128, 129

fund raising, 9, 31, 44, 57, 60, 62–63, 195, 214

Gaither, H. Rowan, 126, 128, 129–30, 131, 146

Gaither Report, 127

Galbraith, John Kenneth, 23, 46, 49, 50, 51, 59, 237, 265; *New Industrial State, The,* 52

Gardner, John, 253

Gary, Elbert, 234, 235–36

Gates, Frederick T., 109–12, 114, 121–23, 124–25

Gay, Edwin F., 188

Gelb, Leslie, 154, 154*n*, 174–75, 176, 177, 212, 224, 296–97

General Agreement on Trade and Tariffs, 247, 248

General Education Board, 108, 112, 117, 172

General Electric Company, 244, 255, 257–58

General Foods, 242, 256

General Motors, 257–58, 263

Geneva Conference (on Southeast Asia, 1962), 73

Germany, 198, 199, 246, 248–49, 273, 277, 289; concentration camps in, 248–49; *see also* West Germany

Gerth, Jeff, 93

Gilded Age, 274

Gilman, Daniel C., 33

Gilpatric, Roswell L., 144*n*

Gintis, Herbert, 136

Gladden, Washington, 111

globalism; *see* Internationalism

Godkin lectures (Harvard), 156

Goldwater, Barry, 73, 286, 287, 314

Gomes, Peter, 25–26

Gompers, Samuel, 107, 236

Goodale, James C., 81

Goodwin, Richard, 23

Gordon, Kermit, 140–41, 154, 159–60, 173–74, 179

Gordon, Lincoln, 59

Graham, Billy, 292

Graham, Katherine ("Kay"), 77

Grant, Ulysses S., 274

Gray Areas, Gray Areas projects, 138, 139–40, 141, 142

Great Britain, 6–7, 8, 186, 187, 199, 227, 247, 279, 312

Great Depression, 166–67, 239, 240, 250, 253, 274, 275, 277, 281

Great Society, 22, 30, 52, 62, 64, 140, 149, 291, 318

Greece, 199

Greene, Jerome D., 46, 114–15, 118, 123–24, 163

Greenfield, James, 81, 82, 82*n*

Greenspan, Alan, 180

Groton School, 39, 49, 206, 275

Gwin, Catherine, 215

Hagler, Jon, 151

Halberstam, David, 205; *Best and the Brightest, The,* 49

Haldeman, H. R., 76, 174, 175, 293

Halperin, Morton, 296–97

Hamilton, Alexander, Hamiltonians, 233, 234

Hanna, Mark, 232

Harding, Warren Gamaliel, 164, 190, 273, 274, 275

Harkness, Edward Stephen, 36

Harper, John D., 256

Harper, William R., 33

Harriman, Averell, 199

Harris, Huntington, 301

Harris, Sidney, 262

Hart, A. G., 250

Hartman, Robert, 156, 157

Harvard Business School, 30, 31, 54, 56, 60, 61, 63, 126, 238, 244, 256

Harvard Classics, 34

Harvard College, 18, 21–65, 77, 90, 101, 114, 124, 131–32, 138, 147, 156, 162, 173, 182, 187, 188, 206, 207, 218, 240, 241, 266, 275, 279, 280, 285, 287, 289, 299, 300, 316, 327; and academic freedom, 22; admission policies, 16, 32–35; anti-Semitism at, 38–41, 48; club system at, 36–37; curriculum reform at, 22; elective system, 15–16, 36; endowments and funding, 22, 60, 62–63; as Establishment symbol, 21, 49, 50; liberalism at, 12–16, 22, 27–32, 49–50; primacy of, 21–22; quota system at, 38–41; religious factionalism at, 41–48; service tradition at, 49–58; student protests at, 22, 23–27, 52; Unitarians at, 12–16, 45, 46

Harvard Congregational Presbyterian Student Fellowship, 46

Harvard Corporation, 36, 40, 41, 45–46, 52, 114, 123, 162

Harvard *Crimson,* 25, 44–45

Harvard Divinity School, 162, 42

Harvard Faculty Club, 46, 312

Harvard Graduate School of Education, 143

Harvard Lampoon, 37

Harvard Law School, 52, 61, 137, 270, 278, 290

INDEX

Harvard Liberal Union, 46
Harvard Memorial Church, 40, 44, 45–46, 47, 48
Harvard School of Public Administration, 56–58, 60, 61, 137, 279; *see also* Kennedy School of Government
Hauge, Gabriel, 203, 208
Hayakawa, S. I., 224
Heald, Henry, 131–32, 137, 138, 140, 146–47
Heard, Alexander, 143, 148, 150
Hechinger, Fred, 89
Hedge, Levi, 13
Heilbroner, Robert, 260–61
Heiskill, Marian Sulzberger, 150
Heller, Walter W., 50, 172
Henderson, Leon, 250
Hersh, Seymour, 93
Herzog, Paul, 58
Herzog Report, 58
Hesburgh, Theodore, 212
Hewlett-Packard, 319
Higginson, Henry L., 123–24
Hills, Carla, 178
Hills, Roderick, 178
Hispanics, 137, 138, 293
Hiss, Alger, 287, 288, 289–90, 291, 316
Hitler, Adolf, 41, 239, 247, 261
Hoffman, Paul Gray, 127, 128, 146, 231, 240–42, 243, 244–46, 248, 258, 265, 281
Hoffmann, Stanley, 49, 205, 212; *Primacy or World Order*, 213, 213n
Hofstadter, Richard, 238
Holmes, Oliver Wendell, 279
Hoover, Calvin Bryce, 246–47, 248–49, 265; "International Trade and Domestic Employment," 246
Hoover, Herbert, 164, 186, 274–75, 277, 279, 309–10
Hoover, Roland, 159
Hopkins, Harry, 250
hostages (American), 309
House, Edward M., 186
House Armed Services Committee, 296
House Banking and Currency Committee, 134
House Ways and Means Committee, 134
Howe, Daniel Walker, *Unitarian Conscience, The*, 13n
Howe, Frederick, 235
Howe, Harold, 149–50
Howe, Mark DeWolfe, 46
"How Harvard Rules," 52
Hughes, Charles Evans, 271
Hull, Cordell, 171
human rights, 96, 180
Humphrey, George, 282
Humphrey, Hubert H., 286

Humphrey-Hawkins bill, 155, 255
Humphrey School (University of Minnesota), 64
Hunt, E. Howard, 177
Huntington, Samuel P., 101, 304
Hutchins, Robert Maynard, 127, 128, 137, 240–42
Hutchinson, Anne, 27
hypocrisy, 121, 300

IBM, 144n, 145
Ickes, Harold L., 277–78, 281n
Illinois Institute of Technology, 131, 138, 147
India, 51, 59, 127
individualism; *see* Free enterprise
inequality, 136–37, 180
inflation, 22, 181, 216, 252–53, 306, 323
Institute for Government Research, 34, 162–65, 166, 170; *see also* Brookings Institution
Institute for International Affairs, 186–87; *see also* Council on Foreign Relations
Institute for Policy Studies, 205
Institute of Economics, 165, 166
intelligence activities; *see* specific personnel and agencies
Internal Revenue Service, 75; *see also* Taxes
International Bank for Reconstruction and Development; *see* World Bank
International Harvester, 151n
International Health Commission, 120
International Institute of Strategic Studies, 217
internationalism, 127, 171, 185, 186, 193–94, 198, 200, 211–12, 213, 215, 220–21, 231, 246, 248, 281, 294, 295; *see also* Cold War; United States foreign policy
International Monetary Fund, 199, 304
Interstate Commerce Act, 101
Interstate Commerce Commission, 238
Iran, 219, 224–25, 307, 309
isolationism, 76, 171, 185, 189–90, 195–98, 199–200, 203, 220–21, 245n, 247, 275, 281
Israel, 78–79, 258
Italy, 209
Ivy League, 13; *see also* specific universities

Jackson, Andrew, 313
Jacobssen, Per, 200
James, Edwin L. ("Jimmy,") 78
James, William, 15, 34–35, 46
Japan, 198, 199, 246, 275, 301, 302, 303, 304
Javits, Jacob, 94, 144
Jefferson, Thomas, Jeffersonians, 12, 29, 33, 233, 234, 313, 324, 325

343

INDEX

Jews: Eastern European, 37–38; German, 16, 37, 38, 57; at Harvard, 37–39, 39n, 40–41, 45, 47–48, 57; see also anti-Semitism
Joachim, Josef, 161
John Birch Society, 312
Johns Hopkins University, 33–34, 114
Johns-Manville Corporation, 178
Johnson, Hugh S., 167
Johnson, Lyndon Baines, 22, 30, 52, 73–74, 75, 82, 132, 140, 154, 155, 175, 203, 204, 205, 286, 297
Johnson School (University of Texas), 64
Joint Chiefs of Staff, 74
Jones, Jesse, 244–45
Jones, Reginald H., 255
Jordan, David S., 33
Jordan, Hamilton, 305–06
Journal of International Relations, The, 188

Kaplan, J. M., 144n
Kaplan Fund, 144n
Karl, Barry Dean, *Executive Reorganization and Reform in the New Deal*, 169n
Katz, Milton, 137–38
Kaysen, Carl, 49, 50, 59
Kelly, James A., 136
Kelly, Walt, "Pogo," 262
Kennan, George, 71, 200, 202, 203
Kennaway, James, *Bells of Shoreditch, The*, 227n
Kennecott Copper Company, 255
Kennedy, David, 290
Kennedy, Edward M., 23, 25, 26, 27, 97n, 307, 309
Kennedy, John F., 5, 7–8, 22, 23, 25, 26, 30, 50, 51–52, 59, 60, 82, 132, 139–40, 154, 172, 173, 181, 202, 243, 285, 287; Library, 60; Memorial Park, 23
Kennedy, Robert F., 25, 133, 134, 144, 286
Kennedy, Rose Fitzgerald, 25
Kennedy School of Government (Harvard), 23, 23n, 24, 25, 26, 27, 53, 60, 61–65; Center for Science and International Affairs, 62–63; Institute of Politics, 63; Pollack lectures, 316
Keppel, Frederick P., 195
Keynes, John Maynard, 247, 249–50; *Economic Consequences of the Peace*, 248
Keynesians, 30, 50, 170, 172, 250, 251, 252, 265, 282
Khmer Rouge, 218
Khrushchev, Nikita S., 51, 325
King, Martin Luther, 51
Kirbo, Charles, 305
Kirkland, John Thornton, 13
Kissinger, Henry A., 50, 207–08, 208n, 209,

211, 212, 213, 214–15, 217–18, 220, 224–25, 269, 284, 301, 302, 303, 307, 308, 308n–09n; *Nuclear Weapons and Foreign Policy*, 202, 209; *White House Years, The*, 218–19
Kiwanis, 263
Knox, Frank, 276
Knoxville Chronicle, The, 67
Kohnstamm, Max, 302
Koppers Company, 258
Korean War, 62, 201
Korshak, Sidney, 93
Kraft, Joseph, 184
Kristol, Irving, 220
Kuhn, Loeb & Company, 237
Ku Klux Klan, 312

Labor Law Study Committee, 256
labor unions, 10, 79, 121, 165, 170, 233, 234, 236, 239, 241, 253, 254, 257, 264, 292, 293, 318, 321; see also Ludlow Massacre; specific leaders and legislation
LaFollette, Robert M., 115, 278
laissez-faire economics; see Capitalism; Free enterprise
Lake, Anthony, 214n
Lambert, Samuel, 298
Lamont, Thomas W., 186
Lance, Bert, 305
Landon, Alfred M., 281
Lanouette, William, 178
LaRouche, Lyndon, Jr., 312
Lasch, Christopher, 32
Lash, Joseph, 279
Laski, Harold, 279
Latin America, 152; see also specific countries
Lawson, John R., 116–18
Lazard Freres, 144
League of Nations, 185, 186, 189–90, 194, 273, 274
LeBoutellier, John, *Harvard Hates America: The Odyssey of a Born-Again American*, 30–31
Leffingwell, Russell C., 184–85, 190–91
Leigh, Benjamin Watkins, 234
Lend-Lease program, 170
Lenin, V. I., 7, 193
Leverett, John, 28
Levi Strauss, C., 151n
Lewis, Flora, 217
Lewis, Fulton, Jr., 127
Liberal Christianity; see Unitarianism
liberalism, liberals, 20, 25, 27, 28–29, 43, 50, 52, 65, 79, 84, 92, 95, 97, 127, 153, 156, 157, 159, 172, 173, 181, 212, 232. 272, 278, 290, 297, 321, 322

344

INDEX

libertarianism, libertarians, 319–20; *see also* Free enterprise
Lilienthal, David E., 144*n*
Lilly Foundation, 211
Lincoln Center for the Performing Arts, 143
Lindblom, Charles, 263–64
Lindsay, John V., 133, 145, 146
Links Club, 129
Linowitz, Sol, 152
Lippmann, Walter, 15, 16–18, 199, 265; *Preface to Morals, A,* 16–18
Littauer, Lucius, 56–57
Littauer Center (Harvard), 57–58
Littauer fellowships, 137
Little Rock school integration, 283
Lloyd, Henry Demarest, 227
Local Initiatives Support Commission, 151*n*
Lockheed Aircraft bribery scandals, 302
Lodge, Henry Cabot, 5, 203, 289
Loeb, William, 308
Lord, Day, and Lord, 80
Lord, Winston, 184, 185, 214–15, 220, 221, 223, 268, 269
Lovett, Robert A., 162, 199, 277, 285
Low, Seth, 236
Lowden, Frank, 196
Lowell, Abbott Lawrence, 35–36, 37, 38–40, 41
Lowry, W. McNeil, 140
Luce, Henry, 242, 245
Ludlow Massacre, 115–20
Lusher, David, 172
Luther, Martin, 104
Lynn, Lawrence, 214*n*

MacAvoy, Paul, 178
McCabe, Ralph, 242
McCarthy, Eugene, 286
McCarthy, Joseph R., McCarthyism, 7, 22, 30, 41, 42, 49, 127–28, 130, 131, 133, 171, 199, 200, 201, 206, 220, 287, 288, 289–90. 291, 314, 326
McCloy, John J., 128–29, 132, 150, 151, 171, 199, 202, 203, 225, 266–67, 277, 285
McCord, James, 298
McCormick, Anne O'Hare, 72*n*
McCormick, Cyrus, 238
McCosh, James, 33
McCracken, Paul, 178
MacDonald, Ramsay, 188
McGovern, George S., 76, 92, 286, 291, 293
McGraw-Hill Book Company, 213*n*
Mackenzie King, William Lyon, 118–19
McKinley, William, 274

MacLaury, Bruce, 154, 157, 158, 182
MacLeish, Archibald, 31–32
Macmillan, Harold, 174
McNamara, Robert S., 60, 175, 297
Macy's, 242–43
Madison Avenue Presbyterian Church, 44
Magruder, Jeb Stuart, 177
Mallory, Walter H., 193, 195–96, 197
Manchester Union Leader, The, 308
Mankato State College, 137
Manning, Bayless, 185, 205, 206, 210, 211–12, 214, 215, 221, 222
Manning, Robert A., 304
Mao Tse-tung, 291–92, 316
Mardian, Robert, 82
Markel, Lester, 80
market economy; *see* Free enterprise
Marshall, Dorothy, 151
Marshall, George C., 199
Marshall Plan, 49, 127, 146, 171, 199, 200, 219, 248, 281, 287
Marxists, 122, 136, 193, 226, 279, 312–13, 318; *see also* Communism; Communist party
Massachusetts Bay Colony, 27
Massachusetts Institute of Technology, 50, 126, 146, 170
Mather, Cotton, 28
Mather, Increase, 28
Mattson, Walter, 82*n*
May, Ernest R., 62
May Group, 62
Mead, Margaret, 262
Meese, Edwin 3d, 307–08
Mellon Foundation, 211
Mellon Trust, 171
Merz, Charles, 78
Metropolitan Museum of Art, 18
Metropolitan Opera, 18
Meyer, Andre, 144
Milbank, Tweed, Hadley & McCloy, 277
Miller, Charles R., 69–70, 71, 78
Miller, Perry, 47
Millet, Jean François, 107
Mills, Wilbur, 134
Minarik, Joseph, 155, 157, 158
Mints, Lloyd, 250
"missile gap," 283, 284
Mitchell, John, 82–83
Mobil Oil Corporation, 97*n*, 257–58
Model Cities programs, 141
Moore, George S., 144*n*, 145
Moore, Maurice T. ("Tex"), 129
Morgan, J. P., 68, 108; House of Morgan, 234, 236, 237
Morgan Guaranty Trust Company, 321
Morgenthau, Henry, 248, 250
Morison, Robert S., 45

Morison, Samuel Eliot, 32, 42
Morris, Roger, 214*n*
Moulton, Harold G., 166–67, 168–69, 172, 179
Moynihan, Daniel Patrick, 89–91, 221, 224
mugwumpery, 34*n*, 270, 309
Munich Agreement, 195
Murphy, Thomas A., 263–64
Museum of Modern Art, 18
Muskie, Edward S., 309
Mussolini, Benito, 261

NAACP, 138
Nagorski, Zygmunt, 184, 209, 222
Nast, Thomas, 232
Nation, The, 245*n*
National Association of Manufacturers, 236–37, 238, 245*n*, 255, 281
National City Bank of New York, 234, 237; *see* Citicorp/Citibank
National Civic Federation, 236–37, 241, 274
National Commission on Water Quality, 255
National Council of Churches, 45
National Education Association, 298
National Founders Association, 236
nationalism, nativism, 74–75, 200, 213, 216, 220–21, 230, 275, 295, 296, 297, 300, 302, 314
National Journal, The, 178
National Labor Relations Act, 239
National Recovery Administration, 167
National Resources Planning Board, 169*n*
National Review, The, 184
National Security Council, 214
Nation's Business, The, 228
NATO, 199, 202, 281
NBC, 78
"neoconservativism," "neoconservatives," 319–20
Neustadt, Richard E., 23, 60, 61–62
neutron bomb, 304
"New Class," 263
New Deal, 30, 57, 64, 153, 156, 167–68, 170, 171, 239, 244, 250, 276, 278, 279, 287, 291, 315
New Directions, 304
New Economics, 282, 284; *see also* specific economists
New England Courant, 28
New England Quarterly, 42
New Establishment, 297
New Frontier, 7–8, 23, 30, 64, 291
New Jersey Bell Telephone Company, 241
New Majority, 295–96, 297
New Nationalism, 272, 277
New Republic, 46, 164, 232, 245*n*
New Statesman and Nation, The, 6–7
Newsweek, 44

New York Central Railroad, 70
New York City fiscal crisis, 321–22
New York City school decentralization, 142; *see also* Ocean Hill–Brownsville school district
New Yorker, The, 102*n*
New York Evening Post, The, 188
New York Mercury, 68
New York Review, 49
New York state legislature, 115
New York Stock Exchange, 37; Stock Exchange Advisory Committee, 260
New York Times, The, 3–4, 5, 18, 39, 66–103, 132, 154*n*, 175*n*, 182, 194, 196, 215, 217, 220, 248, 249, 254, 296, 299, 300, 307, 316, 327; business coverage, business bias, 67, 69, 86–87, 88, 93, 95–97, 98–99, 100; *Business Day,* 93; editors and editorials, 67, 69–71, 75, 78, 84–91, 93, 95, 96, 97–98; Establishment role, 92–103; features, 102, 103; history of, 67–71; as leader, 66–67, 68, 79, 99–100, 103; and Nixon, 75–78, 81–82, 83, 92, 100; Op Ed department, 88, 91, 96, 209; Pentagon Papers coverage, 80–84, 85; profitability of, 66, 87–88, 93, 102; Vietnam coverage, 4–5, 71–75, 85, 100
New York Times Company, 82*n*, 86, 87, 88, 98
New York University, 131, 147
Ngo Dinh Diem, 3, 4–5
Ngo Dinh Nhu, 5
Nhu family, 3
Nicaragua, 219, 274
Nielsen, Waldemar, 128–29, 130–31; *Endangered Sector, The,* 19*n*
Nitze, Paul, 220
Nixon, Richard M., xi–xii, 20, 75–78, 79, 90, 92, 100, 101, 146, 153, 154, 178, 179, 207, 208, 211, 218, 219, 252, 255, 261, 281, 283–84, 294, 300, 306, 307; and Brookings, 160, 174–77; "enemies list," 296–97; foreign policy, 75, 82, 207–08, 214, 218–19, 301–02, 307; *RN; The Memoirs of Richard Nixon,* 175, 176, 287–90, 295, 297–98, 299; on Pentagon Papers, 81–82; as president, 160, 174–77, 291–93, 314, 315–16, 326; *Six Crises,* 290, 291; as vice-president, 288–90; *see also* Watergate
"Nixon Fund," 288
Nobel Prize, 208
Nolting, Frederick E., Jr., 3, 4, 5
nonpartisanship, 10, 19
North American Review, 14
Northern Securities Company, 235
Norton, Andrews, 13, 14
Nourse, Edwin G., 167
Novak, Jeremiah, 304

Nuremberg trials, 249
Nye, Joseph, 212

Oakes, George Washington, 72
Oakes, John B., 3, 4, 5, 72, 75, 80, 85–91, 92, 95, 96, 101, 103
Oakland demonstration project, 139
Oates, James F., Jr., 144n
Oberlin College, 44
O'Brian, John Lord, 44
occupational safety, 301
Ocean-Hill–Brownsville school district, 133, 143; see also Bedford-Stuyvesant entries
Ochs, Adolph S., 67–70, 99, 102–3
Ochs, Effie, 68
Office of Management and Budget, 154, 169 n
Ogden, Rollo, 78
oil crisis, oil embargo, 216, 253
Okun, Arthur, 154, 155–56
Onassis, Jacqueline Kennedy, 23
OSS (Office of Strategic Services), 243, 301
Oxford English Dictionary, 7
Oxford University, 55, 59, 173
Owen, Henry, 301, 302

Packard, David, 149, 319
Pahlavi, Mohammed Reza (Shah of Iran), 224–25
Pakistan, 5
Palestine Liberation Organization, 304
Paley, William, 182, 223, 323; Principles of Moral and Political Philosophy, 8, 9, 10, 11
Panama Canal, 314
Panic of 1907, 237
Paris peace accords (Vietnam), 218–19
Paris Peace Conference (World War I), 185, 186
Parsons, Herbert, 273
Pasvolsky, Leo, 171
Patman, Wright, 133–34
patriotism; see Nationalism
patronage system, 55
Patterson, Ellmore Clark ("Pat"), 321
Patterson, Robert P., 276–77
payroll taxes, 243
peace, 126, 187, 197; see also specific wars, treaties, organizations
Pearl Harbor attack, 197, 243
Pechman, Joseph A., 154, 155, 172, 173
Pegler, Westbrook, 127
Pendleton Act, 55
Penn State University, 258

Pentagon, 60; Internal Security Affairs, 154
Pentagonalism, 301–02
Pentagon Papers, 80–84, 85, 101, 154, 174–76, 212, 296–97, 299
Penthouse, 304
Percy, Charles H., 283
Perkins, Elliott, 36–37, 38
Perkins, George W., 234, 236
Perkins, Thomas Nelson, 36–37, 39
Philippines, 74
Phillips, Kevin, Emerging Republican Majority, The, 293–95
Pipes, Richard, 220
Pittsburgh City Council, 106–07
pluralism, 9–10, 32, 47, 48, 49, 68, 150n, 159, 261, 270
Podhoretz, Norman, 220
Polaris submarines, 284
Political Science Quarterly, 56
politics; see specific leaders and issues
Pollack lectures (Harvard), 316
populism, populists, 20, 30, 134, 220–21, 270, 280, 285, 294, 313–16, 317–18
Porcellian (Harvard club), 31
poverty, 22, 141, 180, 295, 303; see also specific antipoverty projects
Powell, Jody, 305
Presidential campaigns: 1912, 278; 1916, 278; 1920, 278; 1924, 278; 1932, 278, 313; 1936, 278, 281, 313; 1940, 276, 278, 281, 313; 1944, 278, 281, 313; 1948, 281, 313; 1952, 281–83, 288; 1956, 282–83, 288–89; 1960, 283–85, 289; 1964, 73, 286, 1968, 84, 286, 287, 290, 291, 294, 295; 1972, 286, 295, 297, 298, 299, 315–16; 1976, 178, 180, 286, 301, 314; 1980, 261–62, 262n, 307–10, 316
Price, Don K., 58–59, 60, 61, 62, 63, 64
Princeton University, 18, 33, 72, 205
professionalism, 8–9, 15, 16, 17, 25, 31, 33, 34, 50, 51, 52, 53–56, 64, 126, 184, 223, 260, 279
Progressive Era, Progressive party, 65, 150, 164, 232, 234–39, 246, 252, 265, 269–70, 271, 272, 277–78, 318
Proposition 13, 25, 314
Prudential Insurance, 151n
public administration, public service, 31, 33, 50, 51–52, 53–58, 59–65, 124, 159, 165–66, 277, 279, 280
Public Administration Clearing House, 59
Puerto Ricans; see Hispanics
Puritanism, 13, 27, 28
Pusey, Nathan Marsh, 41–45, 46–48, 49, 52

Quakerism, Quakers, 275
Quie, Albert, 156

racism, racial issues, 23–24, 25, 121, 133, 137–38, 180, 189, 270, 272, 273
Raiffa, Howard, 61
Ramo, Simon, 230
RAND Corporation, 18, 64, 80, 126, 146, 175n, 297
Raskin, A. H., 78
Reagan, Ronald, 262, 262n, 300, 307–09, 308n–09n
Red-baiting; see McCarthy, McCarthyism
Reece, Brazilla Carroll, 128, 130
Reed, Joseph V., 225
Reed, Walter, 120
Republican National Committee, 128, 276; Committee on Program and Progress, 283; Platform Committee, 283, 285
Republican party, 31, 34n, 79, 154, 156, 178, 189, 200, 219, 269, 274–75, 280–87, 315; factionalism in, 280–82, 283–84, 285, 289; internationalism in, 199, 273; isolationism in, 189–90, 199–200, 216, 273; "Middle America" in, 262n, 280; rightward movement in, 79, 199–200, 216, 273, 282, 286, 294, 314; see also specific politicians
Resources for the Future, 127
Reston, James, 78, 81, 132, 220
Rhodes scholars, 59, 72
Rivlin, Alice, 156
Robinson, Marshall, 150
Rochester Unemployment Plan, 244
Rockefeller, David, 95–96, 101, 203, 206, 207, 208, 209–10, 214, 216, 217, 224–25, 226, 228–29, 265–67, 290n, 301, 302, 317, 321
Rockefeller, John D., 105, 108, 109–13, 114, 115, 121, 240
Rockefeller, John D., Jr., 109, 113, 114, 115, 116, 118, 119, 162, 238, 269
Rockefeller, John D. 3d, 3, 4, 5, 9, 19, 122
Rockefeller, John D. 4th (Jay), 4
Rockefeler, Laura Spelman, Memorial Fund, 242
Rockefeller, Nelson, 95, 95n, 208, 214, 238, 255, 283–84, 285, 287, 289, 299, 300–01, 304, 306
Rockefeller, William, 238
Rockefeller family, 312, 316
Rockefeller Foundation, 4, 34, 45, 108, 112–15, 117–20, 121, 122–23, 124–25, 126, 151–52, 162–63, 171, 201, 285, 294; board, 114–15
Rockefeller Institute for Medical Research, 108, 110, 112, 114, 124
Rockefeller Sanitary Commission, 112
Rogers, William, 207
Roosa, Robert V., 179–80
Roosevelt, Eleanor, 249
Roosevelt, Franklin Delano, 56, 57, 153, 166–

69, 169n, 170, 177, 197, 239, 242, 244, 250, 275–76, 278, 279, 280, 282, 294, 310, 312
Roosevelt, Theodore, 56, 232, 235–36, 269, 270–71, 272, 273, 275, 277, 278, 309
Root, Elihu, 70, 164, 187, 188, 270
Rose, Wickliffe, 124
Rosenthal, A. M., 78, 81, 82, 83, 84, 85, 88
Rostow, Eugene, 203, 220
Rostow, Walt W., 203, 220
Rothschild, Victor Sydney, 37, 38
Rovere, Richard, "Notes on the Establishment in America," xi, 8, 171, 285
Rowen, Henry, 297
Royce, Josiah, 15
Rubicam, Ray, 242
Ruml, Beardsley, 242–43, 244, 245, 250–52, 258, 265
Rusk, Dean, 203, 285
Russell Sage Foundation, 18, 150

Sachs, Julius, 37
Safire, William, 77–78
St. Louis Post-Dispatch, The, 297
St. Mark's School, 39
St. Paul's School, 39
Salant, Walter S., 172, 173
Salant, William, 172
Sale, Kirkpatrick, Power Shift, 314–15
SALT, 304, 314
Samuelson, Paul, 50, 172
Santayana, George, 15
Sarbin, Hershel, 253–54
Schlesinger, Arthur, Jr., 46, 49, 50, 201
Schlesinger, James R., 306
Schmertz, Herbert, 97n
Schmidt, Benno C., 144n
Schultze, Charles L., 154, 155; Agenda for the Nation, 154; Public Use of Private Interest, The, 156
Scott Paper Company, 242
Seattle Committee on Foreign Relations, 200
Secretary of Health, Education, and Welfare, 253
secularism, 31, 43, 46, 47
Segre, Sergio, 209–10
Seidman, L. William, 178
self-interest, 228, 265, 272, 300
Shakespeare, William, 107
Shanahan, Eileen, 254
Shanker, Albert, 133
Shapiro, Frank, 37–38
Shapiro, Irving S., 254–55, 257–58
Shawcross, William, Sideshow, 215n, 217–18
Sheehan, Neil, 80, 81
Shepardson, Whitney, 187, 191, 196

INDEX

Sheraton, Mimi, 102n
Sherman, John, 231
Sherman Antitrust Act, 101, 231
Shriver, R. Sargent, 140
Shulman, Marshall, 214, 269
Shumway, Van, 296
Silberman, Lawrence H., 178
Simon, William E., 178, 320–21, 320n; *Time for Truth, A,* 319–20, 321–23
Simons, Henry, 250
Sinatra, Frank, 93
Skybolt missile, 62
Slichter, Sumner, 241
Sloan Foundation, 63–64
slush funds, 253
Smith, Adam, 28, 232, 265
Smith, Alfred E., 278
Smith, Hoke, 115
Smith, Mark, 26–27
Smith, Walter Bedell, 288
Smoot-Hawley tariff, 195, 275
Smuts, Jan, 188
Social Democrats, 312–13
socialism, socialists, 31, 106, 128, 165, 259
social responsibilities creed, 32, 34, 53, 105, 106, 121, 125, 136–37, 161, 228–30, 234, 235, 240, 244, 246, 256, 257, 259, 266, 269–70, 271, 274, 277–78, 279, 280, 312, 317, 318, 327
Social Science Research Council, 59
Social Security system, 155, 239, 244
Soedjatmoko (Indonesian Trustee of Ford Foundation), 150n
Sokolsky, George, 127
South Africa, 23–24, 26, 151–52, 188
Soviet Union, 71, 192–93, 194, 202, 219–20, 248, 283, 284, 291, 301, 302; Red Army, 220, 307
Spectator, The, 7
Sputnik, 283, 284
Standard Oil Company, Standard Oil Trust, 108, 111, 112, 113, 114, 235; *see* John D. Rockefeller
Stanford Law School, 205
Stanford University, 18, 33, 266
Statement of Thirty-One Republicans, 273
Steffens, Lincoln, 232
Stein, Herbert, 178, 179, 182, 250
Stendahl, Krister, 47
Stettinius, Edward R., Jr., 170
Stimson, Henry L., 270–77, 278, 279–80, 285, 309
Stimson, Lewis, 271
Strauss, Robert S., 158, 306
Studebaker Company, 127, 146, 240
student demonstrations and radicalism, 22, 23–25, 31, 52, 204
Students for a Democratic Society, 26, 48

Suez crisis, 62
Sulzberger, Arthur Hays, 4, 75, 76, 76n, 78, 79
Sulzberger, Arthur Ochs ("Punch"), 66–67, 75–79, 80, 82, 85, 86–90, 92–95, 96, 97–99, 101, 102
Sulzberger, Iphigene Ochs, 68, 69, 102
Sunbelt, 6, 11, 265, 315
Surrey, Stanley, 59
Survey, The, 113–14
Sutton, Francis X. et al., *American Business Creed, The,* 317n
Sviridoff, Mitchell, 140, 142
Swarthmore College, 173
Swing, John Temple, 208, 221

Taft, Robert A., 276, 281, 287
Taft, William Howard, 113, 161–62, 164, 269, 272, 273, 278
Taft-Hartley bill, 170
Tarbell, Ida, 232
Tardieu, Andre, 188
tariffs, 69, 195, 238, 247, 270, 272; *see also* specific legislation and agreements
taxes, 25, 69, 93, 105, 106, 126, 134, 134n, 135, 155, 158, 164, 173, 181, 243, 245, 250, 251–52, 253, 255, 317
Taylor, A. J. P., 6–7
Taylor, Maxwell, 203
Taylor, Telford, 249
Temple Emanu-El, 96
Tennessee Valley Authority, 144n, 278
Texaco, Inc., 255
Thieu, Nguyen Van, 218
Third Force, 18–19, 100, 325
Third Sector, 9, 19, 122, 149, 300, 318, 323; *see also* specific people, institutions, programs
Third World, 216, 219; *see also* specific countries
Thomas, Franklin, 143–44, 145–47, 148n, 150n, 151–52
Thomas, Hugh, 7
Thomas, Sam, 68
Thompson Ramo Wooldridge (TRW), 230
Tillich, Paul, 44
Time, 44, 302
Times, The (London), 6, 70n, 120
Tobin, James, 50
Tocqueville, Alexis de, 19, 228, 230–31
tolerance, toleration, 13, 46
Tonkin Gulf Resolution, 73
Trade Agreements Act of 1934, 197
Transcendentalism, 14n
Trib, The 320n
Trident International Finance, Inc., 302

349

INDEX

Trilateral Commission, 101, 163, 301, 302–05, 307–08, 310
Trollope, Anthony, *Phineas Redux*, 252
Trotzky, Leon, 7
Truman, Harry S., 62, 127, 167, 177, 199, 277
trusts, 231–32, 235–36; *see also* specific industrialists, legislators, companies
TRW (Thompson Ramo Wooldridge), 230
Tugwell, Rexford Guy, 168
Turkey, 199
Tuskegee Institute, 26
Twain, Mark, 107, 107n
Twentieth Century Fund, 18

Ulasewicz, Tony, 176
Ullman, Richard H., 211, 212, 215, 217
Ungar, Sanford, 83
Union League Club, 70
Union Pacific Railroad, 162
unions; *see* Labor unions
Unitarian church (Massachusetts), Unitarianism, 11, 12–16, 28, 29, 45, 46, 265
United Federation of Teachers, 133
United Hebrew Charities, 37
United Mine Workers, 115, 116
United Nations, 73, 90, 199, 219, 287, 304
U.S. Air Force, 126, 145
U.S. Army, 288
U.S. Chamber of Commerce, 255, 281
U.S. Commerce Department, 243, 244, 257
U.S. Commission on Industrial Relations, 116–18, 119
U.S. Congress, 108, 112, 113–14, 115, 123, 127–28, 133–34, 134n, 164, 168, 169n, 199, 201, 204, 219, 231, 257, 261, 278, 287, 304, 314; *see also* specific congressmen and committees
U.S. Constitution, 75; First Amendment, 11, 101; Fourteenth Amendment, 11
U.S. Department of Defense, 80, 175, 214, 296, 297; *see also* Pentagon Papers
U.S. Department of Energy, 257, 306
U.S. Department of Justice, 82–83
U.S. Department of Labor, 144
U.S. foreign policy, 4, 5, 80, 222–23; bipartisanship in, 199, 201, 273, 276–77; Carter, 216, 224–25, 304–05, 307; Eisenhower, 202, 203; Ford, 300; Johnson, 72–74, 82; Kennedy, 5, 82, 203, 204; Nixon, 75, 82, 207–08, 214, 218–19, 301–02, 307; FDR, 275–76; Truman, 71, 200–01; Wilson, 185–87; *see also* Kissinger, Henry A.; specific wars and treaties
U.S. Foreign Service, 171, 214
U.S. Labor party, 312
U.S. Senate, 113, 115, 186, 190, 258, 273, 276; *see also* specific senators and committees

U.S. State Department, 9, 170, 171, 197, 198, 202, 209, 210, 212, 238, 274, 276, 285; Bureau of Politico-Military Affairs, 154n, Policy Planning Council, 211; Policy Planning Staff, 215
United States Steel Corporation, 232, 234, 255
U.S. Supreme Court, 11, 57, 83, 113, 114, 123, 271, 279, 280, 283; *see also* specific justices
U.S. Treasury Department, 158, 207, 237, 257, 285, 290
University College (London), 120
University of British Columbia Medical School, 120
University of California–Berkeley, 64, 172
University of Chicago, 18, 33, 108, 109, 115, 117, 127, 240, 241, 242, 247, 250, 266
University of Massachusetts, 150
University of Michigan, 33, 64
University of Minnesota, 50; Hubert Humphrey School, 64
University of Texas: Lyndon B. Johnson School, 64
University of Wisconsin, 172
Upgren, Arthur R. and Bissell, Richard M., *Program of Postwar Planning, A*, 243–44
Urban Institute, 143
urban violence, 22

Van Anda, Carr, 70n, 78
Van Arsdale, Harry, 95
Vance, Cyrus, 212, 214, 269, 304, 305, 307, 309
Vandenberg, Arthur K., 199
Vanderbilt, William K., 238
Vanderbilt University, 58, 143
Vanderlip, Frank A., 234, 237
Vernon, Raymond, 138
Versailles Treaty, 185, 195, 199, 248, 273
Vietnam, Vietnam War, 3–5, 22, 26, 52, 62, 71–75, 76, 80, 85, 93, 100, 132, 173, 175, 177, 181, 203–06, 210, 218, 219, 220, 221, 222, 286, 291, 295, 296, 301, 309, 313; Tet offensive, 204; *see also* Pentagon Papers
Vietnam History Task Force, 154
Vietnam Moratorium Committee, 204
Volcker, Paul A., 306
Voorhis, Jerry, 287

Wagner, Richard, 107
Wagner & Baroody, 178
Walker, James, 13
Wallace, George C., 136, 287, 314
Wallace, Henry, 197, 277–78
Wall Street Journal, 149

Walsh, Frank, 119
Walsh, Thomas R., 70n
Wanniski, Jude, 309
war; see specific wars
Warburg, Paul M., 191, 237
Ward, Artemus, 268
Ware, Henry, Jr., 13, 14
Ware, Henry, Sr., 13
War Industries Board, 162, 167; Price Fixing Committee, 162
Warnke, Paul, 214, 269, 297, 304
Warren, Earl, 83
Warren, Jerry, 296
War Resources Board, 169, 170
Washington Post, 77, 83, 92, 100, 184, 297
Washington Times, 163
Washington University, 161, 165
Watanabe, Takeshi, 302
Watergate, 22, 75, 76, 83, 85, 93, 96, 101, 174, 177, 219, 222, 253, 291, 293, 297–300, 309, 314, 315, 326
Watson, Thomas J., Jr., 144n, 145
Watts, William, 214n
wealth, 22, 106, 111; see also specific individuals and organizations
Weaver, Robert C., 138
Weber, Max, *Protestant Ethic and the Spirit of Capitalism, The*, 104–05
Welch, Joseph, 326
welfare, welfae state, 79, 95, 147
Welles, Chris, 97n
Western Europe, 301, 302, 303, 304; see also specific countries
West Germany, 174
Westinghouse Electric Company, 256
Weyerhaeuser Co., 255
White, Andrew D., 33
White, Harry Dexter, 247
White, Morton, 47
White, Theodore H., *Making of the President, 1960, The*, 285
Whitman, Marina von Neumann, 269
Whitney, J. H. and Company, 144n
Whitney (J. H.) Foundation, 143
Whittier College, 287
"Whiz Kids," 64, 126
Wickersham, George W., 113, 187, 269
Wilhelm (Kaiser of Germany), 161
Wilkins, Roger, 91

Williams, Aubrey, 250
Williams College, 12, 50, 173
Willis, Benjamin, 138
Willkie, Wendell L., 281, 281n
Willoughby, William F., 164, 166
Wills, Garry, 294; *Nixon Agonistes*, 315
Wilson, Charles, 228
Wilson, P. W., 194
Wilson, Woodrow, 56, 57, 116, 119, 162, 186, 224, 272, 273, 278
Winthrop & Stimson, 271
witch-hunting; see McCarthy, McCarthyism
women, 72n, 150n, 185, 204, 242, 253
Women's Action Alliance, 143
Wood, Robert E., 196
Woodstock convention, 181
Woolworth, Frank W., 70–71
World Bank, 171, 199, 202, 247, 248, 297
World War I, 39n, 40, 45, 69–71, 72, 161, 162, 164, 170, 185, 199, 200, 238–39, 248, 273, 276, 278–79
World War II, 30, 41, 49, 105, 169–70, 195, 196, 197–98, 199, 206, 210, 212, 219, 240, 243, 244, 245, 247, 248, 252, 266, 276, 277, 281, 301, 313, 318
World War III, 184
WPA, 250
Wriston, Henry, *Diplomacy in a Democracy*, 203
Wriston, Walter, 321
Wyzanski, Charles E., Jr., 128–29

Xerox Corporation, 254

Yale Law School, 240
Yale University, 12, 18, 31, 49, 50, 64, 77, 114, 126, 158, 187, 206, 263, 270, 271, 276, 287
Ylvisaker, Paul, 137–40, 143
Yntema, Theodore, 247, 247n, 250
Yom Kippur War, 253
Young, Andrew, 304
Young, David, 296

Ziff-Davis Publishing Company, 253–54